SCOTTISH HISTORY SOCIETY

SIXTH SERIES

VOLUME 15

Miscellany XVI

Miscellany XVI

Compiled by the Scottish History Society

SCOTTISH HISTORY SOCIETY
2020

THE BOYDELL PRESS

First published 2020

A Scottish History Society publication
in association with The Boydell Press.
The Boydell Press is an imprint of Boydell & Brewer Ltd
PO Box 9, Woodbridge, Suffolk IP12 3DF, UK
and of Boydell & Brewer Inc.
668 Mt Hope Avenue, Rochester, NY 14620–2731, USA
website: www.boydellandbrewer.com

ISBN 978-0-906245-45-3

A catalogue record of this publication is available
from the British Library

This publication is printed on acid-free paper

MIX
Paper from
responsible sources
FSC® C013056

Printed and bound in Great Britain by TJ International Ltd, Padstow, Cornwall

CONTENTS

KING JAMES VI'S ENGLISH SUBSIDY AND DANISH DOWRY ACCOUNTS 1588–96

Edited by Miles Kerr-Peterson and Michael Pearce

INTRODUCTION

...praying you to understand that my greatest desire in this world is to demonstrate to you that all my life I shall be

your very humble and obedient

Anna[1]

So wrote Princess Anna of Denmark, future Queen of Scotland, later of England, Ireland and (nominally, at least) France. Having been married by proxy to King James VI of Scotland at Kronborg, the fleet attempting to bring her to Leith was driven by contrary winds back to the coast of Norway. Anchored at the island of Flekkerøy, an argument then arose between the Danish mariners and the Scottish delegation, on whether to put Anna aboard a smaller ship and make another attempt to cross the wintry seas, as advocated by the Scots, or to turn back to Denmark, and try again in the spring. The outcome of this argument was a compromise which made no one particularly happy, to winter in Oslo, suggested by the head of the Scottish delegation (and Anna's proxy husband), George Keith, Earl Marischal. Exactly what Marischal sought to achieve by this is unclear. He perhaps hoped a more seaworthy Scottish fleet might be sent to take over from the Danes, or, perhaps more likely, he did not want the humiliation of returning to Copenhagen, after receiving so hearty a send-off in the previous month.[2]

Anna's letters arrived in Scotland in the hands of Andrew Sinclair and the Danish diplomat Stene Bille. These two men, or at least Sinclair, urged that a small Scottish vessel, better able to cope with the choppy seas, should

1 The editors wish to sincerely thank Marie-Claude Tucker for her translation of these letters, and Jamie Reid-Baxter for his invaluable comments on them, which can be found in full, with notes, as an appendix.

2 W. Boyd, A. Cameron, M. Giuseppi, J. Mackie and H Meikle, eds, *Calendar of State Papers Relating to Scotland and Mary Queen of Scots 1547–1603*, 13 vols (Edinburgh, 1898–1969) (hereafter *CSP Scot*), x, 167; D. Stevenson, *Scotland's Last Royal Wedding* (Edinburgh, 1997), 86–90.

be sent to retrieve Anna.[3] James, having already fretted for several months, producing a wad of yearning love poetry in the process, made one of the most decisive and heroic decisions of his life. He would do more than just send a ship: he would sail the North Sea himself to reach Anna. And he did: he arrived in Oslo, the couple were married a second time, then they rode along the Norwegian coast, into Sweden, then across the sea to arrive in style at Copenhagen. There James, famously, 'maid guid cheir and drank stoutlie till spring tyme' with his in-laws, while sight-seeing and even guest-lecturing at the University of Copenhagen.[4] Touchingly, James referred to Anna in November 1589 as the 'sweetest fruit'.[5]

Against the courtly affection expressed by Anna's letters, and the highly romantic gesture by James to speed across the wintry seas, or even the Scandinavian honeymoon, there inevitably arose the much less romantic business of administration. James' heady gesture needed to be organised, staffed and, more importantly, paid for. In part, this is what the documents provided here deal with. Romance is fine in itself, but how many onions are needed for the voyage? How many hams, or how much writing ink will that require? And how much will that all cost? In this case, a barrel full of onions, twenty hams and a quart of ink, at £8, £30 and six shillings respectively. These are all items on the receipts that constitute the price of love in this instance. The materials provided here in this selection, non-exchequer royal accounts, provide exceptional detail for the fitting out of the ship James took to Denmark, and, to a lesser extent, for the journey home. The ship belonged to Robert Jameson of Ayr and we learn elsewhere that it was called the *James Royall*. We gain a fascinating insight into the practical necessities of taking a king across the North Sea, from its decoration with flags, pennants and a new lick of paint, the creation of new cabins, to the full provisions needed for the voyage. Through the mention of sums paid to the 'succour' (sugar) men of Edinburgh for 'confectors' – confectionary and 'sucker' (sugar) – we gain the rather delightful image of the Lord's Annointed, King of Scotland, future king of England, Ireland, and nominally France, sat in an idle moment, enjoying a boiled sweet.

Beyond this glimpse at maritime provisioning, these accounts illustrate for us some of the workings of James' cash flow. All the Stewart monarchs of

3 *CSP Scot*, x, 166–8. For more on Stene Bille, see Thomas Riis, *Should Auld Acquaintance Be Forgot… Scottish–Danish Relations c.1450–1708*, 2 vols (Odense, 1988), ii, 282.

4 James Melville, *Autobiography and Diary 1556–1601*, ed. R. Pitcairn (Edinburgh, 1842), 277.

5 The context of this comes from two letters in the National Records of Scotland (hereafter NRS) SP13/118 & 119: one from James to Sophie of Mecklenburg, and one from Sophie to James, both 26 November 1589, in Latin. Both discussed the weather, past and prospective, and James calls Anna the sweetest fruit – 'your dear daughter is the sweetest fruit' – and looks forward to meeting Sophie, Christian IV and the rest of his new brothers and sisters at Elsinor. Sophie, on her sheet of gilt-edged writing paper, mentions the short winter nights and how three people were embarking to meet James and Anna on 26 November.

Scotland had money issues, indeed the history of almost every royal house in Europe in the early modern period is a story of a crown in need of more cash, seeking new ways to get it, and then dealing with the inevitable political fallout. King James VI of Scotland was no exception and is often seen as a particularly extreme example. The first major crisis of his reign, after all, at least after his minority officially ended, the Ruthven Raid of 1583, was partially a reaction to seemingly out of control crown spending.[6] For his whole life, James is usually portrayed as notoriously illiterate when it came to his finances.

Julian Goodare has certainly shown that James had no qualms about overspending, falling into debt, or even ignoring debts over a long term. This largely fitted with James' conception of kingship: he needed to display largesse, reward political allies and live in a manner befitting a sovereign prince. James did not see it as his problem to worry about balancing books, or to rush to pay off debts to politically marginal merchants or financiers. One major feature of James' finances was the 'hived-off debts', long-term debts resting with financial officers, outwith the scope of the exchequer, which were to be repaid at unspecified times, if at all.[7]

The materials published here are three sets of such hived-off debts, Document Sets One and Two covering the period 1589 to 1590 and Document Set Three covering 1594 to 1596. These list James' expenditure, paid by certain agents, which were usually based on money received from various sources. In the case of these documents, either from Queen Elizabeth's subsidy to James, the Danish dowry received at James' marriage to Anna in 1589, or other substantial gifts and proceeds. These accounts were not included in the treasurer's or exchequer's accounts, but were held semi-officially by one of James' finance ministers. These officers then spent the money received on James' debts, but which they then fell into debt for ('superexpended') once the incoming money was exhausted. They cluster around two major events in James' reign, his marriage to Anne of Denmark in 1589 and the baptism of Prince Henry in 1594. As both necessitated greater royal spending on diplomacy, pagentry and interior decoration, but both also saw the arrival of large sums of dowry or gift money for those occassions, it follows that more spending took place beyond the usual functioning of the exchequer.

Although these accounts were not part of the regular royal accounts, they were audited by financial officers. The exchequer, headed by the separate

6 Steven J. Reid, 'Of Bairns and Bearded Men: James VI and the Ruthven Raid', in Miles Kerr-Peterson and Steven J. Reid, *James VI and Noble Power in Scotland, 1578–1602* (London, 2017), 32–56.

7 Julian Goodare, 'The Debts of James VI of Scotland', *Economic History Review* 62:4 (2009), 926–52.

offices of treasurer and comptroller, did not set financial policy, but were essentially auditing bodies, making sure that royal expenditure was not fraudulently claimed. Most of the crowns' income varied little, while expenses could vary considerably depending on political expediencies. The crown's officers, usually either the treasurer or the comptroller, hence often had to bear the crown's debts from their own resources. They rarely had much choice, although the crown offices usually bought other types of reward, such as landed assets or political influence, that could offset some of the heavy burden.[8] One of the major figures in the following documents is Chancellor John Maitland of Thirlestane, who dominated Scottish politics from the fall of the Ruthven Raid regime until his death in 1596.[9] As chancellor, Maitland was not officially liable for this crown debt; however, it was often expedient for him to do so as his position was political rather than administrative.[10]

In Maitland's block of accounts (Document Set One and partially duplicated in Document Set Two) he was left out of pocket by some £17,824 Scots. Although his accounts were officially registered, it does not seem likely that he was ever repaid. Maitland's superexpenditure pales in comparison with William Ruthven, first Earl of Gowrie's burden of crown debt amounting to £67,488 in 1583. In 1598 the goldsmith Thomas Foulis (the author of part of Document Set 2 and all of Document Set Three) and merchant Robert Jowsie together held £160,522 of crown debts, with no likelihood they would ever be paid back. Sir Robert Melville of Mudochcairnie, mentioned several times in the documents, was superexpended by £35,656 in 1596.[11]

This traditional system of the crown offloading its debts to officers, as represented in Document Sets One and Two, changed in two ways in the 1590s. One was an attempt to ensure royal officers were not personally liable for the crown's debts, the second was to farm debts out to private individuals, like Foulis and Jowsie, which can be seen in Document Set Three.[12] Foulis had been drawn into the royal finances during the preparations for James' marriage to Anna. Foulis had supplied jewels, while Robert Jowsie supplied clothes.[13] They were sent to London in July 1589 on a shopping expedition, and established agents there and a system of English credit. Gradually, through James' lavish spending via them, they were increasingly drawn into

8 Julian Goodare, *State and Society in Early Modern Scotland* (Oxford: 1999), ch. 4, especially 120–32.

9 See Maurice Lee Jnr, *John Maitland of Thirlestane and the Foundation of Stewart Despotism in Scotland* (Princeton, NJ, 1959).

10 Julian Goodare, *The Government of Scotland 1560–1625* (Oxford, 2004), 150–1.

11 Goodare, *State and Society*, 120, 123, 126.

12 Goodare, *State and Society*, 121–3, 126–8, 131.

13 Jowsie, for example, supplied velvet and gold passmenterie for the canopy used by Anna of Denmark in her entry into Edinburgh. Edinburgh City Archives, 'Bailies Accounts, Unlaws 1564–1664', pp. 286–9.

James' bookkeeping.[14] Both Foulis and Jowsie appear in Maitland's accounts. As the king's debts to Foulis mounted, the goldsmith became more invested and hence more involved with James' financial arrangement, so by May 1591 he became responsible for handling James' English subsidy money, money granted by Queen Elizabeth to James, essentially to keep his good favour. This made sense, as Foulis had established a network of agents in London and a considerable amount of debt – English subsidy money could thus service James' English debts, without ever having to go north. This continued until 1595 and the document here represents the last set of accounts by Foulis based on English subsidy money. In 1595 the system broke down and James was forced to ease his spending. In 1596 an eight-man commission, the 'Octavians', were formed to sort out James' finances and they made some good initial inroads. In the following year Foulis managed to gain control of royal income and outgoings, coming close to getting some of his money back. Yet the system (and his mental health) broke down in 1598, leaving Foulis bankrupt.[15] Ultimately, very little of the money James owed Foulis was paid back.

These three sets of documents show us a fragment of James' haphazard financial arrangements, and the burdens placed upon officers of state, such as Maitland, and on the crown creditors, such as Foulis, that James owed money to. At the same time, they also provide a fascinating window into court life at the time of, and immediately after, the royal marriage. Most of the accounts reproduced here involved Engish subsidy money in some way, showing the various ways this income stream was used to plug some of James' debts.[16] These documents have not been previously published. Although they have occassionaly been used by historians, as they are physically separated in three different archive collections in two capital cities, they have not been fully considered in their individual entirety, or alongside each other.

The expenditure made while in Denmark is especially remarkable as an example of the expetations of royal largess. These Danish payments were not as businesslike as the other hived-off accounts, because the emphasis was in demonstrative gift-giving. As James wandered about, sampling the delights of

14 Julian Goodare, 'Foulis, Thomas (c.1560–1628)' *Oxford Dictionary of National Biography* (hereafter *ODNB*), reference number 73674 (accessed 27 October 2017). All *ODNB* entries have been consulted at www.oxforddnb.com.

15 Julian Goodare, 'The Octavians', in Kerr-Peterson and Reid, *James VI and Noble Power*, 176–93, especially at 184–5.

16 It should also be noted that some additional records of the subsidy were compiled in a brief memorandum with some particulars taken from Maitland's Danish account (continued within this manuscript). Other notes concern the finances of the wardrobe and Sir William Keith, the Master of Gray, and Robert Joussie. Payments from 1586 to William Schaw Master of Works (see below in this Introduction) for £4000 and £300, in 1591 to Rachaell the English woman were noted from lost accounts. See BL Add. MS 33531 ff.221, 283–90, and a nineteenth-century transcript NRS RH2/2/16, pp. 181–6, 236–8.

this foreign land, his pursemaster would follow to hand out shiny dalers (the Danish currency) to those who put on a show, opened a door, or gave the king a book. We therefore see a much higher density of such rewards than in the domestic treasurer's accounts. As such, the expenditure in Denmark had little to do with subsistence, general household expenses, or extravagance, but a necessary obligation of royal gift-giving. Perhaps everyone understood the dalers would be used like this, and James had little choice. It can thus be argued that it would be a mistake to think the daler account is a record of James' dowry being squandered, as some have suggested.[17] The editors have therefore decided not to convert the Danish dalers and norts into pounds, shillings and pence. To do so would give the wrong impression about James' spending.

THE DOCUMENTS

Document Set One: British Library, Additional MS 22,958: Audited Accounts of John Maitland, Lord Thirlestane 1588–93

Document Set One is now in the British Library. It is not clear how the documents ended up there, but they are likely to have been Maitland's own counter copies of the documents he officially registered, so that he could have formal legal recognition of his expenses in service to James. They all bear the original signatures of the auditors and were written up on 1 March 1595 in the exchequer.[18] The collection consists of seven documents. They are prefaced by the Latin commission under the Great Seal of 26 December 1593, empowering a small group of finance ministers to audit Maitland's accounts, made during the negations and execution of the royal marriage since 1588. Specifically, they consisted of Mark Ker, Lord Newbattle, Sir Robert Melvill of Murdocairny, John Cockburn of Ormistoun, Sir Patrick Vaus of Barnbarroch, David Seton of Parbroath, Sir Richard Cockburn of

17 Maurice Lee suggests, on the other hand, that Maitland kept a strict control of James' expenditure in Denmark, stopping it getting out of control. This also seems unlikely, given how Maitland was unable to curb James' spending within Scotland – it is perhaps the case that James did not need to spend as much when the political expediency was removed while abroad. Maurice Lee Jnr, *John Maitland of Thirlestane*, 205–8.

18 It is not exactly clear where this was at the time. From 1597 the 'Laich Tolbooth', also known as the 'Town's Council House' in Edinburgh were set aside for the use of the exchequer. This may have formalised an existing arrangement, although it is likely that the exchequer building was simply wherever the officers met to hold exchequer meetings, be that Edinburgh's Tolbooth, or the Palace of Holyrood. Records of the Parliament of Scotland (hereafter RPS) A1597/1/6/4, consulted at www.rps.ac.uk and J. Burton and D. Masson, eds, *Register of the Privy Council of Scotland*, 14 vols (Edinburgh, 1877–98) (hereafter *RPCS*), v, 118.

Clerkingtoun, Walter Stewart, commedator of Blantyre, Alexander Hay of Easter Kennet, Mr David Carnegie of Colluthie, Mr Peter Young of Seton and Mr George Young. These eleven men were either finance ministers or lawyers associated with the court of session.[19]

The first part of Maitland's account covers from Spring 1588 to Spring 1589, based on £10,000 received from Sir William Keith of Delny, Master of the King's Wardrobe, which probably represents the proceeds of the earldom of Ross. William was baillie of the earldom and the lordship of Ardmannoch, while his brother, John Keith of Ravenscraig was also baillie for collecting the rents of the earldom.[20] The money was spent on smaller royal debts and gifts for visitors and ambassadors, for which Maitland was left out of pocket by £2,913 16s. 8d. He was reimbursed this money in the second part of the accounts, of 1589, based on £21,753 6s. 8d. received from Sir James Colville of Easter Wemyss, from the English subsidy money. The subsidy was actually £27,000, but Colville had taken £5,246 13s. 4d. to raise a small force to fight for the English in France.[21] Maitland spent the rest on the expenses of the king's cavalry during the Brig o' Dee Rebellion (£4,500) and embassies to Denmark to arrange the royal wedding. He was left out of pocket by £3,477 3s. 4d.

The third part covers Maitland's expenses of the winter of 1589–90, on fitting out and victualling the ship *James Royall* for the king's voyage to Denmark. This cost him a total of £10,938 10s. 2d., for which there was no incoming money at all. Fourth, is an extensive list of James' expenses in Denmark, winter 1589 to spring 1590. These were largely paid from Anna's dowry of 75,000 dalers (the Danish currency) and a 1,000 daler wedding present from Sophie of Mecklenburg-Güstrow, the Queen Mother, but Maitland was still left superexpended by £910 3s. and 4d. Fifth is a discharge from the exchequer of 5 February 1594 saying that Maitland had handed over 54,000 dalers of the dowry (despite him being owed a considerable amount of money by the crown).

Sixth is another set of accounts of 1590 based on £27,000 received from Sir John Carmichael that July from England, more subsidy money, on various small debts and gifts to visitors and ambassadors, which left Maitland out of pocket by a further £2,594 11s. In total Maitland stated his cumulative superexpenditure as £17,824 7s. 10d. Seventh and finally, is a discharge of

19 Fuller information and further reading on these men can be found in notes to the text, especially pp. 17–18 below.

20 *The Exchequer Rolls of Scotland*, 23 vols (Edinburgh, 1878–1908) (hereafter ER), xxii, 229; Miles Kerr-Peterson, 'Sir William Keith of Delny: Courtier, Ambassador and Agent of Noble Power', *Innes Review* 67:2 (2016), 138–58.

21 Julian Goodare, 'James VI's English Subsidy', in Julian Goodare and Michael Lynch, *The Reign of James VI* (East Linton, 2000), 110–25, at 117–18.

the king to Maitland of 20 May 1590, saying that Maitland had been given four diamonds and two rubies to make into rings as gifts to the King and Queen mother of Denmark.

Document Set Two: National Library of Scotland Advocates MS. 29.2.5: Miscellaneous Accounts of John Maitland of Thirlestane and Jean Fleming, Lady Thirlestane, 1588–90

These accounts were kept by Chancellor Maitland and his wife Jean Fleming between 1588 and 1590. These are now kept in the National Library of Scotland. They form part of volume five of the Balcarres Papers. Some entries were included in the audited account in the British Library (Document Set One), but there is additional and complementary material.

First is a copy or draft of the account of money received from Sir William Keith of Delny, varying in its wordings from the audited version. The second item is a receipt from François de Civille, ambassador sent by Henri king of Navarre, for 1200 merks from Maitland, signed 11 September 1589. Before the final choice of the Danish match, there was the possibility that James might marry Catherine de Bourbon, Henri of Navarre's sister, although this was eventually abandoned in favour of good trading relations in Scandinavia.[22] Civille, may have been making a final vain bid for the Navarre marriage, as discussed below. By this time though such a task was probably hopeless, so Civille sought to press his other objective of raising three thousand troops for Navarre.[23] Henri described this as an opportunity to safeguard the Reformed church and give 'most speedy and certain human succour against the imminent attempts of the enemies of God' – 'le plus promt et assure secours que jatans humatnement contre le plus proches effors des enemys de Dieu'.[24]

Third is a set of accounts by Thomas Foulis based on £9,683 9s. 4d. in English gold angels received from Jean Fleming, Lady Thirlestane, dated 20 June 1589. This was used to pay off some debts and to buy silverwork and jewellery for gifts for the upcoming royal marriage celebrations. A number of payments were made to Lady Thirlestane herself, presumably paying off her or her husband's expenditure for the crown. This interesting document possibly relates to the fifth item below.

Fourth, is an inventory of silver by Chancellor Maitland, dated 26 September 1589. This appears to be from a huge consignment of plate gifted by Elizabeth to James, valued at £2000 (sterling) given to Mr John

22 Stevenson, *Scotland's Last Royal Wedding*, 11, 13, 15.

23 See François de Civille, *Discours des causes pour lesquelles le Sieur de Civille se dit avoir été mort, enterré et ressuscité*, Ernest Poret, marquis Bénigne, ed. (Rouen, 1845).

24 A. Cameron, ed., *The Warrender Papers*, 2 vols (Edinburgh, 1931), ii, 90–2.

Colville in London in September 1589, and presumably evaluated by Foulis in Scotland when it arrived on 26 September, the date in the manuscript.[25] On 15 September Andrew Keith, Lord Dingwall had arrived in Scotland, separated from Anna's fleet by a storm. It was initially expected that her ships would be close behind, although no news was heard. On the 28th, James despatched Colonel Stewart to find out. News arrived on 10 October via Andrew Sinclair and Steen Bille. James set sail the following 22 October.[26] At the time Maitland had his silverwork inventoried, he may already have been thinking of putting together an expedition to Scandinavia.

Fifth, is an intriguing document, the compt of the 'Lady Chancellor', dated 1 August 1590. This was based on a total of £25,045 15s. 4ds. received in English 'angels', French 'crowns of the sun', and Spanish 'pistolets', which were to be melted down and re-coined. The Privy Council had ordered a new gold coinage in September 1588, and these coins were minted into thistle nobles, worth £7 6s. 8d. each.[27] In the use of foreign currency this source is similar to the third above, except for the presence of four sorts of coin by country of origin, rather than source. Thomas Foulis was, inter alia, 'sinker of the mint' since 1584, so may have been in charge of this coinage and the spending of gold also, on behalf of Lady Thirlestane, who somehow is represented as providing the gold and also having oversight of the spend, though Foulis does countersign some pages, and some of the entries are in his first person. Other entries mention 'my lady'. Somehow there had been a collection of foreign gold coin for the mint, and Lady Thirlestane was responsible for handing it to the mint, perhaps per pro her husband. Sources of coin might involve foreign powers, or tax and tolls and Scottish revenues, or purchase of coin from merchants – even so we still do not discover the source of funds for buying the foreign gold coin.

Part was spent in August and September, given to various individuals including tailors, workmen and crown officials. This document was composed after James, Anna, Chancellor Maitland and the other Scottish and Danish dignitaries had returned from Denmark. There is no obvious reason why she was fulfilling this task at that moment: Maitland was fit and well and, in the thick of politics.[28] The answer perhaps lies in the well-quoted statement by Thomas Fowler of December 1589 that she was 'a wise woman and half chancellor when he is at home'.[29] Lady Thirlestane was often styled 'Lady

25 *CSP Scot*, x, pp. 160–2.

26 Stevenson, *Scotland's Last Royal Wedding*, 24–30.

27 *RPCS*, iv, 322–3. These foreign coins were all current in Scotland and were circulating freely; see 'Act Anent the Cunyie' RPS, A1591/8/2.

28 See *CSP Scot*, x.

29 *Calendar of Manuscripts of the Marquis of Salisbury preserved at Hatfield House, Hertfordshire*, volume 3: 1583–1589 (London, 1889), 466–7.

Chancellor'. On the face of it, this meant little: Margaret Livingstone, the justice clerk's wife called herself, or was called, Lady Justice Clerk, with no suggestion that she acted in that role.[30] However, here Lady Thirlestane is very clearly undertaking an official role, around and including the time of her husband's absence.

Sixth and last in this set is a copy of Chancellor Maitland's accounts of expenditure based on the £27,000 English subsidy money received from Carmichael, a complementary account to the last document found in set one.

Document Set Three: National Records of Scotland, MS E30/14: Accounts of Thomas Foulis 1594–6

The third document is an account made by the Edinburgh goldsmith and financier Thomas Foulis of money received from Scottish gold mines and the English subsidy. The compt of 1594 to 1596 was based on £4,000 of English money and a little over £7,000 from the master coiner (Cunyeour) and £6,800 from the secretary in English money. Most was spent on jewellery, several pieces of which were given out as gifts. Other expenditure went on expenses for ambassadorial missions. Both were in large part in preparation for the baptism of Prince Henry, such as the piece of alabaster sent from England for the new chapel in Stirling Palace. Foulis was left out of pocket by £51,881 and five pence. This specific sum was acknowledged by the Octavians, James' eight-man exchequer commission set up in 1596.[31] Appended to these are thirteen corresponding vouchers and receipts, from MS E30/15.

Finally, a second appendix comprises two previously unpublished letters of Anna's, mentioned at the start of this introduction found by Dr Jemma Field in British Library Add. MS.19401, folios 141 and 143 and very kindly transcribed and translated by Dr Marie-Claude Tucker.

COMMENTARY ON KEY EVENTS IN THE ACCOUNTS

The King's Marriage Negotiations

One of the most visible presences in the accounts are gifts made to foreign ambassadors. James' possible marriage to a Danish princess had been mooted in 1587, Denmark being a strong trading partner with Scotland, and

30 Edinburgh University Special Collections, Laing II.2.2, 1588–92, an account of cloth supplied to the Lady Justice Clerk.

31 Goodare, 'The Octavians', 184–5.

Protestant, albeit Lutheran rather than Reformed. Negotiations had been conducted by Peter Young and Colonel William Stewart of Pittenweem and plans were set in motion to send a full ambassadorial mission under George Keith, Earl Marischal, to conclude the marriage and bring the bride, initially Princess Elizabeth, but ultimately Anna. Meanwhile, Chancellor Maitland was pressing for an alternative match to Catherine de Bourbon, sister to the king of Navarre (later Henry IV of France). The merchants of Edinburgh eventually forced James' hand towards Denmark, but these documents show some of the diplomatic wrangling.[32]

Clermont d'Ambroise arrived in Scotland in July 1588 to try and push the Navarre match, and James gave him a jewel worth £533 6s. 8d.[33] Further down the same page James gave 200 crowns (£533 6s. 8d.) to Claude de l'Isle, Seigneur de Marivaux, to relay his sentiments to the king of Navarre. L'Isle had been in Scotland from around the start of autumn 1588, and left by 7 July.[34] Elsewhere in the documents we find François de Civille, who was in Scotland between 10 March to the end of August, who was given 300 crowns (£800).[35] L'Isle and de Civille appear to have been working together in pressing James for the Navarre match.[36]

Sandwiched between the money paid to d'Ambroise and L'Isle though, we find money given to Sir George Beeston, an English naval captain, whose squadron arrived in the Forth in early June. This was not by chance. James was forewarned by Francis Walsingham, and then ordered ports and towns to welcome Beeston and his crew.[37] Beeston's arrival might be interpreted as a case of sixteenth-century 'gunboat diplomacy'. Elizabeth did not approve of James' choice or decision to marry; indeed, one gets the sense that she was thoroughly unhappy not to have been properly consulted on her godson's intentions at all. It is possible that Beeston's ships were there to visibly counter the Navarre diplomats, or perhaps just show to the rest of Europe

32 See Stevenson, *Scotland's Last Royal Wedding*, ch. 1.

33 See p. 61.

34 L'Isle thanked James effusively for a gift in a letter from Lethington dated 2 Sept/23 August 1588, and again from Edinburgh of 14/24 September 1588 (the king was at Stirling), *Warrender Papers*, ii, 73–5 and 76–8. The 200 crowns mentioned in the accounts may have been delivered at Lethington (Lennoxlove, Thirlestane's house) on 23 August 1588, and later a diamond ring in Edinburgh. See p. 23, n. 33.

35 See p. 62.

36 See *CSP Scot.*, x, 97.

37 This order is in the unpublished Treasurer's Accounts, NRS E21/105, June 1589. The published versions, *Accounts of the Lord High Treasurer of Scotland*, 13 vols (Edinburgh, 1877–1916), are hereafter referred to as TA. English ambassador William Ashby reported that the Scots were suspicious about the purpose of the English fleet's visit; but James VI was content enough with their presence (as Ashby writes again on 8 June). James dispatched Sir William Keith to greet Beeston. British Library, Cotton Caligula D I/439, 3 June 1589. Note that this letter was not published by the editors of *CSP Scot.*

that Scotland was under the English thumb whichever way James married. So the fleet in the Forth might be intended to show that James' marriage would not change the balance of power in Europe.

The King's Highland Genealogy

One of the more tantalising things to appear in two of the accounts is the payment of £43 to a 'Highlandman' for a 'cairt' or 'table of all the genologie of all the kingis of Scotland'.[38] The exact significance of this is unclear, but very interesting. We may speculate whether this may have been in preparation for the wedding celebrations, which included the display of pictures of James' genealogy, which had also been a feature of James' own entry in to Edinburgh in 1579.[39] In medieval Scotland there had been a tradition of reading the king's genealogy in Gaelic at coronations, described for the coronation of Alexander III in 1249.[40] It is unknown if this tradition died out or continued. But why ask a highlander? The king's genealogy could be readily found in any published History of Scotland, as by Fordun, Boece or Buchanan.

The celebrations aside, this may have been an act of cross-referencing for James, to compare the Highland tradition to the published histories. He may have been keen to dispute the stories of kingly deposition used by George Buchanan to underline the desirability of deposing tyrannical kings. James' *Trew Law of Free Monarchies* utterly rejected Buchanan's notion that subjects could oppose an anointed monarch.[41] To deepen the mystery further, in February 1593 James paid Walter 'Colhoun' (Colquhoun) 'for making a cairt of genealogie to his hienes of his gracis predecessors'. Walter received £85 10s.[42] Why a second chart was needed is unclear, as is whether Walter was the same genealogist as 1589. Indeed, very little information on Colquhoun is apparent at all.

38 See pp. 22, 61.

39 A few of this type of picture survive to this day, such as the famous portrait of James I. Eventually this phenomenon found its most extensive expression in Jacob de Wet II's 1684 Long Gallery paintings in Holyroodhouse. For a discussion of James' entries, see Michael Lynch, 'The Reassertion of Princely Power in Scotland: the Reigns of Mary, Queen of Scots and King James VI', in Martin Gosman, Alasdair MacDonald and Aro Vanderjagt, eds, *Princes and Princely Culture 1450–1650*, vol. 1 (Leiden, 2003), 199–238 at 222–3.

40 See Dauvit Broun, 'The Genealogy of the King of Scots as Charter and Panegyric', in J. Reuben David and S. Bhattacharya, eds, *Copper, Parchment, and Stone: Studies in the Sources for Landholding and Lordship in Early Medieval Bengal and Medieval Scotland* (Glasgow, 2016), ch. 7.

41 See Jenny Wormald, 'James VI and I, *Basilikon Doron* and *the Trew Law of Free Monarchies*: the Scottish Context and the English Translation', in Linda Levy Peck, ed., *The Mental World of the Jacobean Court* (Cambridge, 1991), 36–54.

42 NRS E22/9, f. 44r.

Men 'taken by the Turk'

James' spending in Denmark consisted of things which historians might expect, such as paying trumpeters, for gifts to the captain and staff of various castles or palaces, and payments for leisure pursuits. One of the more intriguing recurring costs, linked to money given to his chaplain Mr David Lindsay to give to the poor, are payments made to men 'taken with the Turk'. We see at least six men given money (possibly seven for a man 'taken' in France, although it is not said by whom); a poor man, a Polishman, a man with a testimonial from the king of Poland that he was 'a gentilman tain and mutilate with the turk', some persons described as 'Armeinianis' and two further 'uther' men. Giving money to such men was no doubt part of the usual charitable giving expected of monarchs and nobles, but may have had a special interest to James, given his composition of his poem on the Battle of Lepanto, where the forces of (Roman Catholic) Christianity had defeated the navy of the Ottoman Turks. That poem was probably composed in 1585, although it was not published until 1604.[43]

Architectural Interest

The accounts include several payments to William Schaw, who had served as master of works since December 1583, and oversaw all royal building. He went to Denmark with the king and was sent home early to direct operations to prepare Holyroodhouse and Anna's reception. Schaw was given 800 dalers from the dowry money to hire James Gourlay's ship for his return and £666 13s. 4d. from the English subsidy of 1589, and £1,666 13s. 4d. from the subsidy of 1590, both for works at Holyroodhouse. Schaw was also given money from the gold coined and accounted for by Lady Thirlestane, totalling £2,000, and at £1,000 by the treasurer for work at Anna's residence at Dunfermline Abbey. The majority of the money allocated to Schaw for building works came from the subsidy with few payments made from the treasurer's accounts, and this may have been the case in other years, although Foulis' account of 1594 includes only an alabaster stone for the new Chapel Royal at Stirling, and lead for the roof of Linlithgow Palace, to be delivered to Sir Roger Aston, with no other record of the expense of the chapel.[44]

Schaw arrived in Scotland on 16 March 1590 bringing instructions from James for the order and ceremony of the royal reception. Building work

43 James Craigie, ed., *The Poems of James VI of Scotland*, 2 vols (Edinburgh, 1955), i, xlvii–xlviii.

44 A. Juhala, 'Household and Court of King James VI of Scotland', 121–55, discusses payments in treasurers's accounts for the upkeep of palaces, and see J.T. Gibson-Craig, *Papers Relative to the Marriage of King James the Sixth of Scotland* (Edinburgh, 1828), 15–17, for payments to Schaw from the treasurer's accounts, including textiles and upholstery during Anna's coronation.

required at Holyroodhouse included the completion of a new gallery quarter or wing, and specific accommodation for the Danish party in the bishop of Orkney's house, Lady Gowrie's lodging, and Kinloch's house, to be furnished by the responsibility of several courtiers.[45] Schaw also brought a letter from James to the Privy Council reminding them of the urgency of work at the abbey.[46] A 'Dutch' or German 'turnour' called Frederick, presumably a woodworker, was given six dalers and sent to Scotland with Schaw. Perhaps a woodworker was required to fit a chapel suitable for Anna. Elsewhere he is mentioned in royal household accounts as the 'Dutch wright' who ate at the second table for Danish men in the queen's Master Household's hall.[47]

Schaw was also Chamberlain of Dunfermline for Anna from 27 June 1593.[48] He would have supervised the conversion of the monastic guest house as a royal lodging and the reconstruction of the precinct gatehouse as a new Queen's House in 1600, which became her 'ordinar residence', and may have reflected the queen's taste and Danish architecture at Kronborg and Frederiksborg.[49] Schaw also oversaw and signed Anna's household books, in 1598 twice commenting on the poor quality of ale.[50] Schaw was known by report in England as Catholic, as were several others of Anna's household.[51] As a New Year's gift in 1595 he was given a 'hinger', a hat badge in the form of a salamander set with diamonds. This gift was a presumably a reward for his various services to the queen.

Editorial Conventions

In order to produce a readable edition, line breaks have not been preserved and several blocks of text have been broken up into their individual items. The letters i/j and v/u/w have been given according to modern usage. Common abbreviations or contractions, such as qlk, wt and Matie have been silently expanded. Some entries running over two pages have been

45 Maureen Meikle, 280: 'Anna of Denmark's Coronation and Entry into Edinburgh, 1590', in J. Goodare and A.A. MacDonald, *Sixteenth-Century Scotland: Essays in Honour of Michael Lynch* (Leiden, 2008), 280: also Gibson-Craig, *Papers Relative to the Marriage of King James*, 29–34.

46 G. Simpson, 'The Personal Letters of James VI', in Goodare & Lynch, *The Reign of James VI*, 150–3.

47 National Library of Scotland (hereafter NLS) Adv. MS. 34.2.17, f. 135v.

48 W. Macray, 'Third Report on the Royal Archives of Denmark', *Appendix to the 47th Annual Report of the Deputy Keeper of Records* (London, 1886), 34.

49 A. Mackechnie, 'The Royal Palace of Dunfermline', in Richard Fawcett, *Royal Dunfermline* (Edinburgh, 2005), 119–26: D. Howard, *Scottish Architecture 1560–1660* (Edinburgh, 1995), 26–9.

50 NRS E31/6: *Report on the Manuscripts of Col. David Milne Home of Wedderburn Castle* (London, 1902), 70–1.

51 *CSP Scot.*, xii, 228.

united onto the previous page. Thorns have been rendered as 'th', yoghs as 'y's. Proper nouns have been silently capitalised. Most 'mid sentence' capital letters at the start of words have been silently changed to lower case, although ones intended to mark a new sentence or clause have been retained. Some of the page edges in the original documents have been damaged, and small parts of the text lost. Where possible, the lost or damaged text has been silently restored and footnotes have been supplied to indicate on which pages this has occurred. Other editoral notes can be found in the footnotes.

Currencies have been given in their original form. There were 12 pennies to the shilling, 20 shillings to the pound. A merk was two-thirds of a pound, 13s. 4d. In this period £12 Scots were roughly worth £1 English sterling. A crown was usually worth 5 shillings. The crowns used in Thomas Foulis' accounts are English, worth 5 shillings sterling, and £3 Scots. A thistle noble was a Scots coin, worth £7 6s. 8d. Scots. A rose noble was an English coin worth £7 6s. 8d. Scots. A large part of Anna's dowry seems to have been paid in these coins, as many were used while James was in Denmark. An angel was an English coin worth 90 shillings Scots or £4 10s.; 'angellis of gwne hoillis' is sometimes used to describe these coins in the accounts.[52] As the English angels have St Michael on one side and a ship on the other, 'gun hoill' is presumably meaning 'gunwale', somehow preferred to the more obvious 'ship angel', but perhaps a distinguishing feature of a warship. See also R. W. Cochran-Patrick, *Records of the Coinage of Scotland* (Edinburgh, 1876), p. 267.

A Danish daler was worth roughly £2 8s. Scots. The notation 't.' has been used below, in reference to the 'thaler' upon which it was based. This is done to avoid confusion with 'd.' for pennies or the moder dollar '$'. 'Norts' were either coins vauled at one quarter of a daler, or literally one quarter of a daler coin. This text is unusual in using the word 'nort' for the Danish 'ort'. An ort was worth 24 skillings in this period and the daler 64 skillings. See O. Degn, *The Sound Toll of Elsinore* (Copenhagen, 2017), pp. 150–2. They were more commonly referred to as 'orts' in Scottish sources, the word sometimes referring to the fourth part of anything (see www.dsl.ac.uk/entry/dost/ort, accessed 19 September 2018). The word is derived from the word 'ørte' meaning weight, in much the same as the English/Scots 'pound'.

A column has been added to these transcriptions repeating the inventory sums in arabic numerals, to help the reader follow the expenditure, but also to allow easier comparison between entries. Saving the dalers and norts in the accounts made in Denmark and Norway, totals in crowns or other coins have been converted into pounds, shillings and pence. In a few instances, entries have been left as crowns when they are part of a summarised sub-list within the account.

52 Below, p. 62.

Dates are left as found in the text. It should be noted that before 1600 the year started on 25 March, so mentions of 'February 1593' in the text, for instance, should be read as February 1594 and where relevant are followed by the new style date in square brackets [1594]. Discussion of historical context in the introduction and the notes treat 1 January as the year's beginning.

TRANSCRIPTION

Document Set One

British Library: Additional MS. 22,958

[f.1r][1]Commissio

Jacobus dei gratia Rex Scotorum Omnibus probis hominibus suis ad quos presentes Litterae peruenerint Salutem. Sciatis Quia me post nostram perfectam etatem viginti qumque annorum completam et generalem revocationem fecimus constituimus et ordinavimus ac tenere presentis facimus constituimus et ordinamus nostros fidelissimos consiliaros Marcum dominum Newbottle[2], dominum Robertum Melvile de Muridocarny militem nostrum thesaurarum deputatum[3] dominum Johannes Cokburne de Remestoun militem nostres justiciaries clericum[4], dominum Patricum Vaus de Barnbarroch militem unum senatorum nostri collegii justiciis[5], Davidem Seytoun de Parbrocth nostrorum computorum rotulatorem[6], dominum Ricardum Cokburne de Clerkingtoun nostrum Secretarum[7], Walterum commendatarum de Blantyre nostri secreti sigilli custodem[8], Alexandrum Hay de Eister Kennet nostrorum rotulorum registri ac consilii clericum[9], Magistrum Davidem Carnegie de Culluthie[10], magistrum Petrum Young de

1 This page is damaged along the right-hand side. The text has been silently restored where the meaning has been obvious, and from common formulations of this sort of commission.

2 Mark Ker, Lord Newbattle (1559–1609). Later Earl of Lothian. Gentleman of the chamber from 1580 and lord of session from 1584. Margaret Sanderson, 'Ker [Kerr], Mark, first earl of Lothian (b. in or before 1599, d. 1609)', *ODNB* [15462, accessed 27 October 2017].

3 Sir Robert Melvill of Murdocairny (1528–1621). Later first Lord Melville. Treasurer depute from 1582. During James' trip to Denmark, Melville served as acting chancellor. R.R. Zulager, 'Melville, Robert, first Lord Melville (1527/8–1621)', *ODNB* [18550, accessed 27 October 2017].

4 John Cockburn of Ormistoun, justice clerk from 1591. Juhala, 'Household', 337.

5 Sir Patrick Vaus of Barnbarroch (d. 1597). Lord of session from 1576, Vaus had joined Peter Young in a mission to Denmark regarding the royal marriage in 1587. Davie Horsburgh, 'Vaus [Vans], Sir Patrick, Lord Barnbarroch (d. 1597)', *ODNB* [28101, accessed 27 October 2017].

6 David Seton of Parbroath, Chamberlain from 1590, comptroller 1588–96. Juhala, 'Household', 329, 336.

7 Sir Richard Cockburn of Clerkingtoun, secretary 1591–6. Juhala, 'Household', 336.

8 Walter Stewart commedator of Blantyre (d. 1617), childhood friend of King James, courtier and keeper of the Privy Seal from 1582. R.R. Zulager, 'Stewart, Walter, first Lord Blantyre (d. 1617)', *ODNB* [26513, accessed 27 October 2017].

9 Alexander Hay of Easter Kennet (d.1594), clerk register from 1579 and interim secretary while James was in Denmark in 1589. R.R. Zulager, 'Hay, Alexander, of Easter Kennet (d. 1594)', *ODNB* [12703, accessed 27 October 2017].

10 Mr David Carnegie of Colluthie (d. 1598), holder of various fiscal offices and from 1586 a regular auditor of the exchequer. Vivienne Larminie, 'Carnegie, David, of Colluthie and Kinnaird (d. 1598), *ODNB* [69925, accessed 27 October 2017].

Seytoun nostrum elemosinarum[11], Magistrum Georgii Young archidiacoum Sanctiandrois[12] -------------------------

vel quoscumque eorum quatuor coniunctim auditores recepto omnium et quorumcumque receptorum summarum monetes taxationum integrarum seu novarum casualitatum, Totalium, bonorum, rerum aliarumque summarum monetes quarumcunque per nostrum fidelissimum consanguineum et consilarum Joannem dominum Thirlestane[13] res cancellarum nostrum receptis quocumque tempore retroacto nobis incumbeum dictique nostri predilocti consanguinci et consularii debursationumet expensarum per eundem in nostro servitio et negetiitam infra regnum nostorum quia in patriis Novergis et Danniis in nostro comitatu remanentis et reddentis per ipsum debursatis et expositis Daudo concendendo et committendo eisdem nostris auditoribus vel quibuscumque eorum quatuor coniunctim nostram plenariam liberam et integram potestatem et speciale mandatum nostra et singular dicta computa overactionis exonerations et expensis earundem audiendi, allocandi, et exonerandi, et ad hunc effectum quocumque dio seu diobus loco sen locis prout eis videbitur expediens conveniendi et assignandi, Et generaliter omnia et singula ques dictis auditoribus spectant seu attient gerendi et exercendi firmum atque stabile habenum et habiturum totum et quicquid dicti auditores vel quicumque eorum quatuor coniunctim in premissis rite duxerint faciend. QUARE universis et singulis quorum interest vel interesse poterit stricte precipimus et mandamus quatenus dictis nostris auditoribus computorum praedictis vel quibuscumque eorum quatuor … sius officiariis et ministries in omnibus et singulis permissa tangentibus prompte pareant respondeant et intendant sub omni pena ques competere poterit in hac parte Datum sub testimonie nostri magni sigilli apud Halirudhous vicesimo sexto die mensis decembris Anno domini millesimo quadringentesimo novogisamo tertio et regni nostri vicesimo septimo

Per signaturem S.D.N. regis subscript.

Broad Translation

Commission

James by the grace of God, King of Scots, gives Greetings to all his worthy men wherever this letter reaches. Know ye that I have reached my pefect age of twenty-five years and have made, constituted and ordained a general revocation, and now make, constitute and ordain to hold by this present

11 Mr Peter Young of Seton (1544–1628), schoolmaster for King James alongside George Buchanan. Young was central to the negotiations with Denmark over the royal marriage. Master almoner to the king from 1577. Davie Horsburgh, 'Young, Sir Peter (1544–1628)' *ODNB* [30277, accessed 27 October 2017].

12 Mr George Young, secretary depute 1580–97. Juhala, 'Household', 336.

13 John Maitland of Thirlestane (1543–95). See Introduction.

order, our most faithful councillors Mark Lord Newbattle, Sir Robert Melville of Murdocairny treasurer deputy, Sir John Cockburn of Ormiston Justice Clerk, Sir Patrick Vaus of Barnbarroch senator of our College of Justice, David Seton of Parbroath our comptroller, Sir Richard Cockburn of Clerkington our secretary, Walter Commendator of Blantyre keeper of our privy seal, Alexander Hay of Easter Kennet our clerk of register roll and council, Master David Carnegy of Colluthy, Master Peter Young of Seton our almoner, Master George Young Archdeacon of Saint Andrews, or at least four of them jointly, as auditors, to recieve the whole taxation money, new fiscal casualities, and whatever other money recieved by our most faithful cousin and councellor John Lord Thirlstane, our chancellor, recieved whenever occupying our said office, and also our cousin and councillor's payments and expenditure made in our service and the negotiation during our resort in the countries of Norway and Denmark, as well as when preparing in our country, and on our return, all spent by him, and then compiled, then submitted here to our auditors, or at least four of them jointly, having our full and free integral power and special mandate, and so this said account, its payments, exonerations and expenses must be audited, allocated and exonerated, and to this effect these accounts are to be seen on whatever day or days, place or places that must be assigned and convened, and generally, all and singular of these said auditors, they are to oversee or attend to the carrying out and exercising of it, and the firm and stable conducting and total handling, and the said auditors, or whichever four of them convened, with precise conduct will draw to a conclusion. Therefore all together and singularly they will have power between them that we prescribe and mandate to our said auditors of the aforesaid accounts, or whichever four of them... these officers and administrators all together and singularly having deliberated, they may appear, answer and extend these accounts under penalty which may be able to come together in that part. Given under the sign of our great seal at Holyroodhouse 26 April 1593, and of our reign 27 years, Signed by our most serene majesty.

Accounts of Chancellor Maitland: Spring 1588 to Spring 1589

[f.2r]14

The compt of Johnne Lord Thirlstane chancellar of Scotland the sowme of ten thowsand punds money given be him fra Sir William Kith of Delneis[15] knycht according to his compt of thre thowsand pund stirling quhilk the

14 This page is badly damaged. The text has been reconstructed where possible. A duplicate copy, possibly the draft, can be found later, pp. 59–61, and is referred to in these notes as the Advocates text.

15 Sir William Keith of Delny (d. 1602), master of the wardrobe at this time. See Miles Kerr-Peterson, 'Sir William Keith of Delny', 138–58.

[damaged] fra the comptar in the yeir of god J^m v^c four scoir [damaged] maid before the indetors under writtin. They ar to say Mark Lord of Newbottle Sir Robert Melvill of Murdocairny knight thesaurear depute John Cokburne of Ormistoun knight clerk of the justiciarie Sir Patrick Vaus of Barinbarrauche knycht ane of the senators of the colledge of justice David Seytoun of Parbroch comptroller Sir Richard Cokburne of Clerkingtoun younger sectretair Walter commedatour of Blantyre kepair of the previe seill Alexander Hay of Eister Kennat clerk Register Mr David Carnegey of Culluthy Mr Peter Young of Seytoun maister elemosmar to our soveraine lord Mr George Young archdeane of Sanct Androws Be his hienes commissioun under the testimoniall of the greit seill speciallie constituet In the chekker at Edinburgh the first day of Marche the yeir of God j^m v^c fourscoir threttene yeiris [1594].

Charge

The comptar chargis him with the sowme of ten thowsand pund ressavit fra Sir William Keith of Delneis knycht at the kings majesteis command	x^m lib	(£10,000)

Summa patet

Discharge

In the first the comptar aucht to be dischargit of the sowme of sevin thowsand thre hundredth threttie thre punds sex schillinegs aucht pennies debursit be him at the kings majesteis commandment particularlie heirefter expremit		(£7,300 6s. 8d.)
That is to say allowit to the comptar in part of payment of ane debt awand to him be his majestie conteinit in his hienes obligatioun of the dait at Edinburgh the vj day of Aprile 1588 yeiris sein upoun compt tua thowsand pund		(£2,000)
Item to Charlis Pigne laquay[16] according to his compt auchtene punds threttene shillings [f.2v] aucht penneis		(£18 13s. 8d.)
Item to Mr George Young at his majesteis commandment	vj^c Lxvj li xiij s iiij d	(£666 13s. 4d.)

16 Lackey, a footman. 'Piggie' is recorded as a lackey in the royal household between at least 1583 and 1593. Juhala, 'Household', 323. In the Advocates version of the text, the sum was paid to a Charles Forteviot, who is recorded as lackey to Prince Henry; see *ER*, xxiii, 309. It is likely that 'piggie' was the nickname of Forteviot. One of the two texts contain an error, as he is paid £18 13s. 8d. here, but £18 13s 4d in the Advocates manuscript.

Item to Mr Richard Cokburne youngar of Clerkingtoun quhen he past to England with the Laird of Eister Wemys[17]

vj^c Lxvj li xiij s iiij d (£666 13s. 4d.)

Item the xxiij of november 1588 to William Hendersoun[18]

xxiiij li viij s (£24 8s.)

Item that same day to Johnne Windegattis[19]

xxij li (£22)

Item the xxv of november to Andro Melvill[20] master houshald

j^c ij li xiij s iiij d (£102 8s. 4d.)

Item to Mr Patrik Galloway[21] at tua severall tymes the ane in november 1588 the uther the vij of Maii efter his majesteis returning from the north[22]

ij^c Lxxxxv li (£295)

Item to Adriane Dammane[23] and some workmen Flemyngis

ij^c Lxvj li xiij s iij d (£266 8s. 3d.)

17 James Colville of Easter Wemyss (1551–1629), Master of the Household 1579–81, although he continued to serve in the court thereafter. He served as ambassador to England in 1589, in an attempt to have Elizbaeth fulfil the promises made to James during the Armada crisis of 1588. Juhala, 'Household', 113, 310; Arthur H. Williamson, 'Colville, James, first Lord Colville of Culross (c. 1551–1629)', *ODNB* [67449, accessed 27 October 2017]. Sir Richard Cockburn was in London in April 1589, *CSP Scot.*, iv, 21.

18 William Henderson, marshal of the king's house 1589–1604. Juhala, 'Household', 317. The Advocates manuscript version of this text records that this payment was for furnishing the king's house.

19 John Wingate, master caterer 1582–5. Juhala, 'Household', 312. The 'catour' was an officer of the king's household buying food; Gibson-Craig, *Papers Relative to the Marriage of King James*, 34, *ER*, vol. 22 (1903), 33.

20 Sir Andrew Melville of Garvock, extraordinary Master of the Household 1589–1605. He served the terms of Martinmas 1588 and Whitsun 1589. He was the brother to Melville of Halhill and Murdocairnie. Juhala, 'Household', 310; *CSP Scot.*, x, 372; *ER*, vol. 22, 31. The Advocates version of this text mentions Melville's furnishing of the king's house.

21 Mr Patrick Galloway, minister of the Kirk, who served the royal household 1590–1604. Juhala, 'Household', 317.

22 Returning from the north refers to the Brig o' Dee rebellion of the earls of Huntly, Errol and Crawford. The Advocates version of this text specifically mentions returning from 'the Brig of Dey'.

23 Adrian Damman van Bijsterveld, was a representive of the United Provinces/Dutch republic in Scotland, and served for a time as a regent at the newly founded University of Edinburgh, from 1590 to 1594. See Esther Mijers, "'Addicted to Puritanism": Philosophical and Theological Relations between Scotland and the United Provinces in

Item the third of februar to Patrik Murray[24] be his majesties commandiment being direct to the north toward my Lord of Huntlie[25] twentie crownis
Inde Liij li vj s viij d (£53 6s. 8d.)

Item send to his majestie be Mr Richard Cokburn[26] to be gevin to the Englis huntaris[27] tua hundreth crownis
Inde v^{c} xxxiij li vj s viij d (£533 6s. 8d.)

Item to ane helendman[28] that gaif to his majestie ane table of the genologie of all the kingis of Scotland sex thirsall noblis inde
xLiiij li (£44)

Item gevin to his majesteis self divers and sundrie tymes in the said 1588 yeir and a part of the 1589 ane hundreth four scoir threttene thirsell noblis[29]
inde j^{m} iiij^{c} xv li vj s viij d (£1,415 6s. 8d.)

Item part for a jowell that was gevin to Monssoir de Cleremont[30]
v^{c} xxxiij li vj s viij d (£533 6s. 8d.)

Item to the marineris that was in Sir George Bistonis[31] ship callit the Vangard j^{c} crownis
inde ij^{c} Lxvi li xiij s iiij d (£266 13s. 4d.)

the First Half of the Seventeenth Century', *History of Universities* XXIX/s (2016), 69–95 at 77.

24 Probably Patrick Murray of Geanies, brother to Sir David Murray of Gospertie, royal server or servant 1582–93, gentleman of the chamber 1594–7. Juhala, 'Household', 253, 311, 313.

25 George Gordon, sixth Earl of Huntly (1562–1636). On 29 June 1590 Robert Bowes mentioned that Patrick Murray would be sent north to Huntly with a letter from the king. *CSP Scot.*, x, 334–5.

26 Mr Richard Cockburn, probably a different man to Sir Richard Cockburn of Clerkington already mentioned, was a gentleman of the chamber 1588–92. Juhala, 'Household', 313.

27 On 16 March 1588/9 James VI stayed in bed at Holyroodhouse after hunting the hare on the previous day, *CSP Scot.*, x, 6, 9. For the English hunters, see Juhala, 'Household', 325.

28 See Introduction for a discussion of this entry. In the Advocates version the 'table' is described as a 'cairt'.

29 The Advocates version of this text tells us that this was for the king to play cards.

30 Clermont d'Amboise was a Hugenot, and arrived in Scotland in July 1588, in an attempt to persuade James to marry into the house of Navarre. *CSP Scot.*, ix, 586; *Calendar of letters and state papers relating to English affairs: preserved principally in the Archives of Simancas*, 4 vols (London, 1892–9), iv, 406.

31 Sir George Beeston, 1520–1601, was an English naval captain and member of parliament. He commanded the Vanguard during the Armada campaign. Beeston's ship arrived in the Firth of Forth on 1 June 1589 and a couple more English ships arrived in the following days. On 5 June, a party was sent from the ship for provisions, and to see Edinburgh. Three of their number went drinking with some Scots, but an argument led to the wounding of

Item for a great tablet set with diamontis gevin to the said Sir George

iij^c lxxiij li vj s viij d (£373 6s. 8d.)

Item to ane Englis huntar twentie crownis

inde Liij li vj s viij d (£53 6s. 8d.)

As the kings majesties lettre of ressait and discharge sein upoun compt beris

vij^m iij^c xxxiij lib vj s viij d (£7,333 6s. 8d.)

And of thre hundreth crownis deliverit at command of his majesteis precept to the to the laird of Eister Wemys[32] extending to the sowme of

viij^c lib (£800)

And of tua hundreth crownis deliverit to Monssoir de Lile[33] sonne to the baillie of Orleance bring directed from his majestie to the King of Navarre Extending to

v^c xxxiij li vj s viij d (£533 6s. 8d.)

And of three scoir tua crownis send to Berwick to Monssoir de Nassau[34] be his majesteis command

j^c Lxv li vj s viij d (£165 6s. 8d.)

And of twentie crownis gevin to Mr George Young[35] to be gevin to Cuthbert[36] the huntar

Liij li vj s viij d (£54 6s. 8d.)

one of the Englishmen. As they returned to Leith they were set upon by some Spaniards, and Beeston's 'trumpet' (trumpeter) was killed in the fray. The matter was eventually settled by the king. Beeston's ship left Leith on 16 June. 'BEESTON, Sir George (c.1520–1601), of Beeston, Cheshire', in *The History of Parliament: the House of Commons 1558–1603*, ed. P.W. Hasler (London, 1981); *CSP Scot.*, x, 98, 106, 122–3. The draft version of the text (see p. 61) calls Sir George 'Sir John Bestoun'.

32 James Colville of Easter Wemyss, involved in diplomacy with the king of Navarre, ambassador to France, 9 December 1586. *RPCS*, iv, 127.

33 Jérôme Groslot, Sieur de l'Isle, was sent to Scotland in 1589 by the king of Navarre to advocate for James' marriage to his daughter instead of the Denmark match. He left Scotland by 7 July. *CSP Scot.*, x, 37, 116. Cameron, *Warrender Papers*, ii, 81–17: H. Aubert, *Correspondance de Théodore de Bèze*, XVI, 1575 (Geneva, 1993), 189–91.

34 Maurice of Nassau, 1567–1625, Prince of Orange from 1618.

35 Mr George Young, ambassador to Denmark in 1588, elemosinar in 1590, *CSP Scot.*, x, 374.

36 James seems to have employed several English hunters, including Cuthbert Armour, mentioned in 1584. Juhala, 'Household', 324. Cuthbert was paid much more than 'Robert the English hunter', who recieved £13 6s. 8d., mentioned in the exchequer. See ER, vol. 22, 71, 236. These hunters may have been bought to Scotland, or even met by chance near the border.

And of fyftie punds be his majesteis precept to Mr Johne Geddie[37]		
	L lib	(£50)
	Lateris viij^{m} ix^{c} xxxv li vj s viij d	(£8,935 6s. 8d.)
[f.3r][38] And of a hundreth threttie thre punds sex schilling aught penneis to Archibald Carmichaell[39] to be gevin to capitane Carliles[40] man quha come with a present and advertisement from him out of Ireland		
	j^{c} xxxiij li vj s viij d	(£133 6s. 8d.)
And of fyftie four punds ten schilling to Archibald Arnot[41] burges of Falkland for furnitor to certane huntaris according to his compt		
	Liiij li	(£54)
And of four scoir four angellis deliverit at his majesties command to Sir William Keith master of the gardrob		
	iij^{c} Lxiiij li	(£364)
And of tua hundreth thre scoir sex punds thretteine schilling four penneis to Roger Ashtoun[42] to be deliverit to his majestie being in Stiruiling[43] in the said monet of october		
	ij^{c} Lxvj li x xiij s iiij d	(£266 13s. 4d.)
And of ane hundreth thre scoir punds to the said Roger to gif to ane Inglis poet namit Mr Briton[44]		
	j^{c} Lx li	(£160)

37 Mr John Geddie, one of the king's servitors, mentioned 1585 and 1591. Servitor to Queen Anna in 1592. Juhala, 'Household', 316, 330, 343, 351.

38 This page has some water damage, obliterating the page edge. The missing parts of the text, mostly the tallies, have been silently supplied.

39 Archibald Carmichael of Edrom was ambassador to Denmark in 1588, or Archibald Carmichael, meantioned as cornet of the royal guard, mentioned in June 1587, later appointed collector of the voluntary subsidy of the nobles and prelates; *RPCS*, iv, 185.

40 Captain Christopher Carleill (d. 1593) was an English soldier and sailor, who had fought in the Low Countries in the 1570s. He was made governor of Carrickfergus in Ireland in 1587. He was sent to Ostend in 1589. D.J.B. Trim, 'Carleill, Christopher (1551?–1593)', *ODNB* [4668, accessed 27 October 2017].

41 Archibald Arnot in Falkland heritor of the Kirkland of Kinglassy, *RPCS*, iv, 409, 410. Archibald Arnot, testament dated 20 March 1592, and is mentioned in relation to his late wife in Christiane Fairny in August 1591. Francis Grant, *The Commissariot Record of Edinburgh Register of Testaments, Part 1* (Edinburgh, 1897), 13, 90.

42 Roger Aston (d. 1612), gentleman of the chamber 1581–1601. Juhala, 'Household', 313.

43 Stirling. This is either another instance where the scribe changed his 'i' and 'r' around to render this 'Striuling', or it could be 'Striveling', a common spelling at the time.

44 Possibly poet Nicholas Breton (1545–1626), who claimed to have visited James. Theo van

And allowed to the comptar the sowme of thre thowsand punds money of this realme awand to him for sundrie sowmes debursit be him to the kings majestie and at his hienes commandment in the yeir of God j^{m} v^{c} foir scoir aucht yeiris and of befoir contenit in his hienes write and obligatioun of the dait the tent day of ~~Julii~~ Junii 1588 yeiris as the sume sene upoun compt berris

iij^{m} libs	(£3,000)
parle iij^{m} ix^{c} Lxxviij li x s	(£3,978 10s.)
Summa of this haill discharge xij^{m} ix^{c} xiij li xvj s viij d	(£12,913 16s. 8d.)
And sa is the comptar superexpendit ij^{m} ix^{c} xiij li xvj s viij d	(£2.913 16s. 8d.)

tenet Clericus registri[45]

James R

Newbotle Blantyre SRobert Melvill Chancellarius BArribarrache
L Hume Parbrothe comptroller M PYoung RYoung Culluthy

Heijnsbergen, 'Masks of Revelation and 'the "female" tongues of men': Montgomerie, Christian Lyndsay, and the Writing Game at the Scottish Renaissance Court', in Theo van Heijnsbergen and Nicola Royan, eds, *Literature, Letters and the Canonical in Early Modern Scotland* (East Linton, 2002), 90–110, at 73–4.

45 Cls Reg' silently expanded to 'Clericus Registri'. This refers to Sir John Skene of Curriehill (c. 1540–1617), appointed clerk register on 19 September 1594. See Murray Athol, 'Skene, Sir John, of Curriehill (c.1540–1617)', *ODNB* [25669, accessed 23 March 2017].

Accounts of Chancellor Maitland: 1589

[f.4r][46] The compt of Johnne Lord Thirlestane chancellar of Scotland of the sowme of twentie ane thowsand sevin hundreth fyftie three punds sex schillings aucht penneis scottis money ressavit be him at our soverane lords command fra William Colvile servand to James Colville of Eister Wemys being a part of the money quhilk the said James ressavit in England in the monet of [left blank] the yeir of god j^{m} four scoir [left blank] yeiris Maid be the said lord chancellar at [damaged] [left blank] day of [left blank] the yeir of god j^{m} v^{c} foir scoir [left blank] yeiris Befoir the auditors underwrittin Thay ar to say Mark lord of Newbottle Sir Robert Melvill of Murdocannay knycht thesaurar depute Sir Johnne Cokburne of Ormistoun clerk of the justiciarie Sir Patrik Vaus of Barinbannauch knicht ane of the senatoris of the college of justice David Setoun of Parbroth comptroller Sir Richard Cokburne of Clerkingtoun younger secetair Walter commendatair of Blantyre kepair of the privie seall Alexander Hay of Eister Kennat clerk of the register Mr David Carnegie of Culluthy Mr Peter Young of Seytoun maister elemosuiair to our soveraine lord Mr George Young archideane of Sanct Androis Be his hienes commissioun under the testimonial of the great seill speciallie constitute in the chekker at Edinburh the first day of march the yeir of god j^{m} v^{c} fourscoir threttene yeiris [1594].

Charge

The comptar chargis him with the sowme of twentie ane thowsand sevin hundreth fyftie thre punds sex schilling aucht penneis scottis money ressavit be him as is abovewrittin

xxj^{m} vij^{c} Liij li vj s viij d (£25,753 6s. 8d.)

Summa huius oneracionis patet

[f.4v]discharge

Item in the first allowit to the comptar the sowme of ij^{m} ix^{c} xiij li xvj s viij d quhairin he was superexpendit in the sicte of his last compt maid be him of the ten thowsand pund scotts money ressavit be him fra Sir William Keith

ij^{m} ix^{c} xiij li xvj s viij d (£2,913 16s. 8d.)

46 This page is also damaged, so the missing text has been silently supplied as far as possible.

Item the comptar aucht to be dischargit of the sowme of ten thowsand punds deliverit be him at our soverane lords comand to George erle Marshell[47] as principall ambassador directed in denmark for contracting of his hienes mariage

x^{m} li (£10,000)

And of fyve thowsand punds deliverit at his hienes command to Sir William Keith of Delneis knycht Master of his majesteis gardrobe in part of pament of his heines claits[48] furneissit be the said Sir William

v^{m} li (£5,000)

And of four thowsand fyve hundreth punds deliverit at his heines command to captaine William Home[49] captaine of horsmen for the wagis of him and his cumpany in severall monethis[50]

iiij^{m} v^{c} li (£4,500)

And of ane thowsand punds deliverit be the comptar at his hienes command to John Fentoun[51] comptroller clerk in name of David Setoun of Parbroith comptroller in the support of his office

j^{m} li (£1,000)

And of ane thowsand punds deliverit be the comptar at his hienes command to Sir Robert Melvile of Murdocarney knycht thesairar deput to the support of his office

j^{m} li (£1,000)

And of ane thowsand marks deliverit be the comptar at his majesteis command to William Schaw[52] master of work to his hienes in part of pament of the expensis of the said work to a compt

vj^{c} Lxvj li viij s iiij d (£666 8s. 4d.)

47 George Keith, fifth Earl Marischal, 1554–1623. For his role in the marriage negotiations, see Miles Kerr-Peterson, 'Politics and Protestant Lordship in North East Scotland during the Reign of James VI: The Life of George Keith, fourth Earl Marischal, 1554–1623' (University of Glasgow, PhD thesis, 2016), ch. 3.

48 Clothes.

49 William Home, lieutenant of the guard, 1586, master of the stable 1591–5, gentleman of the chamber 1595–9. Juhala, 'Household', 311, 313, 326.

50 This refers to their wages during the Brig o' Dee Rebellion.

51 John Fenton, comptroller clerk, 1562–1616. Juhala, 'Household', 312.

52 William Schaw, master of works, 1583–1602. Juhala, 'Household', 312.

And of fyftie punds deliverit be the comptar at his majesteis command to Andro lord of Dingwall[53] to be gevin be him to a Swadin L li (£50)

Summa of this full discharge xxv^{m} j^{c} xxx li x s (£25,160 10s)

And sua is the comptar superexpendit in this compt iij^{m} iiij^{c} Lxxvij li iij s iiij d (£3,477 3s. 4d.)

tenet Clericus registri
James R

M PYoung SRobert Mellvill Newbottle
RYoung Parbrothe comtroller Blantyre
BArubarrache Culluthy R Chancellarius JCokburne

Accounts for fitting out the James Royall: Winter 1589–90

[f.5r][54] The compt of Johne Lord Thirlestane chancellar of Scotland of all sowmes furneist and debursit be him at our soverane lords speciall command and directioun In the expensis and chargis of his majestie and his company in his voyage first Norroway and then to Denmark for his heines mariage in the monethis of october november december januar and februar in the yeir of god j^{m} v^{c} four scoir nyne yeiris maid befoir the auditors underwrittin Thay ar to say Mark lord of Newbottle Sir Robert Melville of Murdocairny knycht thesuarair depute Sir John Cokburne of Ormistoun clerk of the justiciarie Sir Patrik Vaus of Barinbarrauch knycht ane of the senatoris of the college of justice David Setoun of Parbroth comptroller Sir Richard Cokburne of Clerkingtoun younger secetair Walter commendatair of Blantyre kepair of the privie seall Alexander Hay of Eister Kennat clerk of the register Mr David Carnegie of Culluthy Mr Peter Young of Seytoun maister elemosuiair to our soveraine lord Mr George Young archideane of Sanctandrois Be his hienes commissioun under the testimoniall of the great seill speciallie constitute In the chekker at Edinburh the first day of March the yeir of god j^{m} v^{c} fourscoir threttene yeiris [1594].

Memorand the comptar maid the haill expensis and debursing under writtin conteinit in this compt upoun his awne propir money and credite at the speciall and earnest disyer of our soverine lord without any sowmes of money of his majesties ressavit of befoir for that effect

53 Andrew Keith, Lord Dingwall (d. 1606), sometime mercenary then courtier in Sweden, who returned to Scotland in 1583. See Steve Murdoch, *Network North* (Leiden, 2006), 98–9, 255, and Kerr-Peterson, 'Politics and Protestant Lordship', ch. 2.

54 This page is also damaged, although not as badly as some of the others. The missing text has been silently supplied.

In the first part and debursit be the comptar to Robert Jamesone[55] burges of Air for the fraucht of his ship to his majesteis use be the space of tua monethis in his passing and retunring ilk moneth ane thowsand punds

inde ij^{m} li (£2,000)

Item to Robert Quhyte, skipper

xL li (£40)

Item four pilottis ilk ane xv li

inde Lx li (£40)

Item to James Rokney cannonar[56]

xx li (£20)

Item to Johne Chisholme[57] commisser of the artailzerie[58] for dressing mounting and putting the ordinance on burde

xxviij li (£28)

Item for stemmyng to be syde clouthis top claits and uther ornamentis to the ship for freinyeis silk bukkrum lyningis and uther necessarie things thairto and making thairof

ij^{c} xxij li xiij s x d[59] (£222 8s. 10d.)

Lateris ij^{m} iiij^{c} xx li xiij s x d. (£2,420 13s. 10d.)

[f.5v] Item for taftie[60] to be flaggis enseyngnis stremars and samkynis for silk tueill and uther things necessarie thairto and for making thairof

ij^{c} Lxxx li (£280)

55 Jameson's ship was called the *James Royall* and was later one of the six ships to bring the king back from Scandinavia. This may have been the same 'best' and 'sufficient weirlyke ship' 'that maist commodiouslie and reddilie mycht be fundin within the heavin or raid or Air' that was fitted out for the use of Sir William Stewart of Carstairs, with 120 hagbutters at the direction of the Privy Council in June 1588 to pursue the rebellious Lord Maxwell. We later see Robert Jameson described as 'burgess of Ayr and royal servant' mentioned on 26 January 1607, when his son John and daughter Margaret were legitimated under the Great Seal. W. Dickson, J. Paul, J. Stevenson and J. Thomson, eds, *Registrum Magni Sigilli Regum Scotorum*, 8 vols (Edinburgh, 1882–1914) (hereafter RMS), vol. 1593–1608, p. 669, no. 1839; *RPCS*, iv, 309, 485.

56 James Rocknow was a royal gunner in the garrison of Edinburgh Castle; see Accounts of the Treasurer of Scotland, vol. 13 (Edinburgh, 1978), 404.

57 John Chisholm was comptroller of the ordinance for Queen Mary and was reappointed to the position in 1579 after the Marian Civil War. He was resident of the King's Wark in Leith from 1564. *RPCS*, iii, 191, 205; RPS 1567/4/15; 1592/4/155.

58 Artillery.

59 Includes silk and buckram for making flags and pennants.

60 Taffeta.

Item to a painter for painting of the ship[61]	xx li	(£20)
Item for daillis garronis sparris and uther tymmer for naills lokks bands and irne work and uther necessies for making of pantreis sellars ease rowmes caveis and for office housses in the said ship for repairing her and working thairof	Lxxxxvij li v s	(£97 5s.)
Item for lanternis	iiij li	(£4)
Item for trein plaittis quhyte and reid for dishis trunscheours and coppis	v li	(£5)
Item for xv^{m} bisquit baiks at twentie pund the thousand	inde iij^{c} li	(£300)
Item four chalder floure at sevin marks the boll	inde ij^{c} Lxxxxviij li xiijs iv d	(£298 13s. 4d.)
Item fyftie bolls meill thairof ten bollis twyis scheild at thre li the boll and fourtie bollis uther at four marks the boll	inde j^{c} xxxvj li xiij s iiij d	(£136 13s. 4d.)
Item for aucht cast of Inglis beir at thre scoir four pund the last	v^{c} xij li	(£512)
Item for sex cast of aill at fourtie aucht pund the last	inde ij^{c} Lxxxviij li	(£288)
Item for threttie martis at ten pund the pece	inde iij^{c} li	(£300)
Item for xxx mutoun bouk to salt price of the pece fourtie schillings	inde Lx li	(£60)
Item for thre dosoun of geiss to salt	xiij li xviij s	(£13 18s.)
Item for threttene geiss to baik	v li viij s	(£5 8s.)

61 The act for rigging out of the ships for James' return voyage specified the colours red and yellow. *RPCS*, iv, 469.

Item for twentie cunning to baik

viij li (£8)

Item for tua dosoun of capoins to baik

ix li xij s (£9 12s.)

Item for flour butter eggis plundames & utheris necessars and for baiking thairof

xxij li xvij s (£12 17s.)

Item for twentie pece of baikin beiff with the furnisching and baking thairof

x li (£10)

Item for tua hundreth keling price of the hundredth fourtene pund

inde xxviij li (£28)

Item for tua hundreth lyng at sextene pund ten schilling the hundreth

inde xxxiij li (£33)

Item for tua hundreth skait at sextene pund ten schilling the hundreth

inde xxxiij li (£33)

Item for tua barrell of salmond

xL li (£40)

Lateris ij^{m} v^{c} v li vj s viij d (£2505 6s. 8d.)

[f.6r] Item for xxx bollis of salt to salt the martis mutonis geiss and to be barrellit for all uther uses at auchtene schilhing the boll

inde xx viij li (£28)

Item for twentie four stane of cheis

xxiiij li (£24)

Item for tua barrell of better conteinying threttie stane at xl s the stane

inde Lx li (£60)

Item to the suker man for xij pund weght of confectors at threttie schilling the pund

inde xviij li (£18)

Item for thre stone wight of sucker at auchtene schilling the pund

inde xliij li iiij s (£43 4s.)

Item for sex pund of ginger at sex schiling aucht penneis the pund	inde xl s	(£2)
Item for four pund of pepper at threttie schilling the pund	inde vj li	(£6)
Item for thre barrill of apillis at four pund the barrell	inde xij li	(£12)
Item ane barrell of unyeouns	viij li	(£8)
Item for tua barrel of vinegar	viij li	(£8)
Item for twentie greit hammis at threttie schillings the pece	inde xxx li	(£30)
Item for tua barrell of bowcaill and carrets	v li	(£5)
Item for nyne scoir caponis to be kepit quik in the ship at aucht schilling the pece	inde Lxxij li	(£72)
Item for twentie stane of great quhyte candill at fourtie tua schilling the stane and ane greit kist to put theme in	inde xliij li xs	(£43 10s.)
Item for four stane of small sservice candill at fourtie tua schilling the stane	inde viij li viij s	(£8 8s.)
Item for thre hundreth plakketts of walx at fyve schilling the pece	inde Lxxxx li	(£80)
Item for a kist to put thame in	xL s	(£2)
Item for a hundreth and a half of torchis at fyve schilling the pece	inde xxv li	(£25)
Item for tua dosoun of lame[62] pottis	xxiiij s	(24s.)

62 'lame' – earthenware.

Item for paper gilt and uther[63]	xL s	(£2)
Item for a quart of ink	vj s	(6s.)
Item for four bollis aittis to the caponis	viij li	(£8)
Item for punschanis barrells drywairis tums[64] and uther treis for the aill flour meill bisquit beif mutoun baikin mixt and keyping of uther things necesssar for the vittualing and uther things requisit and to the cowperis and uther work men for graithing seasoning scadding and dressing of thame	j^{c} xxxiij li vj s viij d	(£1033 6s. 8d.)
	Lateris vj^{c} xxv li xviij s viij d	(£6025 18s. 8d.)
[f.6v] Item for careing of aucht tun of wyne from the abbay to Leith and ane pype of wyne sek[65]	xij li	(£12)
Item for cartis and sleddis to carteris pionners and uther work men for careing and paking of the hall vittualing furnitour of the ship and uther grants and for careing of it to the boittis	xxviij li xij s	(£28 12s.)
Item for hardin for cords woll hay and uther small thingis requiste for the packing	xiij li ix s	(£13 9s.)
Item for sex gallonis of medera wyne	xxij li	(£22)
Item for boittis to cary the haill geir and furnitor on burde to the ship to James Lun[66] for lying aucht dayis in Leith with his boit and to the boittis that caryeit his majestie and the cumpany aburde	Liij li	(£53)

63 This entry is best read 'for paper: gilt and other (i.e other types of paper)'. It is unclear if any of James' gilt-edged letters survive. James wrote to Sophie of Denmark from Oslo with plain paper: she wrote to him with gilt paper; NRS SP13/118, 119.

64 'tum' – a type of barrel.

65 The Palace of Holyrood. 'Sek' means sack, the type of wine.

66 Possibly James Lunn, pensioner Ferryman at Queensferry, 1484–1588. Juhala, 'Household', 328.

Item for lance stalffis		
	xxij li	(£22)
Item for powder		
	Lxxxiij li	(£83)
Item for luntis		
	vj li	(£6)
Item for leid		
	iiij li	(£4)
Item for a clok a Jupe a doublat a pair of breiks tua pair of schanks for pasments and furnitour and making of thame for ane hatt and serks and schone to the trumpettour for ane bandroll and stringis to his trumpett		
	Lxxxxj li	(£91)
Item to the said trumpettor at his imbarking thre rose nobles		
	inde xxij li	(£22)
Item for claithis to him		
	xj li	(£11)
Item to George Strauchen[67] for kists to pak the tapestries in	viij li	(£8)
Item gevin to his majestie and debursit for his hienes expensis in Norraway and Denmark till his majesteis tocher was ressavit quhilk was the [left blank] day of Februar 1589[68]		
	v^{m} li	(£5,000)
	parle v^{m} iij^{c} Lxxxvj li xj s	(£5,386 11s.)
Summa of thir haill expenssis contenit in thir tua laiffis extending x^{m} ix^{c} xxxviij li x s ij d Quhilk being eikit to the super expenssis of this		(£10,938)

[f.7r] compt maid of the money ressavit fra James Colvile of Eister Wemys, the haill sowme quhairin the comptar is superexpendit be this compt extendis to fourtene thowsand thre hundreth fyvetene punds threttene schilling sex pennies. tenet Clericus registri

67 George Strachan, 'tapisier' or keeper of the tapestries 1582–1604. Juhala, 'Household', 316.

68 I.e. this £5,000 was loaned by Maitland to James for use in Norway and Denmark until he received the cash dowry in February 1590. Payments from the dowry in dalers and 'norts' are accounted in the next set of accounts.

James R

Robert Melville Blantyre Newbottle Chancellarius JCokburne
Parbrothe controller Culluthy BArnbarrache GYoung MGYoung

Accounts Made in Denmark, Winter 1589 to Spring 1590

[f.8r] The compt of Johne Lord Thirlestane chancellar of Scotland of all money pertaining to our soverane lord and ressaivit in his name in the realme of Denmark and debursit and spendit at his majesteis command alsweill in the said realme of Denmark as efter his majesteis returning thairfra preceiding the first day of Junii the year of god j^m v^c Lxxxx yeiris Befoir the auditors underwrittin Thay ar to say Mark lord of Newbottle Sir Robert Melville of Murdocairny knycht thesuarair depute Sir John Cokburne of Ormistoun knycht clerk of the justiciarie Sir Patrik Vaus of Barinbannauch knycht ane of the senatoris of the college of justice David Setoun of Parbroth comptroller Sir Richard Cokburne of Clerkingtoun younger secetair Walter commendatair of Blantyre kepair of the privie seall Alexander Hay of Eister Kennat clerk of the Register Mr David Carnegie of Culluthy Mr Peter Young of Seytoun maister elemosinar to our soveraine lord Mr George Young archideane of Sanctandrois Be his hienes commissioun under the testimoniall of the great seill speciallie constitute in the chekker at Edinburh the first day of march the yeir of god j^m v^c fourscoir threttene yeiris [1594].

Charge

In the first the comptar chargis him with the sowme of thre scoir fyftene thowsand daleris ressavit be him fra Christophe Walkindorst[69] rent maister of Denmark as the tocher contractit and promitit to our soverane lord with the maist illuster princes Anna be the grace of God Quene of Scottis his dearest spous

Lxxv^m dalers (75,000t.)

And with the sowme of ten thowsand daleris ressavit be the comptar fra the maist vertious princes Sophia[70] be the grace of god Quene of Denmark mother to our soverane lady in name and to the behuif of our soverane lord

x^m daleris (10,000t.)

Summa of the haill charge

Lxxxv^m daleris (85,000t.)

69 ChristofferValkendorf (1525–1601), one of the Danish regency council, who had contributed to the marriage negotiations. Stevenson, *Scotland's Last Royal Wedding*, 126.

70 Sophie of Mecklenburg-Güstrow, Queen of Denmark (1557–1631).

[f.8v]discharge and expensis

In the first the comptar aucht to be dischargit of sex thowsand and threttie dalers deliveret be him at our souverine Lord command to George erle Marschell to pay and releve the sowme for quhilk Frederik Lyell[71] become cautioun for jowell, bocht be his majesteis command deliverit to the Queins hienes the tyme of the contracting of the mariage

vj^{m} xxx dalers (6,030t.)

And of ane thowsand sex hundreth thre scoir sex daleris half daler deliverit be his majesteis command to Sir Lewes Bellenden of Auchnowle[72] knycht justice clerk directed in commissioun out of Denmark to the queens majestie of England

j^{m} vj^{c} Lxvj dalers j half daler (1,666½t.)

And of thrie thowsand dalers deliverit be his majesties command to Sir Johne Carmichall of that ilk[73] a part of quhilk sowme was deliverit to him for a cheinyie and a ring and the same cheinyie gevin to Hendrie Goldensterne[74] captaine of Balhous and the ring to his wyff

iij^{m} daleris (3,000t.)

And of aucht hundreth daleris deliverit be his majesteis command to William Schaw master of work quhairof he suld gif to James Gourlaw[75] skipper for the fraucht of his schip returning in scotland ane thowsand marks scotts and the rest to be imployed for reparatioun of the abbay of Halirudehous againe his majesteis hame cuming

viij^{c} daleris (800t.)

71 Frederick Lyall (1536–1601) was the son of Alexander Lyall, a Scottish-born mayor of Elsinor, who also came to occupy the same position from 1591. He was a councillor and merchant of the town, and appears to have helped Marischal finance the purchase of a jewel for Anna during the marriage settlement. Riis, *Should Auld Acquaintance be Forgot…*, ii., 231–2.

72 Sir Lewis Bellenden of Auchnoull, Justice Clerk 1577–1591. Juhala, 'Household', 337.

73 Sir John Carmichael of that ilk, Master of the Stable 1585–93, Captain of the guard 1592–6. Juhala, 'Household', 310–11.

74 Henrik Gyldenstjerne, governor of Bohus Castle. Stevenson, *Scotland's Last Royal Wedding*, 40, 129.

75 James Gorlay, skipper of one of the king's ships is mentioned again in 1590, arriving in Aberdeen with Andrew Keith, Lord Dingwall. *RPCS*, iv, 505.

And of aucht hundreth and threttris daleris deliverit at his majesteis command to Sir William Keith of Delneis knycht for claithis furnist and maid to his majestie in Denmark[76]

viij^c xxx daleris (830t.)

And of tua hundreth daleris deliverit at his majesteis command to captaine Arnot[77] quha was derected from Scotland to Denmark to his majestie

ij^c daleris (200t.)

And of fyve hundreth daleris deliverit at his majesteis command to Robert Dog directed to pas to Loubecque[78] to by pulder quhilk was brocht hame and deliverit to the captaine of the castell of Edinburt[79]

v^c daleris (500t.)

And of tua hundreth fourscoir sevintene daleris ane nort deliverit at his majesteis command for xiij last and aucht barrell of Rostorg beir[80]

ij^c Lxxxxvij dalers j nort (297t. 1n.)

And of ane hundreth and twentie daleris deliverit to Andro Sinclar[81] to by fyve veschell

j^c xx dalers (120t.)

Lateris xiij^m iiij^c xliij daleris half daler j nort (4,444½t. 1n.)

76 NRS E35/13 mentions William Keith of Delny a couple of times but only for fabric delivered back in his time as Master of the Wardrobe, and in a retrospective payment for the minor components of an outfit in 'argentin graye sattin' that Delny delivered to James in Denmark. Perhaps Delny produced several new outfits in Denmark, but only this one was not fully paid for, or maybe this was special. While in Denmark Delny was dismissed from his office in the Wardrobe. See Kerr-Peterson, 'Sir William Keith of Delny'.

77 Captain Robert Arnot of the royal guard 1586–91. Later servitor to Queen Anna's chamber. Juhala, 'Household', 326, 330.

78 Lubeck.

79 Sir James Home of Coldenknows, Captain of Edinburgh Castle from 1585. *RPCS*, iv, 33, 36, 89.

80 Probably Rostock beer.

81 Andrew Sinclair (1555–1625), third son of the fifth Lord Sinclair. In 1591 he decided to remain in Denmark at the royal court, serving in the administration, in the army and as ambassador. Riis, *Should Auld Acquaintance Be Forgot…*, ii., 74; Stevenson, *Scotland's Last Royal Wedding*, 126.

[f.9r] And of ane thowsand ane hundreth daleris deliverit be his majesteis command to ane wyff of Holand for tua jowells ane of quhilk gevin to the chancelar of Denmark[82] and nyne hundreth daleris the uther gevin at his majesteis command to a gentilman thair

j^{m} j^{c} daleris (1,100t.)

And of five thowsand daleris deliverit be his majesteis command for the cheinyeis quhilk war distribute to sundrie noblemen and gentilmen of Denmark that gaif attendance at court during his majesteis remaining thair

v^{m} daleris (5,000t.)

And of four thowsand daleris deliverit be his majesteis command for jowells quhilk was gevin to the princes being at the Duk of Brunswicks mariage[83] and ane of theme gevin to the admirall of Denmark at his cuming to Scotland

iiij^{m} daleris (4,000t.)

And of thre hundreth daleris gevin for a cheinyie maid of fyne gold that was deliverit to the chancellar of Denmark with the jowell forisaid

iij^{c} dalers (300t.)

And of tua hundreth daleris is be his majesteis command to the captaine of the castell of Coupmanhavin to be distribut amangis the servands thair

ij^{c} daleris (200t.)

And of ane hundreth daleris gevin be his majesteis command to the captaine of Friddrickburgt to be distribut amangis the officers and servands thair

j^{c} daleris (100t.)

And of tua thowsand daleris gevin be his majesteis command to the officers soldiers and haill servands in the castell of Coroniburgt[84]

ij^{m} daleris (2,000t.)

82 Niels Kaas (1534–94), chancellor of Denmark from 1573. Stevenson, *Scotland's Last Royal Wedding*, 123.

83 The marriage between Elizabeth (Anna's older sister, 1573–1626) and Henry Julius, Duke of Brunswick-Lüneburg (1564–1613) was held on 19 April 1590.

84 Kronborg.

And of twentie rose noblis that was borravit and gevin out be the kings command viz to the men that mak the fyre work sex rose noblis to ane bryde that was mareit within the castell of Coroniburgt sex rose noblis to Ramelius[85] tua men that deliverit the ten thowsand daleris sex rose noblis to William Stewart that he gaif to the king tua rose noblis extending to

Lxxv daleris (75t.)

And of twentie tua daleris and ane half givin at the kings command to a pure man that was tane with the turk sex rose noblis extending to

xxij dalers j half (22½t.)

Item of four daleris gevin for a kist to put the daleris in

iiij daleris (4t.)

And of four daleris gevin upoun the 20 of februar 1589 to his majestie to play at the carts

iiij daleris (4t.)

And of fyftie sex daleris ane nort gevin to John Gib[86] at the kings command that he debursit

Lvj dalers j nort (56t. 1n.)

lateris xvj^{m} viij^{c} lxj daler half dolder j nort (16,861½t. 1n.)

[f.9v] And of four dolours gevin to the kings tua trumpettours at his heines command

iiij daleris (4t.)

And of twentie daleris gevin at his majesteis command to Mr David Lyndsay[87] to gif furth to the poore

xx daleris (20t.)

And of twelf daleris gevin to the said Mr David to gif tua poore men

xij daleris (12t.)

And of four daleris gevin to a wright that suld ga hame to Scotland

iiij daleris (4t.)

85 Henrik Ramel (1550–1610), councillor and chamberlain to the Danish king, he had served as ambassador to Scotland during the marriage negotiations. Stevenson, *Scotland's Last Royal Wedding*, 10, 124.

86 John Gib, valet 1576–1601. Juhala, 'Household', 314.

87 Mr David Lindsay (d. 1613), James' chaplain while in Denmark and minister of South Leith 1560–1613. Stevenson, *Scotland's Last Royal Wedding*, 127.

And of ane daler gevin to the bowris[88] that careit the kists with the silver from Elsinure to Coupmanhavin	j daler	(1t.)
And of ane half daler gevin to four pioneris that caryed up the kists with the silver from the toun to the castell	j half daler	(½t.)
And of fyvetene daleris gevin to William Stewart to gif the king to play four rose noblis extending to	xv daleris	(15t.)
And of auchtene daleris the 23 of Februar gevin to Mr George Young[89] to pay for buks to the king	xviij daleris	(18t.)
And of tua rose noblis the 24 of Februar gevin to a turnour	vij daleris	(7t.)
And of ten daleris gevin to the man that furit[90] the king out of Wairberie[91]	x daleris	(10t.)
And of four daleris gevin to tua Scottis skipperis that was passand hame in James Gourlawis bark	iiij daleris	(4t.)
And of tua daleris ane half gevin to Mr Richard Cokburn that he gaif out for the kings majestie tua crownis extending to	ij daleris j half	(2½t.)
And of tua daleris ane haf gevin to William Stewart that he gaif out for the king	ij daleris	(2t.)
And of sex daleris gevin to the turnour[92] that past hame with William Schaw	vj daleris	(6t.)

88 This probably means bearers.

89 Young (see p. 18, n. 12 and p. 23, n. 35 respectively), had already been in Denmark with the mission of the Earl Marischal, before King James arrived.

90 Ferried.

91 Varberg, where James travelled from 9 to 14 January 1590, before travelling on to Falkenburgh. Stevenson, *Scotland's Last Royal Wedding*, 97.

92 Frederick the turner. See Introduction.

And of twentie daleris gevin on the 26 of februar to George Strauchen

	xx daleris	(20t.)

And of auchtene daleris gevin for painting gold

	xviij daleris	(18t.)

And of threttene daleris and half the last of februar gevin to Mr George Young to pay for four greit books to the king

	xiij daleris	(13t.)

And of ellevin daleris the 20 of marche gevin to John Gib that he gaif the king to play

	xj daleris	(11t.)

And of fyftie fyve daleris gevin to Mr George Young to pay for books cost to the king

	Lv daleris	(55t.)

And of ellevin daleris ane nort gevin to a scottis man callit Andro Robertsoun[93] that presented the king ane book thre rose noblis extending to

	xj daleris j nort	(11t. 1n.)
	Lateris ij^{c} xxxv daleris half daleris j nort	(235½t. 1n.)

[f.10r] And of auchtene daleris gevin to Jame Murray to gif the king to play four rose noblis and thre daleris extending to

	xviij daleris	(18t.)

And of twentie thre daleris ane half gevin to John Nasmyth[94] at the kings command conforme to his compt debursit be him

	xxiij daleris j half	(23½t.)

And of sevin daleris ane half the thrid of marche gevin to Mr Richard Cokburne to gif to William Stewart to gif the skippar of the shippis quhen the king visite thame Mair nor the same rose noblis quhilk he had in keiping befoir that was gevin to Jame Murray to gif the king tua rose noblis extending to

	vij dalers j half	(7½t)

93 Andrew Robertson presented James with a book of his translations of Sir David Lindsay's poems. He was an Aberdonian, long resident in Denmark, and who died sometime around 1592. Thorkild Lyby Christensen, 'Scots in Denmark in the Sixteenth Century', *Scottish Historical Review* 49 (1970), 125–45, at 144; Riis, *Should Auld Acquaintance Be Forgot…*, ii., 200–1.

94 Possibly John Naysmith, royal surgeon 1588–1602. Juhala, 'Household', 313.

And of four scoir tua daleris ane half gevin to Andro Sinclar at the kings command to bestow amang the men of the curie the men that brigit the new ship the workmen in the sundis the men of the munitioun hous and Axile Goldensteinis[95] man that brocht the lettres from Norraway twentie tua rose noblis extending to

Lxxxij dalers j half (82½t.)

And of ten daleris gevin the man that caryed the lettres to William Shaw in Mailstrand[96]

x dalers (10t.)

And of four daleris the 4 of marche gevin to William Stewart to gif the king to play at the mont[97]

iiij daleris (4t.)

And of fyftene daleris the 6 of marche gevin to William Stewart to gif the king to play at the mont four rose noblis extending to

xv daleris (15t.)

And of fyftene dalers the 7 of marche at the kings command gevin to Andro Keith[98] four rose noblis extending to

xv dalers(15t.)

And of twentie tua daleris ane half that same day gevin to Jon Gib to gif his majesteis self sex rose noblis extending to

xxij dalers j half (22½t.)

And of elevin daleris j nort gevin to Mr David Lyndsay quhen the king was in the college at the lessons[99] to gif the portar and pedill[100] thair thre rose noblis extending to

xj dalers j nort (11t. 1n.)

95 Axel Gyldenstierne, Danish governor of Norway and commander of Akershus Castle. Riis, *Should Auld Acquaintance Be Forgot…*, ii., 62; Stevenson, *Scotland's Last Royal Wedding*, 35.

96 Probably Malstrand/Marstrand, north of Gothenburg, Sweden.

97 'mont' – is possibly the game of 'three-card monte', or 'find the lady', where the player must follow a down-turned queen as it and two other cards are shuffled in front of him. The game is a favourite of confidence tricksters, so it is perhaps no surprise James lost his four coins. He lost another coin to the game in an entry further down this page.

98 Probably Andrew Keith, a page, mentioned in 1591. Juhala, 'Household', 315.

99 James visited the University of Copenhagen on 7 March 1590. Stevenson, *Scotland's Last Royal Wedding*, 99.

100 Pedill/Pedel was a university officer, a beadle. In Scots the terms generally denoted the person responsible for managing the buildings.

And of twentie daleris at the kings comand gevin to the man that careit bak the duke of Halstaris[101] lettre

	xx dalers	(20t.)

And of twentie daleris gevin to the Polomane[102] that was tane with the Turk

	xx dalers	(20t.)

And of twentie tua daleris and half gevin to the rent masters tua men that caryed the dolours sex rose noblis extending to

	xxij dalers j half	(22½t.)

And of thre daler thre nort tynt[103] be the king at the mont ane rose noble extending to

	iij dalers iij norts	(3t. 3n.)

And of thrittie dalers the 8 of marche gevin to Mr David Mortoun[104] at the kings command

	xxx dalers	(30t.)
	Lateris iij^{c} v daleris half dalour	(305½t.)

[f.10v] And of ane daler gevin to captaine Murrayis man that brocht the orangis fra the burrow maister of Elsinuor to the kings majestie

	j daler	(1t.)

And of fourtie ane dalers ane nort tynt be the King att the mumchance[105] extending to to xj rose noblis

	xlj dalers j half	(41½t.)

And of thre scoir daleris gevin to John Creithtoun at the kings command to gif Roger

	Lx daleris	(40t.)

And of fyftie daleris gevin to John Nasmyth the 9 of Marche at the kings command

	L daleris.	(50t.)

101 Philip, Duke of Holstein-Gottorp (1570–90).

102 Polishman.

103 Lost.

104 Mr David Morton, usher of the inner chamber 1589–97. Juhala, 'Household', 330.

105 Mumchance was a dice game, a variant of a game called hazard, which involved two players rolling three dice in turn, until certain combinations appeared, the roller of these being the winner. The mumchance variant had the additional rule that the players had to remain silent. Here James lost 11 coins, compared with the five he lost at playing 'mont'.

And of four rose noblis extending to xv daleris at the kings command gevin to Mr David Lyndsay to be gevin to a musiciane for sang books

xv daleris (15t.)

And of threttie daleris at the kings command gevin to John Gib to be gevin to Symon the violar for his book presented to the King

xxx daleris (30t.)

And of sex rose noblis extending to xxij daleris ane half the ij of marche gevin to the keipar of the kirk the organer and musicianis and the ringar of the bellis in Roscule[106]

xxij daleris j half (22½t.)

And of fyftie daleris the 12 of marche gevin to the captaine of Roscule to be distributed amangs the servands thair

L dalers (50t.)

And of for daleris the 13 of marche gevin to the poore in Frederiksburgt

iiij daleris (4t.)

And of auchtene daleris thre nortis gevin to the keiparis of the park and the tua horssis extending to fyve rose noblis

xviiij daleris iij nortis (18t. 3n.)

And of ane rose noble extending to thre dalers thre nortis gevin to the woman that keipit the buk spruse foullis and feissantis[107]

iij daleris iij norts (3t. 3n.)

And of ane rose noble extending to thre daleris iij nortis tynt be his majestie at the cartis

iij daleris iij norts (3t. 3n.)

And of thre rose noblis that same nicht extending to xj daleris j nort in Horsholme gevin to his majestie to play

xj daleris j nort (11t. 1n.)

And of tua rose noblis extending to vij daleris ane half the ƶ 20 of marche gevin to the printer in Tucho Bravis[108] Ile

vij daleris j half (7½t.)

106 Roskild.

107 Pheasants.

108 Tycho Brahe's island of Ven/Hven.

And of thre rose noblis extending to ellevin daleris ane nort gevin to the writchtis masons and workmen of the paper and corne milnis thair

xj daleris j nort (11t. 1n.)

lateris iij^{c} L daleris. (350t.)

[f.11r] And of sex rose noblis extending to twentie tua daleris ane half gevin to the officers and servands of the house

xxij daleris j half (22½t.)

And of thre rose noblis extending to elleven daleris ane nort gevin to the boitman

xj daleris j nort (11t. 1n.)

And of twentie fyve daleris the 23 of marche gevin to Alexander Crawfurd[109] cordiner at the kings command

xxv daleris (25t.)

And of sex rose noblis extending to twentie tua daleris ane half the 26 of march to the king to play at the cartis

xxij dalers j half (22½t.)

And of twentie four angells extending to fyftie four daleris that was borrowit and gevin to William Stewart to gif the king in Elsinure

Liiij daleris (54t.)

And of twentie sevin rose noblis extending to ane hundreth ane daler ane nort the 27 of march quhen the king raid to the hunting gevin to William Stewart at his majesteis command

j^{c} j daler j nort (101t. 1n.)

And with threttie daleris gevin to the doctor[110] that presented the book in Copmanhavin

xxx daleris (30t.)

And of fourtie tua daleris gevin for books to gif the college[111]

xlij daleris (42t.)

And of tuentie fyve daleris gevin for a coup to gif the college[112]

xxv daleris (25t.)

109 Alexander Crawford, James' cordiner 1595–9. Juhala, 'Household', 327.

110 It has not been possible to trace either the book or the doctor.

111 The seven large books were apparently destroyed during the British bombardment of Copenhagen in 1807. Stevenson, *Scotland's Last Royal Wedding*, 130–1.

112 The cup apparently survives, although somewhat battered. Ibid.

And of twentie fyve daleris gevin to the hospitall in Copmanhavin		
	xxv dalers	(25t.)
And of fourtie nyne daleris for the expenssis of Mr George Young and Alexander Trumpet[113], being twyis in Copmanhavin		
	xLix daleris	(49t.)
And of fourtie daleris the 28 of marche at the kings command gevin to Markie Dowgall[114]		
	xL daleris	(40t.)
And of fourtie daleris the last of marche gevin to William Stewart at the kings command		
	xL daleris	(40t.)
And of twelf angells extending to xxvij dalers the first of Aprile at the kings command gevin to the man quha brocht the King of Poollis[115] testimoniall that he was a gentilman tain and mutilat with the Turk		
	xxvij daleris	(27t.)
And of sex rose noblis extending to twentie tua daleris ane half gevin to William Stewart to gif the king to play		
	xxij dalers j half	(22½t.)
And of fourtie thre daleris the 3 of aprile gevin for glassis		
	xLiij daleris	(43t.)
And of four rose noblis gevin to the king to play that he tynt[116] extending to		
	xv daleris xv daleris.	(15t.)
	Lateris v^c Lxxxxv daleris	(595t.)

113 Possibly Alexander Trumpet 'scribe' who witnessed a charter under the Great Seal, alongside the notary public, in March 1586. *RMS*, 1580–93, pp. 305–7, no. 947. Trumpet (sometimes Trumpat) appears to have been a Scottish merchant who settled in Elsinor from 1574 to c. 1585, before returning to Scotland, leaving his family behind, for several years. Desiring to return to his family, he got James to write to Christian IV recommending his return to Denmark on 6 May 1592. Macray, 'Third Report on the Royal Archives of Denmark', 27; Riis, *Should Auld Acquaintance Be Forgot…*, ii., 250

114 It has not been possible to identify this Mark Dougal, Douglas or even MacDougal.

115 Possibly Sigismund III (1566–1632).

116 That he lost.

[f.11v] And of ane daler gevin to Hyerome Bowye[117] to gif for wand creills to put the glass in and for taking in of ane last of beir to the ship

j daler (1t.)

And of aucht daleris the 7 of aprile gevin to Ramsay[118] the trumpettour at the kings command

viij daleris (8t.)

And of tua rose noblis extending to sevin dolours and ane half gevin to the king to play that nycht

vij daleris (7t.)

And of fourtie ane dalers iij norts the 8 of Aprile gevin for j^c Lxvij pund weght of sucker

xLj dalers (41t.)

And of ane daler for tua berrells to put it in and to cary it to the ship

j daler (1t.)

And of ten rose noblis extending to threttie sevin daleris and ane half gevin the king to play

xxxvij daleris j half (37½t.)

And of ten rose noblis extending to threttie sevin daleris ane half gevin to Hyerome Bowye at the kings command

xxxvij dalers j half (37½t.)

And of aucht rose noblis extending to threttie daleris gevin to Frances Galbraith[119] at the kings command

xxx daleris (30t.)

And of ane daler the 9 of Aprile gevin to captaine Durahamis[120] man that brocht the lettre to the king

j daler (1t.)

And of sex rose noblis extending to twentie tua daleris ane half gevin to William Stewart to gif the king to play

xxij daleris j half (22½t.)

117 Jeromy Bowie was the sommelier and also in charge of wine glasses. 'Wand creills' were baskets for glasses. Bowie served 1568–97. Juhala, 'Household', 318. He also imported drinking glasses from Rouen; see NLS Adv. Ms. 29.2.5.

118 William Ramsay, trumpetor 1570–1603. Juhala, 'Household', 322.

119 Francis Galbraith was master of the pantry and bread house, 1588–1603. Juhala, 'Household', 318.

120 This might possibly be Alexander Duram/Durham, lieutenant of the Danish ship Raphaell. *CSP Scot.*, x, 289.

And of twentie rose noblis gevin to William Stewart the ij of aprile to gif the king to play extending to

Lxxv daleris (75t.)

And of ten daleris ane half gevin for daitts and cannell[121] the 13 of Aprile

x daleris j half (10½t.)

And of ane half daler gevin for weying of thame and the suckker and for ane barrell to put thame in

j half daler (½t.)

And of fourtie sex daleris gevin for the setting of four ringis for the fasoning and making of ane cheinyie of xx unce weght

xLvj daleris (46t.)

And of four rose noblis extending to fyvetene daleris gevin to the man that caryed bak the anssir of ane lettre to the duke of Holster[122]

xv daleris (15t.)

And of xLv daleris gevin for thre unce and tua drop weght of gold to set the rings in

xLv daleris (45t.)

And of tua hundreth thre scoir fyvetene dalers gevin for a mirror glas to the queen

ij^{c} Lxxv daleris (275t.)

And of sex daleris gevin to John Nasmyt to buy scrotscheits & confitours[123] to the king to tak to the ship

vj daleris (6t.)

Lateris vj^{c} Lx daleris half daler j nort (660½t. 1n.)

[f.12r] And of threttie fyve daleris gevin for tua appis the 15 of aprile

xxxv daleris (35t.)

And of tua rose noblis extending to fourtie fyve daleris at the kings command gevin to the trumpettours in the castel

xLv daleris (45t.)

121 Dates and cinnamon.

122 Philip, Duke of Holstein-Gottorp (1570–90). Also mentioned at p. 43, n. 101.

123 Scrotchets and confitures.

And of twelf daleris the 18 of april gevin to James Gourlaw to by powder to his schip

xij daleris (12t.)

And of tuelf rose noblis extending to fourtie fyve daleris gevin to thre men that deliverit his majesteis tocher

xLv daleris (45t.)

And of tua daleris gevin to a compter that straik up the barrells and put in the halds

ij daleris (2t.)

And of ten daleris at the kings command gevin to a Frenche cordiner

x daleris (10t.)

And of twentie rose noblis and fyftie dalers gevin to Mr David Lyndsay to be distribute at the kings command

j^c xxv dalers (125t.)

And of twentie dalers the 20 of aprale at the kings command gevin to the Scottis trumpettors

xx daleris (20t.)

And of twentie sex daleris thre norts gevin to Hyerome Bowye to pay for glassis and coks to the barrells

xxvj dalors iij norts (26t. 3n.)

And of fourtie daleris gevin to the Inglis trumpettors

xL daleris (40t.)

And of for rose noblis extending to xv dalers at the kings command gevin in offeirand to the preist[124] in the chapell

xv daleris (15t.)

And of twentie daleris gevin at the kings command to George Home[125]

xx dalers (20t.)

And of sex daleris to Johnne Schaw to by horssis graith to the horssis that was gottin fra the duk of Brunswick[126]

vj dalers (6t.)

124 It has not been possible to identify the name of the chaplain at Kronborg.

125 George Home of Spott, who, while in Denmark, had ousted and replaced Sir William Keith of Delny as Master of the Wardrobe. Kerr-Peterson, 'Sir William Keith of Delny'.

126 Henry Julius, Duke of Brunswick-Lüneburg, 1564–1613.

And of ane hundreth xxxiij daleris thrid part daler gevin for cowpis to gif away
j^c xxxiij dalers 3/part d (133⅓t.)

And of twentie dalers gevin to William Stewart skipper
xx dalers (20t.)

And of four scoir dalers to the colonell
Lxxx dalers (80t.)

And of aucht rose noblis extending to threttie dalers gevin to the tua vautis[127] that fansit in the cloiss
xxx dalers (30t.)

And of xij rose noblis extending to xLv daleris gevin in drink silver to the man that delyverit the duk of Brunswicks horssis
xLv dalers (45t.)

And of twentie dalers gevin to the Armeinianis the xxj of Aprile at the kings command that was tane with the Turk
xx dalers (20t.)

And of xxx dalers gevin to the huntaris
xxx dalers (30t.)

Lateris vij^c Lix daleris half daler 3 part daler j nort (759⅓t. 1n.)

[f.12v] And of ten daleris to the falconeris
x dalers (10t.)

And of twentie daleris to the cophous
xx dalers (20t.)

And of threttie dalers to the palfurnour
xxx dalers (30t.)

And of threttie dalers to Thame that presented the buke of ecclesiastes[128]
xxx dalers (30t.)

Item of twentie daleris to Finlaw[129] and John Kerss[130]
xx daleris (20t.)

Item of foir scoir daleris to the hospitall in Elsinure
Lxxx dalers (80t.)

127 'vaulters' – tumblers with swordplay.

128 It is not quite clear who 'Thame' [them] refers to. This may be an instance of someone presenting a book to the king, but his attendants failing to make a note of who it was.

129 Possibly Finlay Taylor, lackey 1579–95. Juhala, 'Household', 323.

130 John Kers, dichter or groom and fireman of the chamber 1586–95. Juhala, 'Household', 315.

And of thre daleris to Richard Prestoun[131]

iij dalers (3t.)

And of twentie daleris to ane uther man that was tain with the Turk

xx dalers (20t.)

And of twentie tua dolors and ane half to the Brunswick sangster for his book sex rose noblis extending to

xxij daleris j half (22½t.)

And of twentie dalers to the duk of Brunswick maister that presented the Dutche buk

xx dalers (20t.)

And of fyftie daleris to the Frenche scoolmaister

L dalers (50t.)

And of aucht daleris to James Murray[132] the page

viij dalers (8t.)

And of twentie daleris to ane gentilman that was tane in France and recomendit be the duke of Magilburghs chancellar[133]

xx dalers (20t.)

And of sevin daleris to tua men that watchit Colvile

vij dalers (7t.)

And of twentie daleris mair gevin at the kings command to ane uther man taken be Turks[134]

xx dalers (20t.)

And of thre scoir ten daleris to Johnne Gib

Lxx dalers (70t.)

And of sex scoir daleris to the tua vautis that was in Upslo

vj[xx] dalers (120t.)

And of thre scor sex dalers to the duk of Brunswicks trumpettors

Lxvj dalers (66t.)

131 Richard Preston of Haltree, a page 1591–7. Juhala, 'Household', 315.

132 James Murray, 'page of honour' mentioned in 1590. Juhala, 'Household', 331.

133 The Duke of Mecklenburg, although it is unclear whether this is Ulrich, Duke of Mecklenburg-Güstrow (1527–1603) or John, Duke of Mecklenburg-Schwerin (1558–92).

134 'ane uther man taken be turks' is superscript here.

And of tua hundreth dalers gevin to Alexander Trumpet to bring hame tymmer

ij^c daleris (200t.)

And of ten daleris to the officers of the toun

x daleris (10t.)

And of twentie tua daleris to Francis Galbraith to pay for the kings claithis weshing

xxij daleris (22t.)

And of threttie rose noblis extending to ane hundreth xij daleris half daler gevin to the King of Denmark and the duke his brotheris maisteris

j^c xij daleris j half (112½t.)

And of ten rose noblis extending to threttis sevin dolours ane half to Johnne Schaw[135] to gif the foollis

xxxvij dalers (37t.)

Lateris ix^c Lxxxxviij daloris half dalor (998½t.)

[f.13r] And of tua daleris for caraying the silver to the ship

ij daleris (2t.)

And of four rose noblis extending to fyvetene dalers to Hendrie Goldensterns men that presented the hagbut and sword

xv daleris (15t.)

And of fourtie rose noblis extending to sex scoir ten daleris the j of maii gevin at the kings command to the skipperis of the admirall ship the pilotts the trumputtours violeris and kettil drummeris

j^c xxx daleris (130t.)

And of ane hundreth crownis extending to sex scoir sevintene daleris gevin to his majesteis self the xviij of maii

j^c xxxvij daleris (137t.)

And of xL daleris at the kings command gevin to Hendrie Ramellis[136] man

xL daleris (40t.)

135 Possibly John Shaw, who later served as Master of the Stable 1591–2. Juhala, 'Household', 311.

136 Henrik Ramel (1550–1610), see p. 39, n. 85.

And of four hundreth punds deliverit to George Auchinlect[137] for helping to keip the Densemens houssis extending to tua hundreth dalours

ij^{c} dalers (200t.)

And of ane thowsand thre hundreth fyftie sex punds threttene schillings four pennies fyve hundreth crownis for the price of ane cheinye of gold weyand fyve hundreth crownis quhilk was gevin to ane of the Danishe ambassadors extending to

vij^{c} dallers (700t.)

And of fyftie four thowsand daleris deliverit at his majesteis command to David Seytoun of Parbroith his hienes comptroller as he hes confessit upoun compt

Liiij^{m} dalers (54,000t.)

parte Lv^{m} ij^{c} xliiij dalers (55,244t.)

James R

Summa of this haill discharge Lxxxv^{m} iiij^{c} Liiij daleris half dalers thrid part daler ane nort (85,454½t ⅓t. 1n.)

Sa is the compter superexpendit in this compt iiij^{c} Liiij daleris half dalor thrid part daler ane nort extending in scotts money to nyne hundreth ten pundis iij s iiij d (454½t ⅓t. 1n. / £910 3s. 4d.)

Quhilk eikit to the superexpensss of the former compt extendis in the haill to fyvetene thousand tua hundreth four scoir auchtene pundis ellevin shilling (£15,280 11s.)

Tenet Clericus registri

Blantyre SRobert Melvill Chancellarius BArnbarrathe
JCokburne RYoung MPYoung Parbrothe controller Culluthy

Receipt for Unspent Dowry Money: 1590

[f.13v] At Edinburgh the fyft day of februare The yeir of god j^{m} v^{c} fourscoir threttene yeiris [1594] In presens of the lordis of council comperit personallie David Seytoun of Parbroth comptroller to our soverane lord and gave

137 It is not quite clear who this George Auchinleck is, possibly a merchant of either Edinburgh or Leith. A John Auchinleck was a Scottish schoolmaster in Elsinor from 1590. Riis, *Should Auld Acquaintance Be Forgot…*, ii., 210.

in this acquittance and discharge gevin underwrittin subscrivit with his hand desirand the sam to be actit and regrat in the buikis of chekker ad futuram rei memoram

The quhick desire the lordis thocht ressounabill and thairfor do decernit and decernis the said acquittace and discharge to be actit and registrat in the saidis buikis of the chekker to the effect abovewrittin of the quhilk acquittance the tennor follows

I David Seytoun of Parbroith comptroller to our soverane lord be the tennor heirof grantis and to have ressaivit at his hieness command fra ane noble and michtie lord Johnne lord of Thirlestane chancellair of Scotland the soume of fyftie foure thousand Dutche daleris being a part of his hienes tocher And therefoir exoneris quitclaimis and dischargis the said lord chancellor his airis and executoris of the same soume forevir Attour I am content and consentis that this my acquittance be actit and regrat in the buikis of our soverane lordis chekker ad futuram rei memoriam

In witness heirof I have subscrivit this my acquittance with my hand at Edinburgh the fyft day of Februar the yeir of god j^{m} v^{c} fourscoir threttene yeiris [1594] Befoir witness Mark lord of Newbottle, Walter commendatoir of Blantyre Alexander Hay of Eister Kennat clerk of register [obscured] subscribitur Parbroth comptroller Extractum de libris actorum Scottarii per me Alexandrum Hay de Eister Kennat clericum Rotulorum regri ac consilii salute domini nostri Regis sub meis signo et subscriptione manualibus

Alexander Hay

Accounts of Chancellor Maitland: 1590

[f.14r]

The compt of Johnne Lord of Thirlstane chancellar of scotland of the sowme of thre thowsand punds sterling ressavit be Sir Johnne Carmichaell of that ilk knycht in England in the yeir 1590 and deliverit be him at our soverane lords command to the comptar upoun the [left blank] day of [left blank] auditours underweittin. Thay ar to say Mark lord of Newbottle Sir Robert Melvill of Murdocairny knight thesaurar depute Sir Johnne Cokburne of Ormistoun knycht clerk of the Justiciarie Sir Patrick Vaus of Barnibarranche ane of the senatoris of the college of justice David Seytoun of Parbroith comptroller Schir Richard Cokburne of Clerkingtoun youngar secretair Walter commendatour of Blantyre keipar of the previe seill Alexander Hay of Eister Kennat clerk of the register Mr David Carnegie of Calluthy Mr Peter Young of Seytoun mr elemonsanar to our soverane lord Mr George Young archdeane of Sanctandrois Be his hienes commissioun under the testmoniall of the greit seill speciallie constitute In the chekker at Edinburgh the first day of marche the yeir of god j^{m} v^{c} four scoir threttene yeiris [1594].

charge

Item the comptar chargis him self with the said sowme of thre thowsand punds ressavit be him fra the said Sir Johnne Carmichiell of that ilk knycht extending in scottis money at ix s the Inglis schilling to

xxvij^{m} li (£27,000)

Summa patet

[f.14v] discharge

In the first retenit be the said laird of Carmichael gevin out of the said sowme in England as his compt bearis threttie punds nyntene schilling sterlinge

inde ij^{c} Lxxviij li xj s (£277 11s.)

Item retenit be the said laird of Carmichaell be ane precept of his majesteis four hundreth and twentie libs sterling

inde iij^{m} vij^{c} Lxxx libs (£3,780)

Item deliverit to Sir James Sandelands[138] in Dunnfermling at his majesteis command

vj^{m} libs (£6,000)

Item gevin to his majesteis self fyve hundreth crownis

inde j^{m} iij^{c} xxxiij xv s (£1,333 15s.)

Item deliverit to monssir de Civile[139] ambassadour from the King of France thre hundreth crownis

inde viij^{c} libs (£800)

Item to William Shaw Master of work for reparatioun of the abbay of Halirudhous sex hundreth twentie fyve crownis

inde j^{m} vj^{c} Lxvj li xiij s iij d (£1,666 13s. 3d.)

Item thre hundreth thre scoir fyvetene crownis for spyces and uther furnitour to his majesteis banquet extending to

j^{m} libs (£1,000)

138 Sir James Sandilands of Slamanno, gentleman of the chamber 1590–6. Juhala, 'Household', 313.

139 François de Civille (1537–1610), arrived in Scotland 10 March 1589 and left at the end of August. *CSP Scot.*, x, 3, 154.

Item for a jowell to monssir Hoteman[140] ane hundredth crownis	inde ij^{c} Lxvj libs xiij s iiij d	(£266 13s. 4d.)
Item to James Bowsie[141] confett maker at his majesteis command	iiij^{c} libs	(£400)
Item to Helene Somervill spous to Mr Johnne Skene be his majesteis precept	iij^{c} xxxiij li vj s viij d	(£333 6s. 8d.)
Item to Sir Lewes Bellenden of Auchnowle knycht Justice clerk at his majesteis command	ij^{m} libs	(£2,000)
Item to John Wemys[142] younger of Logy at his majesteis command	iij^{c} xxxiij li vj s viij d	(£333 6s. 8d.)
Item a Dense man that come with a present to his majestie from Denmark ane hundreth and threttie dalers changit in gold	inde ij^{c} Lx libs	(£260)
Item to the laird of Parbroith comptroller	vj^{c} libs	(£600)
Item to Robert Jowsie[143] merchant be his majesteis precept	iiij^{m} libs	(£4,000)
Item to Thomas Foullis goldsmyt for certane chenyeis of gold for the quhilk the lairds of Rosling Cragmiller Corstorphin and Reidhall[144] war cautioners to him for his majestie	ij^{m} vj^{c} Lxvj li xiij s viij d	(£2,666 8s. 8d.)

140 Jean Hotman, Marquis de Villers-St-Paul (1552–1636), diplomat for Henri IV, who was in Scotland in August 1589. CSPS, x, 135.

141 This is probably Jacque de Boussie, sugarman working at the 1598 banquet for the Duke of Holstein. Edinburgh City Archives, Town Treasurers Accounts, vol. 2, p. 135.

142 The son of Andrew Wemyss of Logy/Logie. *RMS*, 1580–93, p. 158, no. 516.

143 Robert Jowsie/Jowsye was a merchant of Edinburgh, who supplied the court with fabrics throughout the 1590s. See Introduction for his relationship to royal finances and Thomas Foulis. James sent Jowsie and Foulis to London in 1589 to purchase items for his household. *CSP Scot.*, x, 121. For some of his fabric purchasing, see NRS E35/13.

144 Sir William Sinclair of Roslyn, Sir David Preston of Craigmillar, Sir James Forrester of Corstorphine and Mr Adam Otterburn of Redhall.

Item to Sir James Sandelands to be play salver to his majestie
ij^c Lx li (£260)

Item to a man that come out of Denmark from Ramelius
Lvj li (£61)

Item allowit to the comptair for a part of his expenssis in Denmark
iij^m libs (£3,000)

Lateris xxix^m xxxiiij li xj s (£29,034 11s.)

[f.15r] Item gevin to monssir de Lile ~~for~~ at his majesteis command for furnitour of his voyage in France in his hienes effarris tua hundreth crownis extending to
v^c Lx libs (£560)

parte patet

Summa of this haill discharge xxix^m v^c Lxxxxiiij li xj s (£29,594 11s.)

James R

Sa the comptair is superexpendit in this compt by twa thousand fyve hundreth foir scoir fourtene pundis xj s quhilk being eikit to the superexpenssis of the former compt (£2,594 11s.)

The comptair is superexpendit de claro Sevintene thousand aucht hundreth twenty four pundis sevin schillings ten pennies (£17,824 7s. 10d.)

tenet Clericus registri

James R

Blantyre Newbottle SRobert Melvill Chancellarius RCokburne Parbroche controller Culluthy BArubarrache RYoung M PYoung

Receipt of Jewellery delivered to Maitland: 20 May 1590

[f.16r] Rex

We having consideratioun how our richt trustie and familiar counsellor Johnne lord Thirlstane our chancellar and secretair be our command ressavit fra Sir William Keith of Delneis knicht master of gardrob for the tyme four grit tablit diamantis and tua grit tablit rubies incassit in gold, to put in ringis To be propynit to our derrest mother and brother the Quene and king of Denmark, and uther is princes our allias present with us at our lait being in that realme, hes accordinglie causit set the same and in our sicht and presence geviand describute thame to the saidis princes according to our directioun

and honor Have thairfoir exonerat and dischargit like as be the tennor heirof for our selffis our airis and successors we exoner and discharge our said Chancellair his airis executoris and assignais of the saidis four diamontis and tua rubeis gevin and destribute be him as said is for now and evir Ordaning the lordis auditors of our chekker to allow and defease the same to him in his nixt compt and to insert this present in the books ad perpetuam rei memoriam Subscrivit with our hand at Halirudhous the xx day of May 1590
Collatum cum originali
Tenit
Alexander hay

Document Set Two

NLS Adv. Ms. 29.2.5
Copy/Draft Accounts of Chancellor Maitland: Spring 1588 to Spring 1589
[For notes on this set of accounts, see the British Library duplicate, pages XX–XX]
[f.193v]

[Endorsed] Charge & discharge of 10 thousand markes 1588
Compt of x^m lib.
[f.192r]

The compt of Ten thowsand lib Resaved from Sir William Keithe in October 1588
Charge

x^m lib (£10,000)

Discharge
Debursit at severall tymes and delivered to his majestie as the particular compt maid to his majestie and his majesties recept and acquittaince beiris

vij^m iij^c xxxiij lib vj s viij d (£7,333 6s. 8d.)

Item delivered to the laird of Eister Wemys according to his precept thrie hundrethe crounis

inde viij^c lib (£800)

Item to Monsieur de Lisle sone to the Baillie of Orleans quhen he was directed to the king of Navarre tua hundreth crounes

inde v^c xxxiij lib vj s viij d (£533 6s. 8d.)

Send to Berwick to Monsieur de Nassau be his majesties command thrie scoir tua crounis

inde j^c Lxiij lib vj s viij d (£163 6s. 8d.)

Item to M George Young to be gevin to Cudbert the hunter tuenty crounis

inde Liij lib vj s viij d (£53 6s. 8d.)

Item to Mr Johne Geddye tuentye crounis

inde Liij lib vj s viij d (£53 7s. 8d.)

Item to Archibald Carmichael to be given to Captane Carlilis man that com out of Yrland fyftie crounis

inde j^c xxxiij lib vj s viij d (£133 7s. 8d.)

Item to Archibald Arnot bourges of Falkland according to his compt

Liiij lib xj s (£54 11s.)

[f.192v] Item to Sir William Keythe four scoir four angelis
at iij lib vj s viij d the piece
inde iij^{c} Lxiiij lib ~~xiij s iiij d~~ (£364)

Item to Roger Astoun to beir to his majestie being in
Striveling ane hundreth crounis
inde ij^{c} Lxvj lib xiij s iiij d (£266 8s. 4d.)

Item to the said Roger to give to ane Inglis poet[1]
tuentye rois nobles
inde j^{c} Lx lib xlij lib xiij s viij d (£160)

Summa ix^{m} ix^{c} xiij lib xvj s viij d (£9,913 16s. 8d.)

Sua Restis Lxxxvj lib iij s iiij d[2] (£86 3s. 4d.)

[f.195v]

[Endorsed] Cownt & discharge of the thousand markis
The dowble off the compt of ten^{m} pound ressavit fra Sir Williame Keyth
[f.194r]

Compt of vij^{m} iij^{c} xxxiij lib vj s viij d gevin in in ane article of the compt of ten thousand lib resaved from Sir William Keyth
(£7,333 6s. 8d.)

Item to Charles Forteviot according to his compt
xviij lib xiij s iiij d (£18 13s. 4d.)

Item fournyssed to his majestie to play at the cairtes the
space of ane yeir and half j^{c} lxxxxiij rois noblis
inde ij^{m} j^{c} xxiij merks (£1,415 6s. 8d.)

Item to Mr George Young
ij^{m} merks (£666 13s. 4d.)

Item to Mr Richard Cokburne
ij^{m} merkis (£666 13s. 4d.)

Item to William Henrysoun the xxiiij of November to
fourniss the kings hous according to his compt
xxiiij lib viij s (£24 8s.)

Item that same day to John Winyettis catour
xxij lib (£22)

1 BL Add. 22968 has the same payment and identifies the poet as Nicholas Breton, 'Mr Breton'.

2 The first calculation of the sum and rest was cancelled.

Item to Andro Melvile master houshald for fournissing the hous certane dayis immediatlye thair efter
j^{c} ij lib xiij s iiij d (£102 8s. 4d.)

Item to Mr Patric Gallowaye at tua severall the ane in November 1588 the uther the sevint of May thairefter efter his majestie retournying from the north from the Brig of Dey
ij^{c} lxxxxv lib (£295)

Item to Adrian Damman j^{c} crounis
inde iiij^{c} merkis (£266 8s. 8d.)

Item the 3 of Februar to Patric Murray being directed to the north to my lord of Huntly twenty crownis (£53 6s. 8d.)

Item the xvj of Marche to his majestie to geaven to Inglis huntars ij^{c} crounes
inde viij^{c} merkis (£533 6s. 8d.)

Item to ane hieland man that maid the genealogye of the kingis of Scotland in ane carte sex rois noblis
xLiiij lib (£44)

Item to Monsieur de Clermont ane ~~ring~~ jowell worth ~~tua~~ hundreth crounis
inde viij^{c} merks (£533 6s. 8d.)

[f.194v] Item to the marinars of Sir John Bestouns ane hundreth crounes
inde iiij^{c} merkis (£266 8s. 8d.)

Item ~~ane~~ for ane greit tablet set with diamants to the said Sir Johne j^{c} xL crounes
inde v^{c} Lx lib (£540)

Item to ane Inglis huntar tuentye crounes
inde Lxxx merks (£56 6s. 8d.)

Item allowit to the comptar for det awing be his majestie to him
ij^{m} lib (£2,000)

Summa xj^{m} ij merks viij s (11,002 merks 8s./ £7335 1s. 4d.)

Receipt of Money from François de Civelle: 11 September 1589

Receipt to Chancellor Maitland from François de Civelle ambassador of the king of Navarre, 11 September 1589
[f.196v]

[Endorsed] France de Civille discharge of viij^{c} li[3]
[f.196r]

I Francis de Civill ambassador for the kings majestie of France and Navar Grantes me be the tenour heirof to haiff ressavit fra the hands of nobill Lord Sir Jhone Maitland of Thirlstane knight, chancellor of Scotland and secretar to the kings majesie of Scotland the soume of twelff hundreth merks money of Scotland and that at command of the said kings majestie of Scotland And as thir presens dischargs his Grace therof for evir Subscrivit my hand at Edinburgh the xj day of September 1589 yirs
Francoys de Civille

Accounts of Thomas Foulis: 20 June 1589
[f.197r]

The compt of the gold resawed fra my Lady Thirlestane sene the xx day Junij 1589.
Item to the xxj of Junij resawed fra my lady Thirlestane
nyne hundreth angelllis wayand ix pound four unce fywe
grot[4] wayght and ane half gold of xxiij^{c} viij g fyne.
Mair j^{c} angellis of gwne hoillis[5] weyand j pound
wayght gold of xxiij^{c} fyne.
Item the nynteine day of July resawed ix pound xij unce
angellis gold of xxiij^{c} viij g / fyne.
Mair of guid hoill angellis xij unce xix deneiris xij g /
gold of xxiij^{c} fyne

The quhilk gold abovewrittin being past the Irnis in
xxiij^{c} vij grot makis in passage and stane, four pound
xiiij unce x deneirs at xxix li the unce extendis to
the sowme of nyne thousand sex hundreth four, scoir
auchteine poundis ane schilling viij pennies quhairof
givin twa piece for the assays to the kingis box[6] is
fourteine pound thretteine schilling four pennies Sua
restis nyne thousand sex hundred fourscoir thrie poundis
aucht schilling four pennies

ix^{m} vj^{c} Lxxxiij li viiij s iiij d (£9,683 8s. 4d.)

3 François de Civille. For a discussion of this man, see the Introduction. Also see the next account for this payment.

4 Presumably meaning gross weight.

5 'angellis of gwne hoillis' – see the note on currencies at the end of the Introduction for a discussion of these.

6 The box here refers to where sample proof gold and silver coins were kept and assayed. See *RPCS*, iv, 620.

The quhilk sowmes above writtin depursed as eftir followis
Item ane bassin and ane laver that wes gevin to James Hudsoneweyand lxxij unce fywe grot wayght at xlv s the unce with twa haiffis[7] to thame L s is
j^{c} Lxv li xviij s ij d (£165 18s. 2d.)

Item to Roger Ashtoun
ij^{c} xxviij li (£228)

Item to William Schaw
j^{m} iij^{c} xxxiij li vj s viij d[8] (£1,333 6s. 8d.)

Item to M. Richard Cokburne that was givin to Monseour De Leill[9]
v^{c} xxxiij li vj s viij d (£533 6s. 8d.)

Item in arlis[10] of the silver wark
j^{m} li (£1,000)

Item to my Lady twa hundreth thrissil nobillis
j^{m} iiij^{c} Lxv li xiiij s iiij d (£1,465 14s. 4d.)

Summa of this deliverit four thousand sewin hund~~reth threttie~~ twentie sewin poundis iij s iiij d (£4,727 3s. 4d.)

The rest on uthair syd.
Thomas Ffoullis

[f.197v] Item to my Lady the secound of August
ij^{c} li (£200)

Item mair to Mr James Maitland[11] twentie thrissle nobillis is
j^{c} xLvj li xiij s iiij d (£146 13s. 4d.)

Item to William Schaw
iij^{c} xxxiij li vj s viij d (£333 6s. 8d.)

7 There are three pen strokes before 'halffis' in the manuscript. The James Hudson referred to here is possibly one of the king's violers, one of the five English Hudsons who part of his court. He later served as one of James' merchants in London. Juhala, 'Household', 112, 173, 316.

8 This is part of sum of £3000 paid in instalments for building and repair to royal palaces. See Introduction for a discussion of this. Schaw was also the queen's chamberlain; ER, vol. 22, 403.

9 Sieur de l'Isle, see p. 23, n. 33.

10 This is a kind of deposit.

11 Possibly James Maitland, son of Maitland of Lethington. *CSP Scot.*, x, 814.

Item to James Cranstoun[12]

j^{c} li (£100)

Item j bassin and j laver[13] wayand sex pound xij unc at xliij s the unc extending to twa hundreth threttie sewin poundis twelf schillings and the gilting of thame sex angelis is twentie sex poundis

summa ij^{c} Lxiij li xij s (£263 12s.)

Item aucht trinscheouris wayand iiij pound weyght ane grot weyght and ane half at xliiij s the unce is thrie penneis. The gilting of thame twa angellis viij li xiij s iiijd.

summa j^{c} xLix li xvij s vij d (£149 17s. 7d.)

Item that giwin to Thomas Annand[14] and Heue Lindsay[15] for outreding of my lordis silver plaittis

j^{m} v^{c} li (£1,500)

Item delyverit to my Lady twa thousand twa hundreth thriescoir twa poundis threttine schillings elevin penneis

ij^{m} ij^{c} Lxij li xiij s xj d (£2,262 13s. 11d.)

Summa iiij^{m} ix^{c} Lvj li iij s vj d (£4,956 3s. 6d.)

Summa of the haill depursement is nyne thousand sex hundreth fourscoir thrie poundis aucht schillingis four pennies quhilk makis perfyt payment of the gold befoir written past the Irnis (£9,683 8s. 4d.)

Item resawed to be my lordis silver plaittis[16] conforme to this compt above writtin Imprimis conforme to my obligatioun ane thousand poundis nixt ane thousand fywe hundreth poundis quhilk is in the haill twa thousand fywe hundreth pound (£2,500)

12 Possibly Captain Cranstoun, appointed commander of the king's 50 footguards in January 1592, alongside Sir John Carmichael, commander of 50 guard cavalry. *CSP Scot.*, x, 618.

13 A laver was usually a jug that sat within the basin, often used for washing.

14 Thomas Annand, goldsmith, freeman 1576. J. Munro and H. Steuart Fotheringham, *Edinburgh Goldsmiths Minutes 1525–1700* (Edinburgh, 2006), 386. In his Will and Testament dated 10 March 1592 (he died 6 August 1591 in Dundee), Thomas Foulis owed him £1374-13-4d, Thomas Achesone owed him £94. See NRS ECC8/8/24.

15 Hew Lindsay, goldsmith, freeman 1587. *Edinburgh Goldsmiths Minutes 1525–1700*, 386.

16 The account of 'silver plate' follows overleaf.

Item resawed the laird of Craiganis[17] conforme to my tikat deliver thairupoune for the sowme of twa thousand poundis quhilk is in the haill resawed by me Thomas Foullis preceiding yt The sewintenit of April 1590 is four thousand fywe hundreth pounds money quhilk is payit as eftir followis[18] (£4,500)

[f.198r] Item deliverit ten trincheouris wayand iiij^{xx} ij unc j h j h quarter
Item xij plaittis weyand ij^{c} xlv unce j h unc
Item xij plaittis wayand ij^{c} lj unc j quarter
Item xij plaittis wayand ij^{c} lij unc iij quarter
Item xij plaittis wayand ij^{c} lx viij unc iij quarter
Item xij coveris wayand j^{c} lxx unc iij quarters
Summa ane thousand ane hundreth thrie scoir elevin unc iij quarteris unc at xliiij s the unc is in money twa thousand fywe hundreth thrie scoir sewinteine poundis and sewintene schillingis

ij^{m} v^{c} Lxxvij li xvij s (£2,577 17s.)

Item the gilting of tene trincheouris

xiij li (£13)

Item deliverit ane ring with ane diamont in ane starne that was givin to Monseour Houtman[19], And ane tabillit diamont ring that was given to Monseour de Leill price of the twa fourscoir fourteine crownis is in money

ij^{c} L li xiij s iiij d (£250 13s. 4d.)

Item ane cais of gold for pykteithe price

xxij li (£22)

Item the compt of the oustrage ege[20] with the graithe contenit thairin

j^{c} Lxix li iij s iiij d (£169 3s. 4d.)

Item James Hudsone[21] at Lundoun xx angelles

Lxxxx li (£90)

17 Alexander Cunningham of Craigends, *RPCS*, iv, 526, 537.

18 The rest of the page is blank and cancelled out with a cross.

19 Jean Hotman, Marquis de Villers-St-Paul, see p. 56, n. 140.

20 Ostrich egg. Presumably with silver mounts and contents. An 'ostrix eg coupe garnessit in silver dowble overgilt' is mentioned in a royal inventory of silver by Jeremy Bowie of 28 October 1590. NLS Adv. MS. 34.2.17, f. 28.

21 James Hudson, see p. 63, n. 7.

Item that restit of the ~~partiall~~ wayght of the partiall gilt silver wark ane hundreth fytie nyne unce quhilk is furnished at fourtie schillingis the unc
iij^c xviij li (£318)

Item to my Lady in the castell[22] ane amatyst ring price
v li x s (£5 10s.)

Item ane dische of silver coverit wayand xiiij unce j half unc j half quarter unc at xliiij s the unce is
xxxij li iij s vj d (£32 3s. 6d.)

Item ane tabillit diamont ring price
xL li (£40)

Item the gilt wark that wes tain to brak doun wayis twa hundreth fyftie nyne unce ane half unc quhairfor to be givin for ilk unc xl s extendix to
v^c xix li (£519)

Item mair deliverit to my Lady twa stoippis[23] wayand lxxix unc j quart unc at xl s the unce is
j^c Lix li x s (£159 10s.)

Summa four thousand ~~twa~~ ane hundreth sex <fourscoir augtein li> poundis sewinteine schillingis twa pennies. (£4,198 17s. 2d.)

quhilk being tain of my charge of four thousand fywe hundreth poundis restis on me to be givin ~~twa hundreth fourscoir thretteine~~ thrie hunderithe thrie poundis ij s x d (£303 2s. 10d.)

Thomas Foullis

[added in an informal hand, perhaps by Foulis.]

Item mar delyverit ane pair bracelets
Lxiiij li (£64)

Item the exchange of ane ship
j^c Lxiij li (£163)

Item twa rings
iij li (£3)

The mending of ane capefut[24]
iiij li (£4)

22 This entry may suggest that Lady Thirlestane had an office in Edinburgh castle.

23 Stoup, a jug.

24 'casefut' – perhaps 'compterfut', a kind of dish or platter.

Summa iiij^{m} iiij^{c} xxxj li xvij s iij d (£4,431 17s. 3d.)

[f.198r]

Sua rests be theis compt in Thomas Foullis hand xl threscoir viij li ij s x d. Thomas Foulis compt maid the xxij of August 1590 and allowit the rests auchtand iij^{xx} viij li ij s x d to be suportit to the nixt compt.
The count of the gold receawed 1599

Inventory of Maitland's Silverwork: 26 September 1589
[200v]

[Endorsed] The compt and waight of my Lord chancellaris silver wark. xxvj September 1589
[f.199r]

Partiall[25] gilt

Item four cullet coupis with ane ewer and litill coupes and doubill bell salt fatt. thrie dosin spounis. wayand j^{c} Lxviij unc j half.
Item twa bassins, twa laveris and ane chofeir wayand ij^{c} xxvij unc
Item fourteen trincheours wayand ij^{c} xiij unce.
Item ane basin and ane laver wayand Lxxviij unc j half.
Item that was resavit fra Thomas Foullis the xxvj September 1589. tene trincheoris wayand iiij^{xx} ij unc j half ij half quarter.
Item j silver coupe partiall gilt wayand x unce j half j half quarter
Item twa stoupis partiall gilt wayand [left blank]
Item ane baissin and ane laver gilt chaist and gravin wayand j^{c} vj unc j half.
Item ane greit salt fat coverit and gilt wayand Lj unce j half.
Item thrie coupis with coveris and fywe litill coupis without coveris gilt wayand j^{c} ij unce iust.
Item mair thrie coupis gilt and ane crestaill pot weyand thrie scoir fyve unc Lxv unce[26]
Item fyve coupis gilt weyand xLvij unc j quarter
Item thrie dosin of plaittis and twa dosin of coveris that was givin to his majestie wayand ane thousand iiij^{xx} ix unc j quarter j half.[27]

Accounts of the 'Lady Chancellor': 1 August 1590
[f.202v]

25 'partiall' or perhaps 'parciall' – parcel gilt. Nearby on the page is written 'ff', a capital 'F'. The significance is unclear. The silver plate listed here appears to be a portion of a large assembly of plate valued at £2000 (sterling) given to Mr John Colville in London in September 1589; see *CSP Scotland*, x, 160–2. See the Introduction for more information.

26 This entry and the following one are additions in a less formal hand, perhaps that of Foulis himself.

27 This entry has been added on, in a neat hand. Finally, at the bottom of the page is a mark '690o- ¼'

[Endorsed] my Lady chancelaris count the j of August 1590
[f.201r]

My Ladye chancellaris compt the first day of August 1590

Item resavit thrie houndreth fyftie sevin crounis of the sone weyand tua pound sevin unces thre denieris gold of xxij carettis vj grains fyn att vj s stirlyng the pece extending in sterling money to

j^{c} vij li ij s (£107 2s.)

Item ellevin houndreth and fouretie pistolettis weyand sevin poundis threttene unces twenty ane deneris gold of xxij carrett fyn at vj s sterling the pece soume in sterling money

iij^{c} xlij li (£342)

Item foure hounderth and twentie aucht and ane half angellis of the goun hoill: weyand foure poundis sevin unces thre: deneris gold of xxiij carrett fyn att x s sterling the pece

ij^{c} xiiij li v s (£214 5s.)

Item thre thousand sevin hounderth thre scoir ellevin and and half auld angellis weyand tua stane sevin poundis thre unces tuelf denier gold of xxiij carrottes extendin in sterling money to

j^{m} viij^{c} Lxxxv li xv s (£1,885 15s.)

Summa of thir haill sterling money is

ij^{m} v^{c} xLix li ij s (£2,549 2s.)

Att nyne shillings Scottis the testoun extendis in Scottis sillver to

xxij^{m} ix^{c} xLj li xviij s (£22,941 18s.)

Quhilk haill gold above written being past the irnes in thrissill nobillis extendis to the soume of

xxv^{m} xLv li xv s vj d (£25,45 15s. 6d.)

[f.201v] Compt of the deburssement of the summes befoir writtin in August 1590

Item Thomas Achessone master cunyeour deliver for the working of the haill foursaid gold

ij^{c} Lxxxv li v s (£285 5s.)

Item to Frances Napier[28] for the assying of the pistolettes and crounes

j^{c} ix li vj s viiij d (£109 6s. 8d.)

28 Frances Napier, master assayer of the cunyiehouse, *RPCS*, iv, 418.

Item thrie assayes to the box
xxij li (£22)

Item deliverit in Dunfermelyng to James Sandelandis[29]
vj^{m} li (£6,000)

Item to my lord justice clerk[30]
ij^{m} li (£2,000)

Item to the laird of Logye[31]
iij^{c} xxxiij li vj s viij d (£333 6s. 8d.)

Item to ane Dutche man att your lordships command ane hundreth threttie dollours
ij^{c} Lx li (£260)

Item to Frederick the Dutche turnour[32]
xL lib (£40)

Item to Allexander Anstien[33] taillour
ij^{c} Lxxxxij li xiij s iiij d (£292 13s. 4d.)

Item to Duncan Wallace[34] taillour
j^{c} Lxxiiij li xix s (£174 19s.)

Item to James Scott[35] in Leyth foure scoir and ellevin dollours
j^{c} Lxxxij li (£182)

Item to George Carkettill[36]
Lxxv li (£75)

29 James Sandilands, son of the laird of Calder, first gentleman in the king's chamber. See also p. 55, n. 138.

30 Sir John Skene, justice clerk. See also p. 25, n. 45.

31 Andrew Wemyss of Logy/Logie. See also p. 56, n. 142.

32 Frederick, apparently a woodturner and carver. Payments in BL Add. 22958 show that he came with William Schaw from Denmark. See Introduction.

33 Alexander Austin/Oistiane/Oustean, a tailor and burgess of Edinburgh. He acted as a cautionar (guarantor) for the Earl Marischal during the marriage negotiations, and was burgh commissioner at the convention for the tax for the king's marriage, *RPCS*, iv, 234, 269. His Will is dated 6 July 1604 (died 7 February 1604), NRS ECC8/8/39.

34 This Duncan, surname possible Wallace or Vallange or Wallenge, has not been traced.

35 James Scott in Leith (d. July 1596), collector of the town's petty customs in Leith. Scott was to receive duties to repair the shore, 9 May 1589, J. Marwick, M. Wood and others eds, *Extracts from the records of the Burgh of Edinburgh*, 6 vols (Edinburgh, 1869–92), v, 543. Scott was a 'timberman', importing and selling timber and owned a part cargo of one ship at his death, he dealt with a 'Neilsoun' Dutchman in 'Conisberie' (Königsberg, now Kaliningrad), £60 ships customs and entry silver were due to him. Will dated 18 April 1598, NRS ECC8/8/31.

36 George Carkettill, baillie of Edinburgh. On 2 October 1588 he was sent to declare the town's resolution to Francis Stewart, Earl of Bothwell, that they would not lend him any

Item to Marguerite Arthour[37]

	j^c^ L li	(£150)

Item to William Schaw master of work

	vj^c^ iijxx vj li xiij s 4 d	(£666 13s. 4d.)

Item to Robert Joussie[38] be your lordships command

	iiij^m^ li	(£4,000)

Item to Thomas Foullis for releif of the barrounis

	ij^m^ vj^c^ lxvj li xiij s ij d	(£2,666 13s. 2d.)

Summa debursit to the personis above writtin is

	xvij^m^ ij^c^ lvj li xvij s iiij d	(£17,256 17s. 4d.)
	Sua restis yitt vij^m^ vij^c^ Lxxxix li xvij s viij d	(£7,789 17s. 8d.)

[f.202r] Thrid September 1590

Item deliverit to Olifair Hepburne[39]

	Lxxiij li vj s viij d	(£73 6s. 8d.)

Item to my Lady

	vij^m^ iij^c^ xxxiij li vj s viij d	(£7,333 6s. 8d.)

Item mair

	iij^c^ Lxxxiij li iiij s iiij d	(£383 4s. 4d.)

Summa of the haill recept

	xxv^m^ xLv li xv s vj d	(£25045 15s. 6d.)

Item to the comptrollar at his majesties command

	vj^c^ li	(£600)

Item of the sewin thousand sewin hundreth fourscoir and nyne poundis sewinten schillingis and aucht pennies that was resaved fra Thomas Foullis deleverit to the comptroller sex hundreth poundis. ~~sua restis~~ (£600)

and to Oliphair Hepburne foirsaid

	Lxxiij li vj s viij d	(£73 6s. 8d.)
	Sa restis vij^m^ j^c^ xvj li xj s	(£7,116 11s.)

money. Marwick and Wood, eds, *Extracts from the records of the Burgh of Edinburgh*, v, 530. He also provided a 'cupboard' of silver plate for the town's banquet for the Danish ambassadors. Gibson-Craig, *Papers Relative to the Marriage of King James*, 34.

37 Margaret Arthour was recorded as widow of William Aikin of Dowel, *RPCS*, v, 572, 573.

38 Robert Jowsie; see Introduction.

39 Captain Oliver Hepburn. See William Fraser, *Memorials of the Earls of Haddington*, 2 vols (Edinburgh, 1889), ii, 45.

Item tain out of the sowme above writtin ellewin hundreth markis givin to the succorman and Mr John Skeinis wyff.[40]		(1100 merks/ £733 6s. 8d.)
Gifin[41] to Jhams Cot to pay for the fracht of ane cheip of timir Lij nobillis.[42]		(52 nobles/ £379 6s. 8d.)
Gifin to my lord of Drybrcht for the deutie of the tend of Ladar of the crop lxxxix	xviij nobills	(18 nobles/ £132)
to Andra Durie[43] to bay ane hors	~~sax~~ iiij noblis	(4 nobles/ £29 6s. 8d.)
Item to mak out the soume of four thousand marks xxx noblis	summa ij^{c} xx lib	(£220)
Item tane out fyve hundreth fourtye sax noblis	summa iiij^{m} iiii lib	(£4,004)
Summa sax thousand ane hundreth four scoir aucht poundis		(£6,188)
Sua Restis ane thousand sax hundreth ane pound xvij s viij d		(£1,601 17s. 8d.)

Draft/Copy Accounts of Chancellor Maitland: 1590

[f.204v]

[Endorsed] Counte of the silver receaved fra Carmichell of ane thousand pound sterling

The doubill of the compt of the silver ressavit fra Carmichaell quhilk is to be given in to the chekker

[f.203r]

The compt of thrie thowsand pund Sterling ressavit in England be the Laird of Carmichael extending in Scotts money to xxvij^{m} thousand libs (£27,000)

40 'Succorman' – sugarman, maker of sugar bankets. John Skene's wife was Helen Somerville.

41 The rest of the entries in this page are in an italic hand, perhaps that of Lady Thirlestane.

42 A ship loaded with timber, possibly connected with the arrival of Anna of Denmark. A scaffold/grandstand was built at Leith. The surname could conceivably be 'Kor' and such a person could be a relation of the merchant Clement Cor, but it is more likely that James Scott the Leith timberman previously mentioned was intended.

43 Andrew Durie is perhaps the man mentioned holding a precept of the lands of Nether Grange from the Earl of Huntly as Commendator of Dunfermline, c. 1588. Cosmo Innes, *Registrum de Dunfermelyn* (Edinburgh, 1842), 484.

In primis recevit be the said Laird of Carmichaell gevin out of the said sowme in England as his compt beris threttie pund nynetene schilling striviling

inde ij^{c} iij^{xx} xviij li xj s (£278 11s.)

Item recevit be the said laird of Carmichael be ane precept of his majesties four hundreth and tuentie pund striviling

inde iij^{m} vij^{c} Lxxx li (£3,780)

Item delyverit to Sir James Sandelands

vj^{m} libs (£6,000)

Item payit for fyve hundreth crownis gevin to his majestie quhilks was ressavit be my Lord of Spynie at four merks the piece

inde j^{m} iij^{c} xxxiij li vj s viij d (£1,363 6s. 8d.)

Item to James Bowsie[44] comfett maker at his majesties command

iiij^{c} li (£400)

Item to Helene Somervell spous to Mr John Skene be his majesties precept

iiij^{c} libs (£400)

Item to Sir Lues Bellenden of Auchnowle knycht justice clerk at his majesties command

ij^{m} li (£2,000)

Item to John Wemys youngar of Logy at his majesties command

iij^{c} xxxiij li vj s viij d (£333 6s. 8d.)

Item allowit to the comptars self for a part of the expenses in Denmark

iij^{m} li (£3,000)

Item to a Dense man that come with a present to his majestie out of Denmark at his majesties command ane hundreth ~~crownis at four merks the pece~~ and xxx dolars changit in gold and gevin to him extending to

ij^{c} Lx li (£260)

Item to the comptroller the laird of Parbroith

vj^{c} li (£600)

44 Possibly Jacque de Boussie. See also p. 56, n. 141.

Item to William Schaw master of work at his majesties command
j^{m} li (£1,000)

Item to Robert Jowsie at his majesties command
iiij^{m} li (£4,000)

Item to Thomas Fowlis for releif of certane barronis quha war cautioun to him for his majestie
ij^{m} vj^{c} Lxvj li xiij s iiij d (£2,666 13s. 4d.)

Item to Sir James Sandelands to be play silver to his majestie
ij^{c} Lx li (£260)

Item to ane man of Ramelius[45]
Lvj li (£56)

Item gevin to Monsr de Civile[46] ambassador from the king of France thrie hundreth crownis at four merks the pece
inde viij^{c} li (£800)

[f.203v] Item payit for spyces to Jonet Gottre[47] quhilk war ressavit by Mongo Grahame Master houshald quhen her majestie was looked for to have cumit hame
iij^{c} xxxiij li vj s viij d (£333 6s. 8d.)

Item for a jowell gevin to Monsr Hoteman ane hundreth crounis
inde ij^{c} xvj li xiij s iiij d (£216 13s. 4d.)

Summa xxvij^{m} vij^{c} j li iiij s iiij d (£27,701 4s. 4d.)

Sua is the compter superexpendit vij^{c} j li iiij s iiij d (£701 4s. 4d.)

Item mair to the comptour for his super expenses of the last compt maid of the money ressavit from the laird of Wemys maid and allowit in chekker the xiiij day of August 1590
v^{c} iij^{xx} iij li vj s viij d (£563 6s. 8d.)

45 One of the entourage of Hendrick Ramelius/Ramel, 1550–1610, *Dansk Biografisk Leksicon*, xi, 590–1. Stevenson, *Last Royal Wedding*, 124.

46 Monsieur de Seville. The receipt survives, 11 September 1589 made out to Sir John Maitland, and can be found above, before these sets of accounts.

47 Mungo Graham of Rathemis, Master Household, from 1579 until his death in 1589. Juhala, 'Household', 29, 310.

Summa of the haill

xxviij^{m} ij^{c} iij^{xx} iiij li xj s (£28,264 11s.)

Sua is the comptar superexpendit

j^{m} ij^{c} iij^{xx} iiij li xj s (£1,264 11s.)

Document Set Three

NRS E30/14 Foulis account
Accounts of Thomas Foulis 1594–6

[f.1r][48] The compt of Thomas Foulis burges of Edinburgh and goldsmyth to his majestie of the annuitie of [left blank][49] Ressavit be him be vertew of his hienes commissioun fra the chekker of Ingland in the yeiris of god j^{m} v^{c} fourscoir fourteen and fourscoir fytene yeiris
And of the sowme of sewin thowsand thrie punds saxtene schillingis usuall money of this realme ressavit be him at his majesties command fra Thomas Achesoun master cunyeour to his hienes out of the cunyie hous
And of the dewtie of his tak of the mynnis of Craufurd and Robert Muires of the termes of Mertinmes and Witsonday in the yeir of god j^{m} v^{c} four scoir fyftene yeiris,
And of his debusementis of the samyne and superexpenssis of the ~~sam~~ in and at Edinburgh the [left blank] day of Februar the yeir of god j^{m} v^{c} fourscoir fytene yeiris [1596] In presens of the auditors Alexander lord Urquhart president[50]

Chairge

Item ressavit furth of the Exchakkerhous at Lundoun in July anno 1594 yeiris the sowme of four thowsand pund stirling is in Scottis money

xL^{m} lib[51] (£40,000)

Item ressavit fra Thomas Achesoune master cunyeour in the moneth of October 1594 the sowme of

vij^{m} iij lib xvj s (£7,003 16s.)

Item ressavit fra my lord Secretar in the moneth of December anno 1594 sex hundreth fourscoir punds stirling quhilk is in Scottis money

vj^{m} viij^{c} lib (£6,800)

48 This page has at its top 'No. 19', a nineteenth-century archive reference number.
49 *sic* – 'of England' or the total sum, was probably intended.
50 Alexander Seton, lord Urquhart (1556–1622). Maurice Lee, 'Seton, Alexander, first earl of Dunfermline (1556–1622)', *ODNB* [25113, accessed 23 March 2017].
51 In the margin here: 'nota'.

[f.1v] Item ressavit be his majestis commissioun furth of the exchekker at Lundoun in the moneth of August 1595 yeiris thrie thowsand punds stirling quhilk is in Scottis money

xxx^m lib (£3,000)

Item the compter chairgis him self with the termes of Witsonday and Mertinmes in anno 1595 yeires of the mynnis of Crauford and Robert Muires conforme to his tak and assedatioun thairupoun of the dait At Edinburgh the xix day of Januar 1593 [1594] extending to the sowme of

vj^c Lxvj lib xiij s iij d (£666 13s. 3d.)

Summa of the hail charge extends to foure scoir foure thousand foure hundreth thre scoir ten punds nyne s iiij d (£84,470 9s. 4d.)

Tenet
Clericus Registri
[f.2r] Discharge of the foursaid sowmes Quhairwith the said Thomas Foulis is chargit preceiding the first day of Februar anno four scoir fytene [1596] yeiris as followis.

Item the said Thomas dischargis him with the sowme resten awin to him be his majestie at the faiting[52] of his last compt in Januar anno j^m v^c fourscoir threttine yeiris [1594] as[53] the compt subscrivit be the auditors of the chekker extending to the sowme of

xxxiij^m vj^c xL lib 8 s vj d (£33,640 8s. 6d.)

Item to the tellars and clarkes at Lundoun at the ressait of the annuitie in August 1595 twentie punds sterling is in Scottis money

ij^c lib (£200)

52 Fitting.

53 In the margin here: '3'. This figure in this entry probably includes allowance for a superexpenditure of £36,078 1s. 4d. for clothes supplied to James and Anna by Foulis and Robert Joussie, according to their account audited on 2 February 1593/4; see NRS E35/13, (3) p.1. No general account for the subsidy made by Foulis in January 1593/4 survives. Two subsidy payments of £2000 sterling were made in 1593; see Goodare, 'James VI's English Subsidy', p. 115 from *CSP Scot.*, 13.2 (1969), 742. A Scottish memorandum of the subsidy made in in 1593 has no information for that year; BL Add. MS 33531 ff. 283–290.

Item the said Thomas dischargis him with his furnessing in the monethis of Marche and Aprile anno j^{m} v^{c} fourscoir fourtene yeiris conforme to ane particular compt subscrivit be his majestie as followis

To his majestie the xvj day of Marche 1593 The garnesing of tua greit rubies, twentie four diamontis price in stanes gold and making ane hundreth ten crounes Quhilk jewellis war gevin to hir majestie the aucht of Aprilis 1594 (110 crowns)

Ane greit opall ring quhilk wes send in ane taikin to hir majestie be his majestie

price fyftie crownes (50 crowns)

Item the tent Aprile 1594 delyverit to his majestie tua ringis of a pleik of diamountes price of the tua ane hundreth crownes (100 crowns)

Item the xv day Aprile 1594 debursit to his majestie ane ring of fyve diamountes

price fourscoir crownes (80 crowns)

Summa of the hail particulares thrie hundreth fourtie crounes extendis in Scottis money to

j^{m} xx lib (£1,020)

Lateris xxxiiij^{m} viij^{c} Lx lib viij s vj d (£34,860 8s. 6d.)

[f.2v] Item[54] be his maiesties precept of the dait at Falkland the aucht day of July anno j^{m} v^{c} fourscoir fyftene yeires delyverit to Mr David Foulis[55] ane greit ꝑ diamount ring price tua hundreth crounes is in Scottis money

vj^{C} lib (£600)

Item[56] to Williame Murray[57] conforme to his majesties precept[58] of the dait at Halyruidhous the thrid day of October anno j^{m} v^{c} fourscoir fourtene yeiris certane silver wark as followis

54 Margin: Onerand Mr David Fowlis.

55 Fiona Pogson, 'Foulis, Sir David, first baronet (d. 1642)', *ODNB* [9984, accessed 23 March 2017].

56 Margin: Onerand Wm Murray.

57 William Murray, valet to King James and 'Keeper of the vessels' from 1568 to 1604. Juhala, 'Household', 314, 320.

58 Silver work for Prince Henry. There are two corresponding precepts (included below in the appendix); E30/15/13, endorsed '15', and E30/15/9, endorsed '15' and 'Wm Muraye lxij^{xx}'.

Ane pan, ane ladill, ane trinscheour, tua chandellares all weyand threescoir aucht unces and ane half unce silver at liij s iiij d the unce The haill in maid wark extend to

j[c] Lxxxij lib xiij s	(£182 13s.)

Item[59] delyverit to Sir George Home[60] to ane bonet string of his majesties in the moneth of [left blank] anno 1594 yeiris ane diamount and tua rubies price

xxxiij lib	(£33)

Item[61] delyverit to Andro Melvill maister houshald[62] to his maiestie of reddie money the sowme of tua hundreth fourtene pundis fourtene schillingis In the moneth of August anno ane thowsand fyve hundreth fourscoir fourtene yeiris for furnessing of his majesties hous be and attour the sowme of aucht thowsand sevin hundreth auchtene punds tuelf schillingis four pennies delyverit to him in anno j[m] v[c] fourscoir threttine yeiris and allowit to the compter in anno j[m] v[c] fourscoir threttine yeiris

ij[c] xiiij lib xiiij s	(£214 14s.)
Lateris j[m] Lxxx lib vij s iiij d	(£1,080 7s. 4d.)

[f.3r][63] Item furnessit in gold cheinyeis and silver wark conforme to ane act of counsale of the dait at Halyruidhous the tent day of September anno j[m] v[c] fourscoir fourtene yeiris conforme to ane particulare compt subscrivit be his majestie as followis

Item that wes gevin to Cristianus Bernego and Stephane Beill[64] ambassadors frome the king of Denmark in gold cheinyeis

aucht hundreth crownes	(800 crowns)

Item to Adamus Crusius ambassador from the Duke of Brounisweik ane goldin cheyne

price thrie hundreth crownes	(300 crowns)

59 Margin: Onerand Sir George Hume.

60 Sir George Home of Spott. See also p. 49, n. 125.

61 Margin: Onerand Andro Melvill haill soume.

62 Andrew Melville, master of the king's household. See also p. 21, n. 20.

63 This page is marked '2 fol.'

64 'Stephane Beill' – Steen/Stene Bille (1565–1629) was a widely travelled Danish diplomat, who shuttled accross the North Sea during the marriage negotiations. Stevenson, *Scotland's Last Royal Wedding*, 126.

Item to Joachimus Bassevitius ambassador frome the Duke of Megilburgh ane goldin cheynyie
price thrie hundreth crounes[65] (300 crowns)

Item to the quenis majestie ane Jowell and ane diamount ring
price aucht hundreth fyftie crounes (50 crowns)

Item to Andro Sinclare ane target
iiij^{xx} crounes (80 crowns)

Item to ~~the~~ barone ~~of~~ Brandrod and thesaurer of Zeland[66] ambassadors frome the Law cuntreis of Flanderis tua cheinyeis of gold
price ane thowsand crounes (1000 crowns)

Item to my lord Sussex ambassador frome the quene of Ingland in silver wark all doubill overgilt ane thowsand tua unces at four punds the unce is four thowsand aucht ~~hundreth~~ punds (£4,800)

Item the making of the silver plaites sex hundreth punds (£600)

Summa of the haill conforme to the compt subscrivit be his majestie at Halyruidhous the fourtene day of September anno J^{m} v^{c} fourscoir fourtene yeiris extending to
xiiij^{m} v^{c} Lxxxxviij lib (£14,598)

Item[67] to Robert Jowsie of the annuitie in July anno 1594 ane thowsand aucht hundreth tuentie aucht punds stirling and that in pairt of payment of his furneisment maid to his majestie extending in Scottis money to
xviiij^{m} ij^{c} lxxx lib (£18,280)

Lateris xxxij^{m} viij^{c} Lxxviij li (£32,878)

65 These chains are detailed in the precept E30/15/2, 8 September 1594, below.

66 The names of the ambassadors have been added to a blank space and the remaining space filled with a scribble. The 'The^{s} of Zeland' (silently expanded above) was Jacobus Falkius. These ambassadors' names are given in similar forms in William Fowler, *A true reportarie of the most triumphant, and royal accomplishment of the baptisme of the most excellent, right high, and mightie prince, Frederik Henry* (Edinburgh, 1594).

67 Margin: Onerand Robert Joussie. Robert Jowsie, or Joussie, supplied clothing fabric to the royal wardrobe and was paid with English subsidy. His accounts for the clothes of James and Anna survive; NRS E35/13 &14, this payment is recorded E35/13 (3) p. 2.

[f.2v] Item[68] to Sir Robert Melvill of Murdocairney knycht[69] ane hundreth punds stirling be vertew of his majesties precept of the dait at Halyruidhous the sevint day of Juny 1594 is in Scottis money

	jm lib	(£1,000)

Item[70] to Mr Edward Bruce[71] Ane hundreth punds sterling be vertew of his majestis precept for his relief of his expenses in his wayage in Ingland as the said precept beiris of the dait at Edinburgh the sext day of Juny 1594 is in Scottis money

	jm lib	(£1,000)

Item to Mr David Foulis for making his chairgis towardis Lundoun in anno 1594 be his majesties precept ane hundreth punds stirling as the said precept fillit be his majesties awin hand of the dait at Halyruidhous the [left blank] day of anno 1594 beiris is in Scottis money

	jm lib[72]	(£1,000)

Item payit at Lundoun for aucht ruiffis to hir maiestie in august 1594 tuentie four pund stirling is

	ijc xL lib	(£240)

Item[73] send frome Lundoun be vertew of his maiesties missive ane greit allabast stane quhilk wes to the reparatioun of the chapell of Stirling and certane lead quhilk Roger Astoun ressavit to the palace of Lynlythgow tuentie ane punds stirling is in Scottis money

	ijc x lib[74]	(£210)

68 Margin: Onerand Sir Robert Melwill.

69 Sir Robert Melvill of Murdocairny (1528–1621). See also p. 17, n. 3.

70 Margin: Onerand Mr Eduard Bruce.

71 Edward Bruce (1548–1611), Lord of Session from 1597 to 1603 and Lord Kinloss from 1602. See R.R. Zulager, 'Bruce, Edward, first Lord Kinloss and first Baron Bruce of Kinloss (1548/9–1611)', *ODNB* [3729, accessed 23 March 2017].

72 Precept E30/15/7, 1 March 1595/6, below.

73 Margin: Onerand Roger Aston.

74 Precept E30/15/1, 16 May 1594, below; also 'his Precepte for lead and alabast 1594', printed Henry Paton, John Imrie and John Dunbar, eds, *Accounts of the Master of Works: for building and repairing royal palaces and castles*, 2 vols (Edinburgh, 1957–82), i, 314.

Item[75] for drinking glasses and glass for desertis quhilkis Jerome Bowie and the succour man[76] ressavit tuentie tua punds stirling is in Scottis money

ij^{c} xx lib	(£220)
Lateris iij^{m} vj^{c} Lxx li	(£3,670)

[f.3r][77] Item for the comptaris chargis in passing twys to Lundoun, Remaining thair and returning in September 1594 with the silver wark in ane wagane tua hundreth crownes is

vj^{c} lib	(£600)

Item payit for the said wagan at Lundoun nyne punds stirling is

Lxxxx lib	(£90)

Item lent to his maiestie be the compter in cunyeit money tuelf thowsand punds[78] conforme to ane act of counsale of the dait At Halyruidhous the last day of September fourscoir fourtene yeiris Quhilk wes employit upoun horsmen at the last raid in the north for away putting of the excommunicat erlis

xij^{m} lib	(£12,000)

Item for the annuell of the rent of the said sowme for ane yeir bygane in October last conforme to the said act

j^{m} ij^{c} lib	(£1,200)

Item lent in cunyeit money quhilk wes payit to Williame Home master stabler be vertew of his majesties precept of the dait at Halyruidhous the fourt day of October 1594

ij^{c} lib	(£200)

75 Margin: Onerand Jeromias Bowie.

76 Jeromy or Jerome Bowie was the sommelier; see p. 47, n. 117 and p. 65, n. 20: 'succour man' – sugarman, specialist in sugar works for banquets. See also p. 71, n. 40, and Chancellor Maitland's accounts for the fitting out of James' ship for Denmark.

77 This page is marked at the top with '3.fol.'

78 The page is marked "x" in right hand margin at this point.

Item[79] payit for cheinyeis and goldsmyth wark liftit frome diverss creditours For the quhilkis the compter become particularlie oblist conforme to ane act of counsale of the dait at Halyriudhous the nyntene day of December anno J^{m} v^{c} lxxx fourtene that wes given to the quenis majestie and Duke of Megilburgh extending to

iij^{m} ix^{c} xxxiij lib 6s 8d (£3,933 6s. 8d.)

Lateris xviij^{m} xxiij li vj s viij d (£18,023 6s. 8d.)

[f.4r] Item furnessit to his maiestie in December 1594 conforme to ane particular compt subscrivit be his majestie To wit:

Tua diamount ringis quhilk wes gevin to the gentillmen wes with the Duke of Megilburgh

soume price fourscoir crounes (80 crowns)

To his majesties self ane diamount ring

price fourtie crounes (40 crowns)

To his majestie the xxvj December 1594 ane hinger of diamountes and rubies

price fyftie crounes (50 crowns)

Item that same day delyverit to his majestie ane ring

price threttie crounes (30 crowns)

Summa of the haill tua hundreth crounes is in money

vj^{c} lib (£600)

Item furnessit to his maiestie the first day of Januar 1594 [1595] in new yeir giftis conforme to ane compt subscrivit To wit:

Item ane carcane sett with rubies and perle

price ane hundreth crounes (100 crowns)

Item ane cheinyie of perle

price ane hundreth crounes (100 crowns)

Item ane tablet of gold sett with stanes

price fyftie crounes (50 crowns)

Item ane greit emerod ring

price fourtie crounes (40 crowns)

79 Margin: Onerand Thomas Fowlis for the jowellis. Anna's grandfather, the Duke of Mecklenburgh, Ulrich III, did not come to the baptism, so this chain was given to his proxy.

Item ane ring of allevin diamountis
price ane hundreth tuentie crounes (120 crowns)

Item sevin rings
price of the haill threttie fyve crounes (35 crowns)

Summa of the haill four hundreth fourtie fyve crounes is in money
j^{m} iij^{c} xxxv lib (£1,335)

Item delyverit to his maiestie the tuenty fourth of November 1594 ane greit pointit diamount ring price ane hundreth crounes conforme to his majesties subscription is in money
iij^{c} lib (£300)

Item to Sir George Home ane ring price threttie crownes which wes given to Andro Melvill his wyf at the baptisme of hir barne be his majesties directioun is
Lxxxx lib (£90)

Lateris ij^{m} iij^{c} xxv li (£2,325)

[f.5r][80] Item[81] lent to his maiestie in money in Februar 1594 [1595] quhilk Archibald Prymroiss ressavit be directioun frome Sir George Home
ij^{c} lib (£200)

Item to his maiestie the xxx day of May 1595 be directioun of Sir George Home quhilk wes gevin to my young ladie Mar ane ring of allevin diamountis price ane hundreth crownes
iij^{c} lib (£3200)

Item[82] delyverit to the bischope of Halyruidhous be command frome his majestie quhilk he be his maiesties directioun gaif to [left blank] ane diamont ring price thrie scoir crownes is
j^{c} Lxxx lib (£180)

80 This page is marked at the top '4. fol.'

81 Margin, left: 'onerand Primroiss', right margin: 'onerand Archd Prymroiss'.

82 Margin: Onerand the Abbot of Halyruidhous.

Item to Adriane the painter[83] ane medall with the king and Quenis portrat weyand in gold tuenty crownes Be vertew of his maiesties precept at Halyruidhous the thrid day of October anno 1594 is

Lx lib (£60)

Item[84] delyverit to Gilbert Maistertoune in name of Jhone erle of Mar fyve hundreth punds stirling be vertew of his majesties precept of the dait at Falkland the xviij day of September 1595 quhilk wes assignit to the said erle for entertenement of the prince furth of the annuitie in Ingland in anno 1595 is in Scottis money

v^m lib (£5,000)

Item delyverie to James Hutsoun tua hundreth punds sterling of the said annuitie in anno 1595 Be vertew of his maiesties precept of the dait at Halyruidhous the xxvij of December 1594 subscrivit be his majestie and thrie of his majesties counsalours as the samyne beris is in Scottis money

ij^m lib (£2,000)

Item to the tellars and clerkis in the exchekker at Lundoun at the ressait of the annuitie in August 1595 tuenty pund stirling is in Scottis money[85]

ij^c lib (£200)

Lateris vij^m ix^c xL li (£7,940)

[f.5v] Item to Mr David Foulis tua hundreth punds stirling of the said annuitie to be his furnessing in his majesties affaires towards the quene of Ingland in the moneth of Junij July and August anno 1595 conforme to his majesties precept And the sowme therin fillit up be his majesties awin hand as the said precept of the dait at Halyruidhous the [left blank] day of Junij 1595 beris is in Scottis money

ij^m lib (£2,000)

83 Adrian Vanson (d. 1602) was court painter for James. See M. Apted and S. Hannabuss, *Painters in Scotland 1301–1700* (Edinburgh, 1978), 99. Corresponding Precept, E30/15/3, below.

84 Left margin: 'Onerand Comes Marriy', right margin: 'Onerand comes Marriae'.

85 Robert Joussie recorded the same payment at the London exchequer 'as use is' in 1598; see NRS E35/13, (8), p. 84.

Item[86] to Robert Jowsie merchand burges merchand burges of Edinburgh in pairt of payment of his furnessing of the said annuitie in August 1595 Ane thowsand tuentie punds stirling is in Scottis money[87]

x^{m} ij^{c} lib (£1,200)

Item for the comptaris chairgis and onwaitting upoun the said ressait in anno J^{m} v^{c} Lxxx fytene yeiris fourtie punds stirling is in Scottis money

iiij^{c} lib (£400)

Item to my lord of Menmure[88] conforme to his gift as Master of the mynnis for his fie and dewtie therof in anno 1595 the sowme of

xxxiij lib vj s viij d (£33 6s. 8d.)

Item[89] to Roger Astoun fytie punds stirling for sowmes debursit be him and that be vertew of his majesties precept subscrivit be his majestie of the dait at [left blank] the [left blank] day of [left blank] anno 1595 off the annuitie in anno 1595 is in money

v^{c} lib (£500)

Item to the said Roger Astoun for ane haiknay hors be vertew of his maiesties precept of the dait at Stirling the aucht of September 1595 in money

ij^{c} lib[90] (£200)

Lateris xiij^{m} iij^{c} xxxiij lj vj s viij d (£13,333 6s. 8d.)

[f.6r][91] Item furnessit to his maiestie in December and befoir the sext of Januar anno j^{m} v^{c} fourscoir fytene yeris as ane particular compt subscrivit be his maiestie beiris To wit:

Ane pair of braislettis of gold sett with stanes and perle quhilk wes gevin to the quenis majestie

price ane hundreth thrie scoir crounes (160 crowns)

86 Margin: Onerand Robert Jowssie.

87 For similar payments, see Robert Joussie's account; see NRS E35/13.

88 John Lindsay of Balcarres, lord Menmuir (1552–98), master of metals from May 1592. He approved a tack of mines to Thomas Foulis in January 1594. Alan R. MacDonald, 'Lindsay, John, of Balcarres, Lord Menmuir (1552–1598)', *ODNB* [16705, accessed 23 March 2017].

89 Margin: Onerand Roger Astoun.

90 Precept E30/15/6, 8 September 1595, below.

91 This page is marked at the top '5 fol.'

Item ane greit rubie ring
price threttie crounes (30 crowns)

Item ane tablet all diamountes with ane carcane of diamountes and rubies quhilk wes given to the quene on new yeir day
price fyve hundreth thrie scoir crounes (560 crowns)

Item ane uther tablet of gold set with diamountis and rubies quhilk wes given to Thomas Erskin[92]
price j^c L crounes (150 crowns)

Item ane diamont ring that wes gevin to the littil duchman callit [left blank]
price fyftie crounes (50 crowns)

Item ane uther ring
price xxv crounes (25 crowns)

Item ane hinger of ane salamander sett with diamountes quhilk wes gevin to Williame Schaw[93]
price Lxxxx crounes (90 crowns)

Item ane uther jowell with ane croun all diamountes that wes gevin to the Duke
price Lxxxx crounes (90 crowns)

Item ane tabill diamount ring quhilk wes gevin to Thomas Erskin price tuenty crounes (20 crowns)

Summa of the haill above contenit ane thowsand ane hundreth thrie scoir fyve crounes is in Scottis money iij^m $iiij^c$ Lxxxxv lib (£3,495)

La patet

Summa of this hail discharge unto the first day of Februar 1595 [1596], extends to ane hundreth sevintene thousand fyve hundreth fifty fyve lib nyne s ij d (£117,555 9s. 2d.)

And sua the comptar is superexpendit the soume of thretty thre thousand foure scoir fyve lib vj d (£33,085 6d.)

Tenet
Clericus Registri

92 Thomas Erskine (1566–1639), later viscount Fenton and Earl of Kellie.

93 William Schaw (1550–1604), Master of Work and chamberlain of Dunfermline for Anna of Denmark. See Introduction.

[f.7r] Item furnessit be the Comptar to the Quenis maiestie frome July anno J^{m} v^{c} fourscoir allevin and befoir the first day of December anno j^{m} v^{c} fourscoir tuelf yeiris, the particularis quhairof ar contenit in ane compt subscrivit be hir maiestie at Halyruidhous the sevint day of December anno j^{m} v^{c} fourscoir tuelf yeiris Quhilkis wes not gevin up in compt to the chekkar befoir the dait of thir presentis extending as the said compt beris to four thowsand four hundreth fourscoir sevintene crounes half croun is in Scottis money

xiij^{m} iiij^{c} Lxxxxiij li x s (£13,493 10s.)

Item mair furnesit to hir maiestie be the Compter frome the first of December anno Jm vc fourscoir tuelf yeiris and befoir the threttene day of September anno 1594 yeiris as ane particulare compt the dait at Halyruidhous the said xiij day of September 1594 subscrivit be hir majestie beiris Quhilk is not gevin up in ~~chekker~~ compt in chekker befoir the dait of thir presentis extending as the said compt beiris to ane thowsand sevin hundreth thriescoir sevin crounes half croun is in money

v^{m} iij^{c} ij lib x s (£5,302 10s.)

Summa of the haill debursment ~~for~~ foresaid unto the first day of ~~last~~ Februaris quhairin is

xviij^{m} vij^{c} Lxxxxvj li (£18,796)

Tenet
Clericus Registri

[f.7r] The quhilk sowme of xviij^{m} vij^{c} lxxxxvj punds being addit to the sowme of threttie thrie thowsand foure scoir fyve punds fyve penneis quhilk is the super exppenses of the uther compt contenit in the first syde of the uthir leif preseiding extendes in the haill to fiftie ane thowsand aucht hundred foure scoir ane punds fyve pennyes In the quhilk sowme the comptar is superexpendit unto the first day of Februar 1595 [1596]. (£51,881 5d.)

Tenet
Clericus Registri

Blantyre ASeton Urquhart Culluthy Menmure MHamilton[94]

94 Master Thomas Hamilton; see Julian Goodare, 'Hamilton, Thomas, earl of Melrose and first earl of Haddington (1563–1637)', *ODNB* [12126, accessed 23 March 2017].

Appendix 1

E30/15 Thirteen vouchers or precepts for Thomas Foulis.

E30/15/1 Alabaster stone for Stirling and lead for Linlithgow palace, 16 May 1594.[95]

[Damaged address & seal] To our trusty servitor Thomas Foulis gold smyth presentlie at Londoun[Endorsed] his Parte for lead and alabast 1594

Trusty servitour we greit you hartlie wele having necessarlie ado with certane leid and alabaster for decoratioune and outred of our work heir at Sterling We have taiken occasioun heirby effectuislie to desyre you to by thair at Londoun and send hame heir be the first schip or uthirwise to bring with your selff ane thowsand stane wiecht of leid, and sic forme and quantitie of allabast as salbe sett doun in the paperis heirwith presentit to you, Quhilk we sall not faill to se defrayed and satisfeit to your gude contentment, Quhairin ye sall do ws thankfull and richt acceptable plesur and servive, Thus reposing in your cair and diligence to have thir thingis at ws in all haist for the furtherance of our work we commit you to god from our castell of Sterling the xvj of May 1594

James R

E30/15/2 Gold chains for ambassadors, 8 September 1594.[96]

[Endorsed] 1594. Compt of the giftis gevin to the ambassadors for his maiestie in September 1594 is xiiij^{m} v^{c} Lxxxxviij lib

The aucht day of September anno Jm vc fourscoir fourtene yeiris I undersubscrivand grantes me to haif ressavit fra George Foulis in name and behalf of Thomas Foulis goldsmyth burges of Edinburgh foure chenyies of gold weyand seven scoir unces of gold Thairof tua weyand fourscoir uncis and the uther tua weyand thriescoir unces Be this presens tikett suscrivit with my hand at Edinburgh the said acht day of September anno forsaid Beffoir thir witnessis Williame Buckle and Thomas Weir Quilkis cheynyeis are to be delyverit to the Ambassadors of Denmark presentlie, Cristianne Bernice and Steno Beiale of fourty unce wechts[97] and the uther tua of threttie unce wecht the pece to be delyveret to the Ambassador of the Duk of Brounswik called Adamus Crusius and to the Ambassador of the Duk of Middilburgh callit Joachimus Bassolytius

P Young of Setoun

95 Printed, Paton, *Accounts of the Masters of Work*, i, 314: Payment for lead and alabaster NRS E30/14 f. 2v.

96 Payment for ambassadors' chains recorded NRS E30/14 f. 3v.

97 Margin: the pece.

E30/15/3 A medal of James and Anna for Adrian Vanson, 3 October 1594.[98]
[Endorsed] his Parte for 20 to Adrian the paintar
Rex
Thomas Fowlis our goldmyth It is our will and we command yow, That upoun sicht heirof the anser our painter Adriane of our pictour weyand twentie crownis gold To be thankfullie allowit to yow, in your compt of your debursingis in our service the keping this our precept with his acquittance thairupoun for your warrand Subscrivit with our hand at Haliruidhous the thrid day of October 1594
James R.
I Adrian Vanson painter grante me to haif ressavit the hingar above writtin of the wecht foursaid Be thir presents subscrivit with my hand at Edinburgh the sext day of October anno J^{m} v^{c} fourscoir fourtene yeiris
[Signed] Adrian Van Son painter with my hand.

E30/15/4 Payment to David Foulis, 8 July 1595.[99]
[damaged endorsement] 'ij crounes'
Rex
Thomas Foulis ye shall nocht faill incontinent efter the sicht heirof to delyver to our lovit servitour Mr David Foulis ane dyamant ring of the valeur of twa hundrethe crowns to be imployit as we have gevin him in directioun, quhairanent this precept shalbe unto yow ane sufficientt warrand subscyvit with our hand at Falkland the viij day of July 1595
James R
Ressavit the ring above writtin conforme to the directioun forsaid subscrivit with my hand at Edinburgh the xij July 1595 DFoulis.

E30/15/5 Payment to David Foulis, June 1595, 2 Feb 1596.[100]
Rex. Thomas Foulis and Robt Jowssie ye shal not faill incontinent efter the recept heirof to delyver to our lovit servitour Mr David Foulis the sowme of tua hundreth punds sterling of the first and reddiest ye shal resave this yeir in our name in England quhilk we have allowit to him for his furnishing in this our service quhairin we have imployit him quhairanent this present shalbe unto yow ane sufficient warrand subscryvit with our hand at Halyruidhous the [blank] day of Juny 1595
James R
John Cancellrius[101]
The sowme abovewritten is receavit according to the directioun Edinburgh the second of Februar 1595 [1596], DFoulis.

98 Voucher for payment recorded NRS E30/14 f. 5r.
99 Payment recorded NRS E30/14 f. 2v.
100 Payment recorded NRS E30/14 f. 5v.
101 John Maitland of Thirlestane, Chancellor.

E30/15/6 Payment to Roger Aston for a horse, 8 September 1595.[102]
Rex. Thomas Foulis and Robert Jowsy It is our will and we command you that upoun the sight herof the answer our servitor Rodger Ashetoun of the sowm of thre hundreth merks, for ane hacqueney hors quhilk we have taikin from him to our awin use, Quhilk salbe thankfullie allowed to you upoun compt Kepand thir presens for your warrand, Subscrivit my hand at Sterling castell the viij day of September 1595
James R
Ressavit the soume contenit in this precept and dischargis the said Thomas thairof subscrivit with my hand at Edinburgh the fyft Februar anno 1595 yeires, Roger Aston.

E30/15/7 Payment to David Foulis, 1 March 1596.[103]
[Endorsed] Mr David Foulis for his allowance during his employment in Ingland the first payment next begyng the 3 of Marche 1595 [1596][104]
Skene subscrivit[105] Rex
Thomas Foulis ye shal not faill efter the sight heirof to furnishe to oure weillbelovit servand Mr David Foulis for the first monethe of his imployment in our service the sum of ane hundrethe crounis, and monethlie theirefter the sowme of threscoir quhilk we have grantit to him for his ordinarie allowance during the tyme of his absence in our service quhilks shalbe thankfullie allowit to you of the readiest shalbe resavit of oure annuitie in England Quhairof this present shalbe unto you ane sufficient warrand, subscryvit with our hand at Halyruidhouse the first day of Marche 1595 [1596]
James R
Nota this precept nocht to tak begynning nor haif allowance bot fra the day of Mr David Fowlis away passing furth of Scotland
ASeton Urquhart, Blantyre, JWemis, Ormistoun[106], Mr Almusar, Culluthy, Clericus Registri.

102 Payment recorded NRS E30/14 f. 6r.
103 Voucher for payment to David Foulis recorded NRS E30/14, f. 2v.
104 The endorsements are also marked '4' '4'.
105 The contraction here is 'Skene Sst', which appears several times in this document set. These have all been silently expanded to 'Skene subscrivit'. This is presumably a further accounting check. Sir John Skene of Curriehill (c.1540–1617); see p. 25, n. 45.
106 This transcription is uncertain, as the signature is almost indecipherable. There is just enough to make the assumption that this is Sir John Cockburn of Ormistoun. See p. 17, n. 4.

E30/15/8 Payment to David Foulis, 1 March 1596.[107]
[Endorsed] Warrand to Thomas Foulis ffor Mr David his 1000 lib[108]
Skene subscrivit Rex
Thomas Foulis ye shal not faill incontinent efter the sight heirof to deliver to our weillbelovit Mr David Foulis the sowme of ane hundrithe punds stirling quhilk we have ordanit to be disponit according to oure directtioun gevin to him, quhilk shalbe thankfullie repayit to you of the first and readiest of quhatsomever oure casualities resavit, Quhairanent this present shalbe unto you ane sufficient warrand Subscryvit with oure hand at Halyruidhouse the first of Marche 1595 [1596].
James R
Blantyre

E30/15/9 Silverwork for Prince Henry (& King James makes a joke), 16 August 1595.[109]
[Endorsed] 'William Muraye lxij lib[110]
Skene subscrivit
Thomas Foullis ye sall nocht faill efter the sight heirof to deliver to this berer the princis silverwark quhilk ye wer commandit to provyd for him, Receave heirwithe tua silver chandleris and caus them be helpit and grathin, and send bak with all diligence, sua fair yow well At Striveling castell this xvj day of August 1595
James R
\ I will testifie this is the princes awin mark.[111]

E30/15/10, Instruction to account £400 from the annuity, 10 December 1596.
[endorsed] precept for sterlen[112]
Skene subscrivit Rex
Tresorer and remanent lords of oure exchequer ye shall not faill upon the sight heiroff to allow in the countis of oure last annuitie of England the soume of foure hundrethe poundis stirling quhilk we testifie heirby to have turnit to oure particulare use and imployit for the contentment of oure maist special service Quhairanent this shalbe unto you a sufficient warrand Subscryvit with oure hand at Halyruidhous the tent day of december 1596 this was done be my private direction[113] James R.

107 Payment to David Foulis, NRS E30/14 f. 2v.
108 This page is also marked '8' '8' '8'.
109 Included in payment to William Murray for silver, NRS E30/14 f. 2v.
110 This paged is also marked '15' '15' '15'.
111 James indicates that a diagonal pen stroke on the page was made by the baby Prince Henry.
112 This page is also marked '5' '5'.
113 This is in the hand of King James himself.

E30/15/11 Payment to George Nicolson, 30 July & 20 August 1596.
[Endorsed] Robert Bowes for 300 sterlein[114] ~~Robert Bowes ffor 300 lib sterlen~~
Skene subscrivit Rex
Mr David Foullis we greit yow weill. Quhairas be our former lettre direct to our trustie and weilbelovit Mr Robert Bowes ambassador for our dearest sister and cousine the quene of England we required him to disburse for Mr Johnne Colvill three hundredth poundis sterling for quhilk he hath engaged his credit And sen it standis us in heirof to see him pait of the same These ar therfoir to let yow understand that is our will and pleasour and als to require and mak paiment of the same sowme to George Nicolson[115] in name of the said Mr Robert Bowes And that of the first and readiest of our annuetie to be ressavit be yow this yeir in England Quhilk sowme salbe thankfully allowit to yow kepand the presents with the said George his acquittance for your warrand Subscryvit with our hand at Dunfermling the penult day of July 1596
James R
Blantyre, JLyndesay, Clericus Registri, MrTHamilton[116]

Received by me George Nicolson of Thomas Fowlis and Robert Jowsy burgesses of Edenbrough the soume of thre hundreth pounds sterling in full payment and sattisfactioun of this precept within written in name and behalf of Mr Robert Bowes her majesties ambassador within written whereof I hold myself contented of and herby acquittes and discharges the saids Thomas and Robert Jowsy the said some for ever as witnesses this bill subscribed with my hand the 20th day of August 1596 per me George Nicolson[117]

E30/15/12 Jewellery received from Thomas Foulis, 12 January 1597.
[Endorsed] presept for = 2765[118]
Skene subscrivit
Thesaurer it is our will and we require yow that ye faill not upon the sicht heirof to content and pay to our servitor Thomas Fowllis the sowme underwraittin and that for certen goldwark ressavit be us fra him before the making heirof to wit, ane ring of ane diamond and ane rubie pryce fiftie crownes, ane great table diamond ringe pryce fowrscoire ten crownes, ane ringe of sevin diamonds pryce ane hundrethe and twentie crownes, ane ringe

114 This page is also marked. '6' '6' '6' '7'.

115 The name 'George Nicholson' is inserted in a blank space and two wavy lines fill the rest of the space.

116 Thomas Hamilton, Lord Binning and Earl of Haddington (1563–1637). See p. 86, n. 94. 'Clericus Registri' refers to Sir John Skene of Curriehill (c. 1540–1617).

117 This certification by George Nicholson is faded and damaged.

118 This page is also marked 'ii' 'ii' 'ii'.

of alevinthe diamondis pryce fourscoire crownes Item ane tablet of ane great emerald and ten diamundes pryce tua hundreth and fiftie crowns Item ane karkane set with diamundes rubies and perles pryce tua hundrethe crownes extending in the holl to sewinthe hundreithe fowrscoire ten crownes, at threa punde ten schillinges the crowne is in Scottis mony, tua thowsand sevin hunderithe threa scoire fyve pundes quhilk sowme ye faill not to pay as said is of the first and reddiest quhatsumever our casualities quhairanent this present with the said Thomas discharge sall be yowr sufficient warrand subscryveit with our hand at Halyrudhows the twelthe day of Januar the yeire of god, 1596 [1597].
James R
Crauford, Montroiss, Andro lord Ochiltre, Trakquair, Clericus Registri

E30/15/13 Delivery of Silverware, 7 May 1597.[119]
Skene subscrivit Rex
Thesaurer ye sall caus anser and deliver to our servitor William Morrye ane sillver coupe with the cover and ane sey cais of sillver: with ane trencheor quhairin the salltfatt may stand all for our derrest sone the prynce quhilk ye leif nocht undone quhairanent thir presens sallbe your warrand subscrivit with our hand Halliruidhous the sevint of Maye 1597
James R.

119 Included in payment to William Murray for silver, NRS E30/14 f. 2v. This page is also marked '15'.

Appendix 2

Two Letters from Anna of Denmark to King James 1589[120]

Kindly translated by Marie-Claude Tucker, with additional helpful comments from Jamie Reid-Baxter and Alison Rawles. Please note that Anna's French was not perfect, so her spelling mistakes have been intentionally retained.

BL Add. MS.19401 f.141

Monsieur, vous pourrez cognoistre par ce que vous mandent plus amplement messieurs les ambassadeurs destinés pour ma conduicte en ce voiage, l'extreme devoir faict tant de la part de ceux qu'il vous a pleu d'envoir en dennemarch, que de leur costé, à fin de vous rendre jouissant de l'accomplissement du desir assez tesmoigné par vos lettres, et qu'a ceste intention nous nous sommes desja par quartre ou cinq fois avances en la mer, mais que par vents contraires et autres inconvenients y survenus, avons tousjours esté rejectes aux havres dont estions issus, qui est cause que l'hiver maintenant nous pressant, et la redoubtance de plus grands dangers qui sont tresapparents a contrainct toute ceste compagnie, bien à nostre grand regret et des vostres, qui en sont extremement desplaisants, de prendre une resolution, de ne rien plus attenter pour ceste fois, ains de differer le voiage jusques à la primevere, laquelle saison estant venue, vous pouvez pour bein asseure, moyennant la grace de deiu, que nul empeschement ne retardera plus ~~plus~~ noctre tant souhaiteé entrevue, ce que je prie que puisse estre aves tant d'heur et contentement, que je desire tant que vivrai de demeure.

l'entierement vostre à vous rendre humble obeissance

Anna

Sir, you will, from the more ample reports of the ambassadors sent to accompany me in this voyage, learn of the extreme efforts made by those whom you were pleased to send to Denmark and their party, in order that you might enjoy the fulfilment of the wish amply evidenced in your letters, and that to this intent, we have already put out to sea four or five times but have always been driven back to the harbours from which we had sailed, thanks to contrary winds and other problems which arose at sea, which is the cause why, Winter now hastening down on us, and fearing the evident greater dangers [involved], all this company has been forced, much to our great regret and that of your men who are extremely displeased about it, to take a decision to make no further attempt at this time but to defer the voyage until the Spring: when that season has come, you can be well assured, that by God's grace no impediment shall further delay our so much longed-for meeting, which I pray may be with as much felicity and contentment as I desire all my life to remain

The one who is entirely yours,

Anna

120 We are grateful to Dr Jemma Field for bringing these to our attention.

BL Add. MS.19401 f.143

James' letter to Anna by Stewart (the Prior of Pittenween) is printed in Warrender Papers, *ii, 109-110. The Danish archive has the original copies which have 'le Sieur Stuart' and the location 'Fleckeroe', see Macray, 'Third Report on the Royal Archives of Denmark', 25.*

Monsieur, Combein que par mes precedentes vous aies assez peu apperievoir qu'il n'a tenu à nous que n'aions parachevé nostre voiage encommencé, Si est-ce que ayant depius receu celle quil vous a pleu de m'escrire par le Seigneur avec une singuliere demonstration du grand desir qu'avez que le voiage sauance au plustost, je n'ai sceu omettre d'adiouster ce mot, pour vous remercier de vostre bonne volonté, Vous asseurant que de nostre costé ne sera donné aucun ~~redar~~ retardement, et qu'a ceste fin j'ai esté contente de m'arrester en ce paix de norvege, en attendant une meilleure apportunité de parfaire le susdict voiage, qui sera quand il plaira à deiu de nous en faire la grace, vous priant de voire que le plus grand desir que j'ai enc e monde c'est de vous faire paroistre que toute ma vie ie serai.

vostre bein humble et obeissance.

Anne

Sir, though by my previous letters you have been sufficiently informed that it is not due to us that we have not completed the voyage undertaken, yet having since then received the letter that you have been pleased to write to me by the gentleman, as a special manifestation of your great longing for the voyage to proceed as soon as possible, I could not but add this note to thank you for your good will, assuring you that no delay shall ensue on our part, and to this end, I have been content to stay in this country of Norway, pending a better opportunity to complete the foresaid voyage, which shall be when it shall please God to grant us that grace, praying you to understand that my greatest desire in this world is to demonstrate to you that all my life I shall be

your very humble and obedient

Anna

THE PRINCIPAL OF GLASGOW AGAINST THE COVENANT (1638)

Edited by Salvatore Cipriano

INTRODUCTION

This document is a defence of the King's Covenant written in autumn 1638 by John Strang (1583/4–1654), the principal of the University of Glasgow from 1626 to 1650, with comments and interpolations by James, marquess of Hamilton (1606–49), Charles I's commissioner for Scotland at the beginning of the British Civil Wars.[1] The manuscript is part of the Wodrow Collection in the National Library of Scotland, Edinburgh, and is bound in Wodrow Folio Volume XXXI, item 2, fos 7–24.

The Manuscript and its Historical Context

Strang's treatise is an underutilised source whose title has perhaps prevented further inquiry into its contents. Walter Balcanquhall, the Scottish dean of Rochester, with whom John Strang had been in correspondence in autumn 1638, named the tract 'The Principal of Glasgow Against the Covenant', no doubt to amplify the purported opposition of a leading Scottish intellectual – a university principal – to the Covenanting movement.[2] This title has stuck. The Wodrow Collection finding aid in the National Library of Scotland identifies the manuscript as 'The principal of Glasgow University's arguments against the National Covenant', which suggests that Strang's treatise was a work of anti-Covenanting polemic, similar to the Aberdeen Doctors' writings against the Covenant published during summer 1638.[3] The tract, however,

1 On Strang, see S. Handley, 'Strang, John (1583/4–1654)', *Oxford Dictionary of National Biography* (Oxford, 2004) (*ODNB*) [www.oxforddnb.com/view/article/26632, accessed 15 January 2016].

2 H.M.B. Reid, *The Divinity Principals in the University of Glasgow 1545–1654* (Glasgow, 1917), 282.

3 For an overview of the Aberdeen Doctors' polemics, see J.D. Ogilvie, 'The Aberdeen Doctors and the National Covenant', *Papers of the Edinburgh Bibliographical Society* 11 (1912), 73–86; D. Stewart, 'The "Aberdeen Doctors" and the Covenanters', *Records of the Scottish Church History Society* 22 (1986), 35–44. It is clear that Strang had read the Doctors' work, and he cites them on two occasions in his tract. See National Library of Scotland, Edinburgh

contains little in terms of overt opposition to the National Covenant. To say that it does obscures its contents and reinforces the notion that at the outset of the Scottish Revolution there was a stark Covenanting/anti-Covenanting divide. The reality of the situation was more complex. A substantial portion of Scotland's religious establishment occupied a grey area between support for and opposition to the Covenanting movement. Strang subscribed to the National Covenant only after repeated overtures from Robert Baillie, his friend and eventual colleague at Glasgow; Archibald Johnston of Wariston, the firebrand advocate and co-author of the Covenant; and John Adamson, principal of Edinburgh University. The university principal was among those subscribers whose Covenanting allegiance can be described as lukewarm at best. This document is indicative of the idiosyncratic nature of both support for and opposition to the Covenant.

Historians have nevertheless seized upon the identification of Strang's treatise as anti-Covenanting to illustrate the Glasgow principal's reluctance to support the movement. While Strang certainly had his misgivings, this conceptualisation fails to take into account the manuscript's actual contents.[4] Peter Donald is the only historian to have considered Strang's tract in any detail. He discusses its major points briefly in light of Hamilton's efforts to manage Scottish affairs in the period immediately preceding the opening of the General Assembly at Glasgow, which abolished episcopacy in Scotland, in late November 1638.[5]

But in truth, Strang's tract is a product of the renewed Covenanting agitation that came in the wake of the proclamation of the King's Covenant, Charles I and his Scottish privy councillors' attempt to quell mounting discontent in Scotland in 1638. In April, Wariston and Alexander Henderson, a leading Covenanting minister and co-author of the National Covenant, drew up what was known as the 'Eight Articles', which they had Lord Lorne, the future marquess of Argyll, deliver to court.[6] The Articles pressed the crown to eliminate a number of 'innovations', including the Five Articles of Perth of 1618 (liturgical strictures passed under James VI and I that,

(NLS), John Strang, 'The Principal of Glasgow Against the Covenant', 1638 (hereafter Strang Treatise), Wod.Fol.XXXI fos 17v., 19v. William Wilkie, a regent at Glasgow University under Strang, also requested the Aberdeen Doctors' work from Balcanquhall in October 1638. See R. Baillie, *The Letters and Journals of Robert Baillie*, ed. D. Laing, 3 vols (Edinburgh, 1841), i, 482.

4 See, for instance, S.J. Reid, '"Ane Uniformitie in Doctrine and Good Order": the Scottish Universities in the Age of the Covenant, 1638–1649', *History of Universities* 29/2 (2016), 13–41, at 19 n. 19. See also J. Coutts, *A History of the University of Glasgow from its Foundation in 1451 to 1908* (Glasgow, 1909), 124–5.

5 P. Donald, *An Uncounselled King: Charles I and the Scottish Troubles, 1637–1641* (Cambridge, 1990), 103–4.

6 A. Johnston, *Diary of Sir Archibald Johnston of Wariston, Volume I 1632–1639*, ed. G.M. Paul (Edinburgh, 1911), 330; Donald, *Uncounselled King*, 69–70, 76–7.

among other things, mandated kneeling at communion), the Court of High Commission, the Book of Canons of 1636 and the Prayer Book of 1637, the latter having occasioned the riots in summer 1637 that intensified into revolution.[7] They also called for annual meetings of the General Assembly, a meeting of Parliament and trials of Scotland's bishops.[8] By late summer, Hamilton and several other Scottish privy councillors advised the king to assent to these overtures. Hamilton also advised Charles to order the re-signing of the Negative Confession of 1581, which formed the basis of the National Covenant, alongside a new bond of maintenance. With these measures, it was hoped that the crown would be able to co-opt Covenanting zeal and restore Scotland's trust in the king.

Charles was loath to heed this advice, but by early September 1638 he acquiesced and ordered Hamilton to see to these actions.[9] The proclamation, which became known as the King's Covenant, was promulgated on 22 September 1638. In it, Charles rescinded the Canons, the Prayer Book, the High Commission and 'the practice of thame or anie of thame' in an attempt to 'free all our good subjects of the least suspicion of anie intention in us to innovate anie thing ather in religion or lawes'. The king also discharged the 'urging of the practise' of the Five Articles. Charles then re-authorised subscription to the Negative Confession with a new bond in which subscribers pledged to uphold true religion and the king's majesty. Charles also granted Hamilton the authority to call a 'free' General Assembly to be held in Glasgow in November 1638 – an Assembly that, according to the proclamation, would include bishops – and a Parliament to be held in Edinburgh the following May.[10]

At first glance, Charles's concessions seem substantial. But few Covenanting leaders were convinced of the king's sincerity. Immediately, Wariston, Henderson and the earls of Rothes and Loudon protested the King's Covenant.[11] They began their protest by identifying several limitations in the proclamation. Most significantly, they argued that the King's Covenant did little to allay fears concerning religious innovation. The key discrepancy was that the King's Covenant only discharged the *practice* of innovations like the

7 On the Perth Articles, see L.A.M. Stewart, 'The Political Repercussions of the Five Articles of Perth: a Reassessment of James VI and I's Religious Policies in Scotland', *Sixteenth Century Journal* 38 (2007), 1013–36. On the Prayer Book riots and the growth of the revolution, see A.I. Macinnes, *Charles I and the Making of the Covenanting Movement 1625–1641* (Edinburgh, 1991), 158–77.

8 J. Leslie, Earl of Rothes, *A Relation of Proceedings Concerning the Affairs of the Kirk of Scotland, from August 1637 to July 1638* (Edinburgh, 1830), 96–8, 100–2, 128.

9 Donald, *Uncounselled King*, 92–103; D. Stevenson, *The Scottish Revolution 1637–1644: The Triumph of the Covenanters* (Newton Abbot, 1973), 104–12.

10 P.H. Brown (ed.), *The Register of the Privy Council of Scotland, Vol. 7, 1638–1643*, second series (Edinburgh, 1906), 64–78.

11 Johnston, *Diary*, 390–2.

Canons and Prayer Book, and did not *eliminate* these innovations completely. They could, therefore, be reintroduced. The protest also argued that an extra-ecclesiastical body could not determine membership in the General Assembly, which Charles, via the Scottish Privy Council, had done by insisting that the impending meeting at Glasgow include bishops. The heart of the protest consisted of sixteen reasons as to why those who had already subscribed to the National Covenant could not subscribe to the King's Covenant. It maintained that any subscription to the King's Covenant would supersede the National Covenant, which was intended to be everlasting. Further, the protesters argued that signing the King's Covenant equated to admitting themselves as transgressors, and they could not condemn their subscription of the National Covenant as illegal. Elsewhere, they reasoned that subscribing to the King's Covenant would oblige the Covenanters to uphold the Five Articles of Perth and episcopacy, while the new bond of maintenance was too lenient on Catholicism. In the conclusion, the protesters resolved to maintain the National Covenant and oppose all rival covenants and confessions.[12]

This protestation flummoxed Strang, who was among the King's Covenant's supporters. In Glasgow Strang was not alone in favouring the king's measure, for the presbytery of Glasgow welcomed the proclamation and issued a letter of thanks to Hamilton on 24 September. Strang and three Glasgow University regents were among the letter's signatories.[13] Strang also took further action by penning a response to the Covenanters' protestation, which, according to the manuscript's opening paragraph, he intended for Hamilton's 'privat use and contentment'.[14] The principal had only subscribed to the National Covenant reluctantly, and it is clear that he continued to harbour doubts concerning the nature and direction of the Covenanting movement. Strang was, however, wholly satisfied with the King's Covenant, particularly because it signalled, in his eyes, the supreme magistrate's intention to correct the ills that bred religious instability in Scotland. That his brethren continued to resist the king was puzzling. Strang's riposte was both a point-by-point answer to the Covenanters' protest and a defence of the King's Covenant.

The document is divided into four main sections. The first (fos 7r.–8r.) is an introductory letter 'To his beloved brother J. H'. These initials most likely stand for James, marquess of Hamilton, especially as he provided

12 The protestation is printed in [Charles I], *A Large Declaration Concerning the Late Tumults in Scotland* (London, 1639), 157–73.

13 National Records of Scotland, Edinburgh, Presbytery of Glasgow to Hamilton, 24 Sept. 1638, Hamilton papers, GD406/1/445. The signatories from Glasgow University included Strang and the regents John Rae, William Wilkie and Patrick Maxwell. Signatories from the presbytery included Robert Wilkie, John Maxwell, George Bell the younger, Gavin Forsythe and Hugh Blair.

14 NLS, Strang Treatise, Wod.Fol.XXXI fo. 7r.

comments on the document.[15] In this section, Strang both lamented the Covenanters' rampant 'seperation or discontement' and praised the king's remedies that voided 'thinges unlawfull'.[16] Strang thus early on demonstrated his frustration with the Covenanters' refusal to accept Charles's concessions: 'If he have done this what \can/ he doe more? And shall we when he hath condescended this farre to us, still beare in upoun him, and remaine unsatisfied, lyk some men who deal most hardlie with these who ar most gentle and still crave more of them whom they sie disposed to grant much.'[17] Strang assigned this intransigence to the Covenanters' 'strict dealing' in regards to church government. The king had 'dischairged the innovationes compleined upon' and ordered subscription to the anti-Catholic confession of 1581. If scruples remained, Strang contended, they were due to matters of church government. To this Strang contended that 'No sound divyn' could argue that the Church of Scotland had maintained a strict and unchanging polity, for it had since 1560 oscillated between episcopal and presbyterian organisation. Strang cited Europe's Reformed churches as evidence: even 'the best Reformed churches agrie not among themselves'. In pleading for peace, Strang concluded this section by stating that 'We need not to exspect a perfyt estate of Godis church or of the governament therof heir upon earth.'[18] When compared to his hardline Covenanting brethren, Strang exhibited a marked ambivalence in matters of church government.

In the second section (fos 9r.–13r.), Strang offered eleven reasons in defence of the King's Covenant entitled 'Reasones why all his majesties orthodox subjectis in Scotlande and namelie these who subscryved the late covenant should themselves fullie acquiesce to his majesties late declaration and proclamationes.'[19] Starting with this section, the manuscript becomes paginated. This is significant, for Hamilton's notes and comments punctuate this portion of the tract in one un-paginated folio. In his interpolations, Hamilton referenced these page numbers.[20] Here, Strang reiterated and expanded upon points in his introductory letter, especially regarding

15 In his brief discussion of this document, Henry Reid transcribed the initials as 'J. D.'. He likely confused the extended curvature of the horizontal bar in the 'H' as resembling a 'D'. Because of this, Reid suggested that the tract was addressed to James Durham, the Covenanting army captain and later minister of Blackfriars in Glasgow. This is highly unlikely because in 1638 Durham was sixteen years of age and probably a student at St Andrews. Reid, *Divinity Principals*, 281. On Durham, see K.D. Holfelder, 'Durham, James (1622–1658)', *ODNB* [www.oxforddnb.com/view/ article/8314, accessed 15 January 2016].

16 NLS, Strang Treatise, Wod.Fol.XXXI fo. 7v.

17 Ibid.

18 Ibid., fos 7v–8r

19 Ibid., fo. 9r.

20 Ibid., fo. 10. Fo. 11 is blank.

Charles I's concessions in satisfying the grievances in the Eight Articles.[21] But the most telling part of this section is Strang's comparison of the King's Covenant to the National Covenant. Specifically, Strang contended that the National Covenant had no staying power. It was a temporary solution that addressed current grievances, but it would be 'impractical' in the future. Strang argued that a covenant 'ought to be perpetuall', and that it should be 'lawfullie subscryved by all men at any tyme, & speciallie when it is commandet by authoritie, therby to discerne the orthrodox and hetrodox'. It was also ludicrous to think that those who had already signed the National Covenant could not subscribe to the King's Covenant.[22] Charles's covenant was 'the best and strongest meane, that ever wes agried upoun by publick authoritie, to preserve the puritie of religion'. Strang also noted that a general bond of maintenance without the inclusion of the king had been viewed as dangerous and led to some of his subjects taking exception to the National Covenant. But Charles had taken the 'best course' to make the King's Covenant 'more valid' by removing the separation between the king and his subjects. Thus for Strang, the National Covenant was flawed, while the King's Covenant was in 'no wayes impared'.[23] It needs to be noted here that at no point in this section, or in the tract in general, does Strang label the National Covenant as illegal – at this time, he had subscribed to it. Characterising the National Covenant as illegal would have implicated Strang in an unlawful conspiracy against the king. Rather, Strang more clearly argued that the King's Covenant offered a better path for settling religious dispute in Scotland. His most hostile language was reserved for the Covenanters' protest and not for the National Covenant itself.

In the third section (fos 13v.–16r.), entitled 'Answeris to the reasones objected in the late protestation', Strang responded in turn to each of the three limitations identified in the Covenanters' protest. First, Strang addressed the Covenanters' argument that Charles I's proclamation discharged the use of the Prayer Book and Canons without condemning them. Strang exhibited more faith in the king's intentions, arguing that the King's Covenant also rescinded all statutes secular and ecclesiastical that enacted these innovations. Thus the Covenanters' fears were based 'rather in apprehension and fancie then [*sic*] in realitie and substance'.[24] Next, Strang argued that though Charles had discharged the Five Articles of Perth, the king would not suffer them altered nor abjured because they did not fall under the scope of religious innovation. 'We have sworne', Strang wrote, 'to the uttermost of our power, to stand to the defence of the kinges authoritie, in the defence of

21 Ibid., fo. 9r. On the Eight Articles, see above, notes 6 and 8.

22 NLS, Strang Treatise, Wod.Fol.XXXI fo. 12v.

23 Ibid., fos 9r., 12r.–12v.

24 Ibid., fo. 14r.

the lawes of this kingdome: thairfore we have sworne to defend the kinges authoritie, in the articles of Perth, establisched by the law of the kingdome.'[25] Finally, Strang contended that the protestation against bishops' inclusion at the General Assembly 'is made onlie by such as ar antiepiscopall'. Once again, Strang deferred to the king's judgement, and maintained that Charles believed episcopacy to be 'lawfull and expedient for the church', which legitimated the king's call for bishops to be present at the impending General Assembly. Strang did reason, however, that bishops' attendance at meetings of the Assembly and episcopacy's legality were both subjects that could be debated at the Assembly. His contention was that episcopacy's fate should not be decided *before* the Assembly convened.[26]

The final section (fos 16v.–24r.) is entitled 'Answeris to the particullar reasons objected against the new subscription'. In this section, Strang replied to each of the Covenanters' sixteen reasons for refusing to subscribe to the King's Covenant. He restated many of the arguments found in the previous three sections. Strang contended once more that subscribing to the King's Covenant would not render the National Covenant obsolete, especially because each included the Negative Confession. He reiterated the fact that the King's Covenant represented a concession to the Covenanters: Charles's 'ordinance for a new subscription importeth his gracious condescending to us'.[27] Further, the King's Covenant had royal approbation, which made it wholly lawful in Strang's eyes. This was the central 'defect' in the bond of maintenance in the National Covenant, which was not rooted in royal authority.[28] A general band sanctioned by the king would also do more to counteract Catholicism in Scotland, 'seing poperie is evin now pregnant and powerfull in this land'.[29]

In concluding this final section, Strang defended Charles I's Scottish Privy Councillors, whom the Covenanters in their protest lambasted for introducing the King's Covenant, arguing that, 'there is no place left to the generalitie of any mans conception of the true Faith and Religion, nor to any private interpretation, or mentall reservation'.[30] To this Strang responded:

> Evrie man most belive for himsellf, and know what he beliveth and confesseth in matteris concerning his salvation. No man can in conscience be tyed by an implicit faith to the meaning of any wryt, except onlie the meaning of Godis spirit, in the holie scripture. Nather can it be instancet, that in our kirk, ther ar any diversities of meaninges and interpretationes of the said confession, concerning any matter necessar to faith and salvation.[31]

25 Ibid., fos 14v.–15r.
26 Ibid., fo. 15v.
27 Ibid., fos 16v., 17r., 18r.
28 Ibid., fo.18v.
29 Ibid., fos 18v.–19r.
30 [Charles I], *Large Declaration*, 170.
31 NLS, Strang Treatise, Wod.Fol.XXXI fo. 23r.

This was a stark departure from the more zealous Covenanting divines who championed rigid orthodoxy to the authority of the Kirk. Strang furthermore contended that it was absurd to think that all subscribers of the National Covenant had done so because of their commitment to an acute understanding of the parameters of the Church of Scotland. He argued that 'many thousandis hes subscryved the said confession and [the National] covenant, who ar not acquented with the bookis of discipline, and actis of assemblies the laufulnes also of som assemblies is now contraverted, concerning which ev\e/rie subscryver cannot judge'.[32] The Covenanters' arguments to the contrary were hypocritical.

This document illuminates Strang's thinking on the nature of royal authority, covenanting and church government, and his intention was to argue in favour of the King's Covenant. Indeed, this document is not simply an anti-Covenanting polemic, but instead an argument for the merits of the King's Covenant. When compared with the National Covenant, Strang reasoned that the King's Covenant offered a better solution to alleviate religious pressures in Scotland because it stemmed from the king's authority. Moreover, it is important to reiterate that Strang does not label the National Covenant as illegal at any point in this manuscript, which the Aberdeen Doctors were quick to do. When Strang expressed disdain, it is for the Covenanters' misguided protest against the King's Covenant, and not for the National Covenant itself.

Strang's treatise, his related correspondence with Balcanquhall and the resultant affair over the tract's discovery provides clear evidence that Strang's subscription to the National Covenant was not rooted in any principled commitment to the Covenanting movement. Indeed, the university principal's initial opposition to the Prayer Book did not translate into support for the Covenant. Strang's subscription, rather, came down to political expediency and the urgings of his professional and personal acquaintances. When the King's Covenant was introduced, Strang found an altogether better option to rectify the troubles in Scotland and satisfy his conscience.

Beyond its contents, the fate of the manuscript itself, which had particular bearing on its creator, is also especially intriguing. In autumn 1638, Strang was in correspondence with Hamilton and Balcanquhall. In a letter to William Laud, archbishop of Canterbury and the architect of Charles I's ecclesiastical policy, Balcanquhall spoke of Strang as the 'learnedst covenanter in Scotland'. Hamilton, Balcanquhall and Laud urged Strang's tract to be published and disseminated, which together with the Aberdeen Doctors' works would have done much to advance the cause of the crown in public debate. The king also desired that Strang 'owne what he writ'. But in the

32 Ibid.

charged political and religious climate of late 1638, Strang would not claim authorship. It was too dangerous, and he contended that the work needed revision. In the manuscript's opening paragraph, he wrote that he wished that his treatise not be made public, referring to his writing as 'rude, and undigested lines'.[33] And, when Hamilton attempted to read the piece at the opening the General Assembly at Glasgow, Strang interrupted and blocked its reading.[34]

The tract thus went unpublished and, apparently, unbeknownst to the Covenanters until 1646 when it was discovered, alongside Strang's correspondence with Balcanquhall, following the Battle of Naseby. The documents then came into the possession of the Scottish commissioners at the Westminster Assembly.[35] Their discovery called into question Strang's orthodoxy and his fitness to teach divinity at Glasgow. The General Assembly ordered a review of Strang's teaching dictates to evaluate his orthodoxy, and though a specially appointed committee found minor discrepancies in some of Strang's notes, it uncovered no grave doctrinal errors.[36] Strang was eventually exonerated in 1647, but his days at Glasgow University were numbered. Following this affair, he cut back his teaching and eventually resigned his principalship in April 1650, but not before the General Assembly approved a statement of Strang's orthodoxy. The discovery of this manuscript, in addition to the Engagement's role in sowing discord among the Covenanters, certainly expedited Strang's resignation. But, as the statement of orthodoxy demonstrates, he refused to enter retirement in disgrace.[37]

Strang's Treatise and the Complexities of Covenanting

As historians investigate the complexities of the Covenanting movement with renewed vigour, they would do well to consider further Strang's defence of the King's Covenant. Recent scholarship has moved beyond the high political narrative to evaluate how Scots negotiated and responded to the turbulent confessional politics wrought by the National Covenant.[38] Historians have

33 Baillie, *Letters*, i, 476–7, 482, 490; NLS, Strang Treatise, Wod.Fol.XXXI fo. 7r.

34 Baillie, *Letters*, i, 135.

35 Ibid., i, 479–80.

36 NLS, Supplication of John Strang, 1647, papers and correspondence of the General Assembly, MS 3430 fo. 75; Baillie, *Letters*, ii, 404–5, iii, 5–6; A.F. Mitchell and J. Christie (eds), *The Records of the Commissions of the General Assemblies of the Church of Scotland*, 3 vols (Edinburgh, 1892–1909), i, 191, 192–3.

37 Reid, *Divinity Principals*, 282–7. See also Baillie's life of Strang in the preface to J. Strang, *De Interpretatione & Perfectione Scripturæ* (Rotterdam, 1663); A. Peterkin (ed.), *Records of the Kirk of Scotland, Containing the Acts and Proceedings of the General Assemblies from the Year 1638 Downwards* (Edinburgh, 1843), 482.

38 See especially L.A.M. Stewart, *Rethinking the Scottish Revolution: Covenanted Scotland, 1637–1651* (Oxford, 2016).

already contended that local responses to the National Covenant were more complex than the oversimplified labels of Presbyterian/Episcopalian and Covenanting/Royalist would suggest.[39] And, while scholars have highlighted the existence of an anti-Covenanting royalist party, led by Scottish peers and deriving much of its strength from portions of the Highlands and northeast,[40] it is clear that Strang occupied a grey area between 'Covenanting' and 'Royalist'. While no committed Covenanter would necessarily claim to be anti-monarchy – especially during the early years of the Covenanting movement – there was nonetheless a constellation of attitudes towards royal government and its position in relation to the church.

Strang's treatise should also be considered in light of the Calvinist resistance theories that had infiltrated early modern Scotland. There was no shortage of Covenanters who readily subscribed to Calvinist theories of resistance against magistrates who overstepped their constitutional bounds. The writings of Henderson, Wariston, George Gillespie and Samuel Rutherford, for example, echoed the resistance theories set down by John Calvin, Theodore Beza, George Buchanan and David Pareus, among others, who argued that it was incumbent upon 'inferior magistrates' – such as the Covenanting elite – to resist 'superior magistrates' – such as the king – who transgressed in their power.[41] Henderson also justified taking up arms against Charles I in his 'Instructions for Defensive Arms' of 1639, published in 1642.[42] The covenant or 'federal' theology that pervaded Scotland in the early seventeenth century further influenced this thinking and provided added justification for resisting Charles's policies.[43] What is more, this theological tradition, encapsulated in the writings of continental reformers, and particularly in Pareus' commentary

39 C.R. Langley, *Worship, Civil War and Community, 1638–1660* (London, 2016), 13–38.

40 B. Robertson, *Royalists at War in Scotland and Ireland, 1638–1650* (Burlington, VT, 2014), 31–40. See also B. Robertson, 'The Covenanting North of Scotland, 1638–1647', *Innes Review* 61 (2010), 24–51.

41 See e.g. I. M. Smart, 'The Political Ideas of the Scottish Covenanters, 1638–88', *History of Political Thought* 1 (1980), 167–93; J. Coffey, *Politics, Religion and the British Revolutions: The Mind of Samuel Rutherford* (Cambridge, 1997), 146–87; I.W.S. Campbell, 'Calvinist Absolutism: Archbishop James Ussher and Royal Power', *Journal of British Studies* 53 (2014), 588–610, at 600–1. On the development of Calvinist resistance theories and their broader influence, see R.M. Kingdon, 'Calvinism and Resistance Theory, 1550–1580', in J.H. Burns and M. Goldie (eds), *The Cambridge History of Political Thought 1450–1700* (Cambridge, 1991), 193–218.

42 For the manuscript of Henderson's 'Instructions', see NLS, A. Henderson, 'Points to be preached and conversed on to the people of Scotland', 1639, Wod.Fol.XXVII fos 36–8. It was published three years later in London as A. Henderson, *Some Speciall Arguments for the Scottish Subjects Lawfull Defence of Their Religion and Liberty* (London, 1642). These writings came during a period of heightened public debate in Scotland and England as the Scots attempted to justify arming against the king during the Bishops' Wars. See Stevenson, *Scottish Revolution*, 133–7; S. Waurechen, 'Covenanter Propaganda and Conceptualizations of the Public during the Bishops' Wars, 1638–1640', *Historical Journal* 52 (2009), 63–86.

43 M. Steele, 'The "Politick Christian": the Theological Background to the National Covenant',

on Zacharius Ursinus's Heidelberg Catechism, was a feature of Scottish university curricula, which blended the traditional Aristotelian course with the methodological innovations of Calvinist educational reformers such as Petrus Ramus, Johann Heinrich Alsted and Bartholomäus Keckermann.[44] This was the intellectual milieu to which Strang belonged. His opposition to the Prayer Book, which Baillie remarked 'did a great deall of good to further that universall refuseall of the Book which followed', evinces his capacity to recognise and resist royal policy that he felt was damaging to religion in Scotland.[45] And, in his opening letter to Hamilton, Strang stated clearly that a prince's subjects should not fall into 'blind obedience' and accept passively 'all thinges with out any examination of the laufulnes, and equitie of the comand'.[46] But at the same time, Strang was more than willing to accept the remedies in the King's Covenant offered by Charles I, the 'supreme magistrate' to whom he repeatedly referred in his tract, writing that 'No man can do dewtie to god, who rendereth not deuitfull obedience to his king.'[47] Strang, a reluctant signatory of the National Covenant, was clearly situated on the more avowedly monarchist end of seventeenth-century Scotland's political spectrum, believing that his brethren, as loyal subjects to the crown, should end their resistance since Charles had complied with their demands.

Strang's *volte-face* might at first glance appear surprising, especially when compared to the uncompromising stances of prominent Covenanters like Wariston, Henderson and Rutherford. But in truth, Strang's actions speak to Covenanted Scotland's much broader intellectual landscape. As has been recently demonstrated in the case of Robert Baillie, among the Covenanters' leading lights, even the most prominent Covenanting ministers often harboured an array of oftentimes pliable attitudes towards royal authority,

in J. Morrill (ed.), *The Scottish National Covenant in Its British Context* (Edinburgh, 1990), 31–67.

44 H. Hotson, '"A Generall Reformation of Common Learning" and its Reception in the English-speaking world, 1560-1642', in P. Ha and P. Collinson (eds), *The Reception of Continental Reformation in Britain* (Oxford, 2010), 193–228, at 195–200; Reid, '"Ane Uniformitie"'; 'Reformed Scholasticism, Proto-empiricism and the Intellectual "Long Reformation" in Scotland: the Philosophy of the "Aberdeen Doctors", c. 1619–c. 1641', in J. McCallum (ed.), *Scotland's Long Reformation: New Perspectives on Scottish Religion, c. 1500– c. 1660* (Leiden, 2016), 149–78. For examples of contemporary curricula at the Scottish universities see, for Edinburgh, Edinburgh University Archives, The Discipline of the College of Edinburgh, 3 Dec. 1628, Edinburgh University Register, IN1/GOV/CRT/Da.21/1 pp. 39–53; A. Morgan and R.K. Hannay (eds), *University of Edinburgh Charters, Statutes, and Acts of the Town Council and Senatus 1583–1853* (Edinburgh, 1937), 110–15. For Aberdeen, see C. Innes (ed.), *Fasti Aberdonenses: Selections from the Records of the University and King's College of Aberdeen* (Aberdeen, 1854), 225–31. For a proposed curriculum for Glasgow, see Baillie, *Letters*, ii, 463–7.

45 Baillie, *Letters*, i, 29.

46 NLS, Strang Treatise, Wod.Fol.XXXI fo. 7r.

47 Ibid., fo. 21r.

church government, liturgy and covenanting, the strength of which were tested frequently by the events of the period; Strang was no different.[48] Intellectual rigidity among the Covenanters was not necessarily the norm.

Given the evidence that points to a wider diversity of opinions regarding royal authority and church government among the Covenanting elite, scholars would perhaps also do well to probe further the nature and impact of the King's Covenant, which is often relegated to brief mentions in the narrative of the Covenanting revolution.[49] Beyond the northeast of Scotland and Glasgow, Charles I's proposals largely failed to find support.[50] But Strang's tract problematises the King's Covenant's supposed impotence, especially among Scotland's intellectual elite. Tellingly, at the General Assembly at Glasgow, which met in November–December 1638, commissioners addressed the existence of the King's Covenant directly. In addition to affixing what was known as the 'Glasgow Declaration' to the swearing of the National Covenant – an oath that clearly identified the Five Articles of Perth and episcopacy as abjured – the Assembly's commissioners passed an act that stated:

> [I]n the meane time, least any should fall under the danger of a contradictorie oath, and bring the wrath of God upon themselves and the land, for the abuse of his Name and Covenant; The Assembly by their Ecclesiasticall authority, prohibiteth and dischargeth, that no member of this Kirk swear or subscribe the said Confession, so far wreasted to a contrare meaning, under paine of all Ecclesiasticall censure: but that they subscribe the confession of Faith, renewed in Februar, with the Declaration of the Assembly set down in the former Act.[51]

Subscribing to 'contradictorie' oaths like the King's Covenant was made illegal, for doing so would have consequences of a divine scale. In ensconcing the legality of the National Covenant at the Glasgow Assembly, the Covenanters barred support for the King's Covenant and other rival covenants. Strang's writing had been kept secret, but such a punitive policy suggests the potential threat, real or imagined, that the King's Covenant posed

48 A.D. Campbell, 'Episcopacy in the Mind of Robert Baillie, 1637–1662', *Scottish Historical Review* 93 (2014), 29–55; *The Life and Works of Robert Baillie (1602–1662): Politics, Religion and Record-Keeping in the British Civil Wars* (Woodbridge, 2017).

49 Kisteen MacKenzie's study of the legal parameters of the King's Covenant is a notable exception. See K.M. MacKenzie, 'Restoring the Nation? Hamilton and the Politics of the National Covenant', *International Review of Scottish Studies* 36 (2011), 67–91. On the reception of the King's Covenant in Glasgow, see A. Lind, 'Battle in the Burgh: Glasgow during the British Civil Wars, c. 1638–1651', *Journal of the Northern Renaissance* (forthcoming, 2020).

50 Stevenson, *Scottish Revolution*, 110–11; Macinnes, *Covenanting Movement*, 185–6; W. Makey, *The Church of the Covenant 1637–1651: Revolution and Social Change in Scotland* (Edinburgh, 1979), 34–6. For a more detailed discussion of the genesis of the King's Covenant, see Donald, *Uncounselled King*, 89–105.

51 Peterkin (ed.), *Records of the Kirk*, 40.

to the Covenanting movement. Indeed, with the absence of the Aberdeen Doctors at the Glasgow Assembly, Strang was also among the few dissidents present to organise opposition the Covenanters' agenda, and he sought to increase Glasgow University's representation at the assembly to ensure that the commissioners were 'non-covenanters'. The commission, however, was rejected, while Strang, as mentioned above, did not allow his treatise to be made public.[52] The rejection of Strang and the university's commission, combined with the Glasgow Declaration, neutralised what remained of the opposition to the Covenanters' agenda at the Glasgow Assembly.

Strang's tract in support of the King's Covenant demonstrates the currency that Charles I's proclamation could have among subscribers to the National Covenant: there was potential for substantial intra-Covenanting disagreement and dispute in the early stages of the Covenanting movement, while commitment to the National Covenant could be ambivalent and disingenuous. The document thus provides important insight into the trials, negotiations and ideological disputes that marked of the early days of the Scottish Revolution.

Editorial Conventions

This transcription has maintained the idiosyncrasies of Strang's spelling and diction, much of which reflected common seventeenth-century Scottish conventions. Though in draft form, there are noticeably few contractions and little usage of special characters. Where they are used, they have been silently expanded using contemporary spelling. Strang made the most use of the thorn: thus 'y^{e}/ye', 'y^{t}/yat', 'ayr' and 'nayr' have been silently expanded as 'the', 'that', 'ather' (either) and 'nather' (neither), respectively. The usual contractions and conventions 'matie' (majestie), 'on' (one), 'be' (by) and 'o^{r}' (our), in addition to contractions for place names ('Dund' for Dundee and 'Ede' for Edinburgh) have also been expanded. Common Scots shorthands such as 'qch' and 'qhlk' do not feature in this text.

Early modern conventions, including the long s and double f, have been modernised. Throughout the text Strang regularly interchanged 'w' and 'u', with 'w' functioning as a 'u' and vice versa. This quirk has been modernised in the transcription: thus 'ws' has been rendered as 'us', 'wpon' as 'upon', 'awthoritie' as 'authoritie', 'yow' as 'you' and so on, in order to assist in readability. Latin phrases are interspersed throughout the manuscript and have been transcribed in italics. Capitalisation, paragraphing and punctuation have been modernised.

52 On Strang and the Glasgow Assembly, see S. Cipriano, 'Seminaries of Identity: The Universities of Scotland and Ireland in the Age of British Revolution' (Fordham University, PhD thesis, 2018), 93–7; Lind, 'Battle in the Burgh'.

The draft form of this manuscript explains the fair amount of additions and deletions within the body of the text. The author's deletion of text is marked with a ~~strike through~~. Superscript additions are signalled by \ / in order to give the reader a sense of how Strang amended and added to his treatise throughout its writing. Illegibility of text owing to damage, manuscript binding or otherwise is indicated by '…' and a corresponding footnote. Smaller gaps in the text are marked with [ ]. Strang made many marginal additions to the body of the text, which he marked in-text with 'X' or 'X°'. These marginal additions are designated with < >, and are included within the body of the text, replacing the 'X' and 'X°' markers, so as to not interrupt the flow of reading.

With respect to marginal additions, special attention needs to be drawn to the addition of text on fo. 17v. In the body, Strang includes a marker 'X°' whose marginalia alerts the reader to a paragraph of text located under the letter 'A' on fo. 24v. of the manuscript, after the conclusion. This text is meant to be read in the body of fo. 17v., and has been included there and designated with < > and a corresponding footnote.

Throughout the text, Strang over-lined a number of passages for emphasis. For formatting purposes, to assist in readability and to maintain the author's emphases, the over-lined passages have been underlined in the transcription.

The headings of the four main sections, which are discussed above, are given in bold so as to highlight for the reader the division of the text, especially as to when Strang addressed the Covenanters' protestation directly. When pagination begins on fo. 9r., page numbers are added next to the corresponding folio (e.g. 'fo. 9r./p. 1'). These are the page numbers that Hamilton referred to in his notes on fos 10r.–10v., which are un-paginated. Hamilton's notes are transcribed in italics and indented so as to differentiate clearly for the reader a break in Strang's writing. A footnote also indicates the temporary change in authorship. In this interpolation, contractions have been silently expanded, but otherwise the rough nature of Hamilton's spelling, punctuation and organisation has been maintained.

Throughout the text, Strang cited key events in Scotland's post-Reformation ecclesiastical history, referenced contemporary debates within the Kirk and drew on classical parables in support of his position. These in-text references are expanded upon in footnotes to contribute to the reader's understanding of Strang's treatise.

Acknowledgements

I wish to recognise and thank several colleagues who provided assistance at various times throughout the long road from transcription to publication. Chris Langley was most encouraging when I first considered the idea of transcribing and editing Strang's treatise, and he graciously provided comments and suggestions on earlier drafts of both the introduction and transcription. Christopher Maginn and Jonathan Woods lent me their expert palaeographical advice as I attempted to negotiate some of Strang's more difficult handwriting and phraseology. Andrew Lind shared his expertise on Scottish royalism during the British Civil Wars as I revised for publication. The Scottish History Society's anonymous reviewers provided important and useful feedback on an earlier draft of the work, while John McCallum has been most helpful and conscientious in facilitating the publication of this piece.

TRANSCRIPTION

NLS, Wod.Fol.XXXI item no. 2, fos 7–24

fo. 7r.

To his beloved brother J. H.

The perturbation and division of the state of this kingdome, dear brother, being so manifest, and lamentable, and the danger that may ensew therupon, so iminent and fearfull, I confesse with you, it is the parte of everie good patriot to searche the causes therof; and contribute his best endevoures, for removeing the sam and to furn~~h~~ise al the remeid he can, wherby everie thing may be reduced to ordor without which no good, no peace, no exercise of honestie, and religion is to be expected. As King Croesus his sonne, allthogh dumb from his infancie, had his mouth opened, with a loude and articulat voice, to intreat for his fatheris lyf, in his extreme danger:[1] so these that have bein hithertilles accustomed to silence, oght to speik in this present perill of our countrey, and father of our countrey, for there saftie. But ~~to judge~~ <though being> conscious to my selfe of my infancie and ineptitude, I dare not presume, to speak in publick: yet for your privat use and contentment I have adventured to communicat my mynd to you in these rude, and undigested lynes.

If the memberis of our naturall bodie be out of there proper joynt or place, or draw everie one \from/ another, that which is due to another, and withdraw there comon help one from another, the whole bodie must of necessitie com to ruine: even so it fareth with the politick body, which is conteined and preserved, be the same proportion, and harmonie of all the partes. Now the present truble of our estate semeth to proceid from a certane disjunction betwix the head and the memberis: which whether or not, it may now be helped, and the tyme and occasione presentlie offered doeth admit, and requyre a redintegration of there solid union, is dilligentlie to be considerit. God and nature hes set such proper places and merches to the supreme governor whether one or moe of any state, and to the subjectis therof: that to the former is given the right \and/ power of commanding, and to the other is recommended the verteu of obedience: in both which, as in al humane affaires, there may be defectes, and error. And as this ~~religion~~ <religion[2]> is the greatest, and of most importance of al otheres: so there may fall furth therin the most pernicius error, tending to the perversion of

1 This references the tale of Croesus, the sixth-century BCE Lydian king, whose eldest son was born mute yet found his voice for the first time just as a Persian soldier was about to kill Croesus. By speaking up, the son ultimately saved his father's life. See Herodotus, *The Histories: Oxford World's Classics*, trans. R. Waterfield (Oxford, 1998), 39.

2 The tape of the manuscript binding obscures most of the word in the margin, so that all that

all thinges. The error most considerable upoun the superior parte, is ather upoun the one extremitie a neglect of the state, or a too lax government, and commandement: wherby wicked men ar emboldened, and the better sort ather may \be/ corupted or endangered, and a way opened of licentiousnes to al violent humors: or upoun the other extremitie a too stark, and severe overruling, ather in commanding that which is unlawfull, or laying upoun ther subjectis too heavie burdenes. Upoun the parte of the subjectis may be ather on the one syd, contumacie, or disobedience, a most comon faultt, wherunto we are all naturallie inclyned, specialie wher ruleres are most gentle, and humane: or on the other syd the faultes of subjectis may be a blind obedience, doeing all thinges with out any examination of the lawfulnes, and equitie of the comand; and so under goeing a slavisch yoik, no lesse unprofitable to the comander, then to them who ar commanded: yet nevertheles for the passive part thereof, never to be imputed to any as ~~a~~ fault, but rather ~~hath~~ \is/ an high point of Christianitie, wherby suffering for well doeing in obeying God, rather then man, is recomended. And as for active obedience, when it is not against faith, and honestie, but onlie trublesome and heavie to our selfe, it semeth it can not be condemned ~~onto both~~ the groundes of Christiane religion, which comandes us <u>when we ar compelled to goe with any on myle, to go with him tuain;</u> and both religion, and philosophie recomendenth to us a passinge from our owne right for peaces sake.

fo. 7v.

These thinges being premitted for groundes, let us indifferentlie consider and judge, if this seperation or discontentment proceid, and goe on, to what partie it may be specialie imputed. As for the parte of our king we neid not to questione the one extremitie, wherein princes may shill by neglecting there subjectis, or by useing too great lenitie. That is not the matter compleined upoun. All the discontentment is conceved to proceid from the other extremitie (which yet no man upon his conscience dare impute to his majestie in respect of his knowen integr~~e~~itie, justice, and meiknes~~)~~, ~~but to som sinistrous informations and counsels~~) we esteime that latelie thinges unlawfull have bein comanded, and urged without ordor, against the lawes and customes of this kindgome. If it be so, what remeid can be found by the prince for correcting such an excesse <(although it wer granted)> but to recall and repeal his commandementis, and to deal gentlie with his subjectis. And hes not our king done so? Has he not recalled and annulled all his proclamationes which wer griveous to us, and removed our grevances mentioned in our supplications, and granted us the sam lawfull meanes,

is visible is '-ion'. Because the deleted word is certainly 'religion', it is likely religion that also appears in the margin.

which we desyr, to redresse all our evilles? If he have done this what \can/ he doe more? And shall we when he hath condescended this farre to us, still beare in upoun him, and remaine unsatisfied, lyk some men who deal most hardlie with these who ar most gentle and still crave more of them whom they sie disposed to grant much.

This too strict dealing hath deceved many, and hath made them losse all, which they might have gained. And what shall our king, and strangeris, and other indifferent men think, if ~~who~~ \we/ yealding nothing to his majestie schew as great tokenes of our discontentment now, as if he had granted nothing to us. I grant against articles of faith (although we may suffer for them) yet we must not yeald to any mortall man. In other thinges there may be a greater latitude of mutuall toleration for peaces cause. Seing his majestie hath dischairged the innovationes compleined upon, and not only hath allowed, but comanded us to subscryve the confession of faith made against papistes, agreable to the puritie of our reformation, no man can say that now alteration of our religion, or authorizeing of poperie is intendet. If there remaine any other matter of controversie among us, it must be concerning the outward ordor and governement of the church, and in thinges of that nature. No sound divyn will deny, bot there may be diversitie of judgmentis *salva fide et charitate*. Heirin the best Reformed churches agrie not among themselves. Nather in this churche of Scotland hath there bein ever a constant and durable agriement in such thinges. As for example from the begining of our reformation, about the yeir 1560, to the year 1581, the authoritie of bischopes and superintendentis (litle different from bischopes) was acknawledgit. In the year 1581 presbiteries began to be institute: and yet in the year 1590 presbiteres wer not universallie planted as appeirett, by an act of generall assemblie at Edinburgh in August 1590: and they wer not confirmed in parliament befour the year 1592. In the meane tyme about the year 1584 the presbiteriall governament was assaulted, and a course taken by authoritie, to establish episcopacie. Som bischopes wer created, ~~by authoritie~~ but within few yeares discharged. In the generall assemblie, at Dundee, the year 1597 ther was an introduction made for bischopes againe, under the name of the commissionares

fo. 8r.
for the church, which was so prosequte by degries, the yeares following, that at lenth the estate of the bischopes was fullie restored in the parliament ~~was~~ <and in the generall assemblie 1610 ratified by the parliament 1612 there titles> ~~ther titles~~ was acknawledged, and there authoritie, and power ~~and there authoritie and power~~ in the discipline of the church particulerlie was establisched, concerning receving of presentationes, admission and deposition of ministeres, excomunication, moderation of presbitries and

synodes et ct. annulling the act ~~annulling the act~~ of parliament 1592 and al other actes made in the contrary.[3] Notwithstanding of all this varietie, according to the diversitie of tymes, and differences of mens judgmentis in church governament in everie tyme, yet (praised be God) unitie, and peace, with puritie of doctrine hes bein ever preserved in our church, without heresie, and shisme. And why should we not all now also (although there be among us discrepance of judgments in these and such lyk tymes) forbear on another in love and endevor to keip the unitie of the spirit in the bond of peace? Although in such matteres som be ~~e~~ otherwise mynded then otheris. Nevertheles wherto we have alreadie attaned let us walk by the same rule: let us mynd the same thing.

~~We ar deficent in many thinges~~, We need not to exspect a perfyt estate of Godis church or of the governament therof heir upon earth. <We ar deficient in many thinges,> offences must be, abusses and disvaleris easilie do creap in the church; no man, nor estate of man is frie of corruptiones. It becometh all men, according to there vocation, to endevor, that defectes may be amendit, enormities redressed, vyce punished, and everie good ordor establisched but by a lawfull and ordinar way, ~~when it may be had at extraordinar tymes, and ocasiones an extraordinar course may be allowed: such as our necessitie, and exigence hath latelie enforced us to use.~~ But by the mercie of god, and goodnes of our prince, the ordinarie way is open and patent to us. ~~And, I hope, more and more, shall be~~, if the fault be not in our selves.[4] It is his majesties good pleasure, that we be now in as good estait, and have as much libertie, as we have ever had these 30 yeires bygane, or more (and

3 Strang here references the capricious nature of the Kirk's polity during the reign of James VI, and indeed, the contentious relationship between the Kirk, a succession of regents and the king himself in the late sixteenth century. It is impossible to recount these events fully in a footnote, but it is important to offer a general outline that highlights the growth of royal power in the Kirk and the resurgence of bishops in the ecclesiastical hierarchy. Between 1560 and 1580, the Kirk maintained a hierarchical, episcopal structure where bishops existed haphazardly alongside post-Reformation superintendents. The General Assemblies of 1580 and 1581, anti-episcopal in tenor, resolved to divide the Kirk into fifty presbyteries, though this measure was never approved by the Scottish Parliament; indeed, in 1584, during the earl of Arran's regency, Parliament passed the 'Black Act' that affirmed the king's jurisdiction over the church and banned presbyteries and meetings of the General Assembly that were not called by the crown, though presbyteries were reinstated in 1586. In 1592, Parliament passed the 'Golden Act' that endorsed the presbyterian system, though in the May 1597 meeting of the General Assembly at Dundee, with James present, the king signaled his intention to take control of the Kirk and affirm the rule of bishops. The 1610 General Assembly at Glasgow, populated with commissioners approved by bishops, was controlled by the king's Scottish councillors and restored the power of bishops and reasserted the king's supremacy in the church. These acts were ratified by Parliament in 1612. See A.R. MacDonald, *The Jacobean Kirk, 1567–1625: Sovereignty, Polity, and Liturgy* (Aldershot, 1998).

4 Given Strang's deletion, this clause seems to conclude the preceding sentence.

God knaweth few nationes have had the lyk) and ther fore now we have no more cause of an extraordinar stirre, then we had all that tyme before. But should so moderat our zeal, specialie in matteris of that nature, that by an extraordinar course, we mak not a commotion of the state, to the danger of his majesties honor, and hazard of the peace of the cuntrie the least violation wherof produceth a thousind tymes greater vyces, crymes and notorious eviles, then ar these that we would reforme, supponing them to be as evill as some estemeth. Which will be the less excusable on our parte, if it shall be manifest that his majestie by his late proclamatione hath done, what he can, to remove our feares, and doubtes, to satisfie our complaintes, and no wayes to prejudge our libertie, nor stop the ordinar course of justice, and judgment. I confesse that to me may be well applyed that saying *qui panca videt cito indicat*. For truelie I sie bot few thinges, and know no more, then that which is published to all. If there be any greater mysteries, which ar comunicat onlie to few, as I am altogether ignorant therof; so am I unable to judge of the same, but am allwayes prone to judge charitablie, and protest in Gods presence, that I have no other send heirin, but Gods glorie, and the conservation of trueth, and peace, within this kingdome. Let us al consider well, and the lord give us understanding in all thinges.

fo. 8v.
Blank

fo. 9r./p. 1

Reasones why all his majesties orthodox subjectis in Scotlande and namelie these who subscryved the late covenant should themselves fullie acquiesce to his majesties late declaration and proclamationes and speciallie touching the subscription of the confession of faith and generall band thairin mentionat with an answer to the reasons objectet in the late protestatione to the contrary

Reasones for acquiescing

1. The kinges majestie by his late declaration and proclamationes hath not only given satisfaction to all the supplicationes, complaintes and protestationes made in this publick bussines, before the subscryving of the covenant (for these only concerned the book of service, the book of canones and high commission which now ar discharged) but also hes satisfied the wholl intention of the covenant which consisteth in three partes. 1. The short confession 2. An enumeration of diverse actis of parliament 3. An application to the innovationes and feared evilles with a generall band of mutuall assistance. The first his majestie hes commandet to be renewed: for the second

he secureth us against all innovation of lawes: for the thrid he removethe the feared evillis generallie concerned and particularlie mentioned in the said supplicationes, complaintes, and protestations. And generallie against whatsoever evilles, or innovationes, can be feared, or \for/ complaintes made upon any personnes, his majestie hath granted all the remeid that can be craved from him, viz a frie generall assemblie and parliament: and also hes condescendet to a band of mantinance and mutuall assistance more sure then that which is conteined in the late covenant, in ~~sua~~\so/farre as the authoritie of his majestie and counsell is adjoyned.

2. The covenanteris with comon consent haveing comprysit ther overturis for settleing of this church, and kindgome, in a~~n~~ solid, and durable peace, in eight articles (which although~~t~~ they professed to be the least that could be asked ~~yet~~ \yet/ no man doubted, if they wer granted, that they would acquiesce and rest contented) his majestie hath given satisfaction to them all partlie by an expresse grant of diverse of them, partlie by the induction of a frie generall assemblie and parliament to the censure wherof all persones ar made lyable and by which all disordouris may be rectified.[5]

3. In the comon supplication made to his majesties commissionar for induction of a frie generall assemblie and parliament, it was declared, that the grant therof would undoubtedlie redresse all our evillis, settill the peace of the churche, and kingdome, and procure he cheirfullnes of obedience, that

fo. 9v./p. 2

that is due to be randrit to his majestie; which since his majestie hath now ~~gr~~ granted he hath reasone to expect the frute promised.

4. His majestie hath not only granted that which was condescendet to be sufficient for redressing all our evillis and settleing peace, to wit frie generall assemblie, and parliament: but also to facilitat the proceidingis of both, and to shew his awin willingnes to remove the fearis, and doubtis of his peopill concerning innovation of religion and lawes, hath dischairged the book of service, the book of canones, and heigh commissione, hath annulled and rescindit all actis of councell, proclamationes, et \etc./ made for establisching them or any of them, hath dispensed with the practice of the articles of perth, hath declared the bischopes, and all others persones civill and ecclesiastick to be subject to the generall assemblie, hath appoynted a frie entres, to all

5 This refers to the 'Eight Articles', written by Alexander Henderson and Archibald Johnston of Wariston in April 1638, which urged the crown to eliminate the Prayer Book, Canons, High Commission and Five Articles of Perth and to call a meeting of the General Assembly and Parliament. See Rothes, *Relation*, 96–8.

that are to enter to the ministrie, without oathes not warranded by act of parliament.

X X X

5. In respect the schort confession of faith subscryved by King James and his houshold the yeir 1580, and the generall band of mantinance of the true religion and the kinges persone maid the yeir 1589 is the verie ground and paterne of the late covenant:[6] lyk as in the said covenant the said confession is verbatim premitted as most agreable to the puritie of our reformation, and proponed as a soverane remeid against all popisch erroris, and against all innovationes, and evillis compleined upone: which is declared there, <u>to be contrary to the said confession, and that the present and succeiding generationes in this land are bound to keip the said confession, so solemnlie subscryvit and sworne to be heirtofore, by all persones of all estaites</u>. Lyk as all men of note and learning, who subscryved the late covenant, and persuaded otheris to subscryve the sam, hes ever professed publicklie and privatlie (which is also signified in printed answeris and reasones) that the said covenant differreth nothing in substance from the said confession and generall band: and that therfore <u>it is warranded by the sam authoritie, and that our progenitoris by the lyk oath hath obiged us to the substance and tenor of the oath of this covenant</u>. Wherfore his majestie, by his ordinance to subscryve and renew the said confession, and generall band, hath given a most undoubted prooff of his pious intention, never to admitt any change or alteration of our religion and of his constant resolution to mantine the sam.

fo. 10r.[7]

pag 2 + if ane \+/ bot \+/ learne are the rest till the closing the parentisen:

+ then \maybe/ shuld be + efter the yeir 1581, they begane to urge the institution of presbetars,

page the 3 + by all as as Covenanters / our Covenant of September which which

6 Strang refers here to the 'Negative' or 'King's' Confession of 1580/1, which drew on the Scots Confession of 1560 and was subscribed by James VI. The Negative Confession was conjoined with a general bond of mutual assistance against popery in 1589/90. The Negative Confession was also repeated in the National Covenant and the King's Covenant. See J.E.A. Dawson, 'Bonding, Religious Allegiance and Covenanting', in S. Boardman and J. Goodare (eds), *Kings, Lords and Men in Scotland and Britain, 1300–1625: Essays in Honour of Jenny Wormald* (Edinburgh, 2014), 155–72, at 167–9; Stewart, *Rethinking the Scottish Revolution*, 90–6.

7 The following two folios (10r–10v) are in Hamilton's hand.

we mead the worthill belife was the \entir/ ground of our Covenant: being no waayes impared

p. 4 & : Covenant : altered, to thatt whic is in parentisis + as in all things

p 7 in the letter end ther of, + bot in aleaged \way/ & wher the mening and sense is fair and perspicuous

11 and itt may be in the opinion of the answeres good a nufe

13 the figours has we Covenanters have thought tho bot others think not so /

14 att the mark ø[8] *f...*[9] *for divers of the breidring if not all of them, who wer assembled that morning, be for both the proclamation, and protestation was mead, att the gray freires Church, doe affirme, thatt ther was a message sent unto them, frome the othere 3 tabiles, desyring them to send up one of ther number to joyne with the othir 3 in the protestation which thatt efter noune was to be mead against his majesties proclamation, bot thatt the wholl briddring did absolutlie refyuse so to doe aleging thatt they knew nothing fitt to be protested against, and thatt unles the other tabilles would send doune unto them the prottest which they meant to make thatt they might advyse*

fo. 10v.
concerning the thing to be protested against they wold not send anie of ther number to proteste in ther names, which answer of ther being delivered efter 12 of the clock, they \desoving ther/ meting and reassemled to gadder \no more/ thatt day and yeitt thatt on that efter noun Master Hanrie Rollige[10] *with out anie warrant or deputation from the assemblie of the bridring did suthlie and incuriouslie protest in ther name, protest against his majesties most gracious proclamation: not onlie contrarie to ther mynds bot expreslie against ther order and resolution taken att ther morning meitting, for which manie the bridring do hoope to have him condinglie punished att the generall assemblie, as they them selfes doe affirme and aught*

in the sam page att the 20

which divers, ar of opinion that the protestation simeth to ascrybe to our Covenant,

8 This mark likely corresponds to the mark midway through fo. 17v/p. 14. At this juncture in the treatise, Strang interpolated an additional paragraph within the text's body. See n. 18 for further explanation.

9 This word is faded/unfinished, and it appears to have been wiped away due the existence of ink smudges.

10 This is a likely reference to Henry Rollock, minister of Trinity Kirk, Edinburgh, who was a member of the Tables' committee of ministers. See Stevenson, *Scottish Revolution*, 82–3.

for thes word of the prottestation which affirme our Covenant to be saled from heaven by the fyre of the spiritt as they have given ocasion to manie of our selfes to charg itt wit nonsence as to being abill to make ani \by anie/ gramaticall construction to make sence of them, & so which is infinitlie wors they have given ocasion to manie of to thinke thatt they tend not onlie to pop…[11] *bot agri neir to blasphemi, for they desyre to knowe what can be more said of the bookes of holy scripture bot that they penned manie of them wer inspyred frome heaven by the spirit \and the bookes themselfe speaks by that same spiritt/ and from bott from us, ever to asscrybe eather shuch inspiration, or \shuch/ infallibilitet to our Covenant*

fo. 11r.
Blank

fo. 11v.
Blank

fo. 12r./p. 3
6. Seing it is confessed, that it is regnised, there should be an comon covenant in this countrie, for confession of true religion, and mantenance therof, and of the kinges person, and estaitt: and no man will deny, that it is most to be wisched that his majestie would concurr therto with his authoritie. And seing the late covenant is framed in such a maner, as it wer impertinent to desyr his majestie to ~~subsceyve, or~~ authorize the sam in *ijsdem terminis*, becaus besyd other reasones, first it semeth to condem in som poyntis, the order and practice of the church of Ingland: nixt becaus it appeireth to be maid in opposition to the king, and the proceidinges of his majestie, and \his/ councell, it being relative to supplicationes and complaintes (alleadged to be misregardet by authoritie) and \to/ the protestationes made against his majesties proclamationis. And \seing/ his majestie is content to concurre with his subjectis, in that confession, and generall band, which is acknawledgit to \be/ one in substance with this said covenant, and more honorable for his majestie, it becometh his majesties subjectis, with all thankfulnes, to acquiesce therto, speciallie seing it is not expected, that a better way, or an other forme of covenant, comon to his majestie, and his subjectis, can be condecendid unto.

7. Seing a generall band of subjectis, for mutuall defence, and assistance without the king (allthough not against him) appeireth to be dangerous, at the least dishonorable unto authoritie; and for this cause not onlie his majeste,

[11] The crease in the manuscript binding obscures the end of this line. The cut-off word is likely 'poperie'.

but many good Christianes hath tacken exception against the covenant: his majestie by his late ordinance, hath tacken the best course, to remove the said exception, supplie the defect, at the least to mak the said band more valid in the sellff, and clear to the world: so that herby the occasion of the dangerous separation betwix his majestie and his subjectis, is removed by the best way that can be devysed, our covenant is no wayes impared, but much betterit; speciallie seing all the examples we find in the scripturis of publick covenantis of the pepill, concerning religion, hath allwayes bein made with the consent, and authoritie of the suprem magistrat.

8. Seing we professe, that we have subscryved the late covenant, <u>in obedience to the comandement of god, conforme to the practice of the godlie in former tymes and according to the laudable</u>

fo. 12v./p. 4

<u>example of our religious progenitoris which was warranded by the act act of councell</u>, soe can we refuse to subscryve the same confession, and band, which is ordained by the sam act of councell, and whairof we have the sam laudable example above specifiet of our progenitoris. And acording to the comandement of god, practice of the godlie in former tymes, we ar obliged to obey our superioris in all thaire lawfull commandementis.

9. The covenant latlie subscryvit is so particularlie accommadat to the present tymes and occasiones, that the innovationes and evilles compleined upon, or feared, being removed (as alreadie they ar or schortlie we hope shall be) it will be impertinent to renew the same, in the sam termes, within twentie or threttie yearis. But the confession of the faith of the Church of Scotland is, and ought to be perpetuall: and is or should be comon to all Reformed churches of the world and therfore may be lawfullie subscryved by all men at any tyme, & speciallie when it is commandet by authoritie, therby to discerne the orthrodox and hetrodox, pure professoris and heretickes living togither. And therfore it appeareth to be absurd to say, that \it/ might have bein subscryved by us, the last year, bot not this year: and that now also it may be subscryved by these who have not subscryved the covenant, bot not by these who have subscryved the covenant.

10. The said confession of faith and generall band being altogether agreable to godis word, is the best and strongest meane, that ever wes agried upoun by publick authoritie, to preserve the puritie of religion, mantine the professoris of it, resist our adversaries, and namlie papistis, ther erroris and practices: and most wisched by the godliest, most zealous, and ~~preceis~~ \precise/ in this land to be renewed by his majesties authoritie. Which since it hath pleased his majestie to enjoyn (fore against the will, not onlie of papistes, but of som

amoung our sellffis, who esteimed this confessione to be too stark) how glaidlie should we all, who have no exception against any matter therin conteined, obey his majestie the nurse father of our church, in so lawfull and pious an comand; if in any

fo. 13r./p. 5
thing, contrarilie in this, it apeareth we should obey for conscience saik. This confession and band was enjoyned by ~~his majestie~~ \King James/ his councell, and generall assemblie, to be sybscryved ~~not onlie for that tyme, but also for all tyme coming~~. And who ever doubted befour thir late dayes, haveing no scruple in the matter, to obey the kinges comendement, in subscryving of the sam? Such an example wes never hard in any age heirtofore to refuise at the comandement of authoritie to sybscryve an orthodox confession.

11. If we refuse to subscryve this confession we depryve our selfes of the best meanes which we have to discerne papistes and tack ordor with them. For so ther shall be no constant confession of faith in our church, which any will be bound, or can be urgit to subscryve. Seing no man will or can be urgit by authoritie to subscryve our covenant, and it is not perpetuall for all ages as is said: and seing the commandement and ordinance is comon to all, we can urge no man therby to subscryve that, which \we/ refuse to doe our sellffis. And by this sam reasone we refuse to subscryve this confession, we must refuse to subscryve all ~~uthr~~ \other/ confessiones of faith in the world made befor our covenant anno 1638.

fo. 13v./p. 6

Answeris to the reasones objected in the late protestation

The summe of all that is alleadgit for useing a protestation against his majesties late proclamation is becaus in the said proclamation 1. Sumthinges therin tendeth to the prelimitation of a frie generall assemblie 2. Sum~~thing~~\things/ tendeth to the prejudice of the late covenant.

Concerning the former poynt, first, a thriefold instance is objected of prelimitationes imported by the said proclamation. Nixt sex reasones subjoynes why we should not acquiesce to any prelimitation.

The reasons usit to schaw that his majesties proclamation importeth these prelimitationes, ar for the most part taken not from any wordis conteinet in the proclamation, bot from these thinges, which ar challenged to be ommitted: not from that which it sayeth, but from that which it sayeth not. This is ane hard and strange inferrence, to inferr a prelimitation of a generall assemblie, becaus in the proclamation this, or this is not said, this is said and no more and who can speak or wryt, but sumthinges will enter in the mynd of the hearer or reader which he findeth to be ~~ommitted~~ omitted.

Concerning the first prelimitation

That his majestie doethe ascrybe all the late distractiones of this church and comon wealth to our conceved fearis of innovation of religion and lawes as to the cause and occasion therof, by what consequence will it follow

fo. 14r./p. 7

that the cause of our feares are said to be rather in apprehension and fancie then in realitie and substance? Sum conceaveth feares without cause therfor all conceved feares ar causles: and whosoever mentioneth conceveth feares mentioneth causles feares. This is *captio a consequente*. A generall word is well chosen in any dealling betwix pairties when the particular ~~m~~ might be mor contraverted. And what althought his majestie being conscious to himsellff of his awin upright meaning did think that in som thinges we feared more then neidet, what reasone have we to stand with our prince upoun such an expression?

X X X

The late proclamation dischairgeth not onlie the practice of the book of service and canones but also themselffis and not onlie rescindes the actis made for establisching of our practice but also anullis and rescindes all actis of councell, proclamationis, and all other actis and deides whatsomever, that hath bein made, or publisched, for establisching of them, or any of them, and declared to be null, and to have no force, nor effect in tyme cuming. And therfor to object the proclamation ather maid 19 of Februarij at Stirlling, or fourt of July at Edinburgh~~e~~, semeth to be impertinent, and unkyndlie dealling: and far mor to defect to ~~an~~ \a/ worse sense, then apperinglie is meaned, the wordis of the said proclamation made the 4 of Julij as if his majestie had declaired therin, that he had purpose to bring these bookis in our church in a fair and legall way: whairas the wordis used in that proclamation, rather doeth import the contrary.[12] For therin all actis made

12 These refer to two royal proclamations. In the first, delivered by the Scottish Privy Council at Stirling on 19 February 1638, Charles took full responsibility for drafting and sanctioning the Prayer Book, refused to rescind its use, denounced the petitions, supplications and riots against the Prayer Book and forbade meetings of supplicants. Charles's 4 July proclamation, published by Hamilton in Edinburgh, again demanded that his subjects obey his commands, but the king also intimated his intention to potentially discharge the High Commission, Prayer Book and Canons and grant a meeting of a General Assembly and Parliament.

in favor~~it~~ of the service book ~~et~~ \etc/ are dischairged, and assurance given that his majestie will never urge the receving of the said bookis or any other thing of that nature but by such a fair and legall way as shall satisfie his subjects. His majestie speaketh not onlie of the said bookis, but to give greater contentment he addeth any lyk thing of that nateure. If such a fair and legall way to bring in these bookes as shall satisfie his subjectis cannot be expected speciallie after our covenant, this is but in fair wordis, to signifie his majesties intention, never to bring in these bookis. But what neid we to contravert upoun these wordis seing his majestie now be expresse wordes hes given satisfaction therto by his late ~~proclamat~~ proclamation?

The comparing of his majesties former proclamationes with the last servethe greatlie for our ~~confermation~~ \confirmation/ to declair his majesties willingnes

fo. 14v./p. 8
to satisfie the doubtis and desyris of his ~~guid~~ people in s~~om~~\so/ fare as he hes procedit from one degrie to an other, untill no man in his poynt can justlie be requyred for all preceding actis and proclamationes concerning these bookes being now anulled by the sam authoritie, by which they wer made, and without any reservation, they ar so extinguished, as if they had never bein made: and so no argument is to be drawn from them ather for establisching or approbation of the said bookis. Hence therfair ther can be inferred no ground of any predetermination prejudiciall to the fridome of the generall assemblie and parliament: unlesse these who favor the bookis of service and canonis might alleadge that his majestie hath made a prejudice against them, and ~~oppen an~~ \opened a/ way to the assemblie, to give out the lyk sentance for dischairging of them.

Concerning the second prelimitation

In all the kinges proclamation it is not said that the articles of Perth ar establisched by the actis of parliament and generall assemblie, but that his majestie doeth frie his subjectis from censour and pain, notwithstanding of any thing conteined in the actis of parliament or generall assemblie, to the contrary. Is this all the fault that perhappes Perthes assemblie is called a generall assemblie, or that it is called an act of parliament by which these articles wer confirmed? Suppon both that assemblie and parliament to be null, this phraise will never import them to be valid *lognendum cum vulgo.*

For these proclamations, see *RPCS 1638–1643*, 3–4, 32–4. See also Stevenson, *Scottish Revolution*, 80–1, 97–8; Donald, *Uncounselled King*, 62–3, 86–7.

Who absteineth to call sum councellis by the name of generall councellis, which ar reprobat, as *concilum a riminense, ephesiminum secundum* ~~and utheris, which ar to be termed rather conciliaballe then worthie~~. Butt it wes not the kinges part in ~~the~~ \his/ proclamationes to precendence ather that assemblie or parliament. And quho would have thought befour this tyme, except a great favorer of Perthis assemblie, that his majestie by dispensing with the articles of Perth and dischairging censoure or paines therupon, had committed a great fault, such as ~~his~~ \this/ to prejudge the libertie of an assemble following and what consequence is this? Because his majestie hes dischairget the urgeing of the practice of Perth articles and all paines and censouris thairupon: thairfoir his intenion is that they should stand...et[13] the consequent be true or false, certanlie ther consequence is faultie

fo. 15r./p. 9

~~fauls~~ and the contrary be ~~als~~ \as/ probablie inferred. Som frameth the objection after this maner: his majestie hath declared in his proclamation, that he hath not any intention to innovat any thing, ather in religion or lawes: bot the articles of Perth concerneth the religion and ar establisched by law: thairfoir his majestie hes an intention for the standing of the actis of the assemblie, and parliament, appoynting the articles of Perth. A brave argument forsoothe, wheras is more in the conclusion then in the premisses. All that can be probablie inferred upon these premisses is that his majestie hath not an intention to alter the articles of Perth: but not, that he hath an intention, no to alter them, or \not/ to suffer them to be altered (there is a great difference betwix these I have not ane intention to doe this, and my intention is not to doe this) ~~but~~ but nather the one, nor the other can be inferred upoun the wordis of his majesties proclamation, be any benigne interpreter: wherof the sense is plane, that first, wheras we complein of the innovation of religion and lawes, by the introduction of the bookis of service, and canonis and high commission, nixt of the distraction made by the articles of Perth. Concerning the first, his majestie frieth us of any suspition of his intention to innovat any thing in religion and lawes. Concerning the second, he dispenseth with the articles of Perth and dischairges the urgeing of them, as ~~give~~ \if/ he would say to us: not onlie shall ye be frie of any danger which ye feare be innovation of religion and lawes, but also from these articles thinges which ar griveous to you, notwithstanding of any thing conteined in the law, or generall assemblie to the contrary. Might not any man with greater ~~cullor~~ \colour/ inferre from our covenant thus. We have sworne, to the uttermost of our power, to stand to the defence of the kinges authoritie, in the defence of the lawes of this kingdome: thairfore we have

13 A tear in the page obscures the first part of this word.

sworne to defend the kinges authoritie, in the articles of Perth, establisched by the law of the kingdome. Away with such naughtie ~~subtallities~~, subtileties to be captions of wordis, ~~wher…nis~~[14] ~~have second simpill meaning is plane~~

Concerning the thrid prelimitation

No better is that argument: becaus his majestie in the proclamation ordaineth all his subjectis to be lyable to the tryell and censour of the generall assemblie, and parliament; and for the frie entrie of ministeris, that no other oath be administred to them, then that which is conteined in the act of parli

fo. 15v./p. 10

ament. Therfore by this proclamation episcopacie is stronglie establisched. Can an evill conclusion (as this is supposed to be) be deduced from good premisses, such as non can deny these to be if they pervert not ther meaning, as *ex verie me insi verim* so *ex bonis nie insi benum*. And what although his majestie be of the ~~o~~ppinion, that episcopall governament is lawfull and expedient for the church, the sam being purged from corruptiones? Is it not knawin and allowed, that many hes subscryvit the covenant being of the sam o~~p~~pinion? And shall we not ~~tollerat~~ \tolerat/ that in the kinges majestie, to which we have consented among our selfis? Hence it is too apparent, that this protestation is made onlie by such as ar antiepiscopall, and this is yet mor evident, becaus this is also carped, that by the induction of the parliament and assemblie, prelatis ar warned to be present; and why ought not all persones to be warned that have, or pretendeth to have entresse? And namlie these who ar in possession, speciallie *pendente lite* whither they ought to have enteresse or not. And that they should not have entresse his majestie could not predetermine by his proclamation. But if this be a subject to be disputed in the assemblie, the predetermination appeareth to be made upoun the part of the protesteris, who presupose heir, and in ther thrid protestation directlie declair, that arche bischoppis, and bischopis, have no warrand for ther office in the church: and many of them spair not to say, that episcopacie the sellff is a corruption and abjured by them.

Generall Replyes

Now what although all our chief matteris to be handled in this generall assemblie had bein befour particularlie, and not in an confused generalitie both signified to his majestie in our supplicationes, and by his majestie declaired in his proclamation could this be thought a prejudice to a frie

14 The author's deletion obscures the middle of this word.

generall assemblie, or a strange and uncouth practice? What generall or oecumenick councell was ever indicted, wherof the causses and speciall matteris to be intreated wes not for schawin? It is thought a verie wyse and commendabill course, that in our conventiounes of burrowes celebrat once evrie year, no matter of importance useth to be deliberat upon, and concluded, but that which hes bein proponed in the preceiding convention a year agoe ~~of god~~ and the lyk example we find in dyverse of our generall assemblies.

fo. 16r./p. 11

It was objectit as our argument (althought evlie applyed) against the assemblie of Perth, that the sam was procleamed without any preceiding advertisment given to the presbitries, touching the matteris to be handlet: seing when an assemblie is to be halden *pro re nata*, premonition ought to be granted made in due tyme by his majestie, and the commissionaris of the churches and the occasion sett downe expreslie, to the effect commissioneris might be sent instancted, acording to the qualitie of the bussines to be entreated.

I wisch that pairt of the alleadgence, concerning the prelimitation and predetermination of the freedome of the generall assemblie and parliament, might not be retorted against our sellfes: whill as som object that our subscription of the covenant is rather a prelimitation of the assemblie, then any other deid done by his majestie or prescryved by him to us: lyk as som suspect the choosing of the commissionaris for the generall assemblie efter such a maner, as can not be weill instructed by any preceiding act, and constant practice of the church to be also a prelimitation.

Morover it is said that the appoyntment of a preceiding meiting at Edenburghe of the commissionaris of the generall assemblie seimeth to be an anticipating of the generall assemblie appoynted by his majestie to convein at Glasgow ~~ffinallie~~ \finallie/ seing ther ar secret instructiones for choosing of commissionares for articles to be treited in the assemblie and convoyance of the whole course of proceiding comunicat onlie to these, who ar knawin to be verie disconforme and antiepiscopall, and cairfullie conceilled from otheris, som thinketh this to be no small prelimitation and prejudice to the freedome of the assemblie. To these we have our awne answeris (~~I belive~~) good enough: but such as may move us to be mor equitable, and to be content that prelimitationes be not much objected on ather syd.

Haveing found no sufficent ground of the limitationes alleadgit or ~~prejudiges~~ <prejudices> of the libertie of the assemblie, inrespect of any prelimitatione made by the kinges late proclamation, it is neidles to insist in examining the sex reasones objected against prelimitationes: to which any man of meane judgement may easilie answer, in so far as they ar opposed to his majesties proclamation in the forsaid poyntis. And it is to be wisched that they be not also retorted against the protesteris.

Thair remaineth no other reasones to be answered touching the prejudice of the late covenant alleadgit to be made by the said proclamation, but onlie these which ar objected against the new subscription: to ~~the~~ which we answer as followethe.

fo. 16v./p. 12

Answeris to the particullar reasones objected against the new subscriptioun

1. Thaire is no cause of feare that the late covenant sall be buried in oblivion which hath bein maid so publiklie and solemnlie, and manifested to the world: and wherof ther ar moe monumentis extant, then perhapes can be instancet in any lyk example. And seing the confession and generall band is acknawledgit to be the verie ground, mother, portend, and fountane of our covenant, as is above spent in the sext reasone, it is strange to think that the formar can prejudge or absolve the latter: and ~~give~~ \if/ ther be no reprignance betwix them (*verim vera et bonum bono non reprignat*) how can the subscryving of the one be equivalent to the rendring or rescinding of the other? And if the new subscription import a rescinding and rendering of our former subscription, then nather we nor our posteritie can ever in all tyme cuming subscryve this sam confession of faith which we or our fatheris have ~~befor~~ subscryved or any Christiane befour this tyme. And within few yeires our late covenant being found unproper for the tyme, nather we nor our posteritie can subscryve heirefter, any confession at all which is absurd.

2. All our divines mantine against the Anabaptistes not onlie that we tak not Godis name in vaine bot that we honor god by giveing our oath and that we are bund to give it quhen the magistrat requyrethe unles the matter be impious, which can not be here alleadgit!

Be the new subscription, wherby all Godis peopill in this countrie may concurre with ther king in an harmonie of confession~~e~~ of faith, and of a generall band for manteining of the trew religion and our king, God sall be honored, his name glorified, and by this happie union our fearis of innovationes, suspitiones against our prince, and jealousies among our selfis, being removed, \if/ we goe on unanimouslie and cheirfullie in this bussines,

~~and~~ our joyes shall be fullfilled, Sathan disapoynted, ~~and our gracious king encouraged to grant the mor readilie all our just petitiones.~~[15]

Thair is as great necessitie, as ever ther wes, to urge this new subscription of that confession, which was intended to be an abjuration of poprie, becaus poprie is even now pregnant and powerfull in this land, as it is said in this protestation in the sext reasone following: and now it is most seasonable and reasonabill to re~~m~~ove[16] all jealusies betwix the king and

fo. 17r./p. 13
his subjectis and to bind us togither in the most strict obligation and union, against all the enemies of religion, and of the king. And to pretend becaus we are knowin to be frie of poprie & ther for we have no neid to subscryve the abjuration of poprie, so seimeth to be too slight an evasion which our for fatheris, wherof som of them wer knawine to be as frie of poprie as we, would have bein loath to have alleadgit. But the mor frie we ar from poprie, the mor readilie ought we to subscryve that confession, from which non is exeimed. This is not to multiplie oathes without necessitie. Seing the necessitie, expedience, and new occasion of this new subscription is made manifest. And yet non of us think it any fault, that many nobill men, and utheris, hes multiplied, ~~threttie or fourtie tymes~~ within thrie or four monethes, ther oathes and subscriptiones of the late covenant, for example to otheris.

3. The thrid reasone is coincident with the first, and leaneth upoun a false suppositon: as if the new subscription imported a rendering of the covenant, which is not granted. For if our progenitoris by ther oath to the said confession hath obliged us to the substance and tenor of the late covenant as is acknawledgit, then we, by renewing the oath, can not therby prejudge our covenant. And heirby we ar so far from withdrawing our selfes from our blessed and loyall conjunction; that by the contrary we mak it the mor strong, by the concurrance of his majestie, his counselloris, and other his weill affected subjectis. And who of us would not have thoght this concurrance in the sam confession, together with such a course taken for removeing of these innovationes, a great blessing a yeir agoe?

But wheras som extendeth this reasone yet further, alleadging that we ar bound by the covenant, to promove and adher to evrie thing that is concluded by the meiting of the comissioneris of the covenanteris in Edinburghe; becaus it is said in the covenant, that we sall nather directlie,

15 Given the tenor of the paragraph, it is unclear why the author struck through this last clause.
16 The 'm' in this word appears to be obscured by an ink blotch rather than struck through deliberately.

nor indirectlie suffer our selfis to be devydit from this blessed and loyall conjunction: nor sall cast in any lett or impediment, that may hinder or stay any such resolution, as by comon consent shall be fund to conduce to so grand endis: bot by the contrary shall by all lawfull meanes labour, to promove and further the sam. We have to considder that \it/ hes bein indeid objected by the adversaries of the covenant, and by many who had scruples to …[17] subscryve the sam, that heirby we establisched a perpetuall judicatorie

fo. 17v./p. 14
without the king, and contrary to his lawes, and that we who have subscryvit the sam tye our consciences to the obedience of all the ordinances therof, although against the king, and his lawes, yea although we wer ordained to tack up armes and enter in warfair. But ~~this~~ \the/ consequences perverslie deduced from the wordes of the covenant ~~we~~ \are/ detested by all honest men <and ar indeid contrary to many articles of our covenant, namlie to these wherby we abjure. Usurped authoritie upon the church, the civil magistrat, and the consciences of men, tyrannous lawes made upon indifferent thinges, against our Christiane libertie, generall (that is implicit) fath, and the thrie solemne vowes wherof blind obedience is one: and to these wherby we sweir, that we shall attempt nothing to the dimunition of the kinges greatnes and authoritie, and to be examples to otheris of everie duetie, we owe to God and man.>[18] The covenant speakis of comon consent, that which may conduce to the gud endes and lawfull meanes. The doeing of evrie small convention of comissioneris at Edinburgh, must not be thought ~~that~~ the comon consent of the covenanteris. This protestation was concluddet by a verie few number scarcelie ~~twelve~~ <twentie> ministeris being then conveined att Edinburgh, and also not be the comon advyse of these, as is knowen ~~sall be cleired~~. And although any conclusion be maid by the consent of the most pairt, yet no man can be tyed thairto if it be unlawfull, or against his conscience, although it wer the act of an universall, or oecumenick councell. As an~~e~~ implicit faith, so a blind obedience to any man, or compend of men is justlie condemned by all men of our religion. We can not bind our conscience to the absolute by living or obedience to any, unles we attributt to them an impossibilitie of erring or doeing wrong. Although actis of parliament dischairgeing leagues, bandis, and conventiones of subjectis, without the kinges licence have bein objected against us: yet we

17 The word is almost entirely obscured by a deletion or ink blotch, but given the tenor of the sentence it is likely a mistakenly spelt or extraneous 'sub' that precedes 'subscryve'.

18 This portion of text within the chevrons appears under the letter 'A' on fo. 24v./p. 28 of the manuscript, after Strang's conclusion. It is clear that it was meant to be included at this juncture on fo. 17v./p. 14, for Strang's marker 'X' and corresponding marginalia draw attention to its inclusion: 'and are indeid; sie the last pag at the letter A to wit the 28 pag'.

have allwayes defendit the legalitie of our proceidinges, becaus our band and covenant is one in substance, with that which wes authorized by King James and his councell, and consequentlie warranted by the sam authoritie, and our conventiones after a peaceabill maner in a comon danger of the church and comon wealth for preventing of trubles wes onlie institute, and frequented to present, and prosequte our supplicationes, grivances and complaintes unto authoritie, to receve answeris from his majestie, his commissioner, and councell: and to treat with them concerning the same. And in these thinges we ought to conforme our selfes to such resolutiones as by comon consent should be fund to conduce to so good endis. This, according to our judgment of charitie is the meaning, and purpose of all, and undoubtedlie of the most, who have subscryved the late covenant, in the simplicitie of ther heartis. And so such appeireth to be imported by the answeris maid to the doctoris of Aberdeine:[19] and therfor after his majestie hath given full answer to our complaintes and supplicationes, and speciallie haveing granted a frie generall assemblie, and parliament the onlie ~~suppreme~~ \supreme/ nationall judicatories competent to judge

fo. 18r./p. 15

of nationall causes and proceidinges, and able to redresse all our evilles, to whom it appertineth to find out and determine what is conduceable to so good endes, all our meitinges for consultation touching that comon bussines, should give place therto; ~~and wherfor it y…ng…~~[20] and hither to onlie ar we bound to the said meitinges, and consultations mentionat in the covenant.

4. The new subscription, if we doe no more, can never be ane argument of our recanting and repenting what we have don: nather inferreth it a passing from our supplicationes and complaintes. But rather his majesties ordinance for a new subscription importeth his gracious condescending to us. Nather by subscryving both the covenant and the generall confession, prefer we the one befor the other. And what matter is it which of them we prefer to the other if we prejudge nather of them? Some tyme speciall additionis hath bein fund to prejudge the generall: but the generall can never prejudg, nor tack away that which is indeid specialie comprehendit under it.

19 This refers to the Aberdeen Doctors' anti-Covenanting pamphlet *Generall Demands Concerning the Late Covenant*, published on 20 July 1638, and the Covenanters' reply, the *Answeres*, printed two days later. See *Generall Demands, Concerning the Late Covenant, Together with the Answeres of Those Reverend Brethren to the Sayd Demands: As Also the Replyes of the Foresayd Ministers and Professors to Their Answeres* (Aberdeen, 1638). For bibliographical information on these publications, see Ogilvie, 'Aberdeen Doctors', 83–6.

20 This is the author's deletion as opposed to damage or manuscript binding. The deletion is such that most of the original writing is obscured completely.

Wher as it is said that the new subscription will open the door to the reentrie of the particularis abjured, and to repent our selfes of our cheifest consulationes, and so to be against God and our soulis, all this is deduced from that suposition that the latter subscription doeth evert the former. Which seing it is not proved by any reasone of moment, we deny the sam and affirme the contrary, inrespect of all the reasones preceiding.

5. It hath bein indeid objectit, not that the confession of faith, bot that the mutuall band of defence and assistance against all persones quhatsomever, mentionat in the covenant, was unlawfull, becaus it wanted the warrand of publik authoritie. And although answeris hath bein made to this objection: yet many good Christianes hath not bein satisfied thair with: and therfor as we could have wisched that his majestie had addet his authoritie, so it hath pleased him graciouslie to supplie quhatsomever ~~reall~~ \real/ or suposid defect was in that band, by his awin concurrance, in the generall band now prescryvit by authoritie: wherby all honest menis doubtis may be fullie satisfied. And as this is no finall benefitt, so it is a most forcible motive for our new subscription with the kinges concurrance. The answer made to the objectione above spec[21]

fo. 18v./p. 16

was, that we war not destitute of the warrandes civill, and eclesiastick, which authorizeth the former covenant. Now seing these warrandes wer no uther, but such as concerneth the foursaid confession of faith, and generall band now ordained to be subscryved, how can we think our selfes warran~~d~~ted to subscryve the late covenant, and now to refuse our subscription to the said confession and band? Ther is no reasone to prefer a covenant made with god, farre lesse a band of mutuall asstestance, without the kinges authoritie, *cateris paribus*, to it which is made by the kinges authoritie. Of the latter we have onlie examples in scripture, and none of the former.

6. Seing poperie is evin now pregnant and powerfull in this land, then the renewing of the confessione of faith conteining the abjuration of poperie, in ~~an~~ \a/ verie particular maner, and the band of mantinance against papistes, can not be bot verie seasonable: and seing his majestie hath tacken sufficient ordor for removeing the innovationes and evilles feared or compleined upoun and hes granted for that effect a frie generall assemblie and parliament (which as it is acknawledgit by the mackeris of the protestation will undoubtedlie redres all our evilles) these evilles being removed,

21 The author here writes 'above spec' at the bottom of this folio, which likely means 'above specifiet' or 'specified', a phrase he uses at other points in the tract.

and controversies tacken away, thair is no necessitie of rydding of merchers in these poyntis. Efter debaites ar conciliat, the causes of old querrellis would not be allwayes remembrid. When a man macketh a lawfull purches of his neighbouris landis, he may remove and promove his former marches. Ther ar some pairtes of the covenant disgracefull to some persones, and not \verie/ honorable to the king, as these wordes which hath relation to complaintes neglected, and protestationes. If our grivances be removed, the persones of men and namlie of our king may be spaired. Some regrantes that the names of ancient heretickes, and of ther heresies, which ar now out of use, ar not buried: and the keiping of them in memorie is sometyme ane ocasione of renewing of them by the lyk spiritis: yet from this new subscription intendet, so long as the former is not recalled, so much can not be inferred. The late covenant applyed onlie to the present tyme can onlie serve as a merch for a tyme and for these who subscryvit in this age. Our marches with the papistes must indure, untill poperie be fullie abolisched: which we have not expect untill chryst destroy antichryst with the brightnes of his coming.

fo. 19r./p. 17
Be it so that the obligation of our covenant is perpetuall and the example may conduce for after ages: yet we think it will be inpertinent to our successors to renew it in the sam termis.

If the king and his good people with one mynd and accord goe on in the subscription of the confession and band, papistes had never lesse cause to presume to win ground upoun us, or to be secure them selfis. Nothing is mor abho\r/red of papistes, then the said confession, wherin the erroris ar expreslie abjured: nothinge more feared by them, then the band, wherin his majestie with his subjectis be one league ar bound to resist and supresse papistes with ther whole power. Nothing will be more acceptabill to them, then our opposition to his majestie in this matter, and division among our selfes, which is ther strenth and joy.

Although after the large confession of faith registrat in the actis of parliament, the schort confession wes addet, for the more cleir abjuration of poyntis of poperie: yet the subscription of the one prejudges not the subscription of the other: and no man that hes subscryved the latter can justlie refuse to subscryve the former if he wer urgit by authoritie upon as guid reasones as now we ar: among which this is not of small moment, that thair may be an harmonie of the king and all his gud subjectis, for the profession and mantinence of religion against all heretickes and specialie papistes.

7. The papistes shall heirby be occasioned to renew ther old objection, *annuas et menstruas fides de deo decernunt*, that our faith changeth with the moone,

or once in the yeir, and Reformed churches may justlie wonder at our inconstancie, if we refuse to subscryve the confession of our proud fatheris, and if we now affirme it to be unlawfull for us to subscryve that confession and band which we thought lawfull to subscryve a yeir, a moneth or a day preceiding our late covenant; and our deare freindes I fear will bewail the losse of the peace of the church and kingdome made unnecessarlie, if for this cause allenarlie it be broken.

8. If we judge, mantine and professe that the service book, book of canonis, and uther evillis feared by us ar abjured in the schort confession of faith, we ought the more willinglie subscryve the sam. And if any other think that they may both subscryve the said confession and receve the said bookis, the remidie is prepaired: becaus not onlie the kings majestie with advyse of

fo. 19v./p. 18
his councel, to satisfie our complaintes hath so publicklie dischairged them; but he hath granted us a frie generall assemblie and parliament ~~anent~~ which we acknawledge to be sufficient for redressing all our evilles.

9. It is ~~ane~~ \a/ bold affection to affirme that the religion professed in Scotland in the yeir 1580, and that which is professed heir at this tyme is diverse: and to mak the articles of Perth and episcopacie sensyn introducit in our church to be an innovation of religion and that to say utherwayes wer a formall contradiction to that, which we have sworne in our covenant. How can any man who is in judgment conforme adher to such a protestation seing it was condescendit by comon consent of the covenanteris, that the opinion concerning the laufulnes of episcopacie, and of the articles of Perthe, was no hindrance to subscryve the covenant: as is manifest by the wrytt intituled considerationis according to the groundis of conformitie for these quho ar scrupolous to subscryve the covenant, red and allowed by the whole assemblie of the ministrie conveinet at Edinburghe, the tyme of the first subscryving of the covenant, and by all the dealling therefter used to mak men conforme in ther judgment to subscryve, and by the answeris to the demandes of Aberdine? And not the least part of the ministeris hes subscryvit the covenant in this sam mynd.

If our religion must be esteimed diverse for such poyntis I fear that our church shall be comprysed in too nearow boundis, and far lesse then ever the Donatistes wer.[22] We give too great an advantage to the papistes, who

22 This is a reference to the Donatists, a group that splintered from the early Christian church in the Roman province of Carthage in the fourth century CE, and who were distinctive and controversial for their uncompromising view of the nature of the clergy. During the

objecteth that the protestantis ar devyded in so great a multitud of religiones. And we must be thoght to have an other religion then even our mother church of Geneva had, or hes, wherin some of Perth articles ar observed.

It is no lesse presumption to tak upon us to understand better the kinges mynd, intention, and comandement in this proclamation, then his majesties commissionar and all the lordis of councell, who hes publisched thair declaration in print to the vew of the world. And yet som doubt not affirme that the lordis of his majesties councell hes bein so foolisch, and unconsiderat, as to involve both themselfes, and otheris, who ar to subscryve according to ther example, in a contradiction both to his majesties proclamation, and generall band: as if these tyed us to the religion presentlie professed in this instant yeir of god 1638 and the act of councell comandeth all subjectis to subscryve the confession as it wes meaned at the making and renewing of it anno 1580 and 1589 which objection is groundles and frivolous: not onlie inrespect it importeth our religion to be diverse now, from that which it was then: but becaus his majestie by his proclamation commandethe

fo. 20r./p. 19
us to subscryve the same confession, which wes befor subscryved anno 1580 and 1589 and not any other confession ather in wordes or meaning. And the lordes of councell of purpose to obviat all such obligationis, hes comandet to subscryve the said confession of faith daited the second of Merche 1589 and that according to the sam date and tenor therof, as it wes then professed within this kingdome, together with the generall band datet in anno 1589 and for that effect not onlie the date of the said confession and generall band is particularlie mentioned in the said act: but also in the bodie of the said generall band (which is most contraverted) the date is expreslie annexed, att [ ][23] 1589.

Lett it be granted that not onlie in his majesties judgment, but also that in ~~the~~ verie deid episcopacie and the articles of Perth ar not condemned nor abjured in the said confession (as ~~an~~ \a/ great part of the ministrie of Scotland even of these who have subscryved the covenant ar of the sam mynd) yett it is a most absurd consequence to inferr, that if we should now sweir that confession, we should be obliged by our oath to manteine Perth articles or episcopacie, lett be the corruptiones of the publik governament of

Reformation era, the labels 'Donatism' and 'Donatists' were also employed as rhetorical tools to disparage any number of religious reform movements. See, for instance, P. Biel, 'Bullinger against the Donatists: St Augustine to the Defence of the Zurich Reformed Church', *Journal of Religious History* 16 (1991), 237–46.

23 Here, there is a gap in the line, presumably for a month and a day, but neither is provided.

the church or civil places and policie of kirk men. Nather the kinges majestie nor any man ever alleadgit or can alleadge, that these thinges are included and affirmed in the said confession directlie nor indirectlie. The most that any man can say is that these thinges or som of them ar not excluded nor condemned by the said covenant.

When a man is obliged to give an oath according to the mynd and intention of the exacter he is not obliged to be in the mynd and opinion of the exacter in evrie thing, that the exacter esteimeth not to be incuded in the oath, but onlie in that which he knoweth the exacter to esteim to be included in the oath. Is \it/ not possible that ~~an~~ \a/ confession of faith in most poyntes may be drawin up, wherunto the Lutherans \and these/ of our profession may subscryve, and sweir, retaning thair awne different judgmentis, whether the exacter be a prince of our profession, or theires? ~~and in all a Lutherane prince to this effect could not resist~~ Farre lesse is the intention of the exacter of an oath to be measoured from his awin opinion concerning the thinges to be sworne, but from his purpose, and maner of exhibition therof, for it is possible that a prince may exhibit a confession of faith to be sworne and subscryved by his subjectis, and yet be of a different opinion himsellff, as for example, if a popeisch prince intending to permitt no religion within his dominionis, except onlie the religion of the papistes and protestantis, and willing to mantine the professoris of both schould comand all is subjectis to subscryve ather the confession of the one or the other. Who doubteth bot his protestant subjectis may lawfullie sweir and subscryve to the confession of ther awin religion and that according to the purpose and intention of the exacter, although being of a contrary judgment himself in the matteris that ar sworne?

fo. 20v./p. 20
It is strange that in this protestation it is alleadgid, that in the first parliament halden by King Charles, under the name of the mantinance of religion the forsaid novationes and episcopacie is ratified, wheras in the covenant it is declared, that by this sam act of parliament is ratified the puritie of religion, in doctrine, sacramentis, the libertie and freedome of the church, in all her assemblies, policie, and jurisdiction: to the which the said novationes and episcopacie are declared to be repugnant by the protesteris.

In the late proclamation ther is not conteined any injunction by the king, that all ministeris at ther entrie sall give oathes according to the act of parliament: but his majestie dischairgeth any uther oath to be administred unto them, then that which is conteined in the act of parliament. If episcopacie be dischairged, that oath will also cease, and befour then, ther is no reasone that his majestie should dischairge that oath, speciallie seing no complaint was ever made to his majestie concerning the unlawfullnes therof.

10. The tenth reasone is coincident pairtlie with the eight and partlie with the nynth preceiding and so the answer allreadie given to these serveth also for this.

To object ~~against~~ \againe/ his majesties proclamationes and actes of councell which ar dischairged and nullified is impertinent.

11. All similitudis ar halting, and these that ar brought for the ellevint reasone as much as any, and som of them ar too hautie, although uttered by ~~an~~ \a/ preface of reverance: as these, which ar taken from the Old and New Testament. And all argumentis from similitudis ar faultie, when they ar not used in ~~thes~~ the sam thinges, wherin the comparison is to be institute as it heir appeareth. The old confession, which manifestlie distermineth betwix us and papistes wherby we most openly abjure poperie is not as an merch stone hid in the ground, or lyk a closed hand, or scheathed sword. No prince professedlie popisch would comand his subjectis to subscryve our first confession, unlesse he would comand them to professe our religione and to sweir against his awine profession: farr lesse would he concurre in ~~ane~~ \a/ mutuall band to mantine our religion, to the eversion of his owne religion, and of the professoris therof. If a Jewisch magistrat or king to discerne Mahometanes, or paganes, blasphemeris of the Old Testament, would comand his Christiane subjectis, to subscryve the Old

fo. 21r./p. 21
Testament, without requireing of the new, after they had subscryved both, no well advysed Christiane would rejoyn. Or if a Lutherane prince, to discerne his subjectis from papistes, would injoyne all his subjectis, to subscryve a confessione of these articles, which ar comon to the Lutheranes and us, could any of our professores justlie refuise to subscryve the sam. But in this comandement of our king, and of his councell, the reasones ar more pregnant, as hes bein schawin, the differences ar farr lesse, yea under no substantiall difference at all (so the protesteris have ever professed) and whatsoever difference can be imagined, the remeid is also prescryved by the same ordinance, appoynting a frie generall assemblie and parliament: <u>which will undoubtedlie redresse our evilles</u>.

The examples of old Eleazar, and of the old confessoris, and martyres, is not to the purpose: for nothing heir is commandit which is not most openlie avouched, both by the comanderis, and obeyeris.

12. He that is not forgetfull of his oath made to the covenant, must remember, that he hath sworne, <u>to stand to the defence of the kinges majestie authoritie, in the defence and preservation of the true religione, liberties, and</u>

lawes of this kingdome: and not to attempt any thing to the dimunitione of the kinges authoritie, and to be a good example of evrie deutie to god, and man. And consequentlie to our king no man can doe ~~a~~ deutie to god, who rendereth not deutifull obedience to his king. Whosoever resisteth the power, resisteth the ordinance of god. When by his majesties authoritie, we ar comanded to subscryve an orthodox confession of faith, wherby papistes may be discerned and resisted, and to subscryve a band for the defence and preservation of the true religion, according to the liberties and lawes of this kingome, to refuise our selfes, or to persuad utheris to refuise, and resist, is a matter of ~~consequence~~ conscience.

These who ar conscious to themselfes of no fault or guiltines, is not bound to apply to themselfes that clause concerning the kinges pardon. The king urgeth no confession of a fault from any the doeing of a lawfull deid, injoyned to all in comon, in whom his majestie suspecteth no fault (such as is the subscription requyreth) will never import a confession of fault on our part. Although ther be fault nather in our subscryving of the late covenant, nor in our lawfull meitinges and proceidinges: yet no man can deny, that somtyme in a good cause, men may foull in the maner, and our zeall may debord through ignorance, and that evin in this sam cause ther have bein some disordoris in som persones, by rasch speiches, and violent deides: which the godlie will not justifie: nather is it to be doubted if the king and his subjectis agrie in this comon bussines

fo. 21v./p. 22
that noble men and otheris will desyr an act of oblivion to passe in the nixt parliament for ther better securitie.

13. This reasone appeareth to be added, rather for the number \then/ for the intent, with a too great intention of carping. Who can indeid suspect that our king, who is a lyvelie example of godliness, sobernes and righteousness <is averse> from that point wherin the generall band is said to be deficient (and which if it should have bein added, now is more proper to \be/ adjoyned to the confession of faith nor to the generall band, as is also imported in this sam reasone of the protestaris wher it is said that without this clause we can not now subscryve this confession) lyk it is a bad consequence which no man shall be able to mak good, by any schew of reasone, that if without this clause we subscryve the confession, we loose the bandis to wickedness etc, which may be as justlie objected against our pious fatheris who subscryved the confession without this clause as against us (although they had not our covenant to be ther paterne) and against all other confession of faith extant befour our covenant. And who doubteth but we ar tyed to that part of our covenant by a perpetuall band? His majestie wyslie considerit, that if he had

mad any alteration in the confession of our fatheris, so much magnified in our covenant, that he might have given greater occasion of obloquie. If he had added any thing, howsoever good, and plausible, it might have bein said, why did he not adde more? If he had diminisched it, or changed any wordis or clauss therin, much more might have bein objected. And therfore he hath not altered one syllab in the confession, nather also in the generall band, bot that which was impertinent for our tymes; and yett it is objected that the band now urged to be subscryved conteineth many clauses not so fitting for the present tyme, as that wherin it was subscryved, but no instance is given wherin: and sure it is that many such clauses cannot be found therin and if any be found therin not so fitting for the present tyme, and \as for/ that tyme wherin it wes subscryved: yet it is sufficient that there is no clause therin, which is not fitting, or may be fitting, also for our tyme. And if there be any error in this kynd it may by our selve mendid or oversein. This is *nodum in scripoquarere.*

fo. 22r./p. 23
14. In the narrative of the generall band, nothing is changed, but in so farr as som few lynes ar left out, which ar manifestlie impertinent for our tyme, unlesse we would say, that now we knew of preparationes and poweres of forren enemies, readie for invasion of this realme; and \of/ plottis, and practices of Scottisch papistes conspyring with forren princes, against our countrie, which at that tyme was certanlie understoode. It is strange that in the preceiding reasone, it is objected, that the generall band now to be renewed conteineth many clauses not so fitting the present tyme, as that tyme when it was first subscryved; and yet in this reasone, there is fault found, that these lynes, which unoubtedlie ar unfitting for the present tyme, ar omitted.

Although ther can be no such particular designation made now as was made then, in the said lynes omitted, of the partie, from whom the immenent danger is threatned to our religion: yet non of us doubteth, but that we stand allwayes in danger of our religion, by the adversaries therof in generall, as the pope his ~~suppostes~~ \suppostes/ Jesuites, seminarie preistes ther practices, and all the poweris forren or intestine, whom they ar able to move: and these ar most expreslie designed in the band to be renewed, as our partie from whom the danger is now and allwayes threatned.

And if malice it sellff cannot charge these, who subscryved the covenant to be of that nomber, it would be more then a malicious construction to esteim the sinceir professoris of our religion to be the partie, against whom this generall band is made, and no lesse to lay such ane aspersion upon the honorable and religious lordis of councell, who ar bund to us and with us by so many bandis. Non who loveth, and followeth efter peace and trueth schould suffer such an uncharitable suspition to enter into his mynd. Love is not too suspitious *hic murus aheneus esto, nil conscire sibi*.

15. If a number of these, who subscryved the late covenant, refuise to subscryve the said confession and generall band, as the lordis of his majesties privie counsell hath allreadie subscryved the sam, and many otheris appear-inglie will follow there example, the breache will be the wydde, and the lamentable division of this church more dangerous, som repyning against the ordinance of the king, and his councell; som obeying the sam as most just, pious, and equitable, and \being/ scandalized at there brethren, for refuissing to subscryve the covenant of ther fatheris, and the ground of the late covenant, and so opening a door for the papistes, living amoung us to escaip ther censour. Wheras our comon consent and unanimitie in subscryving would, by the blissing of god, prove the most effectuall meane to preserve trueth and peace in this land, to withstand the comon enemie, and to remove our fearfull and feared divisiones.

fo. 22v./p. 24
And if some would mantine, that the novationes and evilles compleaned upon may consist with the said confession after they had subscryved the sam, the frie generall assemblie and parliament enseuing, which will undoubtedlie redresse all our evilles will provyd that the opinione of these men sall not be prejudiciall to the libertie, and puritie of religion. And wher as it is objected, that the new subscription might mak way to division, inrespect som by verteu of the covenant haveing sworne, to labor by all lawfull meanes, to recover the former libertie, and puritie of religion, otheris might mantine that for puritie, which is allreddie ~~professed~~ establisched: it may be easilie replyed that the sam reasone stryketh as much against the subscription of the late covenant, as against the new subscription \injoyned/ by authoritie for ther is nothing in this kynd that can be said to be alreadie establisched, but that which is ordained by actis of a generall assemblie and parliament, and therin nothing is called in question by any, except episcopall governament, and the fyve articles of Perth assemblie concerning both which poyntis nothing is determined in the late covenant, and expreslie it wes aggried by comon consent, that notwithstanding any man wer persuaded of the lawfullnes of both \these/ yet he may subscryve the covenant. And heir it would be considderit, seing for the subscryving of the covenant a syncretisme or mutuall aggriement was concluded, and allowit betwix men of diverse opiniones concerning conformitie, whither or not it is a divisive motion, and upon whose part, that in the meane tyme the one part doeth condemne the opinionis of the other, publiklie, both in sermones, and protestationes and howsoever, it apertineth to the assemblie, to tack a convenient course, for these and such lyk differences.

16. It is not necessar to admonisch the honorable lordis of councell, professoris of the sam religion with us, that in the oath ther is no place left to mentall reservation: which wer a Jesuitisch trik, contrary to our profession, and the mynd of all honest men. Nather is it to be doubted but that the doctrine, discipline and use of the sacramentis ar sworne, and to be sworne, and the contrary abjured according to the word of God, and the meaning of the church of Scotland agrieable to Godis word, so farre as we can understand. But that any man should professe, sweir, and subscryve the confession of faith without his owin proper conception, understanding, and interpretation, leaning only, by an implicit faith, to the meaning

fo. 23r./p. 25

of the church of Scotland, wer too popische. Evrie man most belive for himsellf, and know what he beliveth and confesseth in matteris concerning his salvation. No man can in conscience be tyed by an implicit faith to the meaning of any wryt, except onlie the meaning of Godis spirit, in the holie scripture. Nather can it be instancet, that in our kirk, ther ar any diversities of meaninges and interpretationes of the said confession, concerning any matter necessar to faith and salvation. And if in any other thinges ther be diversities of meaninges and interpritationes, the sum diversitie or greater as to be found, and hes bein allowit in the subscryveris of the late covenant: as in part it hes bein already instanced.

And if the meanining of the church of Scotland most be gathered out of the bookis of discipline, and actis of assemblie, this will be ~~an~~ \a/ verie uncertane ground. For many thousandis hes subscryved the said confession and covenant, who ar not acquented with the bookis of discipline, and actis of assemblies the lawfulnes also of som assemblies is now contraverted, concerning which ev\e/rie subscryver cannot judge. The one book of discipline conteines sumthing contrary to the other: and that which is ordaned in the first book is retreated in the second. So it is also in ~~all~~ actis of assemblies and there is littlle hope that all who hes subscryved ather the said confession or the late covenant will stand to the bookes of discipline utherwayes non of them could injoy patronages of churches, church landis, tithes nor any other part of the patriomonie of the church, notwithstanding of ther takis, or any other pretext of law whatsomever. Lykwayes, I think there never was, at the least this day ther is no such ruleing elderis and deacones in all Scotland, as is descryved in the said book of discipline. The deacones office expressed ther is not so much to gather almes for the poore, as to receve and distribute the whole patrimonie and rentis of the church, as tithes, rent of church landis etcq. And both elderis, and deacones, as all other ecclesiasticall persones, should be chosen by the judgment and voyce of the eldership or presbitrie and receve ordination by imposition of landis. The ~~rewlling~~ \ruleing/ elderis

schould be chosen *ad vitam*, they schould have no civil place nor power. For the exercise of jurisdiction on both civil and ecclesiastick can not stand in on person ordinarie. Sie the book of discipline the 6 and 8 head from second book. Cap. 1. 3. 6. 8. 9. 12.[24]
Som sayeth what needeth [ ]

[ ][25], what is ther meining who suggesteth this delay intending after a delay to procure an~~e assemblie~~ absolute denyal. His majestie intended

fo. 23v./p. 26
to prepair a fair way, for an ordinar and peaceable meating in a frie generall assemblie, and parliament; and to remove all impedimentis and occasiones of grudge, \suspition/ and distanst, betwix him and his subjectis. If we stand still in way of opposition to his majestie, and the documentis and signes of our seperation be not first taken away, after so much condescending of his majestie, ther is small hope of any peaceable and durable conclusion to be expected from assemblies and parliamentis.

Besyd all the former objectiones, it hath bein too much divulgid or surmised, that by his majesties late proclamation, no secure dealing is intendit, but by fair pretextis to lull us in ~~securitie~~ <sinceir>, that the more easilie afterward, the eviles wherof we complein, may be brought upon us, and in the meane tyme by force of armes his majestie may \be/ avenged upon those who hath opposed.

But if his majestie had any intention averse to our religion, or favorable to poperie, can any man of understanding imagine that his majestie, or any who giveth advyse heirto ar so voyd not onlie of civil honestie, but also of naturall wit, as to enjoyn to his subjectis, such an oath wherby they shall sweir, both against himselfe, and contrary to his designes these sinistrous suspitiones, as we hope they ar farre from these nobillmen, and utheris who have any hand in the said protestation, so should not \be/ harbored in any honest heart.

Concerning fear of armes, it cannot be denyet, but inrespect of the late divisiones, occasioned by these innovationes, there hath bein moved

24 These citations refer to chapters in the *Second Book of Discipline*, printed in 1578. The chapters cited deal with the polity of the Kirk, the admittance of ministers, elders and deacons, the nature and role of the offices of elder and deacon and the Kirk's patrimony. See J. Kirk (ed.), *The Second Book of Discipline: With Introduction and Commentary* (Edinburgh, 1980), 163–72, 178–82, 191–4, 207–12, 230–40.

25 There are two large gaps in the lines that end and begin each paragraph.

dangerous suspitiones, and discontentmentis, betwix his majestie and his subjectis, wherby the whole cuntrie hath bein in fear of warre, and hath made some provision for there defence. But now, seing his majestie according to his peaceable disposition and fatherlie love to his cuntrie, hath taken such course for removeing our feares and grivances, more then ever we expected, as hes satisfied his wyse and religious counselloris, and appearinglie will be allowed by all the Reformed churches in the world, so that not onlie he hath omitted nothing, which any good Christian can object to have bein done to the prejudice of our religion during his raigne wherin he hath not given all possibill satisfaction (unlesse we call the subscription injoyned to the confession of the faith of our pious fatheris prejudice) but also hath eased us, in these thinges, which occasioned our greatest divisiones, in the dayes of his father \of/ most

fo. 24r./p. 27
glorious memorie. And moreover hath remitted and remmied all quarrellis on his parte, we have to consider what meiting for peace we give on our parte: and ~~give~~ \if/ ther be any differences remaining, whether they be of such moment, as by occasione thereof, we should suffer not onlie the peace of our church to be ~~distroubled~~ <disturbed>; but also, that this land be involved in all the calamities of warre, wherunto his majestie may think himselfe necessitat, not for religion directlie, but for such politik consequences, as in all probabilitie we ar to follow upon our divisiones, and prosecuting our intentions against his majesties will; and whether or not we have any examples of martyres, who hath suffered extremitie for any point now contraverted. For if the <cause> ~~course \cause/~~[26] be not such as we would and should give our bodies to be burned for manteinance of the sam, farre lesse by our allowance or procurement should the haill bodie of our cuntrie be cast in the danger of a miserable cumbustion, and desolation, wherby ~~we~~ not onlie our lyfes, bot also \our/ libertie, and religion, which ar deirer to us then our lyfes, may be in hazard, and all the eviles, which we fear, be brought upon us, and the whole kindgome being rent by divisiones, weasted and weakened by intestine truble, may be made a prey to any usurping tyranie, or forran enemie. And all this the more lamentable, that our contraverse shall be with our native king, and such a king as (secluding the consideration of his royall right deryved from a hundredth and sevin progenitores) if it wer left to our libertie, to choose a religious, and righteous king, there is no prince of the world, for his gracious endowments, whom upon our conscience we would compare, let be prefer to him: and at such a tyme, as when we may have the

26 The superscript addition appears to be obscured between the lines, so Strang has instead referred the reader to the word 'cause' in the margin.

fairest afferris, and conditiones for preserving peace and trueth that ever we had, or could expect in our age. O if we knew, even we, at least in this our day, the thinges, which belong to our peace. Now the lord of peace himselfe, give us peace allwayes, by all meanes. Amen.

AN ACCOUNT OF A CONFESSION OF RAISING THE DEVIL AT IRVINE ON 10 FEBRUARY 1682*

Edited by Ciaran Jones

INTRODUCTION

The manuscript is an account of a confession, collected by Sir John Lauder of Fountainhall, of a servant girl to Major-General Robert Montgomerie. The text is dated 10 February 1682, titled 'Ane accompt of ane womans raising the Devill', and can be found in the University of Edinburgh's David Laing manuscript collection.[1] The manuscript occupies 208r–209r of LA. II/89, a bound volume housing a collection of loose, miscellaneous documents relating to the presbyterians and the Covenant from 1631 to 1700. Laing himself may have come into possession of it when he was editing Sir John Lauder of Fountainhall's collection, to which the document, on two, joined folios originally belonged. We know this, because Fountainhall's collection, now held by the National Library of Scotland, contains a concise summary of the servant girl's confession under the heading 'Historical Observes of Memorable Occurents in Church and State from October 1680 to April 1686', which references the text under discussion here.[2]

Around noon on 10 February 1682, Margaret Dougal, a servant girl to Major-General Robert Montgomerie, was accused of stealing some linens by her fellow servants. Feeling angry that she had been accused, and knowing that she had lost something herself, she said to her fellow servants that she would perform a complex divination ritual that would summon the Devil. According to Dougal, the Devil could tell her who had stolen the linens. Later that day, around three in the afternoon, she went to the cellar in the

* I would like to thank Julian Goodare, Alasdair Raffe, Jamie Reid-Baxter and Louise Yeoman for help and advice on an earlier draft of this edition. Thanks are also due to the peer reviewers of the Scottish History Society for their comments and criticisms.

1 Edinburgh University Library (hereafter EUL), Ane accompt of ane womans raising the Devill, Laing MSS, II. 89 fos 208r.–209r.

2 Fountainhall mentions, 'See the full particulars of it in a paper besyde me'. National Library of Scotland (hereafter NLS), MS. 24.4.6., Advocates Library, fos 177r.–177v. The original was also printed in the nineteenth century; J. Lauder, *Historical Observes of Memorable Occurrents in Church and State from October 1680 to April 1686*, eds A. Urquhart and D. Laing (Edinburgh, 1840), 61–2.

Montgomerie household and performed the divination ritual. After she had performed the ritual, she was taken to her bed by a fellow servant where she confessed to Montgomerie to raising the Devil three times. She also confessed to struggling with the Devil; each time she summoned him, he tried to seize her and take her back to hell, while she attempted to control him, forcing him to serve her in the same way a necromancer might have used his superior magical power to get a demon under control, and to channel its abilities in directions that he found useful. Eventually, Dougal managed to resist the Devil by drawing on her magical skills, and she banished him once she had secured knowledge of the stolen goods.

What happened to Margaret Dougal? After telling this confession to the Montgomerie household, the presbytery of Irvine became involved in her case the next day and the minister, along with some of the kirk elders, went to investigate further. Subsequent details of the presbytery's investigation do not survive, but in March the privy council ordered that she be transported from Ayr to Edinburgh for trial.[3] The privy council did not issue a local commission to try her as a witch, but rather got the sheriff deputes of Ayr, William Crichton and Robert Dalrymple, to negotiate her transportation to Edinburgh.[4] A reference in the justiciary court records proves that she was taken to Edinburgh, as on 21 March 1682 the privy council convened the 'comitty for publick affaires', whose role involved preparing and advising on cases to be tried in the justiciary court.[5] The committee of councillors, including the archbishop of St Andrews, Alexander Burnet, and the bishop of Edinburgh, John Paterson, considered her a prisoner for 'alledged raising the Divell', and they ruled that she was 'under some distempter'. They recommended to the prosecuting authorities that her case should 'be dismis[ed]'.[6] It is unclear whether Margaret was brought before the committee, or whether they examined her case without her being present.[7]

There are a couple of points that need to be discussed further. Firstly, it is interesting to note that the committee considered her a prisoner for raising the Devil rather than witchcraft. And secondly, that they felt confident enough to pronounce on her 'distemper' without, as far as one can tell, consulting a physician. It is possible that the committee was actively trying

3 *Register of the Privy Council of Scotland* (hereafter *RPC*), 3rd ser., v. 7, p. 350.

4 Ayrshire Archive Centre (AAC), Receipt by William Creichtoun and Robert Dalrymple, sheriff depute of the Sheriffdom of Air, B6/39/14.

5 National Records of Scotland (hereafter NRS), JC26/60/5; the exact item is unnumbered.

6 NRS, JC26/60/5.

7 Dougal's case was reviewed by the privy council at the same time as Christian Fyfe, a woman accused of assaulting the minister of St Giles, Alexander Ramsay. John Lauder of Fountainhall mentions the council's opinion about Christian Fyfe, but he does not mention anything about Dougal. See J. Lauder, *Historical Notices of Scotish Affairs, Selected from the Manuscripts of Sir John Lauder of Fountainhall*, ed. D. Laing, 2 vols (Edinburgh, 1848), i, 350–1.

to avoid prosecuting Dougal for witchcraft. Indeed, the ruling of this privy council committee reflected similar actions taken by earlier seventeenth-century episcopal figures, some of whom tried to reduce the number of prosecutions for witchcraft in the 1630s.[8] Moreover, Sir George MacKenzie of Rosehaugh, the Lord Advocate in 1682, would have been responsible for prosecuting Dougal when she arrived in Edinburgh. It was well known that MacKenzie urged extreme caution in the pursuit of witches; he had been a young justice depute in the 1661–2 witch-hunt and had witnessed first-hand the 'zeal' of enthusiastic interrogators.[9] It is unlikely that he would have supported prosecuting Dougal for witchcraft and the committee were probably aware of this when deciding Dougal's case.

Previous Commentaries on the Case

Dougal's case has received scholarly attention, most recently from David Mullan and Lizanne Henderson.[10] The latter comments on the uniqueness of Dougal's case, highlighting how uncommon the motif of summoning the Devil is in Scottish witchcraft narratives, and observes that 'it is quite detailed'.[11] The most often cited reference to Dougal's case is found in Charles Kirkpatrick Sharpe's nineteenth-century edition of Robert Law's *Memorialls*.[12] Law's narrative appears to be based on a different and unknown source, and a large majority is paraphrased, which suggests that he may have received verbal information regarding her case, possibly from Montgomerie or from other presbyterians. Law's narrative also includes many discrepancies when compared with the text under consideration. Firstly, and perhaps most importantly, Law did not mention Dougal's name, meaning that she could not be traced by scholars. If Law did indeed receive verbal information, then this would explain why Dougal's name was not mentioned. Secondly, Law assumed that during her divination ritual, Dougal read the 51st Psalm, and chapter 9, verse 19, from the Book of Revelation. In fact, the text of this

8 L.A. Yeoman (ed.), 'Witchcraft Cases from the Register of Commissioners of the Privy Council of Scotland, 1630–1642', in *The Miscellany of the Scottish History Society*, vol. XIII (Edinburgh, 2004), 233–65, at pp. 229–30.

9 G. MacKenzie, *The Laws and Customes of Scotland, in Matters Criminal* (Edinburgh, 1678), 80–108.

10 D.G. Mullan, *Narratives of the Religious Self in Early-Modern Scotland* (Farnham, 2010), 121; L. Henderson, *Witchcraft and Folk Belief in the Age of the Enlightenment: Scotland, 1670–1740* (Basingstoke, 2016), 136–7. Perceptive descriptions have appeared in A.F. McJannet, *The Royal Burgh of Irvine* (Glasgow, 1938), 196–7; and, A. Blair, *Tales of Ayrshire* (London, 1983), 177–8.

11 Henderson, *Witchcraft and Folk Belief*, 136.

12 R. Law, *Memorialls; Or, The Memorable Things That Fell Out Within This Island of Britain from 1638 to 1684*, ed. C.K. Sharpe (Edinburgh, 1818), 219–21. For Law, see *Oxford Dictionary of National Biography* (*ODNB*) [https://doi.org/10.1093/ref:odnb/16152].

edition refers to Revelation 19:19, given as 19:9 in the margin.[13] These distortions could have resulted from the case being transmitted orally.

Law also claimed that Dougal was thrown into prison, where she confessed to Major-General Robert Montgomerie that she had learnt her magical skills from 'Old Doctor Colvin'.[14] This probably refers to Dr Alexander Colville, a wealthy episcopal Ulster clergyman (originally of Inverkeithing), who was reputed to be a warlock.[15] The text under consideration makes no mention of Dougal's imprisonment, and we know that the authorities did not get involved until a day later on 11 February 1682; we can suggest, however, that Dougal may have been confined to a room in the house, and that the individual interrogating Dougal may well have been Major-General Robert Montgomerie. In Law's edition, references to the Devil's appearances are different. Law claimed that in the first instance, the Devil appeared to Dougal 'in a seaman's cloathing, with a blew cape on his head'.[16] This text, however, simply claims that the Devil appeared clothed, and with an old cap on his head, and with some black hair sticking out. Finally, Law did not mention the details of Dougal's alleged conversation and interaction with the Devil, missing large parts of direct speech that took place between Dougal and the Devil, and Dougal and her interrogator, which this manuscript references.[17]

The Questioning Process

Dougal's case appears relatively late in the age of witch-hunting. Although Irvine was not directly experiencing a witch-hunt in the early 1680s, there had recently been two high profile cases that took place nearby. The first was of the bewitchment of George Maxwell of Pollock, which had come before the High Court of Justiciary at Edinburgh in 1677.[18] The second case, in 1679, involved the confessions of the witches from Bo'ness. Confessions of diabolism often appeared in court of justiciary cases once the authorities got their hands on the suspect witch; however, some were recorded in local

13 See below, pp. 149–52, for further discussion.

14 Law, *Memorialls*, pp. 220–1. Colvin is a standard older Scots variant spelling of Colville.

15 J.M. Dickson, 'The Colville Family in Ulster', *Ulster Journal of Archaeology* 5 (1899), 139–45. For recent debates surrounding the Colville family, see J. Reid Baxter, 'The "Real" Dr Alexander Colville of Galgorm', *Familia: Ulster Genealogical Review* 30 (2014), 57–76.

16 Law, *Memorialls*, 220.

17 See below, pp. 148–52, for further discussion.

18 L.H. Willumsen, *Witches of the North: Scotland and Finnmark* (Boston, MA, and Leiden, 2013), 140–6; R.L. Harris, 'Janet Douglas and the Witches of Pollock: the Background of Scepticism in Scotland in the 1670s', in S.R. McKenna (ed.), *Selected Essays in Scottish Language and Literature* (Lewiston, NY, 1992), 97–124.

kirk session or presbytery records.[19] In both instances, the suspect witch was first interrogated by a local authority figure, normally a minister or kirk session elder, before the case moved up the legal hierarchy. Margaret Dougal's confession is particularly interesting insofar as her 'questioning' took place in a more informal setting, before the local authorities became involved. Usually suspect witches were questioned in a more coercive environment, such as the tolbooth. In some cases, we know that accused witches experienced maltreatment and, in a less than representative number of cases, torture. Sleep deprivation was a more common form of interrogatory method, and although it was not necessarily illegal, it certainly degraded the integrity of the accused's mind and body.[20] There is no evidence that Dougal was subjected to either judicial torture or sleep deprivation, as was traditionally employed during witchcraft interrogations. A witch's confession was a patchwork of conversations between the accused and the interrogator, containing sometimes paradoxical or contradictory statements. The confession would then be mediated by a scribe who would write up his notes, occasionally some time after the original interrogation. Thus, the final written version of the confession would often reaffirm the beliefs of both interrogator and accused.[21]

The extant evidence of Dougal's questioning shows that, at the very least, she was interrogated on one day and produced a lengthy and coherent narrative with a beginning, middle and end. Dougal's answers to the interrogator's questions are recorded almost verbatim, suggesting that she was allowed to tell her experience as she saw fit. At the end of the text it is recorded that she was interrogated again on 11 February, probably by local authority figures, as it states that 'the said Margaret who confessed in their presence [minister & elders] as followeth viz,'; the scribe's comma indicates that he intended to continue to copy his notes, although he did not do so. Thus, we are deprived of the chance of comparing the first informal interrogation with another official, legal one. In addition, even though the hand is similar throughout the text, there is a clear difference in style between the 10 and 11 February, with the latter showing a more official, judicial form of writing.

While the identity of the scribe remains elusive, we have better evidence concerning the identity of Dougal's original interrogator, which can account for the difference in style. The primary candidate is Major-General Robert

19 S. Macdonald, 'In Search of the Devil in Fife Witchcraft Cases, 1560–1705', in J. Goodare (ed.), *The Scottish Witch-Hunt in Context* (Manchester, 2002), 33–51, at pp. 35–7.

20 L. Martin, 'The Devil and the Domestic: Witchcraft, Quarrels and Women's Work in Scotland', in Goodare (ed.), *The Scottish Witch-Hunt in Context*, 77.

21 E. Wilby, *The Visions of Isobel Gowdie: Magic, Witchcraft, and Dark Shamanism in Seventeenth-Century Scotland* (Brighton, 2010), 53–81.

Montgomerie. Historically, the Montgomerie family had been involved in witchcraft prosecutions, and the document references a 'me' whom the household servants informed about what had happened in the cellar; this 'me' could very well be Montgomerie. In addition, the casual way the informal questions asked of Dougal on 10 February are recorded suggests that, at least at this stage, this was not a criminal interrogation. So even though the document may have been written up later by a professional scribe, once Dougal had come to the attention of the authorities, her original interrogator was not involved in prosecuting or dealing with magical crimes in any official governmental capacity. Moreover, as already noted, the document specifically states that the local authorities only became aware of the situation on the following day, 11 February, so there is little likelihood that an elder or minister had been present on 10 February.

Dougal and the Devil

The Devil's appearance merits discussion. Dougal claimed that he appeared in three different male forms. First, he appeared as a man with a cap upon his head; next in the shape of a black grim man in black clothing. And finally, as a naked man with a long black tail, including a foot formed like a pig's trotter. The idea of the Devil as a black man and man in black emerged from both popular culture and learned demonology,[22] and it was found across early modern Europe.[23] The Devil's relationship with Margaret Dougal was not centred around the demonic pact and demonological witchcraft, but rather resembled the type of relationship magical practitioners experienced with their spirit-guides, notably fairies.[24] This relationship was morally flexible, emotional and developed over a series of encounters. Unlike in typical witchcraft confessions, the Devil in Dougal's narrative is not presented as her hierarchical master, but rather as a trickster and foolish spirit: his attempts to physically drag Dougal to hell fail as she banished him each time with phrases such as 'Begon yow doge'. Moreover, much like the morally flexible relationships between magical practitioners and supernatural entities, interactions that at first appeared benign could turn violent. In Dougal's case,

22 J. Miller, 'Men in Black: Appearances of the Devil in Early Modern Scottish Witchcraft Discourse', in J. Goodare et al. (eds), *Witchcraft and Belief in Early Modern Scotland* (Basingstoke, 2008), 144–65; L. Henderson, *Witchcraft and Folk Belief*, 131.

23 E. Bever, 'Popular Witch Beliefs and Magical Practices' in B.P. Levack (ed.), *The Oxford Handbook of Witchcraft in Early Modern Europe and Colonia America* (Oxford, 2013), 50–69.

24 Alongside Wilby, *Visions of Isobel Gowdie*, see J. Goodare, 'Boundaries of the Fairy Realm in Scotland', in K. Olsen and J.R. Veenstra (eds), *Airy Nothings: Imagining the Otherworld of Faerie from the Middle Ages to the Age of Reason: Essays in Honour of Alasdair A. MacDonald* (Leiden, 2014), 139–71; E. Wilby, *Cunning Folk and Familiar Spirits: Shamanistic Visionary Traditions in Early Modern British Witchcraft and Magic* (Brighton, 2005), chs 4–6.

she initially summoned him for his help to locate stolen property, and he fulfilled her wish, answering her question each time she raised him. But it is also equally clear that the Devil became more eager to take Dougal to hell with him. In this context, Dougal's Devil not only resembled the folkloric trickster, but he also retained the characteristics of the Prince of Darkness; he was not an entity to be reckoned with lightly. Indeed, on one occasion when Dougal tried to banish him, she claimed that 'shee wanted [lacked] her feathers through fear' – presumably because she was scared of the Devil, and was fearful of what might happen if he managed to overcome her.

Dougal's confession will be useful to scholars interested in linking wider Scottish religious culture with magic, folk belief and witchcraft. Her narrative sheds light on the internalisation of evangelical preaching. She was asked, possibly by Montgomerie himself, how she could speak to the Devil in such an intimate manner. Dougal claimed that even though she did converse with the Devil, she always 'keeped her heart and trust to God': i.e., her commitment was to God, not the Devil. When we take into consideration the fact that she never confessed to entering into a pact with him – and compare her narrative with many accused witches' confessions from the mid-seventeenth-century witch-hunts – it is clear that Dougal did not succumb to his temptations. We could perhaps suggest that, alongside her magical skills, she also considered herself a confident, godly woman, who ran no risk and saw no problem in conversing with the Devil in this manner. This is further reinforced in her comment 'ministers wold doe the same'; a rare statement that suggests Dougal may have had knowledge of ministers' or godly Protestants' confrontations with the Prince of Darkness, some of whom thought that their temptations were divinely imposed or ordained to test their faith.[25] Her comment could, of course, refer to the Rev. Dr Colville himself, from whom Dougal claimed to have learnt her skills.

Popular Magical Practices and Visionary Experience

Dougal's confession contains a wealth of information about popular magical rituals. As already noted, magical practitioners had a complex and emotional relationship with a wide array of spirits – the Devil included – on whom they could call on for aid. Cases of 'raising' or summoning the Devil are

25 There are numerous accounts of ministers and godly Protestants who were plagued by demonic temptation but thought that they were a test of faith. For more, see M.D. Brock, *Satan and the Scots: The Devil in Post-Reformation Scotland, 1560–1700* (London, 2016), chs 3–4; Brock, 'Internalising the Demonic: Satan and the Self in Early Modern Scottish Piety', *Journal of British Studies* 54 (2015), 23–43; Mullan, *Narratives of the Religious Self*, ch. 5; Alec Ryrie, *Being Protestant in Reformation Britain* (Oxford, 2013), ch. 2.

uncommon in Scottish witchcraft narratives,[26] and it was even more uncommon for the summoner to be a woman.[27] Summoning spirits required a great degree of magical knowledge and skill. The practitioner needed to know the right combination of words and spells. Andro Man, for example, allegedly summoned his spirit-guide, Christsonday, by uttering the word 'Benedicte'.[28] Meanwhile the accused witch, Alexander Hamilton, claimed that the Devil told him to use a 'fir stick' and say rise 'foul thief' while beating the ground, in order to raise him.[29]

Margaret Dougal's confession presents us with an almost step-by-step guide as to how to summon the Devil, using a complex ritual. First, she turned the riddle (i.e. sieve) three times anticlockwise. This was a form of divination to locate stolen property. It normally involved balancing the riddle on a pair of shears.[30] Dougal then drew a score around the riddle to act as a magical barrier to protect her from the Devil. Next, to raise him, she uttered the phrase 'Get up you doge', whilst banging her heel on the ground, and then read either verse 19, or verse 9 of chapter 19 of the book of Revelation backward.[31] Both verses may have been used, but it is more likely that Dougal read verse 19, partly because magical practitioners favoured repetition, and partly because the text of verse 19 references 'the beast', whereas verse 9 makes no explicit or implicit reference to the Devil. To dismiss the Devil, Dougal was to cast three black feathers, which seem to have represented lives given to him, on the assumption that he needed a life as payment for each negotiation.

What was Dougal's own understanding, or experience, of the result of the ritual that she had performed? Did she really experience the presence of the Devil, or was she a clever actor who understood what she had to do to persuade her fellow servants that she had done so? Or was it a mixture, in the sense that she may have experienced the Devil in some way, but saw no problem with improving a genuine story with some amateur dramatics? That it was indeed a mixture is suggested by the articulate answers she gave

26 For examples, see L.A. Yeoman and M.B. Wasser (eds), 'The Trial of Geillis Johnstone for Witchcraft, 1614', in *The Miscellany of the Scottish History Society*, vol. XIII (Edinburgh, 2004), 83–146; L. Normand and G. Roberts (eds), *Witchcraft in Early Modern Scotland. James VI's Demonology and the North Berwick Witches* (Exeter, 2000), 148; E.J. Cowan, 'Witch Persecution and Folk Belief in Lowland Scotland: The Devil's Decade', in Goodare et al. (eds), *Witchcraft and Belief in Early Modern Scotland*, 71–95.

27 J. Goodare, 'Men and the Witch-Hunt in Scotland', in A. Rowlands (ed.), *Witchcraft and Masculinities in Early Modern Europe* (Basingstoke, 2009), 149–70 at p. 156.

28 Cowan, 'Witch Persecution and Folk Belief', 84

29 J. Maidment (ed.), *The Spottiswoode Miscellany*, 2 vols (Edinburgh, 1844), ii, p. 62.

30 L. Henderson, '"Detestable Slaves of the Devil": Changing Ideas of Witchcraft in Sixteenth-Century Scotland', in E.J. Cowan and L. Henderson (eds), *A History of Everyday Life in Medieval Scotland, 1000 to 1600* (Edinburgh, 2011), 240.

31 See p. 155 for a discussion of this in the transcription.

during her interrogation. Firstly, there is Dougal's own comment that she never meant to have personally raised the Devil, and the confident, list-like discussion of the ritual she gave, potentially to her fellow-servants, at the beginning of the text suggests that she knew the right words to *convince* them that she had summoned the Devil. However, there is perhaps more evidence to suggest that Dougal did believe she had a visionary experience. The text indicates that, like some visionaries' experiences with spirits, her actual encounter originated involuntarily. When she claimed to her fellow-servant, Jean, that she had accidently summoned the Devil in corporeal form, Dougal stated that 'she wes so extremly terrified that she wes lyke to faint'. Hereafter, her relationship with the Devil proved to be traumatic.

Moreover, visionaries and magical practitioners who claimed to have had actual relationships and experiences with supernatural entities, normally did so based on some emotional encounter that was accompanied by phenomenological and psychological experiences.[32] In the second half of her confession Dougal repeated the ritual to her interrogator, and unlike the list-like description she gave to her fellow servants at the beginning, this time she retold the events with emotion and described psychological and physiological experiences. Firstly, like visionaries, Dougal claimed to have both seen and heard the Devil, and reiterated the direct speech that she had with him. The fact that she could give precise details of the Devil's various humanoid forms – and bearing in mind that her interrogator may not have been learned in demonological theory – further supports the argument that she did believe she had encountered him, and that her confession was not embellished by an authority figure.

In addition, Dougal's relationship with the Devil was based on 'affective response',[33] like the complex and emotional relationships that accused witches and magical practitioners formed with their spirit-guides: if the encounter with the spirit fostered positive emotions, then the relationship sometimes developed over time. However, if the encounter fostered negative emotions, then the relationship might have been short-lived or abandoned altogether. But in both instances, the magical practitioner or witch believed that they had encountered the spirit. Dougal's confession contains some references to her feeling afraid or feared when interacting with the Devil. For instance, when Dougal believed she had summoned the Devil for the first time, she came out 'shaking and trembling and looking alse pale as the clay'; when she summoned him on a second occasion, she 'wes much affrighted' not to transgress the magic score; and when she wanted to banish the Devil

32 J. Goodare, 'Visionaries and Nature Spirits', in B. Mosia (ed.), *Book of Scientific Works of the Conference of Belief Narrative Network of ISFNR, 1–4 October 2014, Zugdidi* (Zugdidi, GA, 2015), 102–16, at p. 105 and p. 108; Wilby, *Cunning Folk*, 244–52.

33 Wilby, *Visions*, 448.

from her, she had misplaced her feathers 'through fear', possibly because she felt scared of him. Dougal's negative emotional responses suggest that, even though her relationship with the Devil may have been short-lived, they underscore the likelihood that she believed she had encountered him.

Conclusions

This manuscript allows researchers to gain some insight into the inner life of a skilled magical practitioner. First and foremost, this edition has given a name to Margaret Dougal: it has restored a sense of dignity to a woman who had simply been known as 'the servant' or 'Irish maid'. While Law's popular commentary has given researchers some insight into the case, this edition has, for the first time, revealed Dougal's 'voice'. As mentioned, her confession was generally unmediated, and without the hindering scribal patterns that far too often permeated typical witchcraft confessions. It is her 'voice' that dominates the text, thus allowing us to examine her emotional state, consider her agenda, and speculate on her experiences. In this sense, her confession separates itself from typical witchcraft narratives that contain the more dominating voices of the interrogator and the scribe – all of which make it hard for researchers to understand the mentality and thought processes of seventeenth-century common folk. Other scholars might find it worthwhile extracting other voices from the text. Among Dougal's voice are the voices of the servants; the first two paragraphs, in particular, seem to be an amalgamation of Dougal's confession and the servants' witness testimony.

This edition can now help scholars pursue a wide array of themes from the perspective of Dougal herself: one of which concerns her identity. It is clear from the record in the *RPC* that she was investigated for a crime, potentially witchcraft, so to some extent we can think of her as an accused witch. Conversely, there is her own statement that she learnt her magical skills from Rev. Dr Alexander Colville in Ireland. Considering this statement, and our brief discussion of popular magical practices and visionary experiences, Dougal may well have identified as a magical practitioner, especially since her relationship with the Devil resembled the type of relationship magical practitioners formed with their spirit-guides. Scholars may be interested in pursuing this connection further, as the David Laing manuscript collection contains more references to magical practitioners interacting with spirits.[34] Moreover, this edition of her confession contributes to the recent scholarship examining the Devil in early modern Scotland, not only from the perspective of demonology, but from religious spirituality: the type of

34 An Ulster minister writes of a young girl's torment and hallucinations. He is unsure if she is communicating with angels or demons. See EUL, Laing MSS, I. 27.

spirituality which has traditionally been seen from the point of view of the godly, not accused witches, magical practitioners and ordinary folk.

Editorial Method

The manuscript is foliated. The transcript preserves all the original capitalisation, but a few other words have been capitalised: for instance, 'Devil', 'Bible' and 'New Testament'. Both abbreviations and contracted words have been silently expanded and extended. Thorn has been transcribed as 'th'; yogh has been transcribed as 'y'. The letters v/u/w have been modernised. Marginal notes have been transferred to footnotes. Scribal corrections have been retained. Punctuation has been silently modernised, allowing researchers to follow the manuscript, especially when direct speech is referenced; paragraphing has been modernised. The title of the edition is editorial.

TRANSCRIPTION

Ane accompt of the raising the Devill by a servant in generall major Montgommeries[1] house in the West country; in February 1682.

[f. 208r] Upon the 10 day of Februarie 1682 Margaret Dowgall confessed that shee raised the Devell; the manner and circumstances of the whole matter are as followeth.

Their wes some linnings[2] in the house lost, and shee by some of the servant women wes blamed for taking of them. Att quhich shee (haveing losed something herself) wes mightily enraged, and said in the kitchine befor noon, in the audeance and presence of two or three persons,[3] that ere twelve a clock att night shee wold know who had taken thesse linnings. Quhairupon shee began and showed them how shee could raise the Devell, and taking the coall ridle[4] in her hand said, 'I must put it three tymes wither shins about, then casting it doun on the ground I must draw a score about it, and if any person please to come in within the score and grip closs to my back, they may see without any danger'. Then said shee, 'I am to have three black feathers to cast in his face, but if he gett three tymes withershins about he will take the person it self'. Next shee said, 'I must chap with my heell upon the ground saying gett up you doge, haveing my book all the whyle by me. Then flinging the feathers in his face, I must knock again and say "be gone you doge", and so he will goe away'.

After this, about 3 a clock, shee told the litle boyes in the kitchen that she wes goeing into the brew house to raise the Devell, and bid them have a dishfull of watter readie. And quhen shee knocked att the door to give them warning, if they wold then look into the watter they should see both the sunne & the moon (though shee not giving them warning, they saw no such thing haveing tryed it). Befor shee went into the brew house, shee asked of her fellow servant, Jean Auld, the key of the door, quhich shee gave her. Shee asked for the ridle and ~~the~~ her New Testament; she [Jean] said they wer both in the brew house. The said Jean leaving her for some space, the litle boyes that wer in the kitchen saw that shee was in the brew house and the door shut, though twice in end shee came out of the brew house to the kitchine,

1 This was Major-General Robert Montgomerie, of Eglinton heritage, who died two years later in 1684. For more on Montgomerie, see *ODNB* [https://doi.org/10.1093/ref:odnb/19064].

2 Linens.

3 She may have been speaking to her fellow servants or someone senior in the household. But it is unlikely that she was speaking to Montgomerie at this point.

4 Sieve.

all shakeing and trembling, girning[5] with her mouth, as the boyes affirmed, and in a great confusion called 'Quickly pull me some feathers out of the black cocks taill', quhich the boy did. The said Jean, comeing afterward with some straw to the door, saw her goeing in to the kitchine, and looking into the door shee saw the ridle lying flat and the Bible with its face dounward, lying upon the back of the ridle. And Dowgall comeing in to the brew house, shaking and trembling and looking alse pale as the clay shee said, 'O I am feared if I wanted[6] all the world after this I shall never raise him again', quhich amazed the poor lasse, saying 'What sayes thou? Hast thou raised the Devell?' 'Yes', said shee, 'and I pray the[e] hold of[f] that place, for I knocked upon it with my heell'. In end she wes so extremly terrified that shee wes lyke to faint, and Jean offering her a drink, shee took a litle of it and grew somewhat better, though she wes yet much consternate[7] and frighted. For, goeing into the kitchen, shee could not sitt or stand in on[e] place, bot sometymes leaning herself, att other tymes running out and in again.

The lasse desyreing her, shee cast her self over upon the her bed, and some of the servants giving me[8] notice, shee acknowledged to me, upon demand, that being provocked with the slander of stealling some cloaths, shee wes moved in her passion to attempt that hellish art of casting the ridle & raising the Devell to inform her about thesse things lost. Although shee did not expect that Satan ~~did~~ should [have] personally appeared to her, bot only shee wold try what wold be the event of thesse charmes with her, quhich shee had severall tymes seen others use in raising up that fowll spirit.[9] However, shee said that in effect he did appear three

tymes upon her useing of thesse charmes viz: shee took the ridle, and wheelling it 3 tymes withershins about, laid it doun on the ground, and haveing read a part of the 19 verse of the 19 chaipter[10] of the [f.208v] Revelation backward, shee laid the Bible upon the ridle.

5 Showing teeth, or snarling.
6 I.e. lacked.
7 Dismayed.
8 The 'me' may imply when Major-General Montgomerie became involved in hearing her confession.
9 The Devil.
10 The King James Bible, chapter 19, verse 19 of Revelation reads, 'And I saw the beast, and the kings of the earth, and their armies, gathered together to make war against him that sat on the horse, and against his army'. In the left-hand margin of the text it states, 'Another relation calls it the 9 v[erse] of that chapter'. Chapter 19, verse 9 reads, 'And he saith unto me, Write, Blessed are they which are called unto the marriage supper of the Lamb. And he saith unto me, These are the true sayings of God'. As mentioned earlier, Law incorrectly identifies chapter 9, verse 19 (9:19). Although this combination of chapter and verse is not mentioned in the manuscript, the text is still noteworthy. Chapter 9, verse 19, reads: 'For

The first tyme shee called him up to the midle[11] with thesse words, stamping with her heell upon the ground, 'Get up you doge'. Upon quhich the floor of the house quaked and, as shee thought, did open quhair ~~she~~ he rose. He had upon his head ane old cape,[12] some litle black hair sticking out, and some cloathes upon him. Then she quickly asked him saying, 'I want[13] such things, who hath them?' And he giveing her some answer, shee flung three black feathers in his face (quhich shee had newly pulled out of a quick cocks taill), saying, 'Begon you doge', quhairupon he disappeared. By this shee wes much affrighted, yet not dareing to transgresse the score till shee had made an end of asking him all, least he should have taken herself, shee began and read a litle more backward. And then on the second tyme shee called upon him as formerly, and he did ryse more then to the midle. And after shee had asked her question, and he giveing some answer, shee wanted her feathers through fear,[14] quhairupon with ane gapeing mouth and cloven tongue he said, 'If thou hast nothing to cast att my mouth, I have something to cast att thine'. Bot after some seeking, shee gott the feathers, and casting them att him ~~shee~~ he evanished.

It is very observeable that about this tyme the servants of the house affirm they saw the doges running about the house howlling and making a great noyse; on[e] of them creeping in att a window, and another goeing to the back of the house quhair she wes, and putting his mouth att a hole in the wall, made a great noyse. But calling him up the 3rd tyme, he rose up in all his body, being naked save on[e] legge, his foot being formed lyke a swynes,[15] haveing withall a black taill behind. And shee bidding him 'Begone Judas', he evanished, saying that if he gott no other prey than the feathers, the next tyme he rose he would take herself.

After shee had told me all this, I asked her how shee could lay the Devell without giving him a lyfe. She answered me, 'Doe ye not know that their is blood and lyfe in a new pulled soft feather?' I asked her if shee wes not affraid least the Devell should take her away and God give her up to him, sieing shee adored and worshipped him, speaking to him so familiarly. Shee said that 'Ministers wold doe the same', and that though shee did such a thing, yet shee alwayes keeped her heart and trust to God. Shee told me moreover

their power is in their mouth, and in their tails: for their tails were like unto serpents, and had heads, and with them they do hurt'.

11 I.e. middle of the ground.

12 Cap.

13 I.e. lack.

14 She was so scared, that in her confusion she had forgotten about the need for her feathers, and mislaid them.

15 Pig.

that shee had been witness to the useing of this art many tymes in Ireland, and that old Doctor Colvill[16] learned her and severall others, bot shee never did it herself befor now.

[f.209r] Irving Februarie 11th[17] 1682
Upon ane report that on[e] Margaret Dowgall had upon the 10 of the said moneth used the devellish art of turning the ridle, raising the Devell, and consulting him about stollen goods, the minister and elders conceiving it their dewtie to enquyre in and anent the truth of the said matter, did send some of their number with the minister to examine the said person viz, Allane Cumming, late provest; Hugh Montgomerie, late bailyie; Thomas McGown and John Gray, merchands, who with Mr John Stirling[18] their minister came to the house of Archibald Dunlope, smyth, and called befor them the said Margaret, who confessed in their presence as followeth viz,[19] &c. It differs not much from the former narrative.[20]

16 See above, n. 12.

17 The manuscript here reads 'ijth'. Normally 'ij' would be 'two'. But the text mentions 'the 10 of the said month', so this date must be later than the 10th. It seems the scribe was momentarily forgetting the difference between roman 'i' and arabic '1'

18 This was the indulged minister of Irvine, John Stirling (1621[?]–83), who had been the minister of Irvine since 1676. See H. Scott, *Fasti Ecclesiae Scoticanae: The Succession of Ministers in the Church of Scotland from the Reformation*, 7 vols (Edinburgh, 1915–28), iii, p. 99.

19 The first scribe stopped writing after the comma, implying that he intended to continue copying his notes.

20 The final words were added in a different hand and in much darker ink. In referring the reader to the 'former narrative', it seems the second scribe did not copy the official confession that Dougal gave before the minister and elders on 11 February. In addition, roughly two-thirds of the page on f. 209r is blank.

ANGELS, GHOSTS AND JOURNEYS TO THE AFTERLIFE: THE 'VERY RARE AND MEMORABLE' STORIES OF JAMES COWAN (1707–10)

Edited by Martha McGill

INTRODUCTION

In the early eighteenth century, the Scottish Presbyterian James Cowan sent three letters to the Glasgow minister and historian Robert Wodrow (1679–1734).[1] The letters described four 'rare and memorable' occurrences: two apparitions of angels; an encounter with a ghost; and the case of a woman who died, journeyed to Heaven, and subsequently revived. The first two letters are undated, but are likely from 1707. This is based on their place within Wodrow's chronologically arranged folio of materials, as well as a reference to James Grierson as being 'lately ordained minister in Tingwall', which happened in September 1706.[2] The third letter was written on 26 April 1710.[3] Three of the four stories actually stemmed from England, but they had circulated in Scotland. Cowan received them from other Scottish ministers, and claimed that they had evoked interest in numerous Scottish gentlemen. This is all the more notable because the stories ranged from being theologically dubious to outright heretical by the standards of Calvinist orthodoxy. This introductory essay will discuss the stories themselves, consider why they came to be circulated, and analyse what they reveal about perceptions of the supernatural world in early eighteenth-century Scotland.[4]

In the last few decades, diverse academic publications have explored the importance of supernatural beliefs within early modern culture. There are

1 National Library of Scotland, Edinburgh (NLS), Wod Fol XXVIII, fos 222–225; Wod.Lett. Qu.II, fo. 143.

2 H. Scott, *Fasti Ecclesiæ Scoticanæ*, 7 vols (Edinburgh, 1915–28), vii, 291.

3 I am grateful to Clare Loughlin for bringing this letter to my attention.

4 In early modern European demonology, 'supernatural' referred to God and his direct actions; 'preternatural' was used for other beings or events that were outside of the natural order. However, as Scottish discussions of these topics did not generally employ the terms 'preternatural' and 'supernatural', I have chosen not to insist on the distinction, and instead to use the term 'supernatural' in its modern sense. For more on this distinction, see S. Clark, *Thinking with Demons: The Idea of Witchcraft in Early Modern Europe* (Oxford, 1997), ch. 10.

numerous excellent studies of Scottish witchcraft.[5] Works have discussed fairies, the Devil, second sight, folk beliefs and ghosts.[6] However, several areas remain under-researched – including angels, which appear in all four of Cowan's stories.[7] For broader contextualisation of the Scottish cases, it is helpful to look to literature on England or Europe. Multiple scholars have examined early modern literary, religious, folkloric and natural philosophical discussions concerning angels.[8] Ghosts have been the subject of several excellent studies, and there are various publications discussing early modern conceptions of the afterlife (although the theme of heavenly journeys has not been widely analysed).[9] Collectively, these works have demonstrated how

5 C. Larner, *Enemies of God: The Witch-Hunt in Scotland* (London, 1981); J. Goodare (ed.), *The Scottish Witch-Hunt in Context* (Manchester, 2002); J. Goodare *et al.* (eds), *Witchcraft and Belief in Early Modern Scotland* (Basingstoke, 2008); B.P. Levack, *Witch-Hunting in Scotland: Law, Politics and Religion* (Abingdon, 2008); J. Goodare (ed.), *Scottish Witches and Witch-Hunters* (Basingstoke, 2013).

6 L. Henderson and E.J. Cowan, *Scottish Fairy Belief: A History* (East Linton, 2001); M.D. Brock, *Satan and the Scots: The Devil in Post-Reformation Scotland, c.1560–1700* (Abingdon, 2016); M. Hunter (ed.), *The Occult Laboratory: Magic, Science, and Second Sight in Late Seventeenth-Century Scotland* (Woodbridge, 2001); L. Henderson, *Witchcraft and Folk Belief in the Age of Enlightenment: Scotland, 1670–1740* (Basingstoke, 2016); M. McGill, *Ghosts in Enlightenment Scotland* (Woodbridge, 2018). See also L. Henderson (ed.), *Fantastical Imaginations: The Supernatural in Scottish History and Culture* (Edinburgh, 2009); J. Goodare and M. McGill (eds), *The Supernatural in Early Modern Scotland* (Manchester, forthcoming, 2021).

7 I have offered some preliminary thoughts on Scottish angels elsewhere: M. McGill, 'Angels, Devils, and Discernment in Early Modern Scotland', in M.D. Brock *et al.* (eds), *Knowing Demons, Knowing Spirits* (Basingstoke, 2018); M. McGill, 'Angels in Early Modern Scotland', in Goodare and McGill (eds), *The Supernatural in Early Modern Scotland*.

8 See, for example, D. Harkness, *John Dee's Conversations with Angels: Cabala, Alchemy, and the End of Nature* (Cambridge, 1999); P. Marshall and A. Walsham (eds), *Angels in the Early Modern World* (Cambridge, 2006); J. Raymond, *Milton's Angels: The Early-Modern Imagination* (Oxford, 2010); A. Walsham, 'Invisible Helpers: Angelic Intervention in Post-Reformation England', *Past & Present* 208 (2010), 77–130; J. Raymond (ed.), *Conversations with Angels: Essays Towards a History of Spiritual Communication, 1100–1700* (Basingstoke, 2011); C. Copeland and J. Machielsen (eds), *Angels of Light? Sanctity and the Discernment of Spirits in the Early Modern Period* (Leiden, 2012); L. Sangha, *Angels and Belief in England, 1480–1700* (London, 2012); D. Oldridge, *The Supernatural in Tudor and Stuart England* (Abingdon, 2016), ch. 5.

9 Useful works include K. Thomas, *Religion and the Decline of Magic: Studies in Popular Beliefs in Sixteenth- and Seventeenth-Century England* (London, 1971), ch. 19; R.C. Finucane, *Ghosts: Appearances of the Dead and Cultural Transformation* (Amherst, NY, 1996); P. Marshall, *Beliefs and the Dead in Reformation England* (Oxford, 2002); O. Davies, *The Haunted: A Social History of Ghosts* (New York, 2007); S. Handley, *Visions of an Unseen World: Ghost Beliefs and Ghost Stories in Eighteenth-Century England* (London, 2007); P. Kapitaniak, *Spectres, Ombres et Fantômes : Discours et Représentations Dramatiques en Angleterre, 1576–1642* (Paris, 2008); T. Chesters, *Ghost Stories in Late Renaissance France: Walking by Night* (Oxford, 2011); Oldridge, *The Supernatural in Tudor and Stuart England*, ch. 6; S. Owens, *The Ghost: A Cultural History* (London, 2017); P.C. Almond, *Heaven and Hell in Enlightenment England* (Cambridge, 1994); C. McDannell and B. Lang, *Heaven: A History*, 2nd edn (New Haven, CT, 2001); P. Marshall, *Invisible Worlds: Death, Religion and the Supernatural in England, 1500–1700* (London, 2017).

the study of the supernatural can reflect more widely on patterns of social development.

There are various sources that offer a window into early modern Scottish beliefs about magical powers and beings. The witch trials contain a wealth of information about sixteenth- and seventeenth-century folk beliefs regarding the supernatural world, and the authorities' demonisation thereof. Ballads, broadsides and pamphlets can be informative, as can kirk session records, letters and visionaries' diaries. The other significant body of sources is educated individuals' records of supernatural stories. The natural philosopher George Sinclair published various accounts in his *Satans Invisible World Discovered* (1685), and Wodrow collected cases that he hoped one day to publish.[10] In the eighteenth century, men including Edward Lhuyd, Martin Martin, John Fraser and Theophilus Insulanus recorded Highland beliefs.[11] The nineteenth and early twentieth centuries saw a surge of antiquarians collating accounts of local folklore, although these stories can rarely be traced back in time with any degree of certainty.[12] Finally, stories of supernatural experiences increasingly appeared in periodicals and other printed works from the late eighteenth century. However, Cowan's letters are exceptionally rich and detailed sources; most stories were recounted in more concise terms. In addition, while many of the early antiquarians maintained a sceptical distance from the stories they reported, Cowan presents a set of stories that educated people were prepared to take seriously.

★★★★★

Cowan came from a family of Presbyterians. His father does not seem to have been a minister, but Cowan describes him as an associate of James Guthrie,

10 George Sinclair, *Satans Invisible World Discovered* (Edinburgh, 1685); Robert Wodrow, *Analecta: Or Materials for a History of Remarkable Providences Mostly Relating to Scotch Ministers and Christians*, ed. M. Leishman, 4 vols (Edinburgh, 1842–3).

11 J. L. Campbell and D. Thomson, *Edward Lhuyd in the Scottish Highlands, 1699–1700* (Oxford, 1963); Martin Martin, *A Description of the Western Isles of Scotland* (London, 1703); John Fraser, 'John Fraser's Deuteroskopia', in Hunter (ed.), *The Occult Laboratory*; Theophilus Insulanus, *A Treatise on the Second Sight, Dreams and Apparitions* (Edinburgh, 1763).

12 The numerous examples include A.M. Grant, *Essays on the Superstitions of the Highlanders of Scotland*, 2 vols (London, 1811); W.G. Stewart, *The Popular Superstitions and Festive Amusements of the Highlanders of Scotland* (Edinburgh, 1823); R. Chambers, *Traditions of Edinburgh* (Edinburgh, 1824); J. MacCulloch, *The Highlands and Western Isles of Scotland*, 4 vols (London, 1824); W. Scott, *Letters on Demonology and Witchcraft* (London, 1830); J.G. Dalyell, *The Darker Superstitions of Scotland: Illustrated from History and Practice* (Edinburgh, 1834); H. Miller, *Scenes and Legends of the North of Scotland: Or, The Traditional History of Cromarty*, 2nd edn (London, 1850); J. F. Campbell, *Popular Tales of the West Highlands*, 4 vols (Edinburgh, 1860–2); A. Carmichael, *Carmina Gadelica*, 2 vols (Edinburgh, 1900); J.G. Campbell, *The Gaelic Otherworld: Superstitions of the Highlands and the Islands*, ed. Ronald Black (Edinburgh, 2005).

the Covenanting minister who was executed in 1661.[13] Cowan himself was licensed by the Presbytery of Haddington in 1700. He thus became a probationer, permitted to preach but not to administer sacraments. The next step – a call to a parish and full ordination – usually took place within a couple of years, but Cowan was not ordained until 1717, when he became a minister in Dundonald, south Ayrshire.[14] In the intervening years he seems to have preached in various locations. He mentions having an 'intimat com[rade] at the profession in Edinburgh', and also speaks of working in Brechin 'upon the supplies' – that is, serving temporarily in vacant holdings. It is possible that Cowan was in poor health, or simply not very good at his job. Following his long-delayed ordination, the kirk session records note his presence at only one meeting, on 13 October 1717.[15] There are no surviving records for 1722–3, but on 5 February 1722 Wodrow wrote that Cowan was to demit, 'not being advised to abide a tryall'. The *Fasti Ecclesiae Scoticanae* records that he stepped down in 1723 'on account of inability or unfitness', and was given an allowance by the parish.[16]

Robert Wodrow was born in Glasgow in 1679. He was the son of James Wodrow, a professor of divinity in the University of Glasgow, and Margaret Hair, daughter of minor laird William Hair from Kilbarchan, Renfrewshire. Having studied at Glasgow University, he was elected to the parish of Eastwood in 1703. Wodrow is best known for his partisan record of Presbyterian persecution, *The History of the Sufferings of the Church of Scotland*, published in two volumes in 1721 and 1722.[17] However, from 1701 he was also engaged in compiling a history of God's favours bestowed on Scotland: *Analecta: Or Materials for a History of Remarkable Providences*. This work remained unfinished when Wodrow died in 1734, but the surviving materials are valuable. They include descriptions of political events, notes on fellow ministers, points of natural history, edifying deathbed scenes, and accounts of monstrous portents and apparitions. For the most part, Wodrow's information came from his parishioners and fellow ministers. He maintained far-reaching networks of correspondence, and his interest in unusual occurrences was probably widely known among early eighteenth-century Scottish ministers.[18]

13 Wodrow, *Analecta*, i, 108; ii, 137.

14 Scott, *Fasti*, iii, 36.

15 National Records of Scotland, Edinburgh (NRS), Dundonald kirk session minutes, CH2/104/2.

16 Wodrow, *Analecta*, ii, 358; Scott, *Fasti*, iii, 36.

17 For more on Wodrow's life, see L.A. Yeoman, 'Wodrow, Robert (1679–1734)', *Oxford DNB*, online edn (Oxford University Press, 2004), https://doi.org/10.1093/ref:odnb/29819 [accessed 2 February 2019].

18 For his correspondence, see Robert Wodrow, *Early Letters of Robert Wodrow, 1698–1709*, ed. L.W. Sharp (Edinburgh, 1937); Robert Wodrow, *The Correspondence of the Rev. Robert Wodrow*, ed. T. M'Crie, 3 vols (Edinburgh, 1842).

Wodrow and Cowan seem to have been on friendly terms. The 1707 letters are headed with R. D. S. (Reverend Dear Sir). The use of the abbreviation suggests a casual correspondence between equals. The subscription is similarly casual; Cowan gives only a contracted 'I am Yours'.[19] In addition, Cowan's margins are modest, and he leaves only horizontal space (not vertical space) before his subscriptions. When addressing social superiors, large margins and significant vertical space before subscriptions were marks of deference.[20] The 1710 letter is somewhat different. Here the paper is quarto-sized, and the letter is signed and dated. The subscription is given in a more conventional format:

I am
R. D. S.

Yours
J. Cowan

The repetition of 'R. D. S.' was polite, as was the use of new lines – but again, we have the abbreviation, and no significant use of vertical space.[21]

Also in 1707, Cowan contributed a passage to Wodrow's *Analecta*. He recounted about twenty stories of strange providences, including cases of prophesying, charming, religious dreams or visions, and appearances of ghosts and the Devil.[22] The 1707 letters could perhaps be read as an addendum. They contain no preamble, no personal news, no date and no signature. There is also no seal or address, and the letters are written on folio-sized paper – that is, large sheets that were rarely sent through the post in this period.[23] Wodrow stored the accounts in a folio of sources, rather than among his correspondence. We can speculate that the letters were delivered in person, and produced specifically in the interests of preservation, perhaps by mutual agreement between Cowan and Wodrow.

However, the 1710 letter suggests that this deliberate preservation was unusual. This letter also has no address or seal, but was not delivered by Cowan himself. Cowan wrote the letter because he had been hindered from

19 On the proscription of abbreviations when writing to superiors, see Antoine de Courtin as quoted in J. Gibson, 'Significant Space in Manuscript Letters', *The Seventeenth Century* 12 (1997), 1–10, at p. 3; S. Walker, 'The Manners of the Page: Prescription and Practice in the Visual Organization of Correspondence', *The Huntington Library Quarterly* 66 (2003), 307–29, at p. 309.

20 J. Daybell, *The Material Letter in Early Modern England: Manuscript Letters and the Culture and Practices of Letter-Writing, 1512–1635* (Basingstoke, 2012), 91–5; Gibson, 'Significant Space in Manuscript Letters', 1–5; Walker, 'The Manners of the Page', 309–22.

21 On the repetition, see Daybell, *The Material Letter in Early Modern England*, 91.

22 Wodrow, *Analecta*, i, 98–118. The manuscript version is at NLS, Wod.Anal.I, 139–182. Only pp. 139–44 are in Cowan's hand.

23 Daybell, *The Material Letter in Early Modern England*, 99–100.

visiting. It thus replaced what was presumably a more common mode of oral communication. There are further reasons to believe that their relationship was generally sustained in person: I have not come across any additional correspondence, but Wodrow apparently had a continued interest in Cowan, noting in 1722 that Cowan had stood down from his post. Cowan's letters seem to offer insight into a mode of discourse – the telling of extraordinary and theologically questionable stories – that most usually took place orally, and almost never made it into the carefully regulated world of print.

★★★★★

To better understand why the stories might have been uncomfortable territory for committed Protestants, we turn now to a more thorough analysis of their contents. The first letter is about an apparition that was clearly meant to be read as an angel. Already, Cowan was on thin ice. After the Reformation, theologians had reformulated the workings of the world of spirits. Most apparitions became manifestations of the Devil. James VI was a proponent of this way of thinking, declaring in his 1597 *Daemonologie* that since Biblical times 'miracles, visions, prophecies, and appearances of angels or good spirites are ceased'.[24] The witch trials also reflect this heavy focus on demonic agency. Accused witches described encounters with fairies, ghosts and the folkloric angel Christsonday, only to be told that they had actually been cavorting with the Devil.[25] There was also growing doubt over whether individuals had guardian angels. Luther was happy to allow for guardian angels, but Calvin declared that 'whether individual angels have been assigned to individual believers for their protection, I dare not affirm with confidence'.[26] Writing in 1656, the Aberdeen theologian William Guild explicitly denied the existence of individual guardian angels, and implied that this was the orthodox Protestant position.[27]

Nevertheless, the idea of angels as a protective force persisted in early modern Protestant culture. Historians such as Laura Sangha, Darren Oldridge and Alexandra Walsham have highlighted the persistence of the protective

24 James VI, *Daemonologie, in Forme of Ane Dialogue*, in J. Craigie and A. Law (eds), *Minor Prose Works of King James VI and I* (Edinburgh, 1982), bk. ii, ch. vii, 37.

25 See J. Goodare, 'Boundaries of the Fairy Realm in Scotland', in K.E. Olsen and J.R. Veenstra (eds), *Airy Nothings: Imagining the Otherworld of Faerie from the Middle Ages to the Age of Reason* (Leiden, 2014), 144–9.

26 E. Cameron, 'Angels, Demons and Everything in Between: Spiritual Beings in Early Modern Europe', in Copeland and Machielsen (eds.), *Angels of Light?*, 36–7; John Calvin, *Calvin: Institutes of the Christian Religion*, ed. J.T. McNeill, trans. F.L. Battles, 2 vols (Philadelphia, PA, 1960), i, bk i, ch. 14:7, p. 167.

27 William Guild, *An Answer to a Popish Pamphlet Called The Touch-Stone of the Reformed Gospell* (Aberdeen, 1656), 214–5.

angel in early modern England.[28] In Scotland, the idea of protective angels was similarly engrained. Sermons and religious tracts described angels watching over humankind, an idea that was reinforced in imagery. Protestant theologians were dubious about the orthodoxy of visual images of angels in church buildings, but some paintings and statues remained, and angels were often represented on tombstones.[29] Wodrow's providences also featured multiple cases of ministers or good Christians being rescued from difficult situations by angelic helpers. The well-known Covenanter Samuel Rutherford was one example. He was said to have fallen down a well when he was about four years old, only to be pulled out by a 'bonny young man'. As there was nobody else in the area at the time, his family concluded that this rescuer was 'noe doubt ane angell'.[30]

The angel in Cowan's account appeared to the minister David Thomson. The letter describes Thomson as being of the 'Episcopall persuasion', although he seems to have worked within the Church of Scotland from his ordination in 1678 to his death in 1702 or 1703, so both before and after the 1689 reinstatement of Presbyterianism.[31] Cowan explained that Thomson was a 'sound Calvinist', and that his father had been a 'zealous Presbiterian minister', thus underlining that he was worthy of divine aid despite (not because of) his Episcopalian leanings. The divine aid came in the form of a 'handsome young gentleman' on horseback. The gentleman guided Thomson across a flooded river, and emerged untouched by the water. He then regaled Thomson with a 'heavenly discourse', predicted that Thomson would die from a fever in his fiftieth year, and vanished.

Angels were understood to be spiritual substances, but they could take on aerial bodies.[32] They generally appeared as beautiful young men (or occasionally children), and could vanish. The fact that the gentleman did not get wet was another clue as to his identity. Around two centuries previously, Paracelsus (1493–1541) had explained:

> He who inherits God's wisdom walks on water without wetting his feet; for in the true art inherited from God, man is like an angel. But what will wet an angel? Nothing. Similarly, nothing will wet the wise man.[33]

The gentleman's prophecy is also indicative of supernatural wisdom. The *Fasti Ecclesiae Scoticanae* gives Thomson's birth and death dates as 1649 and

28 Sangha, *Angels and Belief in England*, esp. ch. 6; Oldridge, *The Supernatural in Tudor and Stuart England*, ch. 5; Walsham, 'Invisible Helpers'.

29 A. Walsham, 'Angels and Idols in England's Long Reformation', in Walsham and Marshall (eds), *Angels in the Early Modern World*; McGill, 'Angels in Early Modern Scotland'.

30 Wodrow, *Analecta*, i, 57; see also ii, 144, 180–1; iii, 89.

31 Scott, *Fasti*, v, 442.

32 There is an interesting discussion of angelic bodies in Raymond, *Milton's Angels*, 169–87.

33 Paracelsus, 'De fundamento scientiarum sapientiaeque', in J. Jacobi (ed.), *Paracelsus: Selected Writings* (Princeton, NJ, 1951), 163.

1702. Cowan writes that he died in 1703. These dates would suggest that Thomson actually lived to between fifty-two and fifty-four.[34] Nevertheless, Cowan records that Thomson's death came about exactly as foretold.

The question of whether or not angels could foretell the future was frequently discussed in Scottish universities in the late seventeenth and early eighteenth centuries.[35] A 1676 metaphysics compendium for students explained that angels knew everything apart from divine mysteries, the future, and the secrets of men's hearts.[36] In theses from 1679, Alexander Cockburn of St Andrews flatly denied that angels could see into the future, excepting those mysteries that God had revealed.[37] Other professors had more complex theories. Lecturing in the 1690s and early 1700s, the Glasgow university professor John Law explained that future events could be divided into three categories.[38] The first category constituted events determined wholly by constant, natural causes, such as lunar eclipses. Angels had perfect knowledge of these events. In the second category were events that had natural causes, but followed inconstant patterns. The air temperature in a given region, for example, would vary according to factors such as winds and storms. Law speculated that angels might be able to predict matters of this sort, but confessed himself uncertain. His colleague John Boyd, who adopted the same three categories, argued that angels were 'often' able to predict these events.[39] The third category comprised freely determined events, including human actions. Only God could foresee these events, and angels could not know of them unless by divine revelation. The date of a man's death would probably fall into the uncertain territory of the second category. In allowing the angel both to appear on earth, and to foretell a relatively complex question about future events, the story was making a bolder declaration about angelic powers than mainstream intellectual culture would generally allow.

*****

If Thomson's story was theologically questionable, the next account was outright heterodox. It concerned a ghost. Angels had a prominent role in

34 Scott, *Fasti*, v, 442.

35 On this issue, see also Cameron, 'Angels, Demons and Everything in Between', 28.

36 Scottish Catholic Archives, Aberdeen, LS/7/10, *Compendium Philosophiae Universae* (1676), sec. 'Compendium metaphysicum'.

37 Alexander Cockburn, *Theses Philosophicae* (Edinburgh, 1679), 9.

38 Glasgow University Library, Glasgow (GUL), MS Gen 873, notes from John Law (1704–5), sec. 'De angelis'. There are similar, earlier versions at GUL, MS 719 and Edinburgh University Library, Dc.8.18.

39 GUL, notes from John Boyd (1696), MS Gen 892, sec. 'Appendix posterior de Deo et angelis'.

Scripture, and thus could never be fully excised from Christian society. Ghosts were different. Defenders of ghosts referenced the biblical story of the witch of Endor, who raised the dead soul of the prophet Samuel.[40] However, Protestants often interpreted Samuel's spirit as an emanation of the Devil. A new orthodoxy was proposed by the Swiss theologian Ludwig Lavater, who published his *De Spectris, Lemuribus et Magnis Atque Insolitis Fragoribus* in 1569 (the English edition, *Of Ghostes and Spirites Walking by Nyght*, appeared in 1572). Lavater argued that most apparitions were the result of trickery, error, or the hallucinogenic fumes of melancholy. The rest were either angels or, more usually, demons.[41] Keith Thomas has written that in the sixteenth century, belief in ghosts became a 'shibboleth' by which Protestants and Catholics might be distinguished.[42] While subsequent historians have disputed this characterisation, there was certainly a fashion within Protestant culture to blame ghost belief on Catholic ignorance or fraudulence.[43]

Cowan's story concerned Mary Tubervill of Wayford, Somerset. Her brother, Daubeney Turbervill (1612–96), was a prominent oculist who treated Queen Anne, and corresponded with the natural philosopher Robert Boyle.[44] I have not found any record of Mary Turbervill's birth or death, but her will was made from St Andrew Holborn (London/Middlesex) in 1702.[45] She was a spinster, and after her brother's death she took over his medical practice. The astronomer and writer Walter Pope, who eulogised Daubeney Turbervill, declared that she had learned from her brother. He added that she practised with 'good Reputation and Success', and he personally held her skill in such high regard that he would 'rely upon her Advice rather than upon any Pretenders or Professors in *London*, or elsewhere'.[46]

According to Cowan's account, Turbervill took a country house fifty miles from London. The landlady of the house had recently died. One evening at twilight, the landlady's ghost appeared. She was hideous and clad in black. A 'noysome smell' was emanating from her. When Turbervill ventured to address her, she swore that if Turbervill had not spoken first 'I

40 1 Samuel 28.

41 Ludwig Lavater, *Of Ghostes and Spirites Walking by Nyght*, trans. Robert Harrison (London, 1572), 16.

42 Thomas, *Religion and the Decline of Magic*, 703.

43 See, for example, Marshall, *Beliefs and the Dead in Reformation England*, 234–42; Chesters, *Ghost Stories in Late Renaissance France*, 103–8; Helen L. Parish, *A Short History of the Reformation* (London, 2018), 150–2.

44 On Daubeney Turbervill, see B. Kaplan, 'Turberville, Daubeney (1612–1696), Physician and Oculist', *Oxford DNB*, online edn, https://doi.org/10.1093/ref:odnb/27823 [accessed 2 February 2019].

45 The National Archives, Kew (TNA), Prob 11/464/369. Her brother's will, made in 1696, can also be seen: TNA, Prob 11/431/438.

46 Walter Pope, *The Life of the Right Reverend Father in God, Seth, Lord Bishop of Salisbury* (London, 1697), 108.

would have torn yow, and thrown yow doun stairs'. She then revealed that she had broken a promise to her late husband by not donating money to the poor. Turbervill found the money hidden in the ceiling of the attic, and took it to the landlady's brother-in-law, who disposed of it as the couple had intended. Thereafter, the ghost reappeared in shining white, with a 'pleasant, beautifull and smileing countenance'. She answered some questions of Turbervill's, stating among other things that she had gone to neither Heaven nor Hell after her death, but had been 'under great horror'. She was then carried away to Heaven by a beautiful young child, in a blaze of glorious light and to the sound of exquisite music.

Other versions of this story seem to have been in circulation. In his 1696 *Miscellanies*, the antiquarian John Aubrey recorded a story, later also reported by Daniel Defoe:

> I must not forget an Apparition in my Country, which appear'd several times to Doctor *Turbervile's* Sister, at *Salisbury*; which is much talk'd of. One Marry'd a second Wife, and contrary to the Agreement and Settlement at the first Wife's Marriage, did wrong the Children by the first Venter. The Settlement was hid behind a Wainscot in the Chamber where the Doctor's Sister did lie: And the Apparition of the first Wife did discover it to her. By which means Right was done to the first Wife's Children. The Apparition told her that she Wandred in the Air, and was now going to God. Dr. *Turbervile* (Oculist) did affirm this to be true.[47]

The details of this story are different, but there are similarities in the ghost's objective, the hidden papers, and the explanation of the ghost's experience after death. A third account appears in a 1695 letter from James Garden, an Episcopalian professor of theology at Aberdeen, to Aubrey:

> I have heard a strange story (which is said to have fallen out 30 or 40 years agoe) of a woman in Salisbury, sister to on Dr. Towrson or Tuberville, I do not well remember his name a phisitian in that city, to whom another woman thatt had been dead 20 years appeared befor all in black, & told her that being in her life time wife to such a man then yet alive in Salisbury, shee had persuaded him to defraud his children of a former marriage in favour of her for which having repented befor her death shee had obtained pardon from God, shee pointed out to the living woman a place in the ceiling of the house wher the rights & evidents of the defrauded children were hid, & desired her to go to him that had been her husband & show him what shee had seen & heard, & desire him in her name, to repair that wrong done by her advice. the living woman obeyed her desire which being done the dead woman appeared to her again clothed in white & allowed her to propose sundry questions concerning religion & the state of the dead all which shee resolved, & particularly told her that she herself had been for 20 years past in a troublesom condition going up & down in the air over hils & dales woods & rivers, & was now going to

47 John Aubrey, *Miscellanies upon the Following Subjects* (London, 1696), 63–4; Daniel Defoe, *An Essay on the History and Reality of Apparitions* (London, 1727), 290–1.

> enjoy her God. If the story is true you cannot be ignorant of it in which case I desire to have a full & distinct relation of it from you.[48]

This account blends elements of Cowan's and Aubrey's versions of the story. Seemingly, Turbervill's account had been in circulation for some time, had travelled widely, and had gained and lost various details along the way.

Let us return to Cowan's version. In some respects, it was a conventional ghost story. There was a folkloric tradition that ghosts could not speak until spoken to. In a humorous 1787 account of popular 'superstitions', Francis Grose declared that ghosts – even the more garrulous female ones – could not begin conversations. He continued:

> The mode of addressing a Ghost is by commanding it, in the name of the Three Persons of the Trinity, to tell you who it is, and what is its business: this it may be necessary to repeat three times; after which it will, in a low and hollow voice, declare its satisfaction at being spoken to, and desire the party addressing it not to be afraid, for it will do him no harm.[49]

This was close to what happened in Turbervill's case: she addressed the ghost in the name of the Lord, and the ghost duly declared her satisfaction and promised not to hurt Turbervill. The ghost's assertion that she could not rest because she had been uncharitable was also a recognised theme in early modern ghost stories. A particularly well-known case was that of Mrs Bretton, recorded by Joseph Glanvill in 1681. Bretton was a lady of 'extraordinary piety' who had lived in Herefordshire, and who returned as a ghost to her maid to ensure that some lands were given to the poor.[50]

The process of questioning the ghost also appeared elsewhere. One example is the account of the ghost of Roger Boyle, first earl of Orrery and brother of Robert Boyle. This story must date from between 1679 (the death of Roger Boyle) and 1691 (the death of Robert Boyle), but it was recorded in 1708. In the story, the ghost of Roger Boyle appeared to one of the Boyle sisters to warn her that some merchants were about to abscond with money that the family had set aside for the poor. She reported the matter to Robert Boyle, who retrieved the money and told her to attempt to question the ghost should he return. When the ghost reappeared, the sister duly commanded him in the name of the Trinity to answer some questions. The ghost complained that his brother was 'too curiouse', but answered her questions: he was in an aerial body; it was impossible for him to explain the state of separate souls; and his own soul was with God.[51]

48 James Garden, 'James Garden's Letters to John Aubrey', in Hunter (ed.), *The Occult Laboratory*, 158.

49 Francis Grose, *Superstitions* in *A Provincial Glossary: With a Collection of Local Proverbs* (London, 1787), 12.

50 Joseph Glanvill, *Saducismus Triumphatus* (London, 1681), 238–41.

51 Wodrow, *Analecta*, i, 126–7.

Turbervill's questions were broadly similar. She began by asking whether the ghost was really the spirit of the landlady, or in fact an apparition of the Devil. The ghost assured Turbervill that she was the true deceased landlady. She further explained that after her death she had been 'under great horror till this business was dispatchd'. With Turbervill's help, she was now free to pass to Heaven. Turbervill also got information about 'some futur event', recalling the popular idea that ghosts had access to privileged knowledge. Another question was deemed 'too curious', and the ghost pinched her arm in punishment.

While some aspects of the story followed conventional patterns, others were decidedly unusual. Common to Aubrey's, Garden's and Cowan's versions of the story is the idea that the ghost had been unable to pass to Heaven or Hell after death. The implication seems to be that the ghost was caught in some torturous intermediate state, and could only be rescued through the assistance of a living person – an idea that is distinctly reminiscent of Catholic purgatorial theology. Even more striking is the way in which the ghost in Cowan's account changed in manner and appearance. Ghosts in early modern England and Scotland hardly ever wore black, and rarely had a smell. Nor did they tend to be aggressive. The landlady's ghost recalls medieval notions of revenants, or risen corpses, which were often ugly and violent.[52] The change in the ghost's clothing, from black to white, was mentioned by both Cowan and Garden. This detail also recalls medieval wisdom: ghosts were thought to undergo this change as they progressed through Purgatory, with their smell likewise improving.[53]

The persistence of purgatorial themes has been downplayed in the English historiography. Sasha Handley declares that Protestant authorities stripped ghost stories of their 'popish associations'. Peter Marshall writes that 'virtually all overt traces of purgatory … had disappeared from English ghost stories outside explicitly Catholic circles by the early part of the seventeenth century'. Owen Davies argues that in post-Reformation England the symbolism of ghosts changing from black to white clothing 'was obviously rendered redundant', while Belinda Lewis states that post-Reformation ghosts were almost invariably presented as coming from Heaven or Hell.[54]

52 On revenants, see N. Caciola, *Afterlives: The Return of the Dead in the Middle Ages* (Ithaca, NY, 2016), pt 2; W. Black, 'Animated Corpses and Bodies with Power in the Scholastic Age', in J. Rollo-Koster (ed.), *Death in Medieval Europe: Death Scripted and Death Choreographed* (Abingdon, 2017); D. Oldridge, *Strange Histories: The Trial of the Pig, the Walking Dead, and Other Matters of Fact from the Medieval and Renaissance Worlds*, 2nd edn (Abingdon, 2018), ch 4.

53 J. Schmitt, *Ghosts in the Middle Ages: The Living and the Dead in Medieval Society* (Chicago, IL, 1998), 204.

54 S. Handley, 'Reclaiming Ghosts in 1690s England', in K. Cooper and J. Gregory (eds), *Signs, Wonders, Miracles: Representations of Divine Power in the Life of the Church* (Woodbridge, 2005),

Francis Young suggests that the association between ghosts and Purgatory became 'something of an embarrassment' even for Catholics.[55] Mary Turbervill's story is not, on its own, evidence of widespread survival of purgatorial themes in ghost stories. However, it is interesting that Turbervill's story was told in the first place, was passed on and discussed by Protestants, and was judged worthy of preservation on multiple occasions. Cowan's informant was Archibald Lundie, the Church of Scotland minister of Saltoun in East Lothian.[56] Garden was interested in the story, and Aubrey and Defoe were prepared to publish a version that was admittedly vaguer, but still implied that the ghost had not gone directly to Heaven or Hell after death. Cowan also mentions 'some gentlemen either of Scotland or England' who were so curious about the story that they had endeavoured to visit Turbervill. Cowan's letter hints that long after the Reformation, medieval conceptions of ghosts and the afterlife lingered, even if they were not usually committed to print.

*****

Cowan's third story describes the resurrection of a pious Sussex lady. James VI held that resurrected corpses were animated by the Devil.[57] However, Wodrow and Sinclair recounted stories of corpses rising again by the hand of Providence, after which they identified sinners or asserted the reality of the afterlife.[58] These resurrections were generally short-term, but there were stories of people who rose again and lived for another few decades. Scotland had its own version of a folk tale, found throughout Europe, in which a grave-robber awakened a recently buried woman while trying to steal her ring. She went on to live a natural lifetime.[59] The resurrection of the Sussex lady seems to have followed this pattern. The main focus of the account was

354; P. Marshall, 'Transformations of the Ghost Story in Post-Reformation England', rev. version in Marshall, *Invisible Worlds*, 171; Davies, *The Haunted*, 22; B. Lewis, 'Protestantism, Pragmatism and Popular Religion: A Case Study of Early Modern Ghosts', in J. Newton and J. Bath (eds), *Early Modern Ghosts* (Durham, 2002), 79.

55 F. Young, *English Catholics and the Supernatural, 1553–1829* (Farnham, 2013), 97. See also Marshall, *Beliefs and the Dead in Reformation England*, 242–5.

56 Archibald Lundie was baptised in 1674. He was ordained in 1696, and died in 1759. Scott, *Fasti*, i, 393.

57 James VI, *Daemonologie*, bk. iii, ch. i, 41.

58 Wodrow, *Analecta*, i, 86–7; iv, 46; i, 117–18; Sinclair, *Satans Invisible World Discovered*, 156–7.

59 J. Bondeson, *Buried Alive: The Terrifying History of Our Most Primal Fear* (New York, 2002), 31–50. In the Scottish version the woman was often said to be Margaret Halcro Erskine, originally from Orkney, who supposedly had an initial 'death' in 1670 or 1674 before finally dying in 1725. Another candidate was Marjory Elphinstone, second wife of Robert Drummond of Carnock, who lived near Inverurie and died in the early seventeenth century. J. Tait, *Two Centuries of Border Church Life*, 2 vols (Kelso, 1889–91), ii, 14–15.

not, however, on the miraculous resurrection, but on the journey to the afterlife that the lady experienced while dead. There was a medieval tradition of individuals being taken on tours through the afterlife.[60] Orthodox Protestantism frowned on experiences of this sort, but several visionaries reported celestial visits, and accounts also appeared in pamphlet literature.[61] Most usually, these accounts aimed to underline the reality of Heaven and Hell, and to stress God's glory.

According to her husband, the Sussex lady was 'the rarest saint in her age'. He was devastated by her death and would not allow her to be buried, despite his friends' reproaches that 'he acted neither like a man nor a Christian'. After three days the lady revived, much to her own displeasure. She summoned the local minister and told her story. After death, her soul flew 'with incredible suiftness' through the walls. She was met by a pair of angels, one with 'something more of a reserved greatness' in his countenance, the other with a 'familiar kyndness'. In their 'delectable society' she took a rapid tour of the Earth. She found that she could hear and see things 'far more exquisitly then when in the body', and could understand foreign languages. They then ascended to Heaven, which she likened to a city. It was dominated by 'that innumerable company of angels and glorified spirits of just men made perfect all praiseing the Redeemer'. The city was glorious, the assembly of angels and departed souls was glorious, the throne was glorious, and the figure of Jesus at the centre was so very glorious that it took her some minutes to be able to look upon him.

Jesus was judging departed souls. The righteous appeared in the company of angels, and were admitted to Heaven. The wicked appeared 'all black and ugly and full of horror' (reminiscent, we might note, of Turbervill's landlady), and were driven back to the gates. From there they were dragged to Hell by devils as they uttered 'fearfull shricks and howlings'. The lady waited for her own judgement, and when it did not come, asked her gentler guardian why it should be delayed. The answer coming to him by revelation, he informed her that she had been sentenced to a 'course of sufferings' on Earth, after which she might return and 'inherit this croun of life'. Her guardians then escorted her back to earth, where she was compelled to re-enter her 'dead stinking Carcass'.

Perhaps there was something folkloric in the motif of the grieving husband drawing his wife back. Scottish ballad culture condemned prolonged

60 P. Marshall, 'Judgement and Repentance in Tudor Manchester: the Celestial Journey of Ellis Hall', rev. version in Marshall, *Invisible Worlds*, 53.

61 See, for example, Wodrow, *Analecta*, i, 51; NRS, vision of Lord Jedburgh, 26 October 1696, GD158/560; experiences of female visionaries discussed in Yeoman, '"Away with the Fairies"', in Henderson (ed.), *Fantastical Imaginations*; *Scotland's Timely Remembrance* (Edinburgh[?], 1717).

grieving, suggesting that it would prevent the departed soul from progressing. In a version of 'The Twa Brothers' (Child 49), recorded in the early nineteenth century, a ghost pleads with his love:

O cease your weeping, my true-love,
And 't will gie peace to me.[62]

In 1811, the author Anne MacVicar Grant recorded a story from the Highlands about a sister who was deeply upset by the death of her brother. She spent every night 'weeping incessantly, and calling in frantic agony on the beloved name'. At length her brother appeared to her in his shroud, wet and shivering. He scolded her for 'rebellion against the decrees of Providence'. He added that had a long journey to make 'through dark and dreary ways' before he could come to the place of rest, and informed her that 'every tear thou sheddest falls on this dark shroud without drying'.[63]

For the most part, however, the Sussex lady's story relies on scriptural precedents. Her resurrection came after she had been dead for three days, like that of Jesus. She was then escorted by angels, like Lazarus.[64] Her vision of Heaven was based on the Book of Revelation. Insofar as one could be orthodox when describing a journey to Heaven, the Sussex lady was. While the Renaissance had celebrated a more human, sensual Heaven, the influence of Calvin and Luther saw Heaven rewritten as a place of eternal praise for God. Over the seventeenth and eighteenth centuries, a theocentric Heaven became the 'orthodox Christian perspective'.[65] The Sussex lady's Heaven accorded with this vision. Her account also refuted unorthodox philosophies such as mortalism, which asserted that the soul slept until the Last Judgement, or the notion that the soul lingered consciously in an intermediate state before the Last Judgement.[66] In contrast to Mary Turbervill's story, the Sussex lady's account left little space for Purgatory. Death was closely followed by judgement, after which the righteous and wicked passed directly into Heaven or Hell. While the lady was required to undergo a 'course of sufferings', this took place on Earth itself, rather than in a spiritual realm.

★★★★★

62 F.J. Child (ed.), *The English and Scottish Popular Ballads*, 5 vols (Boston, MA, 1882–98), i pt ii, p. 440. See McGill, *Ghosts in Enlightenment Scotland*, 162–3.

63 Grant, *Essays on the Superstitions of the Highlanders of Scotland*, i, 178–82 (quotation at p. 181).

64 Luke 16:19–31; Luke 24:7. On angelic escorts, see P. Marshall, 'Angels around the Deathbed: Variations on a Theme in the English Art of Dying', in Walsham and Marshall (eds), *Angels in the Early Modern World*.

65 McDannell and Lang, *Heaven*, 146–55 (quotation at p. 146).

66 On these beliefs, see Almond, *Heaven and Hell in Enlightenment England*, 38–80; B.W. Ball, *The Soul Sleepers: Christian Mortalism from Wycliffe to Priestley* (Cambridge, 2008); M. McGill, 'A Protestant Purgatory?: Visions of an Intermediate State in Eighteenth-century Scotland', *Scottish Historical Review* 97 (2018), 153–86.

The final letter describes an Edinburgh man, John Duncan, who saw a vision of angels while visiting baths in England. Of Duncan, Cowan writes: 'He lives to this present time in Edinburgh; he formerly was, or for present is, a merchand.' He adds: 'I am informed since that Bailie Duncan, who is married to Mr Alexander Hamilton's relict, has a Brother of the same name.' Cowan apparently had some wires crossed here: Bailie Duncan and John Duncan were one and the same. Mr Alexander Hamilton's widow was Helen Eliot. She married John Duncan, a merchant, at Edinburgh in April 1698.[67] Duncan became an Edinburgh bailie, or town official, in 1700. In October 1710 he was elected to the prominent post of Lord Dean of Guilds.[68] We know further that Duncan was a member of the Edinburgh Society for the Reformation of Manners, which was concerned with addressing swearing, drunkenness and other forms of immorality. Daniel Defoe, who would write on angelology in the 1720s, was a friend of Duncan's; Duncan arranged for his invitation into the Society for the Reformation of Manners in 1707.[69]

The story is shorter than the 1707 accounts, and can be summarised concisely. Having risen early one morning, Duncan perceived a pair of angels bearing a sheet. They dragged this sheet through the dew, then squeezed out the water. Duncan heard the words 'So shall God wring out his judgments on this land'. Thereafter he became blind and mute for three days. He waved away doctors, writing on a bit of paper '*Nox dabit consilium*', or 'the night will bring a way'. Sure enough, he recovered unaided, and went on to report the story to a select few acquaintances.

While the angels in Cowan's other stories provided a protective role, these angels were more threatening figures. The angel of judgement was a relatively common motif in early modern culture, despite the unorthodoxy of angelic visitations. Alexandra Walsham has identified tales of judging or avenging angels from both Protestant and Catholic communities in England.[70] In Scotland, Presbyterian visionaries met with angels who warned that God would wreak destruction on the land. Stories of this sort also circulated in pamphlets.[71] Indeed, accounts of God's displeasure (whether or not borne by angels) were so common that there was no need for Duncan to specify why

67 H. Paton (ed.), *The Register of Marriages for the Parish of Edinburgh, 1595–1700* (Edinburgh, 1905), 207.

68 H. Armet (ed.), *Extracts from the Records of the Burgh of Edinburgh, 1689–1701* (Edinburgh, 1962), 270; H. Armet (ed.), *Extracts from the Records of the Burgh of Edinburgh, 1701–1718* (Edinburgh, 1967), 201.

69 C.E. Burch, 'Defoe and the Edinburgh Society for the Reformation of Manners', *Review of English Studies* 16 (1940), 306–12, at p. 312; P.R. Backscheider, *Daniel Defoe: His Life* (Baltimore, MD, 1989), 235–6.

70 Walsham, 'Invisible Helpers', 87–94; A. Walsham, 'Catholic Reformation and the Cult of Angels in Early Modern England', in Raymond (ed.), *Conversations with Angels*, 284–9.

71 McGill, 'Angels in Early Modern Scotland'.

God was proposing to 'wring out his judgments'; there was an established discourse about humankind's sinfulness. Duncan's story also recalled biblical precedents for divine punishment: the 'great quanti[ti]e of water' flowing from the sheet was reminiscent of the Flood.

So overwhelming was this representation of God's anger that it was actively injurious to Duncan, leaving him temporarily blinded and muted. There was a traditional notion that visionaries might lose their powers of sight and speech. For the Catholic saint Teresa of Avila, God could be heard but not seen, as his light would blind a human.[72] There is an echo of this idea in the Sussex lady's initial inability to look at Christ because of the 'brightness of [his] glory'. Protestant visionaries also reported spells of blindness or muteness. The Baptist Sarah Wight, whose visions began in 1647, was struck deaf and blind. Elinor Channel from Surrey, who prophesied in 1654, was mute.[73] This association with an established visionary tradition might have reinforced the validity of Duncan's account for segments of his audience, but it also invited accusations of religious enthusiasm (or excessive religious feeling bordering on superstition).

Cowan underlined that Duncan saw the vision 'with his bodily eyes', as opposed to the 'mind's eye' or the 'spiritual eye'. The lingering effects further demonstrated the physicality of the experience. We might compare this with a snippet of evidence from the Cambuslang evangelical revival of 1742. Catherine Jackson, one of the Cambuslang converts, told a minister that she had seen Christ with 'her bodily eyes'. The Seceders, a religious group who were hostile to the revival, later used this line to condemn the converts as enthusiasts. Ministers who edited the accounts of the Cambuslang converts were careful to avoid language of this sort. Visions could be seen and heard, but with *spiritual* rather than physical senses.[74] Duncan's account had a broadly Christian message, as it emphasised the need for repentance. But as in Cowan's other stories, the details did not necessarily accord with Protestant orthodoxy.

★★★★★

72 R.M. San Juan, 'Dizzying Visions: St Teresa of Jesus and the Embodied Visual Image', in C. Göttler and W. Neuber (eds), *Spirits Unseen: The Representation of Subtle Bodies in Early Modern European Culture* (Leiden, 2008), 265.

73 Henry Jessey, *The Exceeding Riches of Grace Advanced* (London, 1647); Elinor Channel, *A Message from God, by a Dumb Woman to his Highness the Lord Protector*, ed. Arise Evans (London, 1653). On the tradition of muteness among female prophets particularly, see P. Mack, *Visionary Women: Ecstatic Prophecy in Seventeenth-Century England* (Berkeley, CA, 1992), 32–3.

74 D.B. Hindmarsh, *The Evangelical Conversion Narrative: Spiritual Autobiography in Early Modern England* (Oxford, 2005), 220–2 (quotation at p. 222).

To understand Cowan's interest in these stories, we need to reflect more widely on religious culture in the late seventeenth and early eighteenth centuries. From the mid-seventeenth century, there was rising interest in special providences. General providence was God's plan for the universe, drawn up at Creation. Special providences were his spontaneous interventions. In England especially, the civil warfare of the 1640s and early 1650s resulted in a surge in pamphlets detailing prodigious apparitions in the sky, monstrous births and other special providences.[75] By attributing these events to God, writers could demonstrate divine support for particular causes. In late seventeenth-century England, however, special providences began to fall out of fashion.[76] In Scotland, by contrast, accounts of special providences flourished following the 1660 Restoration.[77] The reinstatement of Episcopalianism meant that deposed Presbyterians had particular reason to look for proofs of God's favour. Collections of providences were produced by John Livingstone, Robert Fleming and Robert Law, foreshadowing Wodrow's work.[78] Apparitions were often interpreted as special providences, demonstrating a subtle shift away from the post-Reformation discourse. Instead of being dismissed as diabolic tricks, apparitions were increasingly attributed to divine intervention.

Matters changed with the 1690 reinstatement of Presbyterianism. Wodrow and Cowan certainly retained an interest in apparition stories. However, religious communities increasingly emphasised the evils of enthusiasm. Frequently accused by Episcopalians of enthusiastical tendencies, Presbyterian churchmen emphasised their sobriety: 'We are no wayes led by enthusiastick impulses without the word but walk only by the word, and reject all impulses either contrare to, or beside it, yea not warranted by it.'[79] Alasdair Raffe argues that the period from 1690 to 1730 witnessed 'growing ecclesiological and theological rigidity among Presbyterians', partly in response to Episcopalian and Anglican opposition. David Allan

75 See A. Walsham, *Providence in Early Modern England* (Oxford, 1999); W.E. Burns, *An Age of Wonders: Prodigies, Politics, and Providence in England, 1657–1727* (Manchester, 2002).

76 Walsham, *Providence in Early Modern England*, 333–4; Burns, *An Age of Wonders*, ch. 6 and conclusion.

77 M. McGill and A. Raffe, 'The Uses of Providence in Early Modern Scotland', in Goodare and McGill (eds), *The Supernatural in Early Modern Scotland*.

78 John Livingstone, *Memorable Characteristics, and Remarkable Passages of Divine Providence*, in W.K. Tweedie (ed.), *Select Biographies*, 2 vols (Edinburgh, 1845–7), i, 293–348; Robert Law, *Memorialls: Or the Memorable Things That Fell out Within This Island of Brittain from 1638 to 1684*, ed. C.K. Sharpe (Edinburgh, 1818); Robert Fleming, *The Fulfilling of the Scripture* (Rotterdam, 1669).

79 See M. Heyd, *Be Sober and Reasonable: The Critique of Enthusiasm in the Seventeenth and Early Eighteenth Centuries* (Leiden, 1995), 15–23. The quotation is an answer to George Hickes's 1680 *The Spirit of Popery*, and is cited in A. Raffe, *The Culture of Controversy: Religious Arguments in Scotland, 1660–1714* (Woodbridge, 2012), 138.

similarly notes that 'acute sensitivity to doctrinal error' was an important characteristic of the kirk, and Michael Heyd asserts that a new, 'reasonable' approach to religion developed. As such, 'the conclusion was clear', and was most succinctly expressed by Scots Presbyterian minister James Hog in 1707: 'Visions, voices and Dreams, are no bottom on which we may build, and we ought to cease from regard to them.'[80] This applied even when the visions in question upheld the Presbyterian cause. Jonet Fraser, a Presbyterian visionary from Dumfries who described a glorious visit to Heaven in 1684–5, was compelled in 1691 to confess to her presbytery that she had 'pretended to prophecying and seeing of visions and that she had sinned greatly in being deluded by Satan'.[81]

The second half of the seventeenth century also saw broader challenges to traditional beliefs about the supernatural realm. It was a period of rapid philosophical advancements. The work of René Descartes (1596–1650) became dominant within universities in most Protestant countries, including Scotland.[82] Descartes argued for a mechanistic universe, created by God but left to function according to simple mathematical laws. He was criticised for implying that God did not govern directly on a day-to-day basis, and for proposing a dualistic system of mind and matter that allegedly undervalued spiritual entities.[83] Baruch Spinoza (1632–77) denied the existence of miracles and demons. Thomas Hobbes (1588–1679), John Locke (1632–1704), and the group of English figures commonly termed deists outlined a vision of religion that was dependent on reason rather than revelation.[84] According to Michael Wasser, the growth of the mechanical worldview caused a 'crisis' for demonology, and was instrumental in the decline of the witch trials. After 1662, witch hunting in Scotland gradually faded away. There was one last major hunt, in 1697–1700, but it resulted in a significantly lower percentage of executions than earlier hunts.[85]

80 A. Raffe, 'Presbyterianism, Secularization, and Scottish Politics after the Revolution of 1688–1690', *Historical Journal* 53 (2010), 317–37, at p. 335; D. Allan, *Scotland in the Eighteenth Century: Union and Enlightenment* (Harlow, 2002), 26; Heyd, *Be Sober and Reasonable*, 175–6.

81 Yeoman, '"Away with the Fairies"', 40.

82 C.M. Shepherd, 'Philosophy and Science in the Arts Curriculum of the Scottish Universities in the Seventeenth Century' (University of Edinburgh PhD thesis, 1975), esp. 61–165; A. Raffe, 'Intellectual Change before the Enlightenment: Scotland, the Netherlands and the Reception of Cartesian Thought, 1650–1700', *Scottish Historical Review* 94 (2015), 27, 45–6.

83 J.I. Israel, *Radical Enlightenment: Philosophy and the Making of Modernity, 1650–1750* (Oxford, 2001), 28.

84 See Israel, *Radical Enlightenment*, 218–29; P. Springborg, 'Hobbes on Religion', in T. Sorell (ed.), *The Cambridge Companion to Hobbes* (Cambridge, 1996); N. Wolterstorff, 'Locke's Philosophy of Religion', in V. Chappell (ed.), *Cambridge Companion to Locke* (Cambridge, 1994); J.R. Wigelsworth, *Deism in Enlightenment England: Theology, Politics, and Newtonian Public Science* (Manchester, 2009).

85 M. Wasser, 'The Mechanical World-view and the Decline of Witch-beliefs in Scotland', in Goodare *et al.* (eds), *Witchcraft and Belief in Early Modern Scotland*.

However, these developments raised alarm in certain parts of the Presbyterian establishment. There was a growing perception that 'atheism' (meaning a range of heterodox beliefs) was threatening the foundations of Christian society.[86] Fear of the corrupting influence of atheists led to the execution of the Edinburgh student Thomas Aikenhead in 1697. Aikenhead was accused of having declared (among other things) that 'the Apostles were a company of silly witless fisher-men and ... he wondered the world was so long deluded with their contradictions and nonsense'.[87] In the 1710s and 1720s, persecution continued with the investigation of minister and theologian John Simson for allegedly disseminating heterodox ideas.[88]

Stories of the supernatural could be used to combat the atheist threat. Accounts of witches, angels, ghosts and the afterlife demonstrated that there existed a world of spiritual forces.[89] The trend of publishing these stories began in England, with Henry More's 1652 *An Antidote Against Atheisme*. Subsequent works in the same genre include Joseph Glanvill's *Sadducismus Triumphatus* (1681), Richard Bovet's *Pandaemonium* (1684), and Richard Baxter's *The Certainty of the World of Spirits* (1691). The trend was echoed north of the border. Wodrow explained that in gathering his providences, he was seeking to confirm 'the great foundations of our holy religion'.[90] In the 1690s, Robert Kirk recorded stories of fairies and second sight for the same purpose, while Alexander Telfair published an account of a demonic apparition for 'the Conviction and Confutation of that prevailing Spirit of Atheism and Infidelity in our time'.[91] In 1708, George Mackenzie's *Synopsis Apocalyptica* used miracles and prophecy to refute 'Atheists and Antiscripturists'.[92] George Sinclair followed most closely in the footsteps of his English counterparts; his *Satans Invisible World Discovered* (1685) drew heavily on More and Glanvill. He explained his motives as follows:

86 On the definition of atheism, see M. Hunter and D. Wootton, 'Introduction', in M. Hunter and D. Wootton (eds), *Atheism from the Reformation to the Enlightenment* (Oxford, 1992).

87 M.F. Graham, *The Blasphemies of Thomas Aikenhead: Boundaries of Belief on the Eve of the Enlightenment* (Edinburgh, 2008), 108.

88 See A. Skoczylas, *Mr Simson's Knotty Case: Divinity, Politics, and Due Process in Early Eighteenth-Century Scotland* (Montreal, 2001).

89 See Handley, 'Reclaiming Ghosts in 1690s England'; L. Sangha, '"Incorporeal Substances": Discerning Angels in Later Seventeenth-century England', in Copeland and Machielsen (eds), *Angels of Light?*; McGill, *Ghosts in Enlightenment Scotland*, ch. 2; E. Cameron, *Enchanted Europe: Superstition, Reason, and Religion, 1250–1750* (Oxford, 2010), ch. 17.

90 Wodrow, *The Correspondence of the Rev. Robert Wodrow*, ii, 244; i, 46–59.

91 Robert Kirk, 'Robert Kirk's *The Secret Commonwealth* and his "A Short Treatise of the Scottish-Irish Charms and Spells"', in Hunter (ed.), *The Occult Laboratory*, esp. 96; Alexander Telfair, *A True Relation of an Apparition, Expressions and Actings, of a Spirit* (Edinburgh, 1696), 3. See also Fraser, *'Deuteroskopia'*.

92 George Mackenzie, 'An Essay on the Revelation of St. John', in *Synopsis Apocalyptica: Or, a Short Plain Explication and Application of Daniel's Prophecy and of St. John's Revelation* (Edinburgh, 1708), dedication, i.

> there are a monstruous rable of men, who following the *Hobbesian* and *Spinosian* Principles, slight Religion, and undervalue the Scripture, because there is such an express mention of Spirits and Angels in it, which their thick and plumbeous capacities cannot conceive. Whereupon they think, that all contained in the Universe comes under the notion of things matterial, and bodies only; and consequently, no GOD, no Devil, no Spirit, no Witch.[93]

Cowan hints at this motivation for his letters, declaring one of the stories of interest for those 'who are truely and zealously concerned for the state of religion at this time'. It is perhaps notable that the story of the Sussex lady's journey to the afterlife was passed on by James Webster (1658/9–1720), a minister who played an important role in the persecutions of both Aikenhead and Simson.[94] Despite the pressures of Protestant orthodoxy and the campaign against enthusiasm, a subset of churchmen and philosophers saw value in supernatural stories.

Cowan's letters were not pieces of precise theological polemic, and we should be wary of reading too much into their eschatological implications. As we have seen, the messages of the stories were sometimes inconsistent: Mary Turbervill's story allowed for a purgatorial intermediate state after death, whereas the story of the Sussex lady refuted this possibility. Cowan was reticent about his own feelings regarding the stories. He was reasonably confident about David Thomson's account, but owned that Mary Turbervill's was, in comparison, not 'so very well vouch'd'. He suggested that an 'exact inquiry' should be made to establish the truth of the Sussex lady's story, and encouraged Wodrow to investigate John Duncan's. The stories may have been passed on and recorded despite – rather than because of – their precise messages. Rather than offering a reliable guide to the theology of Cowan or his informants, they indicate how theological flexibility could be justified in the fight against atheism. There was no final consensus on when orthodox supernatural belief became superstition. Cowan's letters are part of an ongoing negotiation on this question, and reflect how religious culture had evolved since the Reformation.

*****

Cowan names seven different individuals who passed on the stories. Six were Presbyterian ministers; the other was a Presbyterian minister's brother. He also mentions 'gentlemen' who had taken an interest in the stories. In at least one case, Wodrow also consulted a fellow minister to confirm Cowan's account. Early modern Scottish religious culture was very much

93 Sinclair, *Satans Invisible World Discovered*, A4v.

94 Graham, *Blasphemies of Thomas Aikenhead*, 121; Skoczylas, *Mr Simson's Knotty Case*, 65–9. James Webster worked as a minister in Libberton, Whitekirk and Tolbooth. Scott, *Fasti*, i, 123.

community-based. David Mullan writes of a 'Puritan brotherhood' who worshipped together, shared religious manuscripts, and were bound by mutual affection.[95] Mullan's focus here is on the late sixteenth and early seventeenth centuries, but throughout the early modern period, Scottish religion – and, especially, Scottish Presbyterianism – was a communal affair. Communities worshipped and repented together. Ministers were answerable to their parishioners, and at the time of Cowan's writing were appointed by them. That there existed networks of communication to discuss extraordinary events is not necessarily surprising. But while Cowan's informants were mainly Presbyterians, three of the four individuals at the centre of the stories probably belonged to different Protestant sects. Two were English. The letters were part of a conversation about the supernatural world that went beyond Presbyterian ministers.

Attitudes towards evidence were changing in the late seventeenth century. Brian P. Levack has shown that the witch trials declined in part because of 'more careful evaluation of evidence': lawyers and judges were increasingly reluctant to accept confessions as adequate proof of guilt.[96] However, there were also forces working in the opposite direction. As special providences became more popular, there was an increased chance that laypeople's experiences with the supernatural would be accepted at face value, rather than being rewritten to imply a diabolic pact. More broadly, scientific culture was placing new emphasis on the value of eyewitness testimony, rather than reference to Scripture or ancient authorities, as a means of establishing scientific truths.[97] Cowan's letters place significant emphasis on the idea of hearing a story from the subject's 'oun mouth', or at least from somebody else who had done so. This, combined with the assurance that the informants were pious and socially respectable, seems to have been his and Wodrow's main criteria in establishing the truth of an account. It was an approach that David Hume would reject in decisive terms half a century later, but Cowan's letters come from a point in time when intellectual culture was experimenting with the authority of experience.[98]

This raises a question about who was controlling representations of the supernatural. It was the duty of ministers to correct unorthodox folk beliefs, but this often ended up being a process of negotiation between local communities and the ecclesiastical authorities.[99] In three out of four of

95 D.G. Mullan, *Scottish Puritanism, 1590–1638* (Oxford, 2000), ch. 1.

96 Levack, *Witch-Hunting in Scotland*, 142.

97 See D. Wootton, *The Invention of Science: A New History of the Scientific Revolution* (New York, 2015), ch. 7.

98 David Hume, *Of Miracles*, sec. 10 in *An Enquiry Concerning Human Understanding.* First published as *Philosophical Essays Concerning Human Understanding* (London, 1748).

99 See M. Todd, *The Culture of Protestantism in Early Modern Scotland* (New Haven, CT, 2002), ch. 7.

Cowan's stories, middle-ranking laypeople were vested with the authority to define and describe the supernatural world. In two of these stories, moreover, the laypeople in question were women. Mary Turbervill took centre stage in her ghost story, and seems to have garnered some measure of fame as a result. The Sussex lady similarly emerged from the pages of her story as a figure of some distinction, and was able to command a minister to be her audience and scribe. Encounters with the supernatural offered women a degree of prestige that might allow them to circumvent the usual social hierarchies, at least in the presence of sympathetic audiences. In 1638, the Scottish prophet Margaret Mitchelson became renowned for her prophecies in favour of the Covenanting cause.[100] In the latter half of the seventeenth century, several further female visionaries recorded encounters with divine power.[101] Cowan's letters demonstrate that even in the early eighteenth century, when the Presbyterian establishment had clamped down on 'Visions, voices and Dreams', the power to shape conceptions of the supernatural world was not restricted to clergymen.

In preserving stories of this sort, Cowan and Wodrow were attaching new importance to laypeople's experiences as a means of understanding the supernatural world. It was a brief, and ultimately unsuccessful, experiment. In subsequent decades, mainstream theological discussions were grounded on Scripture, rather than individual experience.[102] Moreover, as the eighteenth century progressed, lay perceptions of the supernatural increasingly developed independently of the kirk. In the latter part of the century, gothic and romantic authors reshaped popular conceptions of ghosts and other supernatural phenomena. In the nineteenth century, the spiritualist movement granted laypeople control over supernatural forces. And as Lizanne Henderson has demonstrated, popular belief in magical forces continued along its own currents, irrespective of religious orthodoxy.[103] For all Cowan's efforts, popular stories were both too diverse, and too grounded in older traditions, to be contained within a Calvinist framework.

*****

One of the difficulties in identifying broad historical trends is that change is usually met with a backlash, giving the impression that a society is

100 D. Stevenson, 'Mitchelson [Mitchel], Margaret', *Oxford DNB*, online edn, https://doi.org/10.1093/ref:odnb/67842 [accessed 2 February 2019]. I am grateful to Dr Louise Yeoman for allowing me to read her work in progress on Mitchelson.

101 Yeoman, '"Away with the Fairies"'.

102 See C. Kidd, 'The Scottish Enlightenment and the Supernatural', in Henderson (ed.), *Fantastical Imaginations*.

103 Henderson, *Witchcraft and Folk Belief in the Age of Enlightenment.*

moving in two contradictory directions. In the late seventeenth and early eighteenth centuries, there was a growing interest in materialist conceptions of the universe. Correspondingly, a subset of intellectuals began to pay more attention to stories of supernatural encounters. Courts began to interrogate evidence more thoroughly, leading to a decline in witchcraft convictions. Simultaneously, there was a growing interest in the authority of experience as a way of establishing theological truths. Lastly, in an attempt to defend religion, a handful of figures collected stories that defied traditional orthodoxy. As the eighteenth century progressed, the technique of using remarkable providences to combat atheism mostly died away, and the supernatural stories of folk culture continued along a different stream from kirk theology. In attempting to forge an alliance between the two, Cowan's letters reflect a curiously counterintuitive passage in the history of the supernatural.

Editorial Conventions

In making a scholarly edition, elements of the original manuscript are inevitably lost. The physicality of a manuscript, the nuances of handwriting and paper and ink, the use of space on the page: these are all elements that are not easily reproducible. Points of punctuation, spelling or orthography are often modernised, which loses some of the flavour of the original document, but has the advantage of making it more accessible for a modern readership. In this case, I have aimed for a balance between original features and easy readability.

Original spelling has been retained, including the Scots feature of 'w' for 'u', as in 'yow' and 'wp'.[104] I have silently expanded contractions (e.g. þ*t*, w*th*, &). *þ* has been given as *th*. I have sometimes provided letters or words in square brackets to aid comprehension, and have expanded abbreviations in square brackets.

Cowan favours protracted sentences and lengthy blocks of text. I have modernised punctuation insofar as Cowan's style allows, and have inserted paragraphs. Capitalisation has also been modernised, as Cowan's capitalisation is inconsistent, and it is often impossible to distinguish his upper-case and lower-case letters.

The letters are written in a close italic hand, and the presentation is tidy. There are no extensive scribal corrections or marginal notes. The only amendments are forgotten words inserted above the line of text, which have been silently incorporated, and a few minor deletions in case of mistakes,

104 See V. Kniezsa, 'The Origins of Scots Orthography', in C. Jones (ed.), *The Edinburgh History of the Scots Language* (Edinburgh, 1997), 36.

which have been removed. Repeated words on a new page have been deleted.

{…} indicates illegible text. Where it can be inferred this text is supplied; otherwise, dots indicate the approximate number of illegible letters.

TRANSCRIPTION

Letter One

R[everend] D[ear] S[ir]

Mr David Thomson, minister of Kinnell in the shire of Angus, of the Episcopall persuasion, happening to dye in the monneth of June or July 1703, the following story concerning him was reported to me some eight or ten dayes befor his death by Mr John Dowgald, present minister of the gospel at Rescoby,[1] who was his intimat freind and acquaintance and formerly copresbiter with him in the Presbitry of Brechin, who had it from his oun mouth, which is as follows.

Mr David Thomson, after he had past his course at the University, when a youth, was chaplain to this present Earle of Perth, haveing wpon a certain time gone abroad to see freinds about six or seven miles from the Castle of Drummond, as he was returning home being well mounted wpon one of my Lord's horses, there was a river which he was to pass, which by reason of a great fall of rain the day befor was now become unpassible. Wherepon he calls at some people who lived not far from the watersyd to know whether or not the foord was rideable. They told him: 'Sir, we cannot well advyse yow; the water is truly great, but seeing yow are well mounted we think yow may adventure to take it.' Upon which he goes streight forward to the foord with a full resolution to ryd through, but when he was just ready to take the water there comes wp to him a handsome young gentleman of a sweet lovely countenance with something of majesty in it, well equip'd and mounted on a very fine horse, finer then any that ever he saw, who passed by him very swiftly, and springs in befor him into the water, without speaking a word, and who had not gone in twice or thrice the horse's length into the water till both horse and man goes doun, over head and ears, so that Mr Thomson lost sight of both. But immediatly he springs wp, turns the horse's head and comes out, and then addresses Mr Thomson thus: 'Sir, yow see the water is not rydable here. But please to goe along with me a litle further wp the water, and under God I'le conduct yow safely through at another place where it is rydable,' which Mr Thomason with aboundance of assureance and pleasure complyes with.

And when they were come to the place the young gentleman sayes to him: 'Now Sir, I'le take the water befor yow. Follow yow immediatly after and observe the track of my horse exactly without turning in the least to

1 John Dougal was born in 1653. He was called in 1703, and died in 1723. Scott, *Fasti*, v, 302.

the right or left hand, otherways yow are gone.' Which he observing very carefully, it happened that the water came but wp to the horse's belly, and so they came both safely through to the other syd, which was a plain spot of ground, being a moor of about tuo miles in length, and farr from any house. The gentleman then addresses Mr Thomson thus: 'Now Sir, yow have mett with a signale deliverance. Bless God for it, and never forget this day while yow live, for if I had not come wp to yow in the very nick of time when yow were entring the water, yow would undoubtedly have perished. And remember further, that in the fiftyeth year of your age yow will dye of a fever.' And after that he intertain'd him with a heav[en]ly discourse which was very raveshing, and presently evanished so that Mr Thomson could not see him, far nor near, there being neither house nor hole, nor any thicket within sight, or hard at hand where he might have absconded himself. All that I heard Mr Thomson should have observed further concerning this person was that when he came out of the water, there was not one hair either of horse or man wett.

Reverend Sir

This foregoeing story I had from Mr John Dowgald, my very good freind and intimat acquaintance while I stayed at Brechin, where he and his family were dwelling for the present.

About a tuelvemonneth befor Mr Thomson's death, Mr Dougald and I, being both wpon the supplies, were traveling home [to] Brechin, and happening to ryd by Kinnell he was giveing me the character of Mr Thomson, viz: that he was a man of a good sober walk and conversation, a kynd courteous temper, very bookish and intearly devoted to his studys to such a degree that he had lost one of his eyes by excessive reading, a sound Calvinist tho he had complyed with Episcopacy. His father was a zealous Presbiterian minister, I suppose in Fife, which I had from Mr Patrick Tullidaph,[2] who saw Mr Thomson at his house when he was in these bounds wpon the supplyed, at the same time with my self. And so Mr Dowgald, inclineing to touch at Kinnell to see Mr Thomson, wad needs have me to goe alongst with him, which I did not refuse to doe, haveing heard this character, and found that he did answer the same so far as I was capable to know in such a short time, being less then two houres. I found him to be of a very aggreable conversation, and so we parted. About less then a twelve monneth after, I happening to be in Mr Dowgald's house in Brechin where

2 Patrick Tullidelph, who was ordained in 1697 and died in 1709. He was minister of Ferry-Port on Craig, Fife. Scott, *Fasti*, v, 201.

I was frequently, he began thus with me after his usuall and familiar way and manner: 'Billie,[3] I have news to tell yow. Mr David Thomson whom yow and I saw at his hous is dying of a fever, and I have some assureance that he will dye at this time.' I enquired what was the ground of his assureance. He answered: 'Mr Thomson got a warning many years agoe that he wad dye of a fever in the fiftyeth year of his age, and I know of a certainty that he is just now in the fiftyeth year of his age,' and so he told me the whole foregoing story. I answered: 'We must suspend our thought till we see whither he dyes or recovers and the event will determine ws,' which it did, for in 8 or 10 dayes after he dyed. I thought it was not amiss to give yow ane account of these circumstances, particularly this last, and so subjoyn the same to the story. I am

Yours

Sir

The following story is more foraign, no less strange, tho indeed I cannot say so very well vouch'd. My author who reported it to me was Mr Archibald Lundy, minister of the gospell at Saltoun,[4] who I doubt not can give a better and fuller account of it now then when I saw him.

It is concerning one Mrs Turbervill, sister to Mr Turbervile, a famous occulist at London. She lived in a cuntrey house some 50 miles from London, the landlady of which house being lately dead when she came to it. It happened that one evening in the tuilight, as she was comeing out of ane upper chamber and resolving to goe doun stairs, she saw wpon the stairhead a terrible apparition of a woman all in black, with a very ugly face and a countenance full of horror, sending forth a noysom smell, which did not a litle strike Mrs Turbervile with fear and consternation. But passing by the specter she came doun stairs, and thinking it proudence not to reveall to any what she had seen, she betake her self presently to her closet for prayer. And haveing begged the divine protection and indeavoring to blot out of her memory and phansie the frightfull idea of what she had seen, she began to take heart and curage again.

And the nixt night when it was dark she went wp to the same room with a lighted candle in her hand, where the ghost appeared to her again in the same terrible manner as befor, viz: all in black with a horrible ugly countenance, casting out a noysome smell. And which was yet more terrible to her

3 A close friend or comrade.

4 Archibald Lundie was baptised in 1674. He was ordained in 1696, and died in 1759. Scott, *Fasti*, i, 393. Saltoun is in East Lothian.

then befor, the ghost was within the room standing betwixt her and the door, so that now she knew not what way to get out. And therefor she falls doun immediately on her knees and prayes with great fervour that God might preserve her from the assaults of the Evil one, both outward and inward, and that she might be strengthned with faith and courage against naturall fear and unbeleif. And haveing insisted thus in prayer for some litle time she ryses from her knees, and with some boldness and confidence in the divine mercy and protection she bespoak the ghost thus: 'In the name of the Lord what art thow, and why am I so disturbed and affrighted by such a dreadfull appearance? Tho I have bein guilty of many sins, yet I have fled to the mercy of God and merits of Jesus Christ in whom I hop[e] for a compleat pardon of them all, and by the divine guidness I have bein hitherto kept back from gross presumptuous sins, and therefor in the name of the Lord be gone and disturb me no more.'

The ghost answers: 'It's well yow have spocken first, for if yow had not I would have torn yow, and thrown yow doun stairs; and now I'le tell yow what I am, and for what end I have appeared to yow. I am the ghost or spirit of the deceast landlady of this house. My husband and I in our lifetime alotted and mortifyed a considerable soume of monney for the releif of the poor, and my husband dying befor me, on his death injoyned me to apply and dispose of that monney as we had both aggread to befor, which I was willing to doe, but through negligence or forgetfulness left it undone as long as I lived. And now I am under great horror and can be at no rest till it be disposed of, and except yow do what I shall just now enjoyn yow, I will haunt yow continually.' 'What shall I doe?' sayes Mrs Turbervile. The ghost answers: 'Take the candle in your hand and follow me wp the trap stair to the garret, and yow need not be affrayed for I will doe yow no harm,' which she did. When they were there the ghost says: 'The monney's lodged in this garret,' and poynts to the place which was betuein the boards of the roof and the tyle, where there was a rent or slitt in. At which the ghost bids her thrust her arme as far as she could reach towards such a side and there she should find a large napkin full of gold and monney, which none of the world knew of or where it was, except she had appeared to discover it. Which Mrs Turbervile did finds the monney and brings it out, the ghost sayes: 'The soume's intear to the value of so much,' then it sayes: 'Yow must be at the pains and expence of goeing to London with this monney and deliver it to a brother in law of mine, who knows that there was so much monney mortifyed by my husband and me, but knows not what is come of it. And if yow tell him the whole story of my appearing to yow he will belive yow, and enjoyn him from me to dispose of it as it was designed, with certification that if he doe it not I will haunt him continually. And for a reward of your pains and diligence, after yow are returned I will appear once more to yow, but in a glorious manner and not to your terror, and will satisfy your curiosity by answering such questions as yow shall propose to me, but not beyond the number of 5 or 6.' This Mrs Turbervile undertakes to do and so the ghost evanishes.

When she came to London she told the whole story to the gentleman and delivered the monney to him quho found that there was not a farthing wanting. He belived her report, gave her a receipt of the monney, and promised to dispose of it accordingly as was said. After Mrs Turbervile's return, the ghost appears to her again in the day time when she was all alone in a chamber, but then she appeared all in white with a pleasant, beautifull and smileing countenance, and spoak to her thus: 'Now, Mrs, yow have done well. I am now in perfect peace and shall no more truble yow, and am ready to answer your questions.' Mrs Turbervil, who had her thoughts wpon them befor, began with the first, which was this: 'Whither or not are yow the real spirit or ghost of that woman who was mistris of this house, or am I only deceaved with a phantom, or ane apparition of the Devil? If yow be the real spirit of that woman, then seing yow are in the state of the dead then let me know whither or not yow are blessed or damned, and whither yow have bein in Heaven or Hell.' The answer was: 'I am the reall spirit of the late landlady. I am in the state of the dead I{. ...} be, and as for that part of the question whither were yow in Heaven or in Hell, as yet I have bein in neither, but have bein under great horror till this business was dispatchd. Now I am perfectly free of all anxiety and in a state of bliss, and am presently to pass into Heaven, a confirmation of which yow shall have befor I part.'

Mrs Turbervil proposed more questions to the number of five, but our author could give account of none of them but tuo moe, and that composedly and in the general. The one was, as I remember, concerning some futur event quhich she got satisfaction. The other was too curious, for the ghost said: 'Bewar of proposeing that questione, for it's too curious,' and with that gave her a litle nip in the arme which smarted for a time. And then the ghost sayes: 'Now as was promised, for a reward yow shall have a short and swift glance of that glory which I am to pass into,' and immediatly the room shone with a glorious light and she appeared all shineing, and then there appeared a pleasant young child of wonderfull beauty who laid his hand beneath the sole of her foot and so lifted her streight wp from the floor of the chamber till her head reacht the roof. And as she was ascending Mrs Turbervile heard the most melodious sound of musick that ever mortall heard, so excellent that the finest organnall musick in churches when compared with it was but like the gruntling of a sow as she expressed.

Sir, this is the story as I heard it with all the circumstances thereof. Only as I was informed, there were some gentlemen either of Scotland or England who in their way to London were so curious as to goe off their road to see this Mrs Turbervile and to get the confirmation of the story from her oun mouth. I am Yours

Letter Two

R[everend] D[ear] S[ir]

There was a very rare and memorable story which I heard latley at Edinburgh and which I thought fitt to communicat to yow, and I doubt not but it will be worth the pains not only of the more cur[i]ous and inquisitive sort of men, but likewayes of those who are truely and zealously concerned for the state of religion at this time, to make exact inquiry into the truth of the same as possible. The story as I heard it is as follows.

There was a worthy lady in England in the countey of Sussex, as I remember, of rare and eminent piety and devotion, who after some sickness happened to dye. Her husband, a pious gentleman, was so affected with sorrow for the loss of so excellent a Christian and so dear a relation, that his greif did swell beyond its due bounds, to such a degree that for three dayes he did neither eat, drink not sleep, or at least did not take so much refreshment as was necessar to sustain nature, but all the while sat pensive, murning over the body of his deceast wife, which was laid wpon the bed, not being as yet put into the coffine. His freinds came frequently to him to take him out of the room, but could not prevail. At last, it being near the fourth day, they began more sharply to chyde him and expostulat with him, telling that by so doeing he acted neither like a man nor a Christian, nor like himself at former times, while he mourned as those who have no hop[e] [he] was so cruel to himself, provocked God and dishonored the body of his dear wife, whose soul, they had reason in all charity to judge, was now in a glorifyd state. He answered: 'Yow nor the world knew not the worth of this woman, who was the rarest saint in her age, for by her prayers she obtaind not only blessings for her self, her family and me in particular, but for the whole Church of God, and therefor how can I but bewail so great a loss at a more than ordinary rait?' They replyed: 'Tho all this be true, yet now seing she is gone it remains that yow say with Abraham of his beloved Sarah, I must bury my dead out of my sight,[5] and so we intreat yow remove, that the last office may be performed which we owe to the ashes of the dead, otherwayes know that of necessity we must take yow hence by force.' He at last condescends to

5 Gen. 23:4.

remove, wpon condition that he might be allowed to stay four houres in the room with the body all alone, the doors being closs shutt, which was granted. While he was there, and when he had no doubt bein at prayer, he takes a steddy view of the body, which was lying with the face open, and perceaves a ruddiness to appear in the lips and cheecks. At which being strangely surprized, he approaches nearer, and takeing a grip of the hand he feells not only a pulse but a warmth, and within a very litle he observes her to open her eyes. Which made him presently to cry out: 'O my dear, are yow alive, or are yow again returned to the liveing?' Wpon which she raises her self, sitts wp streight in the bed, and with a kind of froun spoak to him and answered: 'Yes I am, and no thanks to yow.' 'O then,' sayes he, 'let me know where and in what state yow have been, and what is the state of the dead.' She {rep}lyes: 'Ask me no further concerning these things at present, but call immediatly for the minister of the place and I will reveall to him what I have to say, allowing yow to be witness,' which was done. The minister came, and all in the family were injoyned secrecy, but none allowed to be present with her when she gave the account but the minister and her own husband. She desyred the minister to take paper and to write from her mouth what she was to say, and thus she began:

'I was really dead, and in the state of the dead. My soul was actually dislodged and separated from my body, and I perceaved that my soul flew with incredible suiftness through the thickest pairt of the wall of this room, meeting with no resistance therefrom, no more then when men walk or run through a mist or fog, and infinitly less. Presently,' says she, 'I was attended by tuo guardian angels, appearing like two beautifull youths of a glorious aspect, a majestick mien mixd with a great deal of sweetness.' She observed in the one something more of a reserved greatness, in the other something more of a tender warmness as it were, and familiar kyndness. Being thus attended by her heavenly guardians she told that she flew with a wonderfull and inconceaveable suiftness through a great pairt of this Earth, and, which is very observable, she said she both heard and saw things, now in this her separat state, as well, nay far more exquisitly then when in the body, for as she was passing through a great many countreys, kingdoms and cities, of all which she could give ane exa{ct} description, she saw the people and what they were doeing and heard what they were saying, and that at a great distance. And which was yet more, she then understood the language of each nation, tho she never knew it befor. When they had taken this short and wonderfull survey of the Earth then they began to mount wp towards Heaven, and in the passage she felt more and more of a heavenly joy, being ravished with the delectable society of her guardians, and with the full assurance of glory.

At last they arived at the gates of that glorious and imperial city of the heavenly Jerusalem. Then makeing a pause, she says: 'But here I must stop, no tongue can tell no heart can conceave, eare hath not heard &c[6] the glory of that place, so that I can give no idea, nor raise any true and just representation of it in your mindes. All I can doe is to referr yow to the description of it given by John the Divine in the 21 chapter of his revelations from the 10 v[erse] and dounward, where it is called a city with great and glorious walls, the nearest resemblance of it I know. Only tho it is called a city it is not really and propperly so, but like unto a city with walls high great and glorious and with many gates.' In at one of whose gates she said she entred, being guarded by the two angels. When she was there the place was all glorious, in the midle whereof she saw visibly and really that innumerable company of angels and glorified spirits of just men made perfect[7] all praiseing the Redeemer. And in the midst of that glorious assembly she saw a glorious hy throne and the glorious Redeemer, the man Christ Jesus really and personally sitting thereon, the brightness of whose glory was so great that for severall minutes she was not able to look wpon him, but afterwards she did with unspeakable joy. She said that he was there judgeing all persons that dyed wpon the Earth, both righteous and wicked, whose souls after death were immediatly sisted befor his throne, and that the judgement of each person was dispatch'd in ane instant. She heard the judge call wpon every person particularly by name and sirname. The righteous came attended with angels, unto whom the judge said: 'Come,' and with a wave of his right hand they passed to that side and were placed there. The wicked appearing all black and ugly and full of horror when they were sisted before the thron, the judge said to them: 'Depart,' and with a wave of his left hand they were driven to the gates, which made them utter fearfull shricks and howlings, and from thence they were taken and convey'd by devils to the place of punishment.

She observed that some of her aquaintances who had dyed after her, and had come in after her, were judged befor her, for she heard the judge call wpon them by name, which made her inquire at her guardian, particularly that one who addressed her with such kyndness and tenderness: 'What may be the reason that the judge calls not wpon me, seing some who have come here after me are judged befor me?' He answeres, haveing it as it seems by revelation: 'Yow are not to be judged at this time. Yow must again return to the Earth and undergo a course of sufferings, but be faithfull unto the death and yow shall inherit this croun of life.[8] And take what yow have mett with as a pledge and earnest of your futur glory.' With that she felt as it were

6 1 Cor. 2:9.
7 Heb. 12:23.
8 James 1:12.

a weight pressing her back to the gates, and when she came there with a greater suiftness then befor she, being alwayes attended by her two guardians, returned to this Earth. Sayes she: 'I came to this house; I saw all the people in the family; I observed their business. I came to the room where my body was lying. I saw my body and my husband sitting by it, and when I looked wpon it I had this murnifull and melancholy reflection: "Must I again reenter that dead stinking carcass, wherein I have sinned and suffred so much?" And heaveing entred into the body I found life, blood, spirits and warmth to spring through all organs.'

She desired the minister to subscrive this written narrative, haveing first done it her self, and desired him to comunicat the same to some few of the ministers of London, whom she named, but only to read it to them without allowing them a coppy, which was done. And if I right remember Mr Robert Fleeming junior was present when it was read, and was the man who wrote ane account of this passage in a letter to Mr James Webster, who told the story to Mr James Grierson, lately ordaind Minister in Tingwall in Zetland, my intimat freind and comerad who was my author.[9] Mr Webster referred him or any to whom he should tell it to Mr Thomas Davidsone, present lecturer in the Tron Church of Edinburgh, in order to further information, unto whom I went and he reported it exactly as I had heard it from Mr Grierson, only with this variation, viz that she should have used the Apostle Paul's words, 'whether in the body or out of the body I know not'.[10] I am

Yours

Letter Three

R[everend] D[ear] S[ir]

I thought to have seen yow at yor house befor yow went east to Edinburgh, but since I was hindred from that I have sent yow here the following narrative which I had from Mr Archibald Lundie, minister of Salton, that so yow may be more particularly informed and more fully satisfied your self from a person in Edinburgh who is a considerable pairt of the subject I am to speak of.

9 Robert Fleming junior was the son of the Robert Fleming who wrote *The Fulfilling of the Scripture*. He had settled in London as a minister in 1698, and was still there in 1707. He died in 1716. Scott, *Fasti*, vi, 489–90. James Grierson was born c. 1676; he was ordained 18 Sept. 1706, and died in 1747. Scott, *Fasti*, vii, 291. On Webster, see above.

10 Thomas Davidson was born in Glasgow in 1676, and elected sole lecturer in the Tron Church in 1706. He died in 1760. Scott, *Fasti*, vi, 316. The biblical reference is 2 Cor. 12:3.

About 5 or 6 years agoe, ane Edinburgh gentleman was in England at the baths, who happening to rise airly one morning (whither while he was abroad in the fields or in his oun chamber my author could not determine), when he was fully awake and had all his senses about him, he saw with his bodily eyes a vision of tuo angels in the aire displaying a large white sheet. After that they lighted doun wpon the ground and spread the sheet wpon the grass, which was all wett with dew. Then they drew or trailed it alongst the ground so that the sheet was all over wett and soacked with dew. After that they took the two ends of it and wrange contrar wayes to one another so that a great quanti[ti]e of water was squeesed out of the sheet, which he saw flowing doun wpon the ground. That being done he heard a voice saying: 'So shall God wring out his judgments on this land,' and thus the vision removed, wpon the back of which he turned immediatly dumb and blind and so continowed for three dayes' space. When they brought physitians to him to apply medicines for the recovery of his speech and sight he would not hear of it, but wroat so as they could read this sentence *Nox dabit consilium*,[11] haveing impressions as it seems that that sad effect would not continow long – as it happened accordingly, for in 3 dayes after he saw and spoake as well as formerly.

He communicat the story but to a very few after he came home to Edinburgh. However, Mr Hary Fletcher, Salton's brother,[12] who was Mr Lundy's author, haveing got account of this passage from another hand was not satisfied till he went to Edinburgh and saw the gentleman himself and spoake with him and had it from his oun mouth. When I heard the story, at first my authors, Mr Lundy and his cusine Mr James Barclay, could not tell the gentleman's name. However, they made inquiry at Mr Fletcher, who informed them that the gentleman was indeed loath to communicat the story and to reveall his name; however, Mr Hary told them that his name is Mr John Duncan. He lives to this present time in Edinburgh; he formerly was, or for present is, a merchand. I am informed since that Bailie Duncan, who is married to Mr Alexander Hamilton's relict, has a brother of the same name.[13] I could have got the story from Mr Fletcher himself, haveing the honor of his acquaintance, but comeing away last from Salton abruptly I have sent it to yow with the conveyance there of, as I have it that yow may take your oun way of satisfying your self in the truth of it when yow are now at Edinburgh. I shall be glad if ye meet with the man himself. I am

R[everend] D[ear] S[ir]
Yours
J. Cowan

11 Night will bring a plan.
12 Henry Fletcher, brother of Andrew Fletcher of Saltoun.
13 Cowan seems to be mistaken here; see the discussion above.

Glasgow Aprile 26 1710

This accompt I have shouon to Mr Lundy, minister at Salton, who tells me it's very trou. RW Ed[i]n[burgh][14]

14 In Wodrow's hand.

THE CANONGATE LISTS OF PARISHIONERS (1661 AND 1684/7)

Edited by Alice Glaze

INTRODUCTION

The Canongate Lists of Parishioners comprise three connected parish lists of late seventeenth-century Canongate, a satellite burgh and parish of Edinburgh. The original manuscripts are part of the Church of Scotland collection held at the National Records of Scotland (CH2/122/67, 'List of Parishioners (1661)' and CH2/122/68, 'Lists of Parishioners (1684)'). These two volumes record three parish surveys conducted by the Canongate kirk session in 1661, 1684 and 1687 that each covered one half of the parish's ten quarters, bracketing the Restoration era. The 1661 and 1684 Lists of Parishioners follow the same five quarters beginning at the Canongate tolbooth, and so provide two snapshots of the same neighbourhood one generation apart; the 1687 list completes the parish tour begun three years earlier with the second set of five quarters beginning at Leith Wynd (where Jeffrey Street now stands). The 1684 and 1687 records are enclosed in the same volume and act as one list. Both the 1661 and 1684/7 Lists of Parishioners catalogue the household residents, including adult and adolescent family members, lodgers and servants (but not children), and were used as working documents by the kirk session; the marginalia, written in multiple hands, indicates a system for keeping track of marriages, kirk discipline and migration, among other social issues. These lists have been transcribed in their entirety, and together, they provide important insight into parish and town life during the later seventeenth century. This introduction provides historical context for the lists, explores some of the insights the lists provide through a cross-referencing with the concurrent kirk session records, and indicates possible areas of future study which could utilise them.

Canongate: Burgh and Parish

Human settlement in the area where Canongate now stands dates back to at least the early twelfth century. When David I founded the Augustinian abbey of Holyrood in what became the east end of Canongate in 1128, there was already an established church and resident lay community.[1] David also granted the abbey the right to establish a burgh between it and Edinburgh.[2] This burgh became known as Canongate, after the gait, or walk, of the canons of the abbey.[3] Scottish monarchs stayed at the abbey guesthouse since at least the fifteenth century, and under James IV a 'royal palace of Holyroodhouse' was officially established.[4] The two burghs of Canongate and Edinburgh developed together, albeit unequally, and became closely knit in the medieval and early modern eras. This was in large part determined by their topography: they were hemmed in by the Nor'loch to the north, and by marshlands to the south and east, although the latter were drained in the sixteenth century.[5] Their high streets ran in sequence along the narrow ridge of a volcanic plug, from Edinburgh Castle perched at the top of the ridge down to Holyrood Abbey and the Palace of Holyroodhouse in the marshy valley below, creating the 'Royal Mile' between the castle and palace. The imposing Netherbow Port marked the burghs' border along this conduit.[6] This physical proximity complemented a close economic and social relationship between the burghs: Canongate's burgesses benefitted from the significant and unique privilege of being able to trade in Edinburgh's markets as well as their own without fee or penalty, and in 1639 the relationship became more intertwined when the superiority of the burgh of Canongate was transferred to the city of Edinburgh as part of a debt payment.[7] This close relationship with Edinburgh, and Canongate's place within the region generally, shaped the growth and nature of the burgh and parish.

This unique political and geographic placement made Canongate home to a diverse social spectrum of residents, and the burgh developed a

1 E. Patricia Dennison and Michael Lynch, 'Crown, Capital, and Metropolis: Edinburgh and Canongate: Rise of a Capital and an Urban Court', *Journal of Urban History* 32.1 (2005), 23. According to legend, David saw a large white stag while out hunting, but the beast was chased off by a vision of the holy rood (cross) of Christ, inspiring the name of the abbey.

2 George Smith Pryde, *The Burghs of Scotland, A Critical List* (Oxford, 1965), 37. This establishment of a burgh so close to another existing burgh (Edinburgh) was unique to medieval Scotland. See Dennison and Lynch, 'Crown, Capital, and Metropolis', 24.

3 E. Patricia Dennison, *Holyrood and Canongate: A Thousand Years of History* (Edinburgh, 2005), 5.

4 Dennison and Lynch, 'Crown, Capital, and Metropolis', 25.

5 Dennison and Lynch, 'Crown, Capital, and Metropolis', 26.

6 The border was not this precise, however. The Cowgate parish, immediately west of the southern half of Canongate, was under Edinburgh's jurisdiction, but Potterrow, further to the west and south, was under Canongate's domain, as indicated in the 1687 parish list.

7 Dennison and Lynch, 'Crown, Capital, and Metropolis', 24. After the Reformation the superiority had been transferred from the Abbey of Holyrood to the local Bellenden family, who then sold it to the city council of Edinburgh in 1639. Canongate remained an independent burgh after this 1639 transfer, albeit with Edinburgh input into its governance. It was officially subsumed into Edinburgh in 1856. Pryde, *The Burghs of Scotland, A Critical List*, 60; Dennison and Lynch, 'Crown, Capital, and Metropolis', 40; Dennison, *Holyrood and Canongate*, 50.

complicated reputation. The royal court had established itself around the Palace of Holyroodhouse by the early sixteenth century, and hosting the court and its followers became the burgh's economic mainstay; the palace alone kept a core household staff of nearly six hundred workers in a burgh of perhaps four or five thousand.[8] Many noble families and wealthy burgesses lived there, and the burgh supported various luxury trades that catered to the palace.[9] However, Canongate was also home to many labourers and servants, and it remained a red-light district of the capital region.[10] Despite (or perhaps because of) this latter fact, the parish's kirk session was also known as one of the nation's most rigorous in its disciplining.[11] The social, economic and political stresses of the turbulent seventeenth century disrupted burgh life. With the removal of the royal court to London in 1603, Canongate lost its economic and logistical centre, although the Privy Council still sometimes met at the palace in the king's absence.[12] Increasing political tensions in the early decades of the century were matched with a severe economic downturn and poor crop yields, which developed into a famine that devastated the capital region in the 1620s.[13] The bubonic plague also hit Canongate frequently, with kirk session and testamentary evidence marking 1605–6, 1636 and 1645 as particularly significant years.[14] The 1645

8 Dennison and Lynch, 'Crown, Capital, and Metropolis', 25, 36. E. Patricia Dennison places the population of the Canongate at less than 4,000 while Leah Leneman and Rosalind Mitchison approximate almost 5,000; Helen Dingwall marks the population of the Canongate in the 1690s between 4,200 and 5,500. See Dennison, *Holyrood and Canongate*, 93; Leah Leneman and Rosalind Mitchison, *Sin in the City: Sexuality and Social Control in Urban Scotland 1660–1780* (Edinburgh, 1998), 10; Helen Dingwall, *Late Seventeenth-Century Edinburgh: A Demographic Study* (Aldershot, 1994), 17–19.

9 Walter Makey, 'Edinburgh in Mid-Seventeenth Century', in *The Early Modern Town in Scotland*, ed. Michael Lynch (Edinburgh, 1987), 196; W.H. Makey, 'The Elders of Stow, Liberton, Canongate and St. Cuthberts in the Mid-Seventeenth Century', *Records of the Scottish Church History Society* 17.2 (1970), 158, 163.

10 Michael F. Graham, *The Uses of Reform: "Godly Discipline" and Popular Behavior in Scotland and Beyond, 1560–1610* (Leiden, 1996), 288–9.

11 Graham, *The Uses of Reform*, 99.

12 Dennison and Lynch, 'Crown, Capital, and Metropolis', 39–40; Laura A.M. Stewart, *Urban Politics and the British Civil Wars: Edinburgh, 1617–53* (Leiden, 2006), 5, 105, 205.

13 Michael Flinn, *Scottish Population History* (Cambridge, 1977), 117; Rosalind Mitchison, *The Old Poor Law in Scotland: The Experience of Poverty, 1574–1845* (Edinburgh, 2000), 15–16. See also Laura A.M. Stewart, 'Poor Relief in Edinburgh and the Famine of 1621–24', *International Review of Scottish Studies* 30 (2005), 5–41.

14 See Charles F. Mullett, 'Plague Policy in Scotland, 16th–17th Centuries', *Osiris* 9 (1950), 445–53 *passim*. See also National Records of Scotland (NRS), Edinburgh commissary court records, register of testaments, CC8/8/39 (Margaret Forrest, 1605); CC8/8/42 (Bessie Nimble, 1605); CC8/8/43 (Isobel Lyon, 1607); NRS, CH2/122, Canongate Kirk Session Records (hereafter NRS, CH2/122 CKSR), volume 3, 5 June 1636. In 1625, the kirk session records noted a fast in celebration in part of the end of a plague visitation in England; see NRS, CH2/122, CKSR, volume 2, 23 October 1625. Margaret Sanderson and Charles Mullet have noted that in 1585 there was a 'particularly severe visitation' of the

visitation marked the final but devastating occurrence of the plague in the area, claiming two thousand lives in less than one year.[15] Cromwell's invasion of Scotland also struck Canongate keenly: he and his troops wintered in the burgh in 1650 directly after crushing the Scottish army at nearby Dunbar, stabling their horses in the abandoned royal palace.[16] Church life ground to a halt for the first year of the Cromwellian occupation, and English soldiers frequent the kirk session records, usually associated with social disorder, for the next decade.[17] With the Restoration in 1660, however, the Palace of Holyroodhouse became once again a royal residence under Charles II. Both Charles and his brother James VII/II renovated and improved the palace, and Canongate reclaimed its place as the heart of a royal court. It was during this period of local as well as national restoration that the first parish list was undertaken.

The kirk session also helped set the tone of life as the local religious authority in Canongate, as is reflected in the parish lists. The kirk session was composed of the parish's ministers as well as a representative elder and deacon from each of the ten quarters, and a session clerk. It formed the local level of the Reformed Kirk of Scotland's interlocking system of ecclesiastical courts, working with and feeding into the local presbytery, regional synod and national General Assembly. As noted above, the Canongate kirk session maintained a reputation for rigour and staunchly Reformed practice.[18] This created some religious tensions during the later Restoration period. The Catholic duke of York took up residence at the Palace of Holyroodhouse while in exile from England during the Exclusion Crisis of 1679–82. The palace also hosted a Catholic chapel and a Jesuit college, heightening religious tensions with the majority Protestant burgh population.[19] In 1687, James VII

plague in Edinburgh, and so likely also Canongate. See Margaret H.B. Sanderson, *A Kindly Place? Living in Sixteenth-Century Scotland* (East Linton, 2002), 59; Mullett, 'Plague Policy in Scotland, 16th–17th Centuries', 443–4.

15 Helen M. Dingwall, 'Illness, Disease and Pain', in *A History of Everyday Life in Scotland, 1600 to 1800*, ed. Elizabeth Foyster and Christopher Whatley (Edinburgh, 2010), 112; James Scott Marshall, *The Life and Times of Leith* (Edinburgh, 1986), 66. For the death toll, see NRS, CH2/122, CKSR, volume 3, 3 March 1646. The plague continued to visit frequently in other forms until the 1660s; see Mullett, 'Plague Policy in Scotland, 16th–17th Centuries', 450–3.

16 Dennison, *Holyrood and Canongate*, 91.

17 NRS, CH2/122. CKSR, volume 4, 3 September 1650; 4 July 1651; for an example of the English soldiers as a social disruption, see volume 4, 20 September 1653, where one woman was rebuked for receiving English soldiers in her home and another woman was rebuked for selling drink to English soldiers during the time of sermon.

18 See for instance the firebrand natures of some of the ministers in the earlier seventeenth century. Ronald Selby Wright, *The Kirk in the Canongate* (Edinburgh, 1956), 38–41; Hew Scott, *Fasti Ecclesiae Scoticanae: The Succession of Ministers in the Church of Scotland from the Reformation*, vol. 1: Synod of Lothian and Tweeddale (Edinburgh, 1915), 25.

19 Keith M. Brown, 'Reformation to Union, 1560–1707', in *The New Penguin History of*

and the Privy Council evicted the Canongate parish from worshipping at the abbey church adjacent to the Palace, which was instead renovated into the Chapel Royal; parishioners worshipped at Lady Yester in Edinburgh until the new parish church was finished in 1691.[20] This religious tension, and the relocation, may have been motivating factors for the 1684 and 1687 lists, as the kirk session sought to identify and categorise its parishioners.

The Lists of Parishioners

The Canongate Lists of Parishioners were minister examination rolls, listing parishioners by parish quarter for the communion roll and for catechism.[21] The Canongate lists are among the earliest extant lists in Scotland.[22] The lists comprised the adults of the parish as well as children considered old enough to be catechised, likely twelve years of age and older.[23] As such, relatively few households list groups of people with the same surname, as would be expected for nuclear families: younger children were not listed, and many adolescents were likely working as servants and apprentices outside the family home. The lists do, however, include servants and lodgers, as well as family members; unlike many other contemporary demographic records, they do more than simply list the household heads.[24] The lists were working documents of the church, with additions, deletions and edits made by the ministers, elders and clerk as they undertook the ongoing work of the parish. The volumes were small and portable, for this purpose: the 1661 bound parish list measures 200 x 100 x 15 mm, and the 1684/7 lists, bound as one volume, measure 302 x 105 x 12 mm.[25] The fact that the lists were working documents accounts for the somewhat enigmatic marginalia system used, a type of shorthand that will be explored at more length below; this system seems to have been used in other parish lists.[26] The 1661 parish lists

Scotland, ed. R.A. Houston and W.W.J. Knox (London, 2001), 257–8.

20 Wright, *The Kirk in the Canongate*, 47.

21 Unfortunately, neither the lists nor the concurrent kirk session records provide explicit geographic boundaries for the quarters, although the 'Abbay Quarter' (1661) and 'Potterow Quarter' (1687) help provide general geographic context.

22 The first two were West Kirk (St Cuthberts) in Edinburgh, in 1632 and 1639, and Uphall, in West Lothian, in 1660 and 1670, followed by Canongate in 1661. Flinn, *Scottish Population History*, 68.

23 Flinn, *Scottish Population History*, 65.

24 See, for instance, NRS, CH2/472, Kinghorn Kirk Session Records, volume 1, parish list (1581) beginning on page 249; and Aaron Allen and Cathryn Spence, eds, *Edinburgh Housemails Taxation Book, 1634–1636*, Scottish History Society, 6th edition, volume 9 (Edinburgh, 2014).

25 I am grateful to Alison Lindsay and the Conservation department at the National Records of Scotland for providing me with the physical descriptions of the volumes.

26 Flinn, *Scottish Population History*, 66.

are well marked, with significant additions and deletions made; in contrast the 1684/7 lists contain fewer edits and was perhaps used less frequently as a reference document. In all lists the names were written first, with all the marginalia, as well as other edits, added later. The parish lists give names of 1,359 people in 1661 (96 of whom were scored out), 1,566 names in 1684 (39 scored out) and 1,505 names in 1687 (21 scored out).[27]

The Lists of Parishioners provide important glimpses of daily life in early modern urban Scotland. The parish lists reveal, for instance, the variety of early modern household structures found in a vibrant urban centre. While many households seem to list married couples with one servant (or perhaps lodger), others were more diverse. For example, pages 67 and 68 of the 1661 parish list include one nuclear family (headed by William Auchinleck and Marion Gray); three households with only women listed (Margaret Neilson and Jean Davidson, Geills Alexander and Cristian Shirrilaw, and Marion Jackson and Margaret Stemson); one woman living alone (Elizabeth Stratoun); and a household of several people with unknown connections to each other (Robert Watson, Margaret Peebles, Archibald Stevin, Silvester Leslie and Henrie Smith). This household structural variety is also seen in the 1684/7 parish list: pages 56 and 57 list a nuclear family (headed by William Brotherstanes and Helen Mather), two female-only households (Jonet Jack and Agnes Monro, and Agnes Leitch and Eupham Ffiddes), and two households of unknown connections (John Livingston, Margaret Gibb, Anna Marshell and Elespeth Campbell; and Thomas Crichton, Marjorie Wood, Rachaell Aikenhead and Elespeth Milne). The parish lists provide a snapshot of the surprisingly diverse configurations of household groupings. Further research is needed, however, to reveal some of the connections between these people, as is discussed in more detail below.

The lists also provide evidence of people, especially women, moving between households, giving insight into economic and social networks and mobility in Restoration Scotland. For example, in the 1661 census, Catharene/Katherein McMillan is listed in two neighbouring households on pages 66 and 67, and Issobell Ormond is listed twice on page 74, which might indicate servants moving between houses and changing contracts.[28] Surnames also repeat across households within the quarters, mapping family ties within the urban centre; they also echo between the two parish lists themselves. Members of the distinctively named Badyenoch family, for instance, are easily traced from a nuclear family with one outlying female

27 Entries such as 'Lady Bogies familie' or 'Beggars Lodged' were counted as a single name although they undoubtedly referred to more than one person. Entries such as 'and his lady' were counted as a separate entity, and 'a woman with a child' was counted as two.

28 These could be clerical errors, but in each case the person's name was written in two different hands, which suggests a later edit rather than an error.

relative in 1661 to four separate households in 1684 and 1687. Using the parish lists together, across a generation, can therefore provide an even deeper understanding of both the transience and the settlement patterns characteristic of busy early modern towns.[29]

The Lists of Parishioners' marginalia add further detail to these rich social records. For example, some households in the 1661 parish list are labelled as 'English', perhaps highlighting those residents who were not full members of the kirk. Soldiers and officers are also clearly labelled in both lists, and other names are marked with qualifiers such as 'sick', 'old', 'scolding', 'catechism' and 'blind', each in their own way identifying those in need of the church's special attention. Religious conformity was, as noted above, an area of concern in Restoration Canongate, and the changing religious demographics are reflected in the parish lists: in 1661, two households are listed as including 'papists' (or 'pop'); in 1684 the number rose to six, alongside one Quaker household, and in 1687 there were ten people marked as Catholics in the parish list, all but one of them residing in the fourth quarter. Beggars' lodging is also marked in the 1661 list, and a 'Moor' is listed as living in a deacon's cellar in 1687, providing glimpses into the population diversity of early modern towns.[30] Names in both lists are frequently labelled with 'test' in the margins, indicating that a testificate of good character from another parish was requested or received on behalf of someone wanting to join the parish or marry in Canongate.[31] The marginalia of the lists therefore illuminate patterns of life in the church and in Scottish society during a period of intense social change and community surveillance.

A cross-referencing of the parish lists with other extant records, such as the Canongate kirk session records,[32] provides important details on marriages, neighbours and relationships, and gives some further insight into the marginalia used in the lists, although some aspects of the notation system remain enigmatic. For instance, the 'm' marginalia may indicate recent marriages in the parish. In January 1661, Dugall McFarlane and Catherene Simson had their banns proclaimed, as noted in the kirk session records, and their names are recorded alongside an 'm' notation on page 42.[33] William Brotherstanes and Helene Mathie, whose banns were proclaimed in May, have the same marginalia on page 46, as have Williame Somerwell and Jonet

29 A comparable study in this way is Allen and Spence, eds, *Edinburgh Housemails Taxation Book*.

30 The former is listed simply as 'Beggers Lodged' rather than a named parishioner found housing beggars.

31 For more information on testificates, see R.A. Houston, *Records of a Scottish Village: Lasswade 1650–1750* (Cambridge, 1982), 15–18.

32 Concurrent volumes are NRS, CH2/122, CKSR, volume 4 (1649-68) and volume 7 (1682–8).

33 NRS, CH2/122, CKSR, volume 4, 22 January 1661.

Bennet on page 40, also proclaimed in May.[34] However, this notation system is not consistent across the parish lists. First, it seems that the 1661 parish list, listed in its heading as written in late July, was not fully edited later to note marriages that took place later in the year. Duncan Wright and Jean Stirling had their banns proclaimed in October, but Jean is listed as still living with Magdalen Hog on page 4 on the parish list.[35] Even marriages that took place before the survey are not consistently marked. George Beruick and Jean Beaston were reprimanded by the kirk session elders for their scandalous behaviour together in early June 1661, and their banns were proclaimed soon after, but they are listed together without marginalia on page 54.[36] John Adamson and Jean Murray, whose banns were proclaimed in July 1661, do not have any marginalia next to their names on page 73, although they are listed as heads of a household.[37] More problematically, many more people are listed with 'm' marginalia than could be considered newly married or married at all. The 1684/7 lists do not include any 'm' marginalia. Some other marginalia, while clear, do not seem to correspond to any extant sources. Most of the entries in the parish list with marginalia indicating 'op [date] 1661' or '1662' have no matching record in the kirk session records, the most likely corresponding record.[38] These notes must be referring to another record set, possibly no longer extant. The meaning behind other common marginalia, such as 'a' in 1661, 'b' and 'v' in 1684, and 'ab' in 1687, has not been deciphered. The notations do not correspond systematically with any entries in the kirk session records. The marginalia should therefore be read with caution (and curiosity), as they may have unknown, inconsistent or multiple meanings; more research is needed in order to clarify the system at work. A list of common marginalia for each List is included at the end of this introduction.

Cross-referencing the parish list and kirk session records does, however, provide some important benefits; for instance, it reveals the work of kirk session discipline in its variety of forms. The most common offences prosecuted by the kirk session were sexual in nature (fornication and, more rarely, adultery), but the elders and ministers also disciplined parishioners for Sabbath breach, slander and other offences. In January 1661, Agnes Clerk confessed to the sin of fornication with an Englishman; in March the kirk session elders ordered her to produce a testificate of her marriage, which she did in April. This is likely what prompted the marginalia of 'op' next to

34 NRS, CH2/122, CKSR, volume 4, 7 May 1661; 21 May 1661.

35 NRS, CH2/122, CKSR, volume 4, 1 October 1661. It is possible that they did not move in together immediately upon marriage.

36 NRS, CH2/122, CKSR, volume 4, 11 June 1661; 18 June 1661.

37 NRS, CH2/122, CKSR, volume 4, 21 July 1661.

38 'Op' is a Latin shorthand meaning to look or check.

her name on page 17.[39] In April 1661, Isobel Walker was caught receiving or 'resetting' infamous people into her home, and was rebuked; her entry on page 40 is aptly marked with 'recetie'.[40] Margaret Nesbit was similarly rebuked in November 1661 for receiving infamous people like Margaret Faill in her house in Chapel Close. Her household, listed on page 48, includes an Issobell Fell, who is marked as 'pop' for 'papist' or Catholic, and who could be a relation of Margaret's.[41]

The 1684/7 parish list marginalia matches less consistently with the concurrent kirk session records, and the marginalia is less varied and more obscure or coded than the earlier list, but the parishioners listed do show up in the records. James Tailyor's household, listed on page 35 of the 1684 parish list, received multiple warnings from the kirk session that year: in May his unnamed taverner was ordered to the magistrates for her disobedience, likely for selling drink on the Sabbath; in October, the kirk session warned his servants, including Agnes Dow, to come before the session to be reprimanded; and in November his daughter, Jean Tailyor, was made to sign a public declaration to no longer frequent the company of one John Anderson, under the pain of £100 Scots.[42] Jean may not have adhered to this declaration, as she was referred to the civil magistrates two weeks later.[43] In January 1687, James Sutherland, a soldier in Captain Graham's company, confessed to fornication with Eupham Scotland, under the promise of marriage; four months later he was rebuked for not yet marrying her, although she was 'nightly in his house' and had borne his child. They are listed together on page 127.[44] These interactions with the kirk session are not reflected in any marginalia next to their names. However, cross-referencing the lists and kirk session records still provides important information about the parishioners, such as a rare contextual glimpse of those listed on the parish's poor relief rolls.[45] In May 1684, George Matters, listed on page 6 as the head of a household, had his amount on the poor relief roll augmented by 2s weekly, and Margaret Sim, listed as the head of a household on page 7, was to be given 5s weekly starting in November 1684.[46] These entries provide added context to the study of the lives of those at the margins of Canongate society.

39 NRS, CH2/122, CKSR, volume 4, 22 January 1661; 26 March 1661; 2 April 1661.

40 NRS, CH2/122, CKSR, volume 4, 30 April 1661.

41 NRS, CH2/122, CKSR, volume 4, 5 November 1661.

42 NRS, CH2/122, CKSR, volume 7, 3 May 1684; 3 October 1684; 13 November 1684.

43 NRS, CH2/122, CKSR, volume 7, 27 November 1684.

44 NRS, CH2/122, CKSR, volume 7, 27 January 1687; 28 April 1687. Her surname is shortened in the list to 'Scot'.

45 These rolls may have been recorded separately but are no longer extant as a discrete record; however, changes to the relief rolls were recorded in the main kirk session minutes.

46 NRS, CH2/122, CKSR, volume 7, 1 May 1684; 13 November 1684.

Cross-referencing the parish lists and kirk session records also provides information on neighbours and community life, giving rare geographic context for the cases raised in the kirk session records. For instance, in December 1661, Helen Watson, 'nurse' (likely wet-nurse) employed by John Greenleyis, writer, gave in her bill of complaint to the kirk session against Margaret Cumming, saying that Margaret had called her a 'whoore' and said that Helen's child had two fathers.[47] The parish lists reveal that the two women were neighbours: Helen and John are listed in the same household on page 73, and Margaret nearby on page 74. Although the kirk session elders agreed to look into the complaint, they also referred Helen to the civil magistrates for punishment as she had spoken 'unreverentlie to the elders' when they had tried to reconcile her with Margaret. Helen was ordered to produce a testificate of good behaviour, which was duly noted in her parish list entry.[48] The parish lists and kirk session records also reveal that neighbours could be called on for help. When Margaret Williamson confessed in October 1661 to committing fornication with Nicholas Smith, an Englishman, she brought 'Sara Auchinleck, spouse of William Worsdaill, coatchman' to swear that Nicholas had declared in London in her presence that he was the child's father.[49] Margaret is listed on page 42 with the marginalia of 'test' indicating that the elders still required a testificate of good behaviour from her; Sara and William are listed in the same quarter on page 48. The lists also produce other context for ties of support. When Thomas Hepburne and Marian Smart confessed to fornication under the promise of marriage in December 1661, James Thomson came forward as their cautioner; he is listed as Marian's household head on page 102, and was likely her employer.[50]

Finally, cross-referencing the parish lists and kirk session records reveals not only parishioners' movements between houses, but also possible reasons for those moves. In June 1661, Margaret Harvie confessed before the kirk session that she was pregnant for the third time out of wedlock, and was soundly rebuked; she may have left the parish, as her entry on page 53 of the parish list is crossed out.[51] In October 1661, Patrick Fair of Edinburgh's West Kirk parish and Grace Cunningham of Canongate, had their banns proclaimed; Grace, listed on page 91 of the parish lists, is crossed out, possibly indicating her move to Edinburgh.[52] In December 1661, Robert Anderson and Janet Mure confessed to fornication; it was Janet's second offence, and

47 NRS, CH2/122, CKSR, volume 4, 31 December 1661.
48 NRS, CH2/122, CKSR, volume 4, 31 December 1661.
49 NRS, CH2/122, CKSR, volume 4, 22 October 1661.
50 NRS, CH2/122, CKSR, volume 4, 10 December 1661.
51 NRS, CH2/122, CKSR, volume 4, 23 July 1661.
52 NRS, CH2/122, CKSR, volume 4, 29 October 1661.

she was ordered to complete the repentance process for her first fault in Saltoun in Haddington before returning to Canongate to formally repent for this more recent sin.[53] Both Robert and Janet are crossed out of their household listing on page 81, possibly indicating their move to Saltoun to undertake this process.[54]

These parish lists provide an important resource for a wide variety of historians. Historical demographers and urban historians can use the lists to analyse household size and formation (within the limits of the parish lists, given the lack of children listed), and changes to both across a generation in the five quarters included in both Lists. Family historians can seek out names and relationships in order to reconstruct genealogies. Gender historians can use the lists as a platform on which to study the prevalence of female-headed households and potential 'spinster clusters' in the urban environment.[55] The lists also record important information for ecclesiastical history, listing the elders and deacons in charge of each quarter and revealing the kirk session's methods of pastoral care, community surveillance and discipline. As the parish lists bracket the beginning and end of Charles II's reign, they also provide an important glimpse for political historians into the social composition around the Palace of Holyroodhouse in Restoration Scotland. The lists catalogue aristocratic families and their households residing near the Palace both when it was in disrepair after its use by Cromwell and his soldiers and once it had again risen in prominence under Charles II and James VII/II in the 1680s, showcasing shifting power relations in the later seventeenth century. Cross-referencing the lists with other extant records, such as the burgh court records, criminal court records, or wills and testaments, would provide further insight into the life of the burgh. Indeed, the parish lists are well placed for comparison with the 1687 Canongate Annuity Roll, and information from the 1691 Hearth Tax and 1694 Poll Tax, which cover both Edinburgh and Canongate.[56] Secondary sources, such as archaeological studies, monographs on Edinburgh and Canongate, and examinations of similar demographic records, provide important context.[57] The Lists of

53 NRS, CH2/122, CKSR, volume 4, 17 December 1661.

54 The Saltoun Kirk Session Records are no longer extant for 1661.

55 For context on spinster clusters and female-headed and -owned homes, see Olwen Hufton, 'Women Without Men: Widows and Spinsters in Britain and France in the Eighteenth Century', *French Historical Studies* 9.1 (Spring 1975), 1–22; Cathryn Spence, *Women, Credit, and Debt in Early Modern Scotland* (Manchester, 2016), 129–42; and Alice Glaze, 'Women's Networks of Family, Work, Support and Slander in Canongate, 1600–1660' (PhD dissertation, University of Guelph, 2017), 98–102 and 136–44.

56 For analysis of these records and their uses, see Dingwall, *Late Seventeenth-Century Edinburgh*.

57 Paul Masser *et al.*, 'Excavations at Jeffrey Street, Edinburgh: The Development of Closes and Tenements North of the Royal Mile During the 16th–18th Centuries', *Scottish Archaeological Internet Report* 58 (2014); Dingwall, *Late Seventeenth-Century Edinburgh*; Michael Lynch, *Edinburgh and the Reformation* (Edinburgh; Atlantic Highlands, NJ, 1981); Robert E. Tyson,

Parishioners can be used to shed new light on early modern Scottish life across various lines of study.

Editorial Conventions

Both parish lists have been presented in a slightly modified form from the original for ease of use. Three columns identify original page number, text and marginalia, while footnotes are used for extra-textual information such as noting different handwriting. For clarity, headings listing the parish quarters are bolded and the manuscripts' horizontal strokes delineating households have been replaced with blank rows; thus, each block of names represents a discrete household. Otherwise, the transcription closely follows the manuscripts' style. Names and marginalia scored out in the manuscripts are similarly scored out in the transcription. Original spelling has been maintained, although abbreviations in common names have been written out using square brackets (e.g. 'Marg[are]t'), and angle brackets < > indicate a best guess for illegible handwriting. Yoghs have been replaced with 'y', and the use of u/v has been modernised.

List of Common Marginalia

1661 List of Parishioners

Marginalia	Commentary
a	no clear meaning; no obvious correlation with 'adherent' or 'absolved'
f	no clear meaning
m	may indicate 'marriage'
non sat	likely indicates 'not satisfied' their required repentance
op	indicates 'check' or 'search'
test	indicates 'testificate'
x	no clear meaning
y	no clear meaning

1684 List of Parishioners

Marginalia	Commentary
b	no clear meaning; no obvious correlation with 'baptism'
test	indicates 'testificate'
v	no clear meaning
y	no clear meaning

'Household Size and Structure in a Scottish Burgh: Old Aberdeen in 1636', *Local Population Studies* 40 (1988), 46–54.

1687 List of Parishioners

Marginalia	Commentary
ab	no clear meaning
b	no clear meaning; no obvious correlation with 'baptism'
ig	no clear meaning
put	no clear meaning
test	indicates 'testificate'
v	no clear meaning

TRANSCRIPTION

List of Parishioners (1661)

National Records of Scotland, Canongate Kirk Session Records, CH2/122/67

Page	Text	Marginalia
2	**The names of the families of the one halfe of the Cannongate beginning at the Tolbuith 23 July 1661**	
	James Elders quarter	
	James Weir	
	Jean Gib	
	Helene Weir	
	James Broun	y
	Elspeth Broun	
	Harie Duncan	m
	John Scot	y
	Marie Maclauchan	non sat x viz
	James Wilson	m
	Jean Anderson	m
	John Wilson	y
3	John Johnstoun	a
	Jonet McFarlane	x a
	Edward Hepburn	m
	Catharen Kinghorn	m
	Bessie Hepburn	
	~~Margaret Johnstoun~~	
	Bessie Jackson	test m[1]
	Janet Hutson	Tranent[2]
	John Findlason	test op[3]
	Helene West	
	Alex[ande]r Hoome	

1 Name and marginalia written in different hand.

2 Name and marginalia written in different hand.

3 'Test op' refers to entire household.

	Jean Johnstoun	
	Alex[ande]r Hoome	
	George Hoome	
	Marion Thomson	test op m
4	Williame Forrester	m
	Margaret Watson	op m f
	John Inglis	a a
	John Broun	y
	Magdalen Hog	m
	Jean Stirling	test f op <casle>
	William Gray	a[4] ~~m~~
	Issobell Law	a[5] ~~m~~ a
	Issobell Davidson	m
	Agnes Argo	m
5	James Dick	m
	Geills Mure	x op a
	Jonet Wilson	m
	Barbara Anderson	a a
	Cristian Anderson	a y
	~~Jean Anderson~~	~~a~~
	Robert Anderson	
	Agnes Carnoch	m
	Thomas Trotter	y
6	Andro Williamson	m
	Catharen Clerk	m
	Andro Williamson	y[6]
	William Din	
	Marion Nicoll	m test[7]
	Beatrix Din	

4 'A' written in left margin.
5 'a' written in left margin.
6 Name and marginalia written in different hand.
7 'Test' refers to entire household.

	~~Catharen Corstoun~~	a
	Andro Melvill	m
	Elspeth Bane	m
	Marie Melvill	y
7	James Murray	
	Barbara Murray	
	Issobell Murray	m
	Janet Linton	test op Feb 1662
		ch vis op tamen[8]
	Andro Frater	m
	Cristian Condie	y a
	George Frater	a
	William Wilson	m
	Helene Aitkin	~~a~~ m
	Walter Turpie	a non bale
	Marg[are]t Watson	a m
	John Blaikie	a
	Gilbert Turpie	m
8	John Turpie	a
	Bessie Walker	m
	~~Gilbert Turpie~~	a
	Marion Glen	test
	Alex[ande]r Barclay	y
	George Rollo	m
	Elspeth Craw	m
	James Badyenoch	
	Elspeth Ritchmond	
	Margaret Badyenoch	f op ante
	Williame Badyenoch	
	Issobell Badyenoch	y
	Helene Badyenoch	m
9	Williame Stevin	m

8 Written underneath household names.

	Marion Rae	m
	Catharen Blacator	a m
	John Forrester	a
	Agnes Glendining	a
	Thomas Forrester	a
	Williame Craufurd	test a
	Alex[ande]r Ramsay	test y ~~a~~
	~~Jonet Madser~~	~~test a a~~
	Katherein Kanny[9]	
	Mr James Brown[10]	
	Catharein Hamilton[11]	
	James Craig	
	Elizabeth Forrest	
	Patrick Young	a
	Andro Campell	y
	Sibbla Stewart	test op f m viz
	John Cummyng	y m
	Issobell Cummyng	y test
	~~Elspeth Low~~	f viz
	Janet Clerk	a test[12]
10	John Falconer	a a
	Jean Mowat	b test op[13]
	~~Daniell Broun~~ Malloch	a[14] test pen[15]
	~~Jean Toshoh~~	~~a~~
	David Johnstoun	m
	Dorathie Wood	m
	Thomas Loudian	y
	James Johnstoun	a y

9 Name written in a different hand.
10 Name written in different hand.
11 Name written in different hand.
12 Name and marginalia written in a different hand.
13 'Test op' refers to entire household.
14 'a' written in between forename and surname.
15 'Test pen' refers to entire household.

	Bessie Mow	m
11	James Aitkman	f x <obed ens> tamen
	Catharene Aitkman	viz x
	James Cleghorn	m
	Jean Yetts	m
	Margaret Sim	a non <vubt>
	Issobell Lennox	~~a m~~
	Georg Abernethie	opm g cambell
	Issobell Fairlie	viz
	Georg Abernethie	y
	Andro Abernethie	y
	Robert Meinyies	a
	Catharen Wood	y test[16]
12	Jean Paterson	m
	Margaret Cock	m
	William Cock	y
	Helene Ellot	m
	Margaret Bailyie	m
	Margaret Douglas	m
	Jonet Bailyie	a a
	John Bowie	m
	~~John~~ Jonett[17] Tripna	y
	Antonie Richardson	English[18] a[19] a
	Sussanna Louthian	a test[20]
	John McKune	~~a~~ tun
	Anna Glen	a ~~a~~ m
	~~Margaret Stevin~~	op test <comunion>
	John Simson	x[21] test op Jan 1661[22]

16 'Test' refers to entire household.
17 'Jonett' written in different hand.
18 'English' written as heading above household.
19 'a' written in left margin.
20 'Test' refers to entire household.
21 Name and 'x' written in a different hand.
22 'Test op Jan 1661' refers to entire household.

13	John Topliff	m
	Alison Jackson	a a sick b
	Gawin More	m
	Beatrix Bullen	f m
	George Maters	m <cond of £x>
	Bessie Sinclar	m test op
	Jonet Matters	m
	John Webster	y[23]
	David Walker	m
	Agnes Liverance	m
	John ~~Duncan~~	a
	Rob[er]t Walker	a[24]
	James Elder	
	Bessie Dauson	
	Sara Elder	y
	~~Jonet Walker~~	~~y~~
	William Bennet	m
14	Bessie Futhie	m
	Margaret McKeinyie	m
	Marie McKeinyie	m
	Agnes McKeinyie	m[25] ~~test~~[26]
	David Durehame	m coll
	Jonet Langlands	m test op[27]
	Robert Jackson	m a
	Marjorie Gairnes	x m f test op feb 1662[28]
	John Nimmo	~~a~~ m
	Margaret Broun	a
	Robert Russell	a

23 Name and marginalia written in a different hand.
24 Name and marginalia written in a different hand.
25 Name and marginalia written in a different hand.
26 'Test' refers to entire household.
27 'Test op' refers to entire household.
28 'Test op feb 1662' refers to entire household.

	Adam Duncan	m
	Jonet Milne	op <m privat>
	Rebecka Buchanan	~~y~~ m
	Catharen Duncan	y
	John Wallace	m
15	Jonet Robertson	
	Mr Alex[ande]r Don	
	Margaret Allane	~~test~~
	Nanse Lourie	a op m[29]
	Ephie Bishop	a[30]
	Neill McKeinyie	m
	Marion Deanes	m
	George Suttie	a
	Alex[ande]r Atchison	goodnes[31] m
	Cristian Sked	m
	James Atcheson	y
	Marjorie Dowie	m
16	Margaret Caldwell	~~a~~ m
	Jean Lindsay	m
	Agnes Paterson	a x non <lder>
	Marion Limpetlaw	~~a~~ m
	Barbara Malloch	m
	Issobell Wilson	a x m
	Elizabeth Penny	m
	James Hutcheson	~~good gooding~~[32] m
	Margaret Gordon	m
	Thomas Forfar	y
	~~Elias Liddell~~	
	Marg[are]t Gib	test a

29 Name and marginalia written in a different hand.
30 Name and marginalia written in a different hand.
31 'Goodnes' written above household.
32 'Good gooding' written above household.

17	Alex[ande]r Lowis	n
	Agnes Clerk	n op
	James Lowis	~~a~~
	Alex[ande]r Herreis	y
	Peter Duncan	m
	Bessie Caldwell	m
	Jonet Duncan	y
	James Rodger	m
	Thomas Tours	a a
	Agnes Johnstoun	a viz
	Eupham Allan	~~a~~ m
	Jonet Mershell	m
18	Alex[ande]r Reid	a m
	Jonet Spence	m
	David Spence	a m
	Elizabeth Reid	a a y
	John Nicolson	a <trumpet>
	Barbara Smith	m
	Robert Bellenden	a
	Margaret Furde	m
	Marie Bellenden	m
	David Duncan	a a
	Barbara Tasker	m
	Jonet Duncan	y
	Marjorie Ure	m[33] ~~x a~~ [illegible] viz
19	Hew Christall	m
	Catharene McKell	a a
	Williame Carnagie	o p m
	Margaret Weir	m
	Williame Carnagie	y

33 'm' written between forename and surname.

	Andro Wood	a a
	~~Marg[are]t Edmonstoun~~	test a p m
	Marion Pring<l>	test op Jan 1662[34]
	Gawin Bonckle	m
	Jonet Falconer	m
	James Bonckle	m
	Catharene Bonckle	y
	Robert Cook	m y
	William Hill	test op m[35]
	Robert Reid	a
	Bessie White	m
20	John Kirk	a
	Bessie Allan	x a
	Robert White	m
	Jean Tompiltoun	m
	~~Williame McKean~~	
	Williame McKean	a
	Elspeth Davidson	viz m fath test ad[36]
	James Giffard	a[37]
	Eupham Vetch	a test op[38]
	Janet Neilson	a[39]
21	James Johnstoun	a a
	Cristian Buchanan	m x
	~~Helene Johnstoun~~	
	Elspeth Allan	
	John Wilson	m
	Catharen Wilson	a a

34 Name and marginalia written in a different hand.
35 Name and marginalia written in a different hand.
36 'Fath test ad' refers to entire household.
37 Name and marginalia written in a different hand.
38 Name and marginalia written in a different hand.
39 Name and marginalia written in a different hand.

	John Birnie	a a
	Jonet Fforrest	m
	John Birnie	y
	William Clerk	a a x non k
	Jean Cunynghame	
	Alex[ande]r Clerk	y
	Helene Cuthbertson	y
	John Clerk	y[40]
22	John Davidson	m
	Jonet Wilson	~~x~~ y m
23	Donald McCarra	a m
	Elspeth Malloch	m
	Andro McCarra	a y
	Andro Williamson	a a
	Jonet Scot	m
	Catharen Bowmaker	a
	John Murray	a
	Jonet Adamson	m
	Magdalen Adamson	a a
	~~Jonet Kincaid~~	
	James Millar	m
	Jean Reid	m
	Robert Millar	a y
24	George McReddie	a a
	Issobell Culland	a a
	Issobell McReddie	a a
	John Sanders	a
	Issobell Baine	m test op
	Marg[are]t Sanders	y
	Elspeth Sanders	y
	Thomas Potter	a a

40 Name and marginalia written in a different hand.

	John Williamson	a a
	Elspeth Kinnaird	a m
	Marg[are]t Williamson	a y
25	John Ramsay	a a
	Euphame Maison	a a
	George Mitchell	~~a a~~ m
	Williame Tuedie	a a
	Marie Craigingilt	a m
	John Greinlaw	a a
	Jonet Nimmo	m
	Marion Greinlaw	y
	Margaret Ramsay	a m
26	Margaret Rattray	
	John Davids[41]	
	John Dabson	English[42] a a ~~Alexr~~
	Jonet Rutherfoord	a a
	Jonet More	a
	Marg[are]t Stewart	a
	Jonet Stewart	a y
	John Black	m
	Issobell Black	m
	Jonet Innes	test a a
27	Margaret McIlroy	~~a~~ x op m
	Violet Falconer	
	Jean Wright	y[43]
	Robert Honeyman	a a

41 Name written in a different hand.
42 'English' written as heading above household.
43 Name and marginalia written in a different hand.

	Issobell Couper	m
	John Gellalie	m op
	Sara McKie	a ch x viz m
	John Gellalie	a
	Barbara Gellalie	a
	Alex[ande]r Wilson	a a
	Jonet Plummer	a viz m
	Marg[are]t Mure	x
	Andro Scot	a a
	~~Cristian~~	
28	Margaret Sinclair	m
	John Howie	m
	Alison Haistie	m
	Williame Louristoun	m

Georg Cambells qrter

	Alex[ande]r Mathie	
	Jean Nisbet	
	Jean Mathie	~~m~~ b
	Jonet Archibald	a x test
	D.L. Lamington[44]	
29	Robert Thomson	m
	Marjorie Whyt	x op
	Margaret Thomson	a
	James Boyd	y
	James Byres	y catechism[45]
	John Anderson	a
	Margaret Lauson	
	Margaret Anderson	y
	John Anderson	y
	William Duncan	a x m

44 Name written in a different hand.

45 Name and marginalia written in a different hand.

	Margaret Hunter	x m m
	Helen McKeith	test a
	Jonet Hogg	test see viz Jan 1662 x[46]
30	James Barrie	m
	Issobell Barrie	m
	Helen Hollie	a test[47]
	John Barrie	test a[48]
	Jonet Steill	m op
	George Gairdner	~~a~~ tr
	Catharen Hopkirk	~~a~~ tr a
	Bessie Maxuell	x tr a
	Jean Findlason	y
	Jonet Reid	
	John Midiltoun	a a
	Alison Arthor	m
	James Midiltoun	a a
31	John Lang	a
	Margaret Provand	x test[49] a
	John Gawin	a[50] m
	Margaret Leslie	m coll m
	Jonet Allan	test a a
	Bessie Robertson	a a
	James Craig	a a
	Margaret Louthian	a f x ara
	Andro Scot	x a

46 Name and marginalia written in a different hand.
47 Name and marginalia written in a different hand.
48 Name and marginalia written in a different hand.
49 'Test' refers to entire household.
50 'a' written in between forename and surname.

	Jonet Spence	a a test[51]
	William Brown	test op dec 1662[52]
	Jean Renten	b[53]
32	John Clatchie	m
	Sussana Knight	~~a a~~ op f tr: et off.
	Archibald Arnot	m b
	Margaret Sinclar	m
	Agnes Arnot	x a
	Helene Simpson	test a a
	Robert Smith	a m
	Marion Hepburn	a a
	Margaret Smith	y m
	Bessie Buchanan	(m) test op
	Margaret Findlason	
	Margaret Flucher	test op[54]
33	Helene Dowie	m
	William Fergusson	a
	Lybra Broun	m
	Elspeth Russell	m
	Jonet Ramsay	a a
	Catharen Ramsay	m
	Jonet Thomson	m maried
	John Thomson	a y
	Patrick Rae	m
	Annabell Vaus	m
	William Wardrop	
	Jean Watson	
	Margaret Wardrop	
34	James Reid	a

51 'Test' refers to entire household.

52 Name and marginalia written in a different hand.

53 Name and marginalia written in a different hand.

54 Name and marginalia written in a different hand.

	Elspeth Gib	a m
	Margaret Gairnes	m
	Jonet Thomson	m y
	Andro Fyf	a a
	Janet Thomson[55]	
	Andro Wilkie	a a
	Elspeth Nicolson	a naturix m
	David Ness	a a
	Violet Hoome	~~xa~~ ch m
	Alex[ande]r McBaith	m a a
	Bessie Leslie	a a
35	George Campbell	
	Jonet Gray	
	William Campbell	
	Margaret Johnstoun	m
	James Jounstoun	m
	Geills Duff	viz
	Margaret Duncan	a y
	John Paterson	
	Agnes Lyell	
	Robert Paterson	y
	Marg[are]t Paterson	y a
	Issobell Tailyefeir	test a p for
	Marg[are]t Allan	test x a
	Issobell Makilquham	test op op
36	Jonet Shaw	m
	Bessie Russell	m
	Jonet Russell	y x m
	Robert Cuthbertson	a a
	Marg[are]t Broun	m
	George Cuthbertson	~~x m~~

55 Name written in a different hand.

	Helene Welsh	blind a
	Agnes Broun	viz m
	Barbara Thomson	m b y
	~~John Graham~~	~~a x~~
	~~Jonet Duff~~	~~x~~
	Elspeth Lindsay	x com op <cambise>
	Barbara Skene	m
37	Catharene Harbert	a a
	John Banks	a a
	Walter Malcom	a a
	Issobell Gairdner	m viz
	Jonet Dickie	y
	Marion Dickie	y
	Andro Mitchell	a
	Catharene McMillan	m
	Catharene Williamson	a
	Helene Mitchell	m y
	Marg[are]t Mitchell	y
38	Cristian Tod	m viz
	James Muller	m[56]
	John Gray	x op
	Jonet Clerk	m
	William Brown	m[57]
	William Fry	m viz[58]
	Elizabeth Blair	m
	Margaret Forsyth	b
	Thomas Watson	

56 Name and marginalia written in a different hand.
57 Name and marginalia written in a different hand.
58 Name and marginalia written in a different hand.

	Margaret Broun	
	Jean Watson	b
	John Watson	test op b
	Margaret Broun	b
	Margaret Lyell[59]	
	Nanse Tom	test op[60]
39	Georg Wilson	~~m~~ a
	Margaret Forbes	m
	William Crouden	a a
	Helen Young	test op op y a
	Issobell Wilson	non <vubt>[61] a a
	Agnes Leitch	y x tom:
	James Gray	t
	Robert Gray	y[62]
	Gutritch Wilson	a a
	Margaret Water	x a
	Margaret Wilson	a
	George Whythead	a a
	Margaret Tail	a a
40	Issobell Walker	recetie[63] x susp:
	Robert Deippo	a o
	Euphame Deippo	test a a o
	Robert Carnagie	<coids> op
	Anna Yets	m
	Gabriell Blair	m
	Jonet Aitkin	m
	Williame Someruell	m

59 Name written in a different hand.
60 Name and marginalia written in a different hand.
61 Written in left margin.
62 Name and marginalia written in a different hand.
63 Written above name.

	Jonet Bennet	m
41	William Mure	a a
	Jonet Stewart	a a test a[64]
	Alex[ande]r McKay	x a[65]
	Bessie Leslie	x op a[66]
	Robert Watson	a a
42	Dugall McFarlane	m
	Catharene Simson	m
	Quintene Adam	m
	Williame Gordon	viz
	Jean Anderson	m[67] test seen op Oct 21 1661
	Issobell Stewart	m
	Margaret Wilson	o a sick
	George Hepburne	m
	Jean Dickson	op privat
	Margaret Williamson	viz m test op[68]
	Agnes Ker	m
	Alex[ande]r Downie	y
	Jean Downie	y
	Jonet Millar	m test op Oct 21 1661
43	Robert Forfar	a old viz
	Thomas Millar	a op m
	Agnes Forfar	a x
	Elspeth Wood	m test op
	Thomas Auchinleck	~~a~~ m
	Sara Melvill	viz m test op[69]
	Issobell Young	y m

64 'Test a' refers to entire household.
65 Name and marginalia written in a different hand.
66 Name and marginalia written in a different hand.
67 'M' written in between forename and surname.
68 'Test op' refers to entire household.
69 'Test op' refers to entire household.

	Findlo Tailyor	a
	Marg[are]t Boswall	a
	~~Issobell McKeith~~	~~test a~~
	Issobell Burnett	~~test op viz~~ test op[70]
	William Purdie	~~a a~~ x
	Issobell Henrison	vemfic[71]
	Jonet Purdie	~~venfic~~ y m
	John Purdie	a a
	James Adamson	x <trimbie>
	Cristian Trumble	
	~~Alison Pearstoun~~	~~a a~~
44	Williame Scoullen	m
	Elspeth Logan	x m
	Ladie Jean Lindsay	
	Margaret Hopkirk	
	Cristian Johnstoun	m
	James McMillan	y m
	William McMillan	m y
	~~Anna Trumble~~	test set off op
	Marion MackMillan	test xtr y[72]
	Marie Kincaid	
	Jonet Keir	
	Anna Keir	
	~~Cristian McKie~~	~~test a a~~
	Susana Weer	m[73]
	Marie Peirs	
	Agnes Distan	test op Oct 22 1661
	Jonet Callende	m test Oct 22 1661
	Issobell Mous	m test
45	Catharene McClure	m

70 Name and marginalia written in a different hand.
71 Name and marginalia written in a different hand.
72 Name and marginalia written in a different hand.
73 Name and marginalia written in a different hand.

~~Robert Erskene~~ m
Elspeth Paterson m
Agnes Thomson test
Jean Grame op[74] test op Feb 1662[75]

John Mairtene a a
Jean Douglas m

Jonet McConnell m

Thomas Hunter a
Jonet Cuthbertson m
Jean Dickie y[76]
Abigail Shaw test m[77]

John Lauder a gentl
Margaret Seatoun m test[78]
Margaret Reid test a
Elizabeth Reid test a
Gryssell Campbell test op Dec 1662 m[79]

46 Andro Barron m
Cristan Scot viz <coth>
Alex[ande]r Loch y b
Andro McCall m test[80]

David Hog
Agnes Ramma y
Barbara Hog y
Mary Semson op[81] test[82]

William Brotherstanes m
Helene Mathie m

74 'Op' written in left margin.
75 Name and marginalia written in a different hand.
76 Name and marginalia written in a different hand.
77 Name and marginalia written in a different hand.
78 'Test' refers to entire household.
79 Name and marginalia written in a different hand.
80 'Test' refers to entire household.
81 'Op' written in left margin.
82 Name and marginalia written in a different hand.

	Issobell Cliddisdaill	test m[83]
	Andro Bullman	m
	Barbara Ros	m
	Barbara Ros	y b[84]
	George Will	op[85] a George Will y
	Cristian Harrowar	m
	James Murray	test a[86]
	Elizabeth Carbeth	barn[87] a[88]
47	James Elder	m
	Cristian Fairlie	m
	Robert Bairdner	y b
	Williame Elder	y b
	Catharene Dickson	y
	William W[illia]mson	m
	Issobell Quiges	m
	Jonet Mitchell	x m
	Annas Kincaid	m
	Jonet Bryden	m
	John Law	a a
	Marie Forrest	x adam a
	David Sim	m
	Margaret Fortoun	m
	David Ralstoun	a m
	Margaret Paislay	m
	Catharen Mitchell	m
48	Barbara ~~Purves~~	a
	Bessie Chalmers	

83 Name and marginalia written in a different hand.
84 Name and marginalia written in a different hand.
85 'Op' written in left margin.
86 Name and marginalia written in a different hand.
87 'Barn' written in left margin.
88 Name and marginalia written in a different hand.

Bessie Brok	a x
Elspeth Keir	test m
Catharene Thomson	x <ref> a
Cristian Suintoun	m
Bessie Lunson	test op m[89]
William Worsdaill	m
Sara Auchinleck	m
James Worsdaill	y m[90]
William Worsdaill	y[91]
Margaret Durie	m
Margaret Nisbet	
Issobell Fell	test <genlw> pop ex[92]
Thomas Watson	a x viz m
Agnes Wat	m

49 **James Gibs qrter**

Andro Small	a m
Agnes Kipper	a a a
Margaret Howie	m
Myles Polwart	a
Jean Ogilvie	m
Margaret Keillo[u]r	m f
Jonet Nisbet	a m
Marion Maxuell	a m
Rachaell Maxuell	a m
Catharen Dauling	
Margaret Drummond	

89 Name and marginalia written in a different hand.
90 Name and marginalia written in a different hand.
91 Name and marginalia written in a different hand.
92 Name and marginalia written in a different hand.

50	John Kemp	a a a
	Elspeth Plain	m
	Margaret Pringle	y b
	Edward McCure	m
	Catharen Riddoch	m
	~~Beatrix Smith~~	a a
	Jonet Robertson	test f et off[93]
	Kathalen McCure[94]	
	John Wood	a a a
	Rebecka Dobie	b
	Marie Anderson	m
	Beatrix Smith	a a[95] test op Nov 26 1661[96]
	Agnes Someruell	m
	Lillias Gildie	m
	Jean Purdie	m Margt Far <se viz m>
	Elspeth Blair	m
	~~Issobell Thomson~~	~~test~~
	~~Jonet Sharp~~	~~test op~~
	Jonet Melm	f et aff op[97]
	Alex[ande]r Guthrie	m[98]
51	~~Patrick Levingstoun~~	a
	~~Anna Jackson~~	
	John Cochrane	m
	Margaret Eviot	m
	James Cochrane	
	Robert Penstoun	test m
	James Eccles	m
	Marie Stevinson	m[99] test op Nov 26 1661
	James Deanes	

93 Name and marginalia written in a different hand.
94 Name written in a different hand.
95 Name and marginalia written in a different hand.
96 'Test op Nov 26 1661' refers to entire household.
97 Name and marginalia written in a different hand.
98 Name and marginalia written in a different hand.
99 'M' written in between forename and surname.

	Nicolas Barclay	
	John Deanes	
	William Sibbald	m
	Agnes Scoone	m
	Helene Wightman	
	Bessie Stevinson	x a a
	Marion Lorn	test m
	Alex[ande]r Guthrie	test y x
52	James Tailyo[u]r	a a a
	Issobell Walker	a
	Agnes Tailyo[u]r	a y
	John Tailyo[u]r	a y
	Thomas Paterson	~~m~~ a a
	Barbara Smith	m
	Janet Ratho	a a
	Edward Mos	a a a
	Marion Porteous	m
	William Dry	a a
	Elisabeth Calbrath	test m[100]
53	~~Eliazer Brauch~~	
	~~Agnes Bird~~	
	~~Margaret Harvie~~	~~test~~
	~~Elisabeth Pateson~~	~~test~~[101]
	~~Nanse Skellie~~	~~test~~[102]
	John Crookshank	
	Lilias Fergusson	
	Robert Flemming	op x a a
	Thomas Hoome	y
	John Crookshank	y
	Issobell Trumble	test op
	William Scot[103]	

100 Name and marginalia written in a different hand.
101 Name and marginalia written in a different hand.
102 Name and marginalia written in a different hand
103 Name written in a different hand.

	Thomas Wilson	
	Bessie Morphie	
	~~Issobell Inglis~~	~~test op~~
	Hew Williamson	a a
	Eupham Murray	op a f m
54	Georg Beruick	
	Jean Beastoun	
	Jean Fyff	test op
	Issobell Burgh	young adult[104]
	Jean Rab	n test x f off dan[105]
	Williame Donaldson	a
	Issobell Mershell	a x op
	Williame Donaldson	a y
	John Angas	a a
55	William Ducat	m
	Catharen Spence	x
	Mr John Algee	
	Jonet Dyks	
	Jonet Algee	
	Agnes Shirthrum	
	Jonet Dumbar	
	Mr Alex[ande]r Hutchesons familie	
	John Hamiltoun	m
	William Hamiltoun	m
	Jonet Poole	m
	Marie Hamiltoun	y test op x
	Catharen Hamiltoun	y
	~~Jonet Wilson~~	~~test~~
	Marie Thomson	test op op
	Christian Barclay	a test op [illegible] 1662[106]
	Helein Purdie	x a[107]

104 Name and marginalia written in a different hand.
105 Name and marginalia written in a different hand.
106 Name and marginalia written in a different hand.
107 Name and marginalia written in a different hand.

	Christian Nesmith	m test op[108]
56	William Porteous	b
	Margaret Bog	a
	~~Jonet McCoull~~	
	Gawin Cuthbert	a a
	Marion Inch	m
	Agnes Ker	a a
	Agnes Sheill	a a op <hector camp moth>
	Lucras Robertson	test op op
	Robert Ellot	m
	Magdalen Chirnside	m
	Alison Ellot	m
	Marg[are]t Ellot	m
57	Alex[ande]r Cranstoun	a a
	Jonet Hannay	a a
	Sir William Murray	a
58	Alex[ande]r Fife	a a test[109]
	Marion Craufurd	x a
	James Ore	a non <solet> a
	Agnes Douglas	m <dornik> op
	Harie Ore	a
	Williame Broun	
	his wyf	ig a
	Elspeth Baderstanes	test op Nov 27 1661
	op non videth x	
	Marie Grant	m
	Issobell Thomson	op

108 Name and marginalia written in a different hand.
109 'Test' refers to entire household.

59	Georg Glen	m
	Marg[are]t Simson	m
	Marion Robertson	b
	Alex[ande]r Tours	a a
	Issobell Craufurd	m
	James Glen	m
	Jean Scot	m
60	Jean Kinrod	m[110] under censure
	Elizabeth Weymse	~~a a~~ m viz
	Margaret Murray	m
	Cristian Mar	m ~~test~~
	Mathew McGrain	x op viz
	Marion Samuel	m
	Georg McGrain	a y
	Mathew McGrain	y
	James McGrain	y
	John McClury	y a
	Elspeth Duff	a a a
61	William Denholme	a a
	Barbara Moncreiff	test[111] a a a a
	Phineas Brooks	Ballie Boyd[112]
	Marie ~~Brooks~~ Macklachan	Loun[113] test[114]
	Helene Cunnynghame	test
	Catharene Baird	Martha Inglis x[115] test op a
	James Hall	a

110 'm' written in left margin.
111 'Test' refers to entire household.
112 'Ballie Boyd' written in left margin.
113 'Loun' written in left margin.
114 'Test' refers to entire household.
115 'Martha Inglis x' written in left margin.

	Jean Pearson	a test[116] a
	Mistris Haynes	a
	Catharein Graham	test a a
	Jean Graham	test[117]
	Elizabeth Paterson	test op m[118]
62	Robert Graham	m
	Euphame Merser	m
	Jonet ~~Soutar~~ Mellen[119]	
	Marion Logan	m
	Marie Logan	
	Jean Logan	
	Alex[ande]r Logan	
	Marion Coustoun	test m
63	William Butcher	a
	Catharen Younger	a test
	~~William Younger~~	a
	John Kemp	test a
	Marion Anderson	m[120] facem test op Jan 62
	Agnes Fyf	test a
	~~Jonet Suintoun~~	a test and roll
	Marjorie Young	test viz m
	Andro Allan	m
	Elspeth Blaw	m
	Bartholomew Smith	m
	Jeane Barclay	m
	Margaret Smith	~~a~~ m
	Richard Smith	y b[121]
	James Garland	a a a

116 'Test' refers to entire household.
117 Name and marginalia written in a different hand.
118 Name and marginalia written in a different hand.
119 Surname written in a different hand.
120 'm' written in between forename and surname.
121 Name and marginalia written in a different hand.

	Jonet Wilson	m
	John Garland	y
64	Jean Valein	op Ingl. Videth b
	Rebecka Horner	test op 2 Dec 1661[122]
	Margaret Flint	
	Laurence French	viz m
	Marg[are]t Caldwell	op
	John Simson	
	Andro Millar	m <pobst bqor>
	~~Issobell Haistie~~	test
65	Mungo Malloch	m
	Cristian Gibson	m
	James Walker	m
	William Bairdner	m y
	Marion Cock	~~test non ad apta~~
	Bessie Malloch	non apta
	Mungo Malloch	y
	James Gib	
	Anna Boog	
	James Lourie	
	Georg Thomson	
	~~Agnes Dewar~~	
	Georg Scot	m
	Eupham Smith	m visit
	Jonet Monro	a[123] test viz op Dec 1661 x viz
66	James Veitch	
	Catharen Sibbald	x a
	~~Marg[are]t Haistie~~	
	Williame Cockburn	a a m
	Agnes Watson	x op viz
	Georg Cockburn	a
	Jonet Cockburn	

122 'Test op 2 Dec 1661' refers to entire household.
123 'a' written in between forename and surname.

	Isobell Ray	a scolding a
	Marg[are]t Steidman	off x Conn
	Agnes Mukle	a a
	William Birkinshaw	
	Jonet Hood	
	Thomas Broun	
	Catharen McMillan	test[124]
67	John Wilson	x op m
	Helene Mitchell	viz
	Cristian Wilson	y
	Katherein MckMillan	m[125]
	William Auchinleck	viz op
	Marion Gray	x preist sick
	Marie Auchinleck	y
	Bessie Auchinleck	y
	Margaret Neilson	m
	Jean Davidson	y
	David Lamb	a m
	Catharen Wilson	x op
	Elizabeth Stratoun	m
68	Geills Alex[ande]r	sick
	Cristian Shirrilaw	b
	Robert Watson	
	Margaret Peebles	a sick a
	Archibald Stevin	test y b
	Silvester Leslie	b
	~~Henrie Smith~~	
	Marion Jackson	m
	Margaret Stemson	test op[126]

124 'Test' refers to the entire household.
125 Name and marginalia written in a different hand.
126 Name and marginalia written in a different hand.

69	Georg Heriot	a
	Cristian Balnaves	a
	Gilbert Robertson	a
	~~Barbara Kilpatrick~~	test
	William Bartane	
	~~Helen Bryson~~	~~y~~ a[127]
	Georg Armo[u]r	m
	Anna Ffindla	m
	Henrie Armo[u]r	y
	James Armo[u]r	y
	Alison Chryster	test a
	~~Elspeth Jackson~~	~~test~~
	~~Helene Adie~~	~~test~~
	~~Barbara Flock~~	a a[128]
	Sara Barclay	a a[129]
	Margaret Purves	op y
	Bessie Kilpatrick	sick ~~x~~ m
	Helene Greir	op viz
	John Carbraith	a
	Jean Carbraith	
70	Alex[ande]r Fergusson	a
	Helen Keir	x op x test[130] a
	Andro Scot	m op
	Marjorie Liddikin	viz f x test[131]
	Eupham Black	
	William Hepburn	
	Marg[are]t Wardlaw	
	James Kennedie	m
	Jonet Ker	test viz op

127 Name and marginalia written in a different hand.
128 Name and marginalia written in a different hand.
129 Name and marginalia written in a different hand.
130 'Test' refers to the entire household.
131 'Test' refers to the entire household.

71	Margaret Porterfield	m
	Margaret Hamilton	y
	Barbara Young	a a
	Bessie Steill	m
	John Wilson	x tr non <ad ok>[132]
	Jonet Dickson	op m
	John Wi[l]son	a[133]
	Adam Bennet	m
	Bessie Polwart	m
72	Alex[ande]r Melvill	x m y
	Catheren Melvill	
	Margaret Gellen	test op[134]
	John Lachlane	m
	Jonet Hutcheson	m
	~~Margaret Hutcheson~~	

Gawin Bonkills qrter

	William Barrie	English[135] a a
	Elspeth Tod	a a
	Grissell Strang	a a
	Agnes Barrie	
73	John Greinleyis	
	Elizabeth Cunnynghame	
	William Henryson	b
	Richard Wilkie	y
	~~Margaret McKie~~	~~test~~
	Jonet Hill	test op Dec 16 1661 m
	~~Jonet Clerk~~	test
	Nanse Clerk	test f op[136]

132 Name and marginalia written in a different hand.
133 Name and marginalia written in a different hand.
134 'Test op' refers to entire household.
135 'English' written as heading above household.
136 Name and marginalia written in a different hand.

	Issobell Frazer	test f op com[137]
	Helen Watson	test a a[138]
	John Adamson[139]	
	Jean Murray	
	Barbara Purse	viz
	Hew Hammiltoun	
	Sara Richardson	
	Anna Hamilton[140]	
	James Inglis	a
	Jean Adamson	test op m
	~~Jonet Anderson~~	test op
	Rachel Hepburn	test m[141]
	Sara Richeson	m[142]
74	Francis Wood	m
	Jonet Rodger	m
	Jean Mackne	test[143]
	Alexander Johnstoun	a a Holmglen
	Agnes Abernethie	x op a a
	Issobell Ormond	test op op a a
	Luke Heriot	a a
	Jonet Brotherstanes	op a a
	~~Anna Allan~~	test
	Alison Alex[ande]r[144]	
	Adam Brown	m m test op[145]
	Margaret Cummyng	a m
	Margaret Stevinson	test op 1661
	~~Issobell Ormand~~	

137 Name and marginalia written in a different hand.
138 Name and marginalia written in a different hand.
139 Names and marginalia of entire household written in a different hand.
140 Name written in a different hand.
141 Name and marginalia written in a different hand.
142 Name and marginalia written in a different hand.
143 Name and marginalia written in a different hand.
144 Name written in a different hand.
145 Name and marginalia written in a different hand.

Jonet Pirnie m
William Wilson m
Robert

75 Georg Hay m
Margaret Paterson

James Mak
Issobell Pirnie
Elspeth Adamson off viz x a a

Elizabeth Gray m
and her sister papist

~~James Lockhart~~
~~Margaret Craufurd~~
~~Jonet Hunter test~~[146]

Elspeth Badyenoch m
William Cuningham a a[147]

76 Jonet Cuthbertson m
Rob[er]t Telfare a a

Beggers Lodged

Elizabeth Gordon m
Marjorie Hay y off f
Elisabeth Hay ~~a~~ m[148]

Helene Hoome viz test op a

~~Thomas Rodger~~
~~Issobell Lumsden~~

77 ~~Agnes Mitchell~~
~~Marie Frazer~~
Isobel Pitbroth m Mr Bisset cabls f com:[149]

146 'Test' refers to entire household.
147 Name and marginalia written in a different hand.
148 Name and marginalia written in a different hand.
149 Name and marginalia written in a different hand.

	~~Catharene Young~~	
	~~Alex[ande]r Purdie~~	
	John Monteith	
	Margaret Campbell	
	William Weir	m
	Helene Fortoun	m
	John Bowie	a m
	David Alison	y
	James Burn	m
	Issobell Cochran	m
	James Burn	y
78	Robert Aytoun	
	Marion Aytoun	m
	Alex[ande]r Baxter	test a op f ot off op[150]
	Jonet Bell	a a[151] test
	William Craig	a m
	Elizabeth Parker	a m
	James Craig	a y
	Patrick Fentoun	a a
	Issobell Toshoh	a m
	Edward Toshoh	a a
	Isack Brand	m QHZ[152]
	Jean Caldwell	m
	David McCarra	
	Thomas Scotland	m
	Alex[ande]r Potre[153]	
79	Mr James Nairn familie	
	James Gray[154]	

150 'Test a op f ot off op' refers to entire household.

151 'a a' written in left margin.

152 'QHZ' written above household.

153 Name written in a different hand.

154 Names and marginalia of entire household written in a different hand.

	Bessie Fforrest	
	Patrick Young	
	Andro Cambell	
	George Castell	test viz m
	Alex[ande]r Watson	test op m
	John Dalmahoy	
	Anna Wilbram	
	Thomas Fairbairn	m
	Christian Roy	m[155]
	~~Geilis Wit~~	~~test op~~[156]
	Elisabeth Herring	test viz m[157]
	Robert Lauchlane	of off
	Bessie Broun	a a
	Andro Lauchlane	test op Dec 1661[158]
	Sussanna Lauchlane	b
	Janet Rae	test[159]
	Angus Frazer	a a[160]
	Issobell Cangla	f opign[161] test op d 1661 a a[162]
80	~~John Thomson~~	~~a~~[163]
	~~Barbara Benton~~	~~a~~[164]
	Alex[ande]r Smith	a m
	Issobell Pringle	a a
	Andro Dugall	ign op viz ad a a
	Jonet Buchanan	a a
	John Harper	English[165] a
	Dorathie Duff	

155 Name and marginalia written in a different hand.
156 Name and marginalia written in a different hand.
157 Name and marginalia written in a different hand.
158 'Test op Dec 1661' refers to entire household.
159 Name and marginalia written in a different hand.
160 Name and marginalia written in a different hand.
161 'f opign' written in left margin.
162 Name and marginalia written in a different hand.
163 Name and marginalia written in a different hand.
164 Name and marginalia written in a different hand.
165 'English' written as heading above household.

	Samuel Ginning	English[166]
	Margaret Inglis	a
	Issobell Paterson	test[167]
81	Mr Dinners	English[168]
	Jonet Grant	
	Margaret Henryson	test op d: test m[169]
	~~Robert Anderson~~	
	~~Jonet Mure~~	
	Eupham Short	viz
	James Bellenden	
	Marion Bellenden	a a
	Sara Bellenden	a
	Anna Bellenden	a[170]
	Margaret Johnstoun	a a
	Elspeth Cockburne	a a
	Anna Hume[171]	
	Mary Levington	test
	Rachel Levington	
	Margaret Levingt[on]	
	Martha Tudieman	test a
	Marion Gray	test x a a
82	John Seatoun	
	Barbara Naper	
	John Moreson	a viz op a a
	Jonet Wright	b
	~~Catharen Raston~~[172]	
	Catharen Halm	ill a
	~~John Maners~~	

166 'English' written as heading above household.
167 'Test' refers to entire household.
168 'English' written as heading above household.
169 'Test op d: test m' refers to entire household.
170 Name and marginalia written in a different hand.
171 Names and marginalia of household written in a different hand.
172 Name written in a different hand.

	~~Barbara Robertson~~	
	~~James Maners~~	
	~~John Robertson~~	
	~~Barbara Broun~~	
83	Thomas Lendell	English[173]
	Catharen Ros	<apolet wtin a m o> test[174]
	Margaret Ros[175]	
	Margaret Wilson	
	Jean Bell	m
	George Near	
	John Weir	y
	Magdalen Nicolson	test op x Nack
	Margaret Clerk	test op x[176]
	Margaret Douglas	a a
	Marion White	m couts
	~~John Gray~~	
	~~Bessie Purdie~~	
84	John Shaw	
	Margaret Cunyngham	
	James Barbor	
	Georg Barbor	
	Ester Barbor	
	Agnes Wats	m[177] test op
	Georg Collingson	English[178]
	Marg[are]t Thomson	a
	Issobell Hamiltoun	test[179]
	Ladie Adistoun	
	Margaret Lauder	

173 'English' written as heading above household.
174 'Test' refers to entire household.
175 Name written in a different hand.
176 Name and marginalia written in a different hand.
177 'm' written in between forename and surname.
178 'English' written as heading above household.
179 'Test' refers to entire household.

	Martha Lauder	
	Annable Lauder	
	Martha Anderson	test a
	Barbara Paterson	test m[180]
	Geils Law	y[181]
85	James Skougall	
	Marie Hay	
	Margaret Skougall	
	Elizabeth Alex[ande]r	test ~~a~~ m
	Mistris Young	
	Helene Fogo	m
	Thomas Couling	
	Deborah Maddin	
	Georg Sommeruell	m
	Margaret Couling	y
	John Heriot	non <v reg> x
	Marg[are]t Jack	a a
	Catharen Aytoun	test a a
86	Andro Wilkie	m
	Marion Herring	m
	Bessie Wilkie	b
	James Dick	b
	John Smith	y m
	Jonet Louristoun	y nat: ch: viz
	James Davidson	
	Catharene Tuedie	
	Georg Davidson	~~test a~~
	~~Marg[are]t Frazer~~	
	Issobell Hay	band <spe>[182] test op Jan 1662 x a a[183]
	Jean Perry	test a viz op ada[184]
	Richard Dobie	m

180 Name and marginalia written in a different hand.
181 Name and marginalia written in a different hand.
182 Written in left margin.
183 Name and marginalia written in a different hand.
184 Name and marginalia written in a different hand.

	Jean Johnstoun	m
	Jonet Trotter	a a
	Agnes Pearstoun	a m
	Jonet Mitchell	a m test op[185]
87	Mr William Walker	
	Margaret Ramsay	
	~~Marg[are]t Porrok~~	~~test~~
	Ann Crigchton	b[186]
	John Strauchan	a a
	Cristian Strauchan	x op surdg
	Helene Littiljohn	b
	William Gay	test op[187]
	Janet Urcharct[188]	
	Archibald Logan	
	Marion Melrose	
	William Gay	x op[189]
	Janet Urchart	x a a
	Rob[er]t Johnstoun	a a[190]
	Mary Foster	m test[191]
88	Thomas Elshie	English[192] a
	Bessie Davidson	m
	Mr Alex[ande]r Dick	m
	Marg[are]t Dalyell	m
	Jonet Johnstoun	a a
	~~Marg[are]t Daikere~~	test[193]

185 'Test op' refers to entire household.
186 Name and marginalia written in a different hand.
187 Names and marginalia of household written in a different hand.
188 Name written in a different hand.
189 Names and marginalia of household written in a different hand.
190 Name and marginalia written in a different hand.
191 Name and marginalia written in a different hand.
192 'English' written as heading above household.
193 'Test' refers to Jonet and Margaret.

	Marjory Joy	<covle>[194] test op viz m
89	John Cook	m
	Margaret White	m
	Thomas Murray	y catech m
	~~Anna~~	
	Alex[ande]r Henrysone	m
	Margaret Watson	m
	Richard Henrysone	y m
	Anna Simson	test op d 26 b 1661
	James Mitchell	test op m[195]
	Richard Stachie	English[196] a test[197]
	Margaret Anderson	a
90	Donald Robertson	m[198]
	Margaret Gilgour	viz op
	John Hay	souldior a a[199]
	Issobell Lauder	
	William Borthuik	Collonell Borthuik & his w.
	Elspeth Maxuell	
	Margaret Thomson	viz
	Andro Cowye	
	Jean Logan	
	Jonet Cowye	
	Marg[are]t Cowye	
	Issobell Ker	m
91	Patrik Lintoun	English[200] a
	Marg[are]t Lintoun	a
	~~Allan McRonnald~~	test[201]
	~~Agnes Agnew~~	test

194 Written in left margin.
195 Name and marginalia written in a different hand.
196 'English' written as heading above household.
197 'Test' refers to entire household.
198 Name and marginalia written in a different hand.
199 Name and marginalia written in a different hand.
200 'English' written as heading above household.
201 'Test' refers to entire household.

	George Mount	~~a~~ m
	Jonet Mershell	
	~~Elspeth Dumbar~~	~~test~~
	Barbara Brown	test op x a a[202]
	~~Jonet Ker~~	
	Geills Smith	
	Alex[ande]r Kae	
	Anna Kae	
	Sara Kae	
	Jean Kae	
	~~Grace Cunnyngham~~	
	Jean Oben	test op Dec 30 1661[203]
92	Adam Davidson	m
	Marg[are]t Fergasson	
	James David	a a
	Elspeth Madin	m
	Jean Lindre	test y op ig com a[204]
	John Bartane	m
	Grissell Hannay	m
	Sibbla Lindsay	m
	Euphame Bartane	
	~~Jonet Ald~~	
	~~Margaret Nukyt~~	~~test~~[205]
	Catharein Mackferlin	m Johns sister[206]
	~~William Ros~~	
	~~Elizabeth Kinloch~~	
	~~Cristian Hog~~	test[207]
93	John Mitchell	
	Beatrix Safflay	

202 Name and marginalia written in a different hand.
203 Name and marginalia written in a different hand.
204 Name and marginalia written in a different hand.
205 Name and marginalia written in a different hand.
206 Name and marginalia written in a different hand.
207 'Test' refers to entire household.

	John Clerk	y
	Anna Clerk	y
	Elizabeth Pitscotie	a test a a
	Marie Wood	a viz tamen y
	Jonet Pollok	test [illegible] op a a
	James Gibson	m
	Issobell Hamiltoun	m
	James Herrin[208]	
	Mary Pickston	test[209]
94	Margaret Watson	
	Jean Manson	
	Sara Manson	
	John Logan	
	Agnes Maxuell	test[210]
	~~Jeremiah Berrihill~~	
	Agnes Herreis	b test op m
	John Hepburn	test[211]
	Chrishan Story	test m[212]
	Alex[ande]r West	m
	Alison Mitchell	m
	Flwrish Robertson	
	Catharen Pearstoun	
	John Gray	a belman[213]
	Bessie Purday	viz godhead m[214]
	Marjorie Heysop	f
95	Alex[ande]r Smith	m
	Marion Wilson	
	Adam Broun	

208 Name written in a different hand.
209 Name and marginalia written in a different hand.
210 'Test' refers to entire household.
211 Name and marginalia written in a different hand.
212 Name and marginalia written in a different hand.
213 Name and marginalia written in a different hand.
214 Name and marginalia written in a different hand.

	William Smith	
	Els[p]eth Smith	m[215]
	James Kay	a a
	Catharen Findlason	a a
	Robert Jaffray	
	Thomas Kaidie	a m
	Agnes Mecineis[216]	
	James Forsyth	test m[217]
96	**Abbay Quarter**	
	Alex[ande]r Peirs	
	Barbara Milne	
	James Peirs	
	Issobell Reid	m f works
	~~Elspeth Tunne~~	~~test~~
	Cristian Cleland	
	Mistris Helene Scot	
	Margaret Seatoun	
	Jeane Morine	
	Helene Kinneir	
	Margaret Edgar	
	Anna Hamiltoun	m
	Margaret Hog	a ~~a~~
	Margaret Gildow	y viz
	Edward Obak	
	Rebecka Colvill	
	Eupham Rollok	f x a a
	James Gibson	a
97	Eupham Leith	test a a
	Barbara Peirs	a a
	a woman with a child	test a
	William Hodg	m
	Bessie Broun	~~m a~~

215 Name and marginalia written in a different hand.
216 Name written in a different hand.
217 Name and marginalia written in a different hand.

Patrick Arnot	y m
~~Jean Smith~~	~~test~~
Robert Elleis	
Issobell Dalgleish	f m[218] test op Jan 9 1662[219]
Issobell Reid	x a a
Anna Cockburn	a a

98 Earle Annandaills familie

Patrick Johnstoun	
William Couper	
William Short	
David Stennops	
Adame Loudon	
Angus McKeinyie	
David Kennedie	
John Johnstoun	
Mistris Sara Johnstoun	test a[220]
Anna Johnstoun	
Elizabeth Oswald	
Agnes Anderson	
Marjory Fen	test op Feb 1662[221]
Geilis Atcheson	
Anna Broun	
John Broun	
~~Margaret Lyell~~	test
~~Mark Harlaw~~	test
~~William Cubie~~	test
Issobell White	
James Lowriston[222]	

99 Ro[ber]t Lesses familie

218 'f m' written in left margin.
219 'Test op Jan 9 1662' refers to entire household.
220 'Test a' refers to entire household.
221 name and marginalia written in a different hand.
222 name written in a different hand.

	Jean Byres	m[223]
	Janet Finlaw	m
	James Low	
	John Levingston	
	Ro[ber]t Patrick	
	James Low	
	James Stevinson	m
	Jean Ker	m
	Margaret Stevinson	
	Dinners Thomson	test[224]
	John[225]	
	James Lessills	
	Margaret Wallace	m
	Janet Broun	test op op
	John Wood	viz
	Anna Wood	a a
100	Ladie Angus familie	
	Mathew Hamiltoun	
	Agnes Reid	
	Alison Hamiltoun	m
	Anna Hamiltoun	m
	Agnes Morphie	test op
101	Stephen Cochran	a a
	Jonet Simson	a a
	James Hamiltoun	
	Ann Hamiltoun[226]	
	Ann Hamiltoun[227]	
	Robert Stevinson	y
	Agnes Jack	~~a a~~
	Elizabeth Moreson	test op n 6

223 this and following names and marginalia written in a different hand.
224 'Test' refers to Dinners, James Lessills and Margaret Wallace.
225 Name written in a different hand.
226 Name written in a different hand.
227 Name written in a different hand.

	Stevin Cockran	m[228]
	Janet Simson	m and[229]
102	Earl Craufurds familie	
	James Thomson	m ~~a~~
	Elspeth Robertson	~~a~~ m
	Marion Smart	~~a a~~
	~~Thomas~~ Millar	test a
	Agnes Milne	y test a viz
103	Thomas Kersan	a a
	Catharene Black	~~a~~ m
	William Williamson	a a m the park
	Issobell Brigs	a a
	James Williamson	a a
	Jonet Mitchell	test a a
	James Wilson	gardner prest viz
	Issobell Thomson	a a
	Rachaell Wilson	m a
	Catharen Wilson	a a
	John Murray	~~f et aff~~[230] test op Jan 10 1662
	Grissell Inglis	f et aff[231] m
	Marie Lindsay	test
104	Thomas Gifferd	English[232] g g[233] a a
	Geills Gifferd	a a
	Andro Caldwell	
	Thomas Caldwell	
	Grissell Bruce	
	Barbara McGhie	m
	Gawin Fairlie	test m

228 Names and marginalia of entire household written in a different hand
229 'and' written in left margin below name.
230 'f et aff' written in left margin.
231 'f et aff' written in left margin.
232 'English' written as heading above household.
233 'g g' written in left margin.

Issobell Wallace — test viz m

Hector Campbell
Rachaell Campbell
~~Jonet Kildow~~
~~Margaret Kildow~~
Jean Mairtene
~~Catharene Craufurd~~ — test
Elisabeth Duncan — test y m[234]
Helen Drysdaill — test[235]

105 Margaret Horsburgh — a a

Samuel Brooks — English[236] a a
Jonet Paterson
Elspeth Paterson — x op a a

106 Harie Gib
Marg[are]t Smith
Elspeth Fyf — m
John Fyf — y m
~~Margaret~~ Niveing
Rachael Cockburne — test op x a a
Cristian Hamiltoun — y test x a a

William More — viz op
Issobell Guthrie — a a
Thomas More — test y

Philip Watson — English[237] a a

107 John Allan — a a
Marion Allan — a op viz tamet a a
Alex[ande]r Watson — a a test[238]
Robert Milne — a a
James Lightoun — a a

234 Name and marginalia written in a different hand.
235 Name and marginalia written in a different hand.
236 'English' written as heading above household.
237 'English' written as heading above household.
238 'Test' refers to entire household.

Katherein Milne	test x op viz fa[239]
Robert Pringle	m
Margaret Ker	m
Bessie Tennent	m
John Lock	m
Agnes Tempill	op x a a
Thomas Young	b
Jonet Archibald	m[240]
Marion Young	op x
Issobell Young	a a

239 Name and marginalia written in a different hand.
240 Name and marginalia written in a different hand.

List of Parishioners (1684)

National Records of Scotland, Canongate Kirk Session Records, CH2/122/68

Transcription by Alice Glaze

Page	Text	Marginalia
1	Thom[241]	
	The names of	
	Thomas	
	Eupham Wrigh	
	Alex[ande]r Hepb	
	Anse ~~William William~~	
	~~William Fry~~	
2	[242]	
3	The names of the families of the one half of the parish of Canongate beginning at the Tolbooth, 1684	
	John Grinley	
	Katharen Guthrie	
	Jonet Ramsey	b ~~y~~
	W[illia]m Fforrester	
	Mar[gare]t Fforrester	b
	Ro[ber]t Ballantine	
	Christian Andersone	
	W[illia]m Govan	
	~~Marion Sutherland~~	
	~~Grissell Quiet~~	~~b~~
	Janet Nicolsone	
	John Todd	
	Marg[are]t Fetheringham	
	Ro[ber]t Wilsone	
	Elspet Pollon	
	James Christie	

241 Fragment; page torn.
242 Blank page.

	Agnes Guthrie	
	Agnes Walker	
	W[illia]m Badyenoch	
	Mar[gare]t Clark	
	George Bain	
	Mar[gare]t Paterson	
	Edward Hepburn	
	Elespeth Meldrum	
	Jonet Hepburn	
4	James Thomson	
	Grissell Wilson	
	Abraham Pergilles	
	Katharen Thomson	
	Mathew Gordon	
	Agnes Ellies	
	Marion Lymeburner	test
	James Hog	
	Cristin Bryson	
	Grissell Johnstoun	
	John Stewart	b
	Alex[ande]r Matheson	
	Cristin Auld	
	Walter Munro	
	Mar[gare]t Milin	
	Mar[gare]t Lowen	b
	Alex[ande]r Mackie	b
	Grissell Lawson	
5	Henry Gray	
	Jean Deanes	b
	~~John Haliwell~~	
	Helen Haliwell	

W[illia]m Edmonstoun
Jonet Greenlaw b
Mar[gare]t Edmonstoun

Marg[are]t Ritchie
Eupham Ritchie b
Grissell Hamilton

Elespeth Baine b

Barbara Murray
Jean Grant b

Helen Aitkin b
Peter Kellie
Jonet Dick

Robert Ffowller
Barbara Craighead b

Alex[ande]r Crookshank
Marjorie Adam
Isobell Crookshank

George Grier
Elespbeth Gibson
James Baittie
Annabell Donald

6 Thomas Wilson
Marg[are]t Marr
W[illia]m Wallace
Isobell Moncrieff

Andrew Wright
Jean Law

Marion Rae
Marion and Marg[are]t Wilkies
John Wilkie[243]

243 Name and marginalia written in a different hand.

Agnes Marshell

W[illia]m Cranford
Agnes Clendining
Cornelius Balfower
Ro[ber]t Lawder
Andrew Speiddie
W[illia]m Watson
Eliza[be]th Alex[ande]r test

James Paton
Kat[herine] Cochran
W[illia]m Paton

George Matters
Jonet Fflint
Mary Seaton

Mrs Dunbar
Anna Dunbar
Mar[gare]t Crookshank test rec: b

7 James Aberthethy
Jean Rodger

Alex[ande]r Walker
Jonet Paton

Mar[gare]t Gray
Helen Cowpland test[244]

John Grahame
Elespeth Marshell

Jean Duff
Mar[gare]t Strauchan

David Johnstoun
Dorathy Wood

244 'Test' may refer to the entire household.

Ninian Anderson
Jean Lockhart

John Logan
Alisone Thomson
Mar[gare]t Cleland

James Blaikie
Jonet Creich

Mar[gare]t Sim
W[illia]m Morgan
Elespeth Lennox b

8 Isobell Marshell b

Henry Antonius
Henry Antonius you[nge]r
Jonet Antonius

Adam Grier
Jean Howstoun

Daniell Bain
Mar[gare]t Anderson
Barbara Crook v

Patrick Jackson
Marion Wright

James Burnett
Marjorie Rollo

Isobell Back b
W[illia]m Simson
Mar[gare]t Logan

Elizabeth Parker b
Mar[gare]t Craig

Jonet Allan
Agnes Walker

9	Henry Alison	
	Jean Gordon	
	Alex[ande]r Ar[chibal]d	
	Kat[herine] Jeills	
	James Marshell	
	Mar[gare]t Lowrie	
	Walter Turpie	b
	Mar[gare]t Watsone	b
	Jo[h]n Braidder	test
	Widow Ayton	b
	W[illia]m Ayton	
	Hector Ayton	
	Andrew Barclay	
	Jeanet Johnstoun	b
	Jean Barclay	
	Isobell Taitt	
	Agnes Dobson	
	Leut Coll[onel] Whytefoord	
	Mar[gare]t Sturgeon	papists[245]
10	Jonet Maiden	b
	Jonet Vause	b
	Easter Vause	
	Agnes Cowan	b
	Alex[ande]r Aitcheson	
	Helen Moore	
	Helen Cock	test rec: b
	Isobell Ro[ber]tsone	
	Agnes Jo[h]nstoun	
	James Jack	

245 'Papists' refers to entire household.

Isobell Bissett

Jo[h]n Duncan

Isobell Greenlaw b
Cath[erine] Anderson b

Anna Glen
Jonet McQueen

Mar[gare]t McQueen
Mar[gare]t Rodger b
David Grahame
W[illia]m Thomson
Agnes Oliphant v

11 W[illia]m Logan
Jonet Duncan
James Glen b
Jo[h]n Logan b
Jo[h]n Stevensone
Thomas Jo[h]nston

Hugh Cristell
Mary Sandersone
Alex[ande]r Phinney

Mary Welsh
Geo[rge] Cuthberson
Jean Rishell

James Steedman
Kat[herine] Ker

~~Jo[h]n Chesshyre~~
~~Mar[gare]t Alex[ande]r~~
~~Mar[gare]t Chesshyre~~

Mar[gare]t Sibbald b
Barbara Malloch
Isobell Marshell v

Kat[herine] Bunckle

Helen Ffiddes

Isobell Baillie

Alex[ande]r Adamson
Kat[herine] Cowrier

12 Ro[ber]t Lowristoun
Jean Ralstoun
Agnes Bartleman

Mar[gare]t Lawson
Marg[are]t Anderson b

Nicoll Mitchell
Rachell Mitchell
Mary Mitchell
W[illia]m Anderson

Mrs King
Mar[gare]t King
Mary King
Helen Walker

Ro[ber]t Livingston
Katharen Eresken

Ar[chibal]d Lowristoun
Jonet Ffalconer

Elespeth Davidson
Mar[gare]t Shand

13 Alex[ande]r Baxter
Isobell Wilkie
Alex[ande]r Baxter v
David Baxter b
Isobell Baxter
John Wilkie v
John Wilsone v
Blench Peter v

W[illia]m Manson

Jonet

James Johnstoun
Cristin Buchannan

Bessie Coall

Walter Geddes
Jonet Watsone
Agnes Gibsone
Mrs Kirk papist

Jo[h]n Ffleeming
Mar[gare]t Marshell

Jo[h]n Colvin
Barbara Henderson

Jo[h]n Cooke
Helen Ritchie

Ro[ber]t Alex[ande]r
Jean Culbert
Isobell Ogilvie

14 W[illia]m Clark
Mar[gare]t Broun

James Guthrie
Mar[gare]t Mackie
Jo[h]n Guthrie v
Charles Borrowman
Margaret Walker v

Samwell Lindsay
Agnes Guthrie b

Andrew Lamb
Rachell Caldwell

Mr Jo[h]n Lumsden

Alex[ande]r Livingstoun Ensign

	Agnes	
	Mr Carruddes	
	Rodger Porteous	
	James Hay	
	Mary Scott	
	James Hay	
15	W[illia]m Baxter	
	Mar[gare]t Sheirer	b
	Jonet Blaikie	v
	John Straiton	
	Jean Jamesone	
	Mar[gare]t Jamesone	
	Jean Straiton	
	Anna Hunter	v
	John Garroch	serjent
	Isobell Straiton	
	Mar[gare]t Guy	b
	Mar[gare]t Buchannan	b
	Agnes McIlrie	test nota
	W[illia]m Moorehead	
	Mar[gare]t Bannerman	
	Mar[gare]t Patersone	
	Mar[gare]t Hay	
	James Glen	
	Marion Fforrest	
	Patrick Turnebull	
	Alisone W[illia]msone	
	James Johnstoun	
	Jean Wightman	
16	Kat[herine] Young	v
	Mar[gare]t Purdie	v

W[illia]m Gemmell
Mar[gare]t McIlfie

Peter Lawsone
Marie Irwin

David Allan
Elsepeth

Ro[ber]t Nathannaell
Elespeth Hutton

Marjorie Pilmoore b
W[illia]m Litster b
Elsepeth Ord b
James Ord

Jean Sibbald

Jo[h]n Campbell
Jonet Ffergusone

Ro[ber]t Doeg

Ro[ber]t Molyson
Mar[gare]t Broun

17 George Suttie
Helen Badyenoch b
Mar[gare]t Suttie v
Jo[h]n Meggitt

Jo[h]n Henderson
Cristin Baittie

Kat[herine] Milne v

David Lorimer
Mary Broun

Geo[rge] Mckenyie
Mary Tulloch

Alex[ande]r Towers
Isobell Craufurd

David Bissett
Kat[herine] Milne

W[illia]m Baitts
Agnes Maire b

Thomas Potter
Elespeth Lidsdaile v

18 John Davidson
Mar[gare]t Andersone

John Dicksone
Kat[herine] Jacksone
Annabell Ratterey test

2 Quarter
John Mastertoun Elder
W[illia]m Stennes deacon

Philip Munro
Elizabeth Leitch
George Munro
Agnes Deivy b

Mr Alex[ande]r Strang
Jonet Shepheard

Marijorie White b
Thomas Thomson b
Eupham Thomson
James Malceintosh v

19 ~~John Davidson~~
~~Mar[gare]t Anderson~~

Helen Bissett

John Miller
Bessie Alex[ande]r

Mar[gare]t Alex[ande]r

~~Robert~~ Alex[ande]r Jeills
Isobell Ro[ber]tson

Henry Marwood
Jonet Edward

Ro[ber]t Simsone
Agnes Pearsone

Ro[ber]t Hepburne
Mar[gare]t Hop

John Park
Isobell Craike

James Colvin
James Johnsoun

Alex[ande]r Smith
Anna Gray

John Tweedy
Jonet Armor

20 Alex[ande]r Watson
Agnes Watt

Elespeth Duncan

Donald Malcontosh
Jean Quy b

~~James Smith~~
~~Jonet Wright~~

~~Alex[ande]r McFersone~~
~~Jonet Andersone~~

Alex[ande]r McFarsone
Jonet Andersone

	James McCampin	
	Helen Teckitt	b
	~~Ro[ber]t Somerwell~~	
	Jonet Thomson	
21	Ro[ber]t Jeills	b
	Elespeth Harper	b
	James Colvin	
	Jonet Johnstoun	
	James Thom	test[246]
	Mar[gare]t Jessiman	
	Pat[rick] Stobe	
	Isobell Vause	
	James Crichton	
	Isobell Guthrie	
	James Maire	
	Cristin Hadden	
	Mar[gare]t Mair	
	John Duncan	
	Mar[gare]t Wauch	~~test~~ b
	~~Jo[h]n Campell~~	
	~~Moor Nisbitt~~	test
	W[illia]m Gemmell	
	Marg[are]t McIlfie	
	Jonet Stichell	
	Lawrence Kyle	
	Isobell Cree	
	W[illia]m Peter	
	Elespeth Ale[xande]r	
22	~~Ro[ber]t Ramsay~~	

246 'Test' may refer to entire household.

~~Marion Wilsone~~
~~Anna Ramsay~~

James Burne
[blank] Sutherland

Henry Wilson
Jonet Spence b
Thomas Lowrie
Jonet Stewart b

Thomas Wright
Eupham Paterson b
Agnes Ffairweather

John Lesly
Mar[gare]t Ale[xande]r

Isobell ~~Alex[ande]r~~ Anderson
Isobell Ale[xande]r papists[247]

Alex[ande]r Hay
Mar[gare]t Welsh

George Mitchell
Jonet Smith
Isobell Smith b
Agnes Sutherland b

23 Jo[h]n Sutherland
Mar[gare]t Smith

John Watson b
Marion Moorehead b

Thomas Ro[ber]tson
Isobell Bowman
W[illia]m Ro[ber]tson

Jonet Thomson

247 'Papists' refers to entire household.

~~Agnes Logie~~

Anthoney Ritchison
Susanna Lauchlan

James Richison
Isobell Ffindlay

Thomas Lindsay b
Jonet Anderson
W[illia]m McAdon b
James Scott
Ro[ber]t Murray v

Jonet Miller b
Isobell Rodger b

Jo[h]n Weir
Marie Broun b
Jonet Weir

24 Bessie King
Mar[gare]t Johnstoun
W[illia]m Hannay b
Mar[gare]t Hannay b
John Murdo
John Smith
Jo[h]n Simsone
David McCara b
Mary Maxwell
Eupham Gray n
Ro[ber]t Morison v

Thorlestanes familie
Thomas Carington
Walter Riddell
Agnes Ker
Neill McGie
Jo[h]n Meneses
Bessie Selkirk
Kat[herine] Litlejohn
Marjorie Toshoch b

Countes Carnworths familie

Lady Thomson
Mar[gare]t Nisbet
Marion Towers b

25 Mr W[illia]m Thomson
Jo[h]n Geddes b
Isobell Gilmoore b
Alison Gowrlay b

W[illia]m Livingstoun
Lillias Gardiner
Jonet Donaldson test b
Sara Whyte test

Andrew Smith
Mary Auchinleck b
~~Ro[ber]t Tarbes~~
~~Mathias Durhame~~
~~Jonet Litlejohn~~ test
Ro[ber]t Kirkaldie[248]

W[illia]m Mackie
Marion Barrowman
Jo[h]n Burntfield b
W[illia]m Fforrester v
Kat[herine] Cuthill
Alex[ande]r Mackie v

James Drummond
Agnes Colquhoun

26 W[illia]m Duncan
Isobell Young
Mar[garc]t Scorger test

James Boyd
Isobell Hunter
Agnes Dobsone

248 Name written in a different hand.

	George Wallace	
	Agnes Broun	
	Alex[ande]r Guthrie	
	Helen McKeith	
	John McKillop	
	Jonet Turner	
	W[illia]m Paton	
	Elespeth Hog	
	Mar[gare]t Hunter	
	Alex[ande]r Ffraser	
	Agnes Urquhart	
	W[illia]m Eddie	
	George Marshell	b
	Mar[gare]t Marshell	b
27	Neill Munro	
	Agnes Ramsay	
	Ninian Seaton	
	Mar[gare]t Pollock	
	Jean Whyte	b
	W[illia]m Stennows	
	Jonet Clark	
	George Campbell	
	Thomas Stennows	v
	Mar[gare]t Bramer	b
	Alex[ande]r Logan	b[249]
	Joseph Lorimer	
	Mar[gare]t Stewart	
	Bartholomew Smith	
	Jean Bartleman	b

249 Name and marginalia written in a different hand.

	James Smith	
	Kat[herine] Smith	b
	James McFarlan	
	Agnes Gibsone	
	W[illia]m Broun	
	Elespeth Arthure	
	John Ar[chibal]d	
	Mar[gare]t Gedd	b
	Agnes McKean	
	Thomas Cochran	b
	Helen Thomson	
28	James Rid	b
	Elespeth Gibb	
	Agnes Peittie	
	Donald McCarstoun	
	Cristian Anderson	b
	Jonet Munro	test
	Agnes Leitch	b
	Daniell Smith	
	Isobell McRierie	
	John Kid	
	Mar[gare]t Mortimer	
	Agnes Brock	b
	Elespeth Cromby	
	James Jo[h]nstoun	
	Mar[gare]t Chalmer	b
	Mar[gare]t Broun	
	James Dick	
	Isobell Craik	v

Thomas Bowman
Mar[gare]t Lesly

29 W[illia]m Carnegie b
Mar[gare]t Hamilton
W[illia]m Carnegie you[nge]r v
Elis[abeth] Carnegie b[250]

David Herculus
Isobell Simson

James Johnstoun
Isobell Aikenhead

Alex[ande]r Fferrier
Jonet Ffraser

John Dow
Grissell Davidson

Adam Buchan
Jonet Wilson

Tho[mas] McCorkadaile
Bessie Welsh

Ro[ber]t Granger
Elespeth Thomson

Ro[ber]t Weir
Marion Stewart

James Wirdie
Jonet McFarlan

John Smetton
Mar[gare]t Simson
Mar[gare]t Smetton

30 Jonet Guy b

250 Name and marginalia written in a different hand.

Thomas Corser
Jonet Dickie b[251]

Earle Wintons Lodgeing

John McNaughton
Jean Mitchell b

W[illia]m Hunter
Elespeth Maither
George Clifton
Jean Cleghorn test

Jonet Caimell

Isobell Rodger

James Leith
Cristen Watson

Ro[ber]t Carbraith
Jonet Andersone
John Arbuthnett
Isobell Jacksone

31 John Broun
Jonet Lenders
Mar[gare]t McNab test

Hugh McGie
Agnes Fforsyth
Susanna Heriott
Kat[herine] Stewart

Alex[ande]r Turner
Elespeth Simson

James Lowe
Mar[gare]t Livingstoun

251 Name and marginalia written in a different hand.

	Peter Wanster	
	Bessie Somervaile	
	Jo[seph] Winster	b[252]
	Mary Wanster	
	Anna Cochran	
	James Johnstoun	
	Bessie Watson	
	James Bichett	
	James Shand	
	Lillias Harper	
	Jonet	test
	Alex[ande]r Hamiltoun	ensigne
	Mar[gare]t Cuming	
	Mar[gare]t Russell	
	Ar[chibal]d Jamesoun	
32	Jean Aitkin	
	Jonet Cranstoun	
	Elizabeth Cranstoun	n
	Jonet Sandelands	b
	Daniell Ffraser	
	Jean Lindsay	b
	Jean Cairncrosse	b
	Jonet Paull	test n
	Kenneth McKenyie	
	Jean Weir	b
	Jonet Drummond	
	John Fforbes	
	Jean Cranstoun	
	Mairjorie	
	Lawrence Ord	
	Agnes Innes	

252 Name and marginalia written in a different hand.

Cristen Ord
Elespeth Turpie

Barbara Ross
James Bullman

Jeills Thomson
Mar[gare]t Shipheard b

Geo[rge] Brouster
Agnes Milne

John Donaldson and
Jonet Hepburne b[253]
~~his wife~~

33 W[illia]m Auchenleck
John Baine
Helen Auchenleck
Mar[gare]t Gemmell

Samuell Shotwell
Isobell Ffrench

John Mastertoun
Jeills Airth
Thomas Mastertoun
Alex[ande]r Charles
Marie Airth

Walter Liston
Jean Gordon
Isobell Shaw b
Jo[h]n Painstoun

Thomas Trotter
Anna Bell
Jo[h]n Wonster
W[illia]m Storie v

253 Name and marginalia written in a different hand.

	Pat[rick] Barclay	
	Anna Ogilvie	test[254]
	Isobell Barclay	
	Agnes Baillie	
	Marjorie Cuthbertsone	
	Pat[rick] Black	b
	Nicolas Allan	
34	David Ralstoun	b
	Ffergus Ronald	b
	Eupham Smith	b
	Mar[gare]t Ratterey	b
	Barbara Gardiner	
	Jonet Smith	
	Marjorie Cuthbertsone	n[255]
	James Veatch	b
	Jonet Munro	
	Martha Diblin	
	Jean Murray	
	Jonet Murray	
	Ro[ber]t Graham	b
	Eupham Mercer	
	Mar[gare]t Graham	b
	John Wilson	
	Helen Deanes	
	Jean Trotter	
	James Cochran	

254 'Test' refers to entire household.
255 Name and marginalia written in a different hand.

Kat[herine] Pearson
W[illia]m Cochran
James Cochran
Ro[ber]t McKenlay
Jo[h]n Stevenson
Elizabeth Scott test: rec:
Isobell Broun
James Newtone[256]

35 **Abay Quarter**
Richard Baillie elder

James Tailyor
Isobell Walker
Jean Tailyor
Elespeth Tailyor v
Agnes Dow
~~Andrew Rid~~
Isobell Tailyor v[257]

Agnes Thomsone
Jo[h]n Cuthbertson v
Helen Blaikwood b
Eupham Blaikwood
Isobell Blaikwood b
Isobell Kid b[258]

Bartholomew Cussens and his wife
Christan Elphinstone b[259]
Bessie Norie
Eupham Baird n[260]

John Young
Elespeth Cochran

David Baillie
Jeills Ffalconer

256 Name written in a different hand.
257 Name and marginalia written in a different hand.
258 Name and marginalia written in a different hand.
259 Name and marginalia written in a different hand.
260 Name and marginalia written in a different hand.

W[illia]m Baillie b
John Baillie
Mar[gare]t Webster
~~David Hutchesone~~
Alex[ande]r Young[261]

William Wilson
Jonet Norie

36 Abigall Gibb
James Craig
Tunno Wood
James Manson
Mar[gare]t Dalyell test rec:

Isobell ~~Watson~~ Rid
Mar[gare]t Webster

Mr Laffoss
Elizabeth Kirkland b
Jonet Wilson v
~~Jean Durhame~~
Jonet Andrew v

John Broun
Julian Broun
John Baine b
Agnes
~~Patrick Caspergood~~ test

John Kallender
Mary Rid
Isobell
Thomas

Thomas White
Jean Edmonstoun
Agnes White
Jonet Watson

261 Name written in a different hand.

John Morisone
Helen Hamilton

37 William Wallace
Barbara Thomsone
Marion Thomsone
Jean Castellan

W[illia]m Cairnes
Elizabeth Semple
Sara Hunter
Jean Somervaile
[blank] Kilpatrick

Luke Stirling

Isobell Colt
George Low
Jean Samuell
Cristin Smith

Alex[ande]r Ffarquhar
~~Mar[gare]t Henderson test~~
Eupham Nicoll

Elizabeth Morison
Mar[gare]t Hendersone

John Stevenson
Katharen McClare
Alison Pearston b
Adam Cargill

38 Ar[chibal]d Inglis
Jonet Alex[ande]r

Jo[h]n Johnstoun
Elespeth Bruce
Elespeth Gibb test

Ro[ber]t Naisemith
Helen Andersone

Thomas Ffraser
Jonet McKeenyie
John Logan
Eupham Smith test rec: b

~~James Broun~~
~~Agnes Anderson~~
~~John Primrose~~

Alex[ande]r Meneses
Jonet Speid
Marjorie Meneses
Marijorie Campbell

David Rosse[262]
Jonet Waldie[263]

Thomas Caldwell
Mar[gare]t Cranston
Mar[gare]t Young v
Anna Lithgow

Jo[h]n Mackie
Jonet Spittle
Mar[gare]t Mackie n[264]

39 Theasaures famillie
Tho[mas] Ffraser
Hugh Ewer
Jo[h]n Cowper
W[illia]m Clerk
John Ritchie
Allan Phinick
Jonet Berrie
Mar[gare]t
Anna Clark
Kat[herine] McCommey
Grissell Muire
Mary Ker

262 Name written in a different hand.
263 Name written in a different hand.
264 Name and marginalia written in a different hand.

John Gibson
W[illia]m Heriott
Ro[ber]t Innes
W[illia]m Dalgrave
W[illia]m Wilson
John Gooldy
Alex[ande]r McClure

My Lord Theasaurer deputs
Jo[h]n Logan
W[illia]m Cuthbertson
Jo[h]n Moore
Jonet Burne
Helen Stewart
James Logan
James
Anna

40 Laird Minto and his Lady
Helen Bissett

Grissell Buchan
Anna Veatch

James Broun
Agnes Anderson
John Primrose

~~John~~ George Moore b
Jean Anderson b

Richard Baillie
Marion Smart
James Veatch b
Isobell Wallace b
Marten Robieson
John Potter v

Edward Moss
Mar[gare]t Moss
Alex[ande]r Moss
Mary Moss b
Elespeth W[illia]mson

41	Bartie Gibsons famillie	Quakers
	James W[illia]mson	
	Cristin Guthrie	
	George Weir	
	James Horne	
	Marion Weir	
	Isobell Ffraser	
	Thomas Paton	
	Jonet McCorne	
	Andrew Hunter	
	Agnes Johnstoun	b
	James Galloway	b
	Mar[gare]t Galloway	
	W[illia]m Smith	
	Jean Butter	
	Eupham Smith	test
42	John Crookshank	b
	Lilias Fferguson	b
	David Crookshank	b
	W[illia]m Stevensone	
	Marijorie Moar	
	James Hadden	
	Jeills Mitchell	
	Isobell Dobbie	
	Lady Lergo	
	Lillias Skinner	
	James Burgh	
	Alisone Gemmell	b
	Helen Baillie	b
	Mrs Armand	b
	John Shand	

John Morison
Agnes Young
Helen Stewart

42 Cristin Hog
Agnes Turner

Mar[gare]t Smith
Isobell Somervaile
Mar[gare]t Adamsone
Jonet Wandles test

Elizabeth Lindsay

John Riddoch
Anna Hamilton
Anna Riddoch
Mar[gare]t Riddoch v[265]

John Somervaile
Agnes Somervaile
Jonet Dalyell

Countes of Errolls famillie
Lady Katharen Murray
Mary Johnstoun b
John Arnott b
Jonet Steill b[266]
Thomas McBreir[267]
W[illia]m Stevenson[268]

44 Thomas Weir
Mar[gare]t Ro[ber]tson
Isobell Hastie

Mar[gare]t Don

265 Name and marginalia written in a different hand.
266 Name and marginalia written in a different hand.
267 Name written in a different hand.
268 Name written in a different hand.

7 Quarter
Alex[ande]r Skeene Elder

James Dyckes	
Mar[gare]t Hadden	
Alex[ande]r Fferguson	v
Kat[herine] Broun	test v
Jean Ogilvie	
Jonet Gilbert	
William Baiddie	
Cristin Jackson	test v
Andrew Barron	
Cristin Scott	
W[illia]m Wilson	v
George Black	b
Bessie Graham	
Mar[gare]t Gordon	
45 Widow McCure	
Edward Mcure	b
Alex[ande]r Eiyatt	
Mar[gare]t Drummond	
Collin Rig	
James Burr	
James McBaith	
Alex[ande]r Riach	b
Alex[ande]r Tailyor	b
Mary Auchenleck	v
Serjent Morison	
Jean Maxwell	
Mary Morison	
Agnes Pickard	test
James Hadden	
Magdalen Cleghorne	
James Cook	b
Andrew Templeman	b

	Ro[ber]t Gowrlay	b
	Mar[gare]t Porteous	
	W[illia]m Broun	
	Jonet Duncan	b
	Jean Glass	
	John Drummond	
	Kat[herine] Hepburn	
	Anna Drummond	v
	Helen Drumond	
	Lilias Drummond	v
46	Elizabeth Broun	
	Marion Allan	b
	Cap[tain] Alex[ande]r Livingston	
	Mrs McCalla	
	W[illia]m Patersone	
	Mrs Cook	
	Daniell Morgan	
	Alex[ande]r McKenyie	b
	Marion McKenlay	v
	Isobell Wood	
	Leu[tenan]t Murrayes familie	
	George Dowie	
	~~George Moore~~	
	Anna Cochran	b
	Barbara Simson	test rec: b
	Eupham Steill	test rec: b
	James Charles	
	W[illia]m Ro[ber]tson	
	James Ffraser	
	Jeills Thomson	
	David Chopman	b
	Elespeth McClaren	test
47	John Dalremple	b
	Mar[gare]t Paterson	
	James Mullikin	b

	Helen Aitkin	b
	Isobell Mullikin	
	Barb Mullikin	b
	Andrew Watson	
	Mar[gare]t Ffrench	
	Isobell Walker	
	Mar[gare]t Tailyor	
	Jonet Cuthbertson	
	Alex[ande]r Moor	b
	Isobell ~~Young~~ Broun	test
	Jo[h]n Don	
	Mar[gare]t Harvie	
	Alex[ande]r Seaton	
	Mary Aikenhead	
	Isobell Seaton	
	Jean Seaton	
	James Litlejohn	
	Mar[gare]t Montgomery	
	Mar[gare]t Ffountaine	test
48	James Elder	
	Agnes Dunlap	
	Thomas Stevenson	
	W[illia]m Ker	
	John Aitcheson	
	Mar[gare]t Weymes	
	Mar[gare]t Gilmoore	test
	W[illia]m Ewing	
	Barbara Ffindlay	
	Grissell Aitkin	test b
	James Clark	
	Jean Stirling	
	Bessie Smith	v
	John Thomson	

	Elizabeth Morison	
	John Munro	
	Jean Braikley	b
	John Allan	
	Ninian Douglas	
	Isobell Little	b
	Mar[gare]t Douglas	v
	W[illia]m Dry	b
	Cristen McEddie	
	Kat[herine] Dry	
49	Isobell Marshell	
	Thomas Allan	b
	Mar[gare]t Johnstoun	
	Barbara Smith	b
	Kat[herine] ~~Pedison~~	
	Mary Paterson	b
	Lady Lucias Hamilton	
	Eupham Sauchland	test
	George Hird	
	Elizabeth Baxter	
	Lady Carnwath	elder
	Jonet Achmouttie	
	Ro[ber]t Dalyell	b
	Isobell Chambers	b
	Lady Pitfoddell	
	Cristen Skeen	
	Helen Buggiwall	
50	John Irwin	
	Mary Smith	
	Jonet Irwin	b
	Edward Alison	

	Bessie Russell	b
	W[illia]m Adam	
	Kat[herine] Adam	
	Andrew Thomson	
	Mar[gare]t Tailyor	
	George Ramsay	
	James Smith	
	Beatrix Clink	
	John Griffan	
	Jean Hosey	
	James Ro[ber]tson	
	Mary Trotter	
	Bessie Blaiketer	
	Andrew W[illia]mson	
	Helen Smith	
51	Alex[ande]r Craig	
	Mar[gare]t Gibson	
	Mark Caddell	
	Mr Dewitts famillie	pap[ists]
	Jonet Baird	
	James Scott	
	Jonet Neilson	b
	Anna Neilson	v
	W[illia]m Donaldson	
	Jonet Broun	
	Jo[h]n McGreggor	
	George Bissett	
	Mar[gare]t Cook	
	W[illia]m Pirrie	
	Mar[gare]t Cock	b

	Jonet Yule	
	Walter Colvin	test b
	Mar[gare]t Abercromby	test v
	Alex[ande]r Skeen	
	Barbara Brand	
	Mar[gare]t Arbuthnett	b
	Mar[gare]t Anderson	b
	Elizabeth Drummond	b
	David Wirdie	v
52	John Auchinleck	
	Isobell Ro[ber]tson	
	W[illia]m Ffleck	b
	Jo[h]n Butter	
	W[illia]m Cowan	
	Marion Hadden	
	Jonet Gray	
	Lauderdailes Lodgeings	
	W[illia]m Marche	
	Jean Purdie	
	W[illia]m Burne	b
	Agnes Mullikin	test b
	John Wardrop	
	Mar[gare]t Barron	
	Jean Watson	
	Jo[h]n Dewr	test n
	W[illia]m Imrie	test b
53	Anna Boag	
	Mr Geo[rge] Thomson	
	Isobell Lesly	b
	Jo[h]n Somervaile	
	Mar[gare]t Cristie	
	Andrew Weir	
	Jean Somervaile	b
	Isobell Civiter	test b

Ro[ber]t Henry
Helen Cockburne
James Dinn

Mathew Fforsyth
Helen Burne
Helen Beck

Mungo Malloch
Jonet Litster
W[illia]m Dick
W[illia]m Steill
Marjorie Murray test
Ro[ber]t Duncan
Jonet Black test

54 James Smith b
Elespeth Witheringtoun

Ro[ber]t Watson b
Mar[gare]t Peipbells

Mungo Waldy
Cristin Waldy b

James Hepburne[269]
Marie Letham b[270]

~~Thomas Wood~~
~~Isobell Hodge~~
~~Elizabeth Broun~~

Robert Browne[271]
Elizabeth Dalyiel[272]

John Hog
Isobell Somervaile
Ro[ber]t Ffindlay

269 Name written in a different hand.
270 Name and marginalia written in a different hand.
271 Name written in a different hand.
272 Name written in a different hand.

Ro[ber]t Gowrlay b
Mar[gare]t Paterson test b
Bessie Lockart test v
Agnes Waldy b[273]

Lady Margaret Huntly
J[oh]n Anderson b
Will[iam] Whyte b
Jonet ~~Anderson~~ Henry b

George Henderson
Jean Smith

W[illia]m Strauchan
Mar[gare]t Thom

55 James Ro[ber]tson
Bessie Kid
Bessie Ro[ber]tson

Jonet Smith
Mary Melvin
Mar[gare]t Stoddert

Ro[ber]t Lauchlan b
Sophia Sinclar
Jo[h]n Sinclar v
Jean Lauchlan v

Alex[ande]r Ffindlay
Jonet Bruce

W[illia]m Aynsley
Jonet Ronald b
Jo[h]n Hislop
John Herriott

James Sinclar
Jonet Hog
Barbara Hog

273 Name and marginalia written in a different hand.

Agnes Veatch

56 John Cowpper
Isobell Burnett b

W[illia]m Alison
Agnes Ffowller

Thomas McKenyie
Agnes Baveredge

Jonet Jack b
Agnes Monro

George Wauchop
Isobell Munro
Mar[gare]t Wauchop v
Jonet Mitchell

Agnes Leitch
Eupham Ffiddes

David Hog b
Mar[gare]t Hutcheson

John Lauchlan
Grissell Hall
Mary Moffet v
Jo[h]n Lauchlan

57 **8 Quarter**
John Smith elder
W[illia]m Brotherstanes deacon

W[illia]m Brotherstanes
Helen Mather
James Brotherstanes b
Jonet Brotherstanes b
Jean Brotherstanes b

John Livingston
Mar[gare]t Gibb
Anna Marshell v

	Elespeth Campbell	
	Thomas Crichton	
	Marjorie Wood	
	Rachaell Aikenhead	b
	Elespeth Milne	
	James Mearnes	
	Cristin Towers	
	Mr Andrew Hay	
	Mrs Aikenhead	
	Thomas Matland	
	Jonet Moffett	
	James Johnstoun	
	Jean Wightman	
58	Barbara Smith	
	W[illia]m Elliott	
	Jonet Mullikin	
	James Badyenoch	
	James Miller	
	Jean Armand	
	W[illia]m McGreggor	
	Helen Burne	pap[ist/s][274]
	Mar[gare]t Badyenoch	
	Helen Hill	
	John Wilkie	
	Kat[herine] Wilson	
	James Wilkie	b
	Mary Wilkie	
	Laird Buchaple	and Lady

274 'Papists' may refer to entire household.

	Daniell McKenlay	
	Anna Claperton	test b
	David Preston	
	Cristin Nisbitt	b
	W[illia]m Noble	
	Eupham Dairnly	
59	David Sowtter	
	Jean Ross	
	Mar[gare]t Trotter	b
	W[illia]m Keir	
	Isobell Connell	
	Serjent Poage	
	Elizabeth Hadden	
	Jo[h]n Morison	
	Isobell Rutherfoord	
	Jean Morison	
	Jo[h]n Tod	
	Jonet Buchannan	
	Alex[ande]r Kininmon	
	Lilias Ferguson	
	Hugh Carroch	
	Jean Sommer	
	Elespeth Colling	b
	Kat[herine] Colling	v
	Alex[ande]r Fferguson	b
	Elespeth Ross	
	Bessie Keg	
60	Serjent Stewart	
	Jonet Wright	
	Elespeth Chalmer	

	John Lindsay	Serjent
	Marijorie Stewart	
	Jonet	
	John Fforsyth	
	Susanna Lawson	
	James Gordon	
	Jo[seph] Fforsythe	b[275]
	Will[iam] Fforsythe	b[276]
	this Blank is for Mrs Clow	
	W[illia]m Lendores	
	Isobell Wright	
	Elespeth Edmonstoun	
	Ro[ber]t Dalyell	Ensigne
	Cristin Muddie	
	Isobell Spink	
	Hugh Daniell	b[277]
	Edward Bunckle	b[278]
	Lady Mar[gare]t Hayes famillie	all papists
61	W[illia]m White	
	Anna Delves	
	Kat[herine] Gray	b
	John Brand	
	James Brand	
	John Brand	
	Jean Brand	b
	Ro[ber]t Brand	b
	Isacc Brand	b
	W[illia]m Boreland	v
	Thomas Swinton	b
	Jonet Leyes	v
	Mr Ro[ber]t Scotts familie	

275 Name and marginalia written in a different hand.
276 Name and marginalia written in a different hand.
277 Name and marginalia written in a different hand.
278 Name and marginalia written in a different hand.

Mrs Stirling

Mrs Lindsay
Elespeth Kinloch

Alex[ande]r Dunbar
Mar[gare]t Nisbitt
Anna Dunbar b
Marion Dunbar b
Geo[rge] Fforrest b
James Morice test b

62 Jo[h]n Ffraser
Isobell Ffortoun

John McKay
Jean Malcome

Maunse Craig
Cristin Stewart
Isobell ~~Stewart~~ Chalmer b

John Cochran b
Mary Thomson
~~Bessie~~ Marjorie Cowpland test rec b

Andrew Rae
Mar[gare]t Ralston

Jeremiah Lindsay
Jean Balvaird
Jonet Kinlock

Andrew Jap
Kat[herine] Duncan

Mar[gare]t Wauchop
Agnes Kilpatrick test

Thomas Alex[ande]r
Bessie Davidson

63 Jo[h]n Johnstoun

Mar[gare]t Broun
Mar[gare]t Ro[ber]tson test rec b

Thomas Bannatyne
[blank] Weymes
Jean Bannatyne
Helen Hamilton test rec b

Mr Matthew Ffleeming
Elizabeth Ffleeming
Marjorie Smith test rec b

Bessie Polwart
Jonet Polwart

Alisone Jackson

Ro[ber]t Drummond
Marion Hendersone
Jonet Chisholme
Jean Wightman
Kat[herine] Poag

John McRanken
[blank] Johnstoun
Urcilla Glass test b

John Mustard
Elespeth Craig

64 Henry Grieve
Jonet Wright
Jonet Malcome

Agnes Pringle
Marion Pringle v

Katharen Nisbitt
Magdalen Duncan b
Ro[ber]t Wilson b
James Sim v
Helen Paton

Ro[ber]t Lightbody
Jean Broun

Jo[h]n Bennet
Agnes Mastertoun b

Mr Vanderdorne and wife

Jo[h]n Laing
Mar[gare]t Spence

Jo[h]n Marshell
Jean Guthrie

W[illia]m Clerke[279]
Jean Yetts b
Mar[gare]t Clerke b
Richard Clerke b
Jo[seph] Hunter b
Elspeth Clerke b

65 W[illia]m Calderwood
Beatrix Cunningham
Mar[gare]t Howstoun test

Mr Scott of Gibleston
Cristin Shoner
Elizabeth Hamilton
Anna Burne b
Jo[h]n Stewart

James Tailyefer
Bessie Watt

Jo[h]n Cantley
Isobell Wauch

Thomas Jo[h]nstoun
Barbara Mitchell
W[illia]m Park b

279 Household written in a different hand.

Marion Cuttle test b

W[illia]m Cuming
Helen Craufurd

Mrs Muire

John Ramsay
Jonet Smith

Pat[rick] Milne
Susanna Cowlling

66 Thomas McCampen
Isobell Lowrie b
Mar[gare]t Gordon
Bessie Cooke b

Mrs Lauder
W[illia]m Lauder b
Kat[herine] Duncan v

Jo[h]n Hempfeed
Mary Lennein

Ar[chibal]d McQueen
Elizabeth McQueine
Jean Maitland
Jonet Lukison test
Marne Wilkie v[280]

Mr Jo[h]n Arthur
Elespeth Bryce

Jo[h]n Sinclar
~~Agnes~~ Jonet Cuningham
Jean Sword
Ro[ber]t Shorelay b
Alex[ande]r Glover v

280 Name and marginialia written in a different hand.

John Smith
Agnes Thean
Jo[h]n Moore v
Marion Yester test v
Michaell Archbald v[281]

67 Mr Bruce famillie
Elizabeth

Cristin Strauchan

Jo[h]n Arbuthnet
Isobell Jackson

Jonet Wright

Jo[h]n Umphray
Agnes Mitchell

Henry Sinclar
Jonet Kinghorne
Mar[gare]t Cassie

Alex[ande]r Watson
Lillias Palmer

Jean W[illia]msone

Jo[h]n Davidson
Jonet Lumsden

Kath[erine] Bannatyne[282]
Anna Ottonnelly b[283]

68 James Ffindlayson
Helen Morison
Pat[rick] Ffindlayson
John Sheill
Mar[gare]t

281 Name and marginalia written in a different hand.
282 Name written in a different hand.
283 Name and marginalia written in a different hand.

Ro[ber]t Smith
Sara Liddell
Jo[h]n Alex[ande]r test
Elizabeth Turner

Jo[h]n Paterson
Bessie Lumsden

Jo[h]n Anderson
Helen Clerk

Joseph Smith
Marion Tweedy
Andrew Tweedy
Agnes Broun
Bessie Blackstick test

Thomas Mossie
Mary Jollie b
~~Mary Mosie~~
John Thomson b
~~James Smith test~~
Jean Mosie b[284]

Jo[h]n Henderson
Jean Scott
Isobell Henderson b
James Alex[ande]r

69 Earle Murray

Ffrederick Buchan b
Sara Brand

Anna Toshoch
W[illia]m Harseburgh
Mar[gare]t Dinn

Jo[h]n Ro[ber]tson
Jonet Inglis

284 Name and marginalia written in a different hand.

Jo[h]n Broun

David Taitt
Mar[gare]t Vause
Jo[h]n McKenyie
James Ogilvie
Isobell Cuming v

Isobell Nisbitt

Andrew Small
Mar[gare]t Lightbody b
Eupham Paterson test rec v

John Sheill
Jonet Don
Edward Sheill
James Caskie
W[illia]m Sim

70 Mrs Salamon

John Ruthven
Susanna Ruthven
Jonet Polwart

James Miller
Marion Hutcheson
Ro[ber]t Broun v

James Maw
Helen Davidson

Alex[ande]r Innes
Grissell Howison

Alex[ande]r Kae
Barbara Boyd
Anna Kae
Mary Lesly b
Elespeth ~~Sanders~~ Alex[ande]r b

John Drummond

Kat[herine] Duncan

John Barton
Jean Douglas b

~~David Allan~~
~~Elespeth Cowper~~
~~Marion Hunter~~

71 John Murray
Jonet Napper
Kat[herine] Kirkland test

Andrew Mylles
Sara Angus b

Adam Darling
Sara Barclay

Isobell Wilson
Agnes Edmond test rec v

James Baird
Jonet Moorehead
Grissell Wirshart b

Mr Kickius
Appalonia Hardie
Mary Kickius
George Kickius
Ephraim Kickius b
Kat[herine] Watt: test

George Cristie
Elespeth McCall
W[illia]m McCall b
George Hamilton
Mary Dobbie test v

Elizabeth Oliphant
Agnes Seren test

72 Peter Cock

Anna Trotter

Andrew Clark b
Jonet Broun

James Donaldson
Jean Aitkin
Jean Donaldson

Serjent Currie
Mar[gare]t Lauder
Ro[ber]t Currie
Agnes Currie v

George Taitt
Mary Jo[h]nstoun
Mar[gare]t Henry test

Jacob Johnstoun
Mar[gare]t Bannatyne
W[illia]m Jo[h]nsone

Jo[h]n Fferguson
Mar[gare]t Thomson
Anna Lennox

David Burrell
Elizabeth Smith
Mar[gare]t Burrell
James Cussen v

73 [285]

74 [286]

75 The names of the families of the one half of the parioch of Cannongate
Beginning at the foot of Leeth Wind
Jan[uary] 1687

[285] Blank page.
[286] Blank page.

1 Quarter

John Wilson ab
Isobell Wilson ab

James Fender ab
Elspet Gray sub
Agnes Fender v

Elizabeth Watt sub
Thomas Jack ab

William Barclay b
Katharin Wylie ab
Ro[ber]t Barclay son b[287]

Robert Wylie ab
Agnes Gairnes ab

William Wylie ab
Bessie Wightman ab

George Barclay b ~~ab~~
Marg[are]t Bell ab
Elspet Hutcheson ab

Hugh Walker ab
Janet Dinn b

Geo[rge] Speers ab
Janet Anderson ab
Marg[are]t Anderson ig:
Janet Broun v:

76 James Neelson ab
Margaret Paterson ab

Agnes Stirlen ab
Christian Conn b

287 Name and marginalia written in a different hand.

James Halliburton ab
Elspet Home ab
Mary Halliburton ab

James Morton ab
Margaret Morton ab

William Sommervill ab
Isobell Cumming ab
John Law b
Margaret Markalla b ~~ab~~

Thomas Sharp ab
Elizabeth Sharp ab
James Campbell ab

James Cathie ab
Agnes Hapkin ab

~~James Anderson~~
Marg[are]t Morton ab
Thomas Anderson son b

John Bruce
Agnes Archibald
Agnes Archibald you[nge]r ig
William Thomson v
Marg[are]t Sauchlie v

77 Archibald More ab
Helen Maxwell ab
Archibald More you[nge]r ab
Adam More ab

John Tweddes ab
William ~~Miller~~ ab

Alexander Loch b
Agnes Mitchell ab
Alex[ande]r Loch b[288]

288 Name and marginalia written in a different hand.

	Patrick Douglass	ab
	Magdalen Mitchell	ab
	John Gray	v
	Jean Douglass	b[289]
	Frederick Wallace	ab
	Agnes Mackenlie	b
	James Gairnes	b
	Isobell Mackenlie	ab
	James Richie	ab
	Isobell Hyslop	ab
	Gilbert Richie	ab
	Thomas Purdie	ab
	Marg[are]t Martin	test ab
	Robert Swan	ab
	Isobell Rutherfoord	ab
	John Foubister	ab[290]
	William Foubister	
	Barbara Sutherland	
	John Foubister	you[nge]r
	Isobell Todd	test
	William Foubister	
78	John Thomson	ab
	Marion Grahme	ab
	Andrew Wallace	ab
	Janet Richie	ab
	Agnes Richie	ab
	James Cantley	ab
	Margaret Duncan	ab
	Robert Gardiner	ab
	Margaret Home	ab

289 Name and marginalia written in a different hand.
290 'ab' refers to entire household.

	James Anderson	ab
	Elspet Paton	ab
	Janet Anderson	ab
	Michael Spence	ab
	Marion Bughel	v
	Margaret Gray	b
	John Spence[291]	
	Thomas King	ab
	Margaret Mackeinyie	
	James Moor	b
	Janet Morison	ab
	James Rankin	b
	James Adie	b
	Christian Steven	ab test
	John Moor	b[292]
	William Baird	ab
	Isobell Wightman	ab
	Isobell Baird	
	Margaret Smyth	test
79	John Ispling	ab
	Alison Broun	ab
	Marg[are]t Caruddes	ab
	Margaret Monroe	b
	Janet Monroe	b
	Penelope Monroe	ab
	James Butterfield	ab
	Margaret Butterfield	ab
	George Lyell	ab
	Margaret Macklurg	ab
	David Sim	ab

291 Name written in a different hand.
292 Name and marginalia written in a different hand.

	Isobell Cuthketle	ab
	James Gray	ab b
	Isobell Henry	ab
	Janet Broun	ab
	George Rosse	ab
	Agnes Peter	ab
	John Smyth	ab
	Alexander Grieve	ab
	William Orrock	ab[293]
	Elspet Mitchell	
	Mathew Orrock	
	John Bain	
	Margaret Broun	test
	Robert Cuningham	ab[294]
	Barbara Sands	put b
80	Francis Ash	ab[295]
	Bessie Douglass	
	Thomas Ash	ab[296]
	Anna Cuningham	
	Isobell Ash	
	Isobell Lauchlin	~~ab~~
	Alexander Craig	ab[297]
	Jean Gilmer	
	Janet Bellie	
	James Duff	b
	Margaret Forbes	b

293 'ab' refers to the entire household.
294 'ab' refers to the entire household.
295 'ab' refers to the entire household.
296 'ab' refers to the entire household.
297 'ab' refers to the entire household.

	Andrew Vallange	ab[298]
	Janet Macklearen	
	Patrick Watson	ab
	Margaret Hague	b
	Isobell Mullekin	ab
	Robert Edward	ab[299]
	Martha Bell	
	Martha Lamb	
	Geo[rge] Armo[u]r	
	Elspet Hamilton	ab
	Andrew Small	b
	Isobell Areskin	b
	Jean Small	~~ab~~ b
	Helen Fanholm	~~ab~~
	Andrew Rail	~~ab~~
	David Small	~~ab~~
	James Carmichael	ab
	Marg[are]t Anderson	v
	Tho[mas] Carmichael	ab
81	John Robertson	ab
	Alison Hodge	b
	Archibald Robertson	ab
	Gilbert Sheen	ab
	Isobell Bell	ab
	Marjory Johnston	~~ab~~ ig
	Robert Carmichael	ab
	Elspet Sturgeon	ab
	James Paterson	ab
	Christian Forrest	ab
	John Scott	ab

298 'ab' refers to entire household.
299 'ab' refers to entire household.

	John Broun	b
	John Gilchrist	ab[300]
	Isobell Buchannan	
	Margaret Low	
	Janet Bellram	ab[301]
	Janet Marshell	put b
	Jean Marshell	
	George Beatie	put b ab[302]
	Margaret Miller	v
	Laurence Happertoun	
	Margaret Stevenson	
	David Whyte	ab[303]
	Margaret Whyte	
	David Moor	
	John Hart	
	Janet Whyte	test
82	Walter Rosse	ab[304]
	Janet Mosie	
	Janet Hill	
	Samuel Hill	put b
	Elspet Watt	put b
	George Carmichael	ab[305]
	Isobell Falla	
	James Merston	put b
	Lucretia Thomson	
	David Miller	ab[306]
	Adam Miller	
	Margaret Nicoll	

300 'ab' refers to the entire household.
301 'ab' refers to the entire household.
302 'ab' refers to the entire household.
303 'ab' refers to the entire household.
304 'ab' refers to the entire household.
305 'ab' refers to the entire household.
306 'ab' refers to the entire household.

	James Hough	ab[307]
	Alison Smyth	put b
	James Mackalyean	ab[308]
	Marion Mackgie	
	Isobell Mackalyean	
	Margaret Mackalyean	
	James Mackalyean	put
	James Mackalyean	
	William Davidson	ab[309]
	Isobell Young	
	Donald Mackran	
	Andrew Ramsey	ab
	Anna Abercrombie	ab
	William Anderson	b
	William Mitchell	young
	Bessie Kellie	put b ~~ab~~
83	Alexander Logan	ab[310]
	Jean Straughan	
	James Logan	
	Bethia Logan	
	John Gellitie	
	~~Katherine Mason~~	ab[311]
	Janet Ure	put b
	Nicholas Mackeinyie	
	Robert ~~Poog~~ Monroe	ab[312]
	Margaret Poog	put b
	David Gargill	ab[313]
	Isobell Fiffe	

307 'ab' refers to the entire household.
308 'ab' refers to the entire household.
309 'ab' refers to the entire household.
310 'ab' refers to the entire household.
311 'ab' refers to the entire household.
312 'ab' refers to the entire household.
313 'ab' refers to the entire household.

	William Gargill	
	John Smyth	put ab[314]
	Agnes Wilson	
	John Hutton	
	Robert Grant	
	John Wilson	ab[315]
	~~Margaret [illegible]~~	
	Daniel Forbes	
	Janet Blackstock	test
	Angus Black	ab[316]
	Marg[are]t Heugh	
	John Monroe	ab
	Janet Mackulloch	ab
	Bessie Lauder	ab
	Collen Lauder	v
	Helen Monroe	ab
84	William Dewer	ab[317]
	Janet Cuningham	
	David Clunie	ab
	Grisel Thomson	ab
	Isobell Thomson	v
	Patrick Beatie	ab[318]
	Elspet Mathie	test
	Janet Robison	
	James Thomson	
	Marg[are]t Clerk	
	William Orrock	v
	James Scobie	b

314 'ab' refers to the entire household.
315 'ab' refers to the entire household.
316 'ab' refers to the entire household.
317 'ab' refers to the entire household.
318 'ab' refers to the entire household.

Patrick Innes ab[319]
Margaret Gairnes
James Gordon
Isobell test

James Rennie ab[320]
Marg[are]t Borleans

James Taylor ab[321]
Marg[are]t Scoon
Isobell Darlen

David Broun ab[322]
Isobell Key

William Murray ab[323]
Marg[are]t Kilpatrick
Barbara Hamilton
Agnes Rosse forn: & not yet satisfied

85 Thomas Rae b ab[324]
Margaret Young
William Burden put b

Francis Henderson
Janet Walker
Robert Henderson b
Francis Van-hagen v

William Innes ab
Agnes Moffet ab
William Innes you[nge]r b
Alexander Innes b
James Young ab
Elspet Fleeming test ab

319 'ab' refers to the entire household.
320 'ab' refers to the entire household.
321 'ab' refers to the entire household.
322 'ab' refers to the entire household.
323 'ab' refers to the entire household.
324 'ab' refers to the entire household.

	John Whyte	ab
	Bessie Wilkie	ab
	Richard Whyte	b
	James Ralston	ab
	Helen Durie	ab
	Jean Ralston	b
	Alexander Irvin	ab
	Geo[rge] Coldcleugh	ab[325]
	Julian Reid	
	Helen Whyte	
	Marg[are]t Bennet	ab[326]
	Robert Hacrew	
	Elizabeth Lauson	
	John Forbes	ab[327]
	Janet Hyslop	
	Janet Taylor	put test b
	John Lauder	
86	Zacharias de Fronoy	ab[328]
	Anna Maskle	
	John Walker	
	Christian Whitlaw	put young
	John Mackdougle	ab[329]
	Margaret Allen	
	Mary Smyth	
	Geo[rge] Gleghorn	ab[330]
	Agnes Blair	
	Marion Wilson	test
	Alexander Thomson	ab

325 'ab' refers to the entire household.
326 'ab' refers to the entire household.
327 'ab' refers to the entire household.
328 'ab' refers to the entire household.
329 'ab' refers to the entire household.
330 'ab' refers to the entire household.

	Alexander Henderson	ab
	Mary Bigger	
	William Bigger	
	William Oliphant	
	Marion Dunlap	
	William Taylor	b
	Anna Lindsay	ab
	John Balfour	b
	Bessie Berrie	ig test
	Josiah Johnstoun	p ab[331]
	Marg[are]t Johnston	
	Jean Red	test
	Helen Binnen	
	Robert Monroe	ab
	Daniel Caddel	ab
	Alexander Monroe	ab
	Marg[are]t Baxter	b
87	Thomas Straughan	put b ab[332]
	Isobell Irvin	
	Marg[are]t Broun	test put
	George Seaton	ab
	Alexander Weer	
	Helen Mastertoun	
	Rachel Weer	v
	Janet Gray	ab
	David Berrie	ab
	Marion Dickson	ab
	David Barrie	
	John Berrie	
	David Walker	ab
	[illegible]ken Wood	

331 'ab' refers to the entire household.
332 'ab' refers to the entire household.

	Marion Broun	ab
	Margaret Gilespie[333]	
88	**2 Quarter**	
	John Laing	ab[334]
	Janet Boyd	
	Thomas Ormeston	
	Alexander Robertson	test
	Janet Bruce	
	Mar[gare]t Gilgour	ab
	John Angus	ab[335]
	Sophia Maxwell	
	Rachel Whyte	
	Thomas Aitken	ab[336]
	Elizabeth Davie	
	Mar[gare]t Harrower	test
	John Avis	
	David Avis	
	John Hepburn	put ab[337]
	Isobell Logan	
	John Scouler	
	Marjory Pursell	put test b
	Christian Paton	put b
	Elspet Malloch	ab[338]
	Bessie Malloch	
	William Lang	In deacon McKillans cellar[339] Moor
	Katharin Sim	

333 Name written in a different hand.
334 'ab' refers to the entire household.
335 'ab' refers to the entire household.
336 'ab' refers to the entire household.
337 'ab' refers to the entire household.
338 'ab' refers to the entire household.
339 'In deacon McKillans cellar' in left margin.

89	Andrew Moffet	ab[340]
	Isobell Watson	
	Janet Calander	ab[341]
	Janet Walker	
	Thomas Black	ab[342]
	Beatrix Henrie	
	James Carmichael	ab[343]
	Janet Goodfellow	
	John Currie	ab[344]
	Agnes Pickin	
	Mar[gare]t Thomson	
	Patrick Lauson	
	Janet Mill	test
	David Areskin	ab[345]
	Janet	
	Robert Rankin	ab[346]
	Helen Lauson	
	Elizabeth Fairly	
	Robert Rankin	
	John Marston	ab
	Mary Colvill	ab
	Christian Forbes	ab
	George Borthick	b
90	James Govan	ab put b[347]
	Katharin Balfour	
	Mar[gare]t Johnston	test

340 'ab' refers to the entire household.
341 'ab' refers to the entire household.
342 'ab' refers to the entire household.
343 'ab' refers to the entire household.
344 'ab' refers to the entire household.
345 'ab' refers to the entire household.
346 'ab' refers to the entire household.
347 'ab put b' refers to the entire household.

James Lauson ab[348]
Janet Shaw

Bessie Barrie ab
Jasper ~~Johnston~~ b

Alexander Maxwell ab[349]
Mar[gare]t Johnston
Richard Dalgleish
Robert Allen
Mar[gare]t More
James Cairnes

William Angus ab[350]
Martha Broun

Andrew Small b
Marg[are]t Lightbodie b

David Kennedy ab[351]
Jean Smyth
Anna Bruce test

William Morison ab
Katharin Wallace ab
Jean Cockburn

Helen Craill ab[352]
Barbara Borleans

David Alexander ab[353]
Isobell Law

91 Alexander Scot ab[354]
Euphan Malice

348 'ab' refers to the entire household.
349 'ab' refers to the entire household.
350 'ab' refers to the entire household.
351 'ab' refers to the entire household.
352 'ab' refers to the entire household.
353 'ab' refers to the entire household.
354 'ab' refers to the entire household.

	Charles Rosse	test
	Margaret Hardie	
	James Livingston	ab[355]
	Katharin Brand	
	John Duncan	ab
	Mary Lootfoot	b
	Thomas Miller	ab[356]
	Helen Stevenson	
	Robert Meinyies	
	George Hay	b
	Katharin Traquair	ab
	Alison Wast	b
	Elspet Birnie	ab
	Janet Jellie	ab
	Mr Henry Hetherwick	p
	Isobell Moorice	
	Margaret Bryson	ab
	Thomas Brantfield	ab
	Elspet Paterson	b
92	John Inglis	ab
	Marjory Carrin	ab
	Margaret Sinclare	v
	Margaret Buchannan	test
	Marg[are]t Redman	ab[357]
	Sarah Hutcheson	put young
	~~Helen Hethertreek~~	
	Alexander Home	ab
	Isobell Grant	ab
	Bessie Hogg	b

355 'ab' refers to the entire household.
356 'ab' refers to the entire household.
357 'ab' refers to the entire household.

	Elizabeth Home	b
	Helen Home	b
	David Dinunn	elder ab
	Marion Alison	ab
	Gideon Campbell	b
	Christian Dinun	ab
	Katharin Dinnun	ab
	Sarah Chancellor	test ab
	George Still	ab[358]
	Alison Bowman	
	John Still	
	Isobell Harkel	test
	Laucklin Mackpherson	ab
	Elizabeth Bowers	ab
	Donald Mackpherson	put v
	Marion Craig	test b
	Andrew McFersone	young b[359]
93	Alexander Ferguson	ab
	Helen Kelloch	ab
	Jean Guiler	v
	Thomas Robison	b
	Jean Brotherstanes	test v
	James Craich	ab
	Elizabeth Robertson	ab
	Francis Beuglass	ab
	Elizabeth Greg	b[360]
	George Watson	ab[361]
	Elspet Wright	
	George Dove	ab[362]
	Beatrix Dickson	

358 'ab' refers to the entire household.
359 Name and marginalia written in a different hand.
360 Name and marginalia written in a different hand.
361 'ab' refers to the entire household.
362 'ab' refers to the entire household.

	James Sommers	b
	Elspet Taylor	ab
	Isobell Denham	test
	William Buchannan	ab[363]
	Elspet Lawman	
	Janet Buchannan	
	Andrew Wilson	ab[364]
	Margaret Carmichael	
	James Wilson	
	Janet Andersone	
	Janet Dick	ab
	~~Helen Blair~~	~~test~~
	Margaret Ker	b
	Margaret Adie	ab[365]
94	William Carmichael	ab[366]
	Margaret Wright	
	Margaret Yessimen	
	Margaret Tam	
	William Struther	ab[367]
	Sarah Duncan	
	James Maule	ab[368]
	Elspet Gibb	
	Robert Borthick	
	Sarah Logan	ab[369]
	Sarah Watson	
	Geo[rge] Alexander	ab
	Marion Caruddes	put b

363 'ab' refers to the entire household.
364 'ab' refers to the entire household.
365 Name and marginalia written in a different hand.
366 'ab' refers to the entire household.
367 'ab' refers to the entire household.
368 'ab' refers to the entire household.
369 'ab' refers to the entire household.

Margaret Pofrey ab[370]
Thomas Marshell

James Lesly ab

James Smyth ab
Janet Crosse ab

George Hogg ab
Margaret Bousten b

Alexander Walker ab
Elizabeth Burrell ab
John Ainsly b
James Wilkie b
Agnes Chapeman test ab
Elizabeth Walker b

95 Janet Gibson put b
David Robertson put b
William Kenlie put young
Jean Gawin put ig

Roderick Pedison
Euphan Gullen b
Elspet Kirkland b

Andrew Smyth ab

Janet Balfour ab[371]
Isobell Ferguson

William Sim ab[372]
Bessie Ferguson

George Hyslop ab
Jean Dobie b

John Gray ab

370 'ab' refers to the entire household.
371 'ab' refers to the entire household.
372 'ab' refers to the entire household.

	Marg[are]t Brounlay	b
	Thomas Gray	v
	James Redpeth	ab
	Marg[are]t Baderstanes	b
	Janet Scot	test
	Andrew Rosse	test v
96	Alexander Innes	ab
	Christian Innes	p
	Mary Innes	ab
	Isobell More	
	Margaret Currier	ab
	Archbald Hogg	ab[373]
	Elspet Geddies	
	Francis Hogg	put b
	~~Agnes Sutherland~~	~~test~~
	Jean Thomson	put b
	Agnes Wylie	ab[374]
	William Garvie	
	Jean Pringle	
	George Wilson	ab[375]
	Janet Mathers	
	Barbara Neiper	
	Andrew Watson	b
	Mary Heatly	ab
	Widow Fiffe	pop[ists][376]
	Isobell Spence	
	George Ballantine	
	John Hay	
	Jean Lindsay	old
	Agnes Bain	ig

373 'ab' refers to the entire household.
374 'ab' refers to the entire household.
375 'ab' refers to the entire household.
376 'pop[ists]' refers to the entire household.

	James Rae	baillie
	Helen Sydeserf	
	Elizabeth Rae	
	John Rae	
97	Mary Rae	in the same familie
	Isobell Lawson	ab
	Jean Dauson	ig
	Adam Sydeserf	b
	John Taylor	put b ab[377]
	Helen Samuel	
	John Wright	put b
	Isaack Lees	put ig young
	Janet Dickson	
	Waller Porterfield	
	John Logan	ab
	Alexander Marshell	ab
	John Cant	ab b
	Agnes Smyth	b
	John Ballantine	p
	David Lesly	ab
	Grisel Campbell	ab
	Mris Maitland	ab[378]
	~~Richard Maitland~~	
	Anna Maitland	
	Marg[are]t Maitland	
	Katharin Small	put b
	Mr Francis de Poul	
	Christian Robison	ab
	Lieutennant Livingston	ab[379]
	Elizabeth Hamilton	
	Marg[are]t Dick	
	Marg[are]t Walstoun	test

377 'ab' refers to the entire household.
378 'ab' refers to the entire household.
379 'ab' refers to the entire household.

98	Patrick Castile	ab[380]
	Margaret Pill	
	James Dowell	
	Helen Watson	test
	Marg[are]t Douglasse	ab[381]
	Agnes Mitchell	test
	Bessie Lesly	
	David Dinunn	you[nge]r ab
	Katharin Diddup	ab
	John Murray	v
	~~William Rosse~~	
	Ro[ber]t ~~Rosse~~ Sheills	b
	Katharin Mackpherson	test
	James Murray	ab
	Katharin Fleeming	ab
	John Murray	b
	Marg[are]t Coldwells	b
	Marg[are]t Turner	ab[382]
	Isobell Ithingtoun	
	Margaret Archbald	ab[383]
	James Lyleburn	
	Susanna Morison	
	Barbara Morison	
	William Man	ab
	Marion Leggit	b
	Elizabeth Anderson	b
	Elspet Kid	ab
	~~Walter Scot~~	
	Andrew Symson	b[384]

380 'ab' refers to the entire household.
381 'ab' refers to the entire household.
382 'ab' refers to the entire household.
383 'ab' refers to the entire household.
384 Name and marginalia written in a different hand.

	Christian Bell	ab[385]
	Janet Douglasse	
99	David Pitkeithlie	ab
	Alison Knox	b
	Janet Pilkeithlie	b[386]
	William Cairnes	ab[387]
	Katherin Lamb	
	Myles Holmes	ab
	Jean Lauson	ab
	Elizabeth Allen	test ab
	Jean Carmichael	b
	Christian Stacy	b
	Robert Cowie	ab[388]
	Marg[are]t Fleeming	
	Allan Wallace	ab[389]
	Marg[are]t Anderson	
	Christian Miller	
	Katherin Yeats	ab
	John Allen	b
	Barbara Moodie	v
	Janet Philip	ab[390]
	Jean Forbes	eld[er]
	Marg[are]t Forbes	
	Jean Forbes	you[nge]r
	Alex[ande]r Robertson	ab[391]
	Janet Ker	

385 'ab' refers to the entire household.
386 Name and marginalia written in a different hand.
387 'ab' refers to the entire household.
388 'ab' refers to the entire household.
389 'ab' refers to the entire household.
390 'ab' refers to the entire household.
391 'ab' refers to the entire household.

	Christian Kid	test
	William Mitchell	
	Marion Broun	ab
	William Davidson	ab
	Hugh Mitchell	b
100	Janet Hill	ab
	John Thomson	ab[392]
	Katharin Watson	
	Thomas Red	ab[393]
	Rebekah Cousten	
	William Ferrier	ab
	Marg[are]t Porterfield	ab
	William Ferrier	you[nge]r b
	Marg[are]t Ferrier	b
	John Ferguson	x
	Charlot Morice	
	Richard Barnwell	x
	Emilia Ferguson	
	John Ferguson	
	Janet Inglis	x
	Elizabeth Ferguson	ab[394]
	James Greg	ab[395]
	Isobel Forrest	
	James Geddies	
	Agnes Williamson	test
	Mistris Lumesdane	ab
	Daniel Callard	ab[396]
	Magdalen Dinnet	

392 'ab' refers to the entire household.
393 'ab' refers to the entire household.
394 'ab' refers to the entire household.
395 'ab' refers to the entire household.
396 'ab' refers to the entire household.

	Christian Broadie	test
	Margaret Cameron	
101	Robert Craw	ab[397]
	Barbara Innes	
	Anna Crow	
	Agnes Scot	b
	James Kirkwood	ab[398]
	Elspet Smyth	
102	**3 Quarter**	
	Lady St. Germanes	
	Alexander Thomson	ab
	Lybra Jack	ab
	Isobell Thomson	young
	Alexander Thomson	young
	Jean Wood	ig:
	John Weddel	b
	Patrick Kinninment	ab[399]
	Mary Fyffie	
	Janet Samuell	test
	Janet Robertson	test
	William Clerk	ab
	Agnes Aikman	ab
	William Cairnes	young ig:
	Alexander Johnston	ab
	Adam Scobie	v
	Richard Clerk	b
	Janet Hill	ig:
	David Ker	ab[400]
	Elizabeth Penman	

397 'ab' refers to the entire household.
398 'ab' refers to the entire household.
399 'ab' refers to the entire household.
400 'ab' refers to the entire household.

	Katharin Mackie	
	Isobell Ker	
	John Ker	put young[401]
103	James Cathcart	ab[402]
	Anna Russell	
	Elspet Stevenson	test
	Thomas Bairner	b
	Christian Hay	ab
	John Cock	b
	Bessie Lauson	ab
	James Ferguson	ab
	John Anderson	ab
	John Riuch	ab
	Geo[rge] Stobb	ab
	Janet Henderson	ab[403]
	Barbara Wallace	
	James Anderson	
	John Leggit	
	William Hadden	
	Marg[are]t Wallace	v
	Marg[are]t Wallace	ab
	Andrew Neelson	ab
	Mris Hay	b
	Mary Hay	ab
	Katharin Hay	ab
	Jean Clerk	b
	~~Jack Henderson~~	
104	Robert Paton	ab[404]
	~~John Paton~~	
	Janet Henderson	
	William Paton	

401 Name and marginalia written in a different hand.
402 'ab' refers to the entire household.
403 'ab' refers to the entire household.
404 'ab' refers to the entire household.

	Daniel Davidson	ab[405]
	Mary Red	
	Isobell Hyslop	test put ig
	John Clunie	
	Mris Murray	
	Margaret Murray	ab
	James Murray	ab
	Margaret Smyth	b
	Margaret Rob	b
	John Paton	ab
	John Paton	ab
	Christian Red	b
	William Fleeming	ab[406]
	Bessie Fyffe	
	James Lauder	ab[407]
	Agnes More	
	Andrew Pringle	ab[408]
	Sarah Henderson	
	John Mortoun	
	Mris Stevenson	
105	Alexander Fairly	ab[409]
	Jean Oliphant	
	John Couper	put b ab[410]
	Jean Aiken	
	Alex[ande]r Gairnes	~~test~~ put b
	Mary Fyfe	
	Tho[mas] Barrowman	v

405 'ab' refers to the entire household.
406 'ab' refers to the entire household.
407 'ab' refers to the entire household.
408 'ab' refers to the entire household.
409 'ab' refers to the entire household.
410 'ab' refers to the entire household.

	Margaret Nesmith	ab
	William Gordon	b
	Jean Anderson	ab
	John Wright	b
	Archibald Gordon	b
	Marg[are]t Gordon	ab
	Robert Dodds	ab[411]
	Agnes Anderson	
	Robert Mitchell	ab
	Isobell Small	b
	Margaret Marshell	ab[412]
	Janet Black	
	Grisel Macknab	
106	Thomas Red	ab
	Elizabeth Wauch	b
	~~Helen Cockburn~~	~~test~~
	John Paterson	
	Helen Kinneir	
	James Sim	ab
	James Cochren	b
	Barbara Bird	b
	Monsieur Allar	ab[413]
	& his wife	
	Robert Paterson	ab[414]
	Katharin Allen	
	Christian Ramsey	test put
	Hardens family	ab[415]
	Robert Scot	put b

411 'ab' refers to the entire household.
412 'ab' refers to the entire household.
413 'ab' refers to the entire household.
414 'ab' refers to the entire household.
415 'ab' refers to the entire household.

	William Morison	
	Geo[rge] Flesher	
	James Forrester	
	William Wight	
	Janet Bennerman	test
	Alex[ande]r Ogilvie	Not[416]
	Mary Moslie	
	Anna Dundradd	
	Geo[rge] Scot	test
	Lillias Ronald	test
	Margaret Kermuck	test
107	Gilbert Somervill	ab[417]
	Katharin Sanderson	
	James Mason	
	Jean Mason	
	James Robison	ab[418]
	Margaret Sanderson	
	Alexander Stewart	
	Euphan Cromartie	
	Widow Donn	ab[419]
	Bessie Donn	
	Marg[are]t Crookshanks	
	James Caskie	
	James Stewart	ab[420]
	Isobell Morton	
	Mary Mark	
	My L. Livingstones family	
	John Wilson	ab[421]
	Geo[rge] Broun	
	Geo[rge] Martin	

416 Marginalia runs into page crease.
417 'ab' refers to the entire household.
418 'ab' refers to the entire household.
419 'ab' refers to the entire household.
420 'ab' refers to the entire household.
421 'ab' refers to the entire household.

	John Livingston	
	Henry Stroud	
	Andrew Sutherland	
	Anna Livingston	
	Janet Balk	
	Jean Stewart	
108	Widow Irvin	ab[422]
	Jean Irvin	
	Giles Pillins	ab[423]
	Marjory Kitchen	test
	Arthur Henderson	ab
	Maus Johnstoun	ab
	Alexander Seaton	ab
	Alexander Rae	b
	Margaret Tait	b young
	Margaret Straughan	test b
	Mris Hague	Nota ab[424]
	Mary Grier	test
	Eberna Hague	
	James Paterson	x[425]
	Alison Graham	
	Mris Hastie	ab
	Agnes Davidson	ab
	Barbara Davidson	b
	John Smyth	ab
	Margaret Hamilton	ab
	Robert Burrell	b
	Bessie Johnston	ab
	Elspet Joy	b

422 'ab' refers to the entire household.
423 'ab' refers to the entire household.
424 'ab' refers to the entire household.
425 'x' refers to the entire household.

	William Hepburn	ab[426]
	Isobell Dounie	
	Margaret Wilson	
109	John Cochren	ab
	Katharin Tennent	ab
	William Dauson	b
	Andrew Dauson	b
	Andrew Baill	young[427]
	Thomas Barrowman	you[nge]r
	Martha Forrester	ab
	Nathaniel Adamson	v
	Charles Barrowman	ab
	Robert Gibb	v
	Janet Litlejohn	v
	Patrick Burrell	ab[428]
	Mary Barr	
	Thomas Elliot	
	John Mill	ab[429]
	Magdalen Grahme	
	Charles Broun	ab[430]
	Margaret Williamson	
	John Craich	ab[431]
	Isobell Wilson	
	Janet Martin	test
	Hugh Williamson	ab[432]
	Euphan Murray	put v
	John Watson	ab

426 'ab' refers to the entire household.
427 Name and marginalia written in a different hand.
428 'ab' refers to the entire household.
429 'ab' refers to the entire household.
430 'ab' refers to the entire household.
431 'ab' refers to the entire household.
432 'ab' refers to the entire household.

	Janet Adam	ab
	James Cutbert	b
	Tho[mas] Casslelaw	b
	Elspet Buchannan	ab
110	James Johnston	put b ab[433]
	Bessie Cumming	
	Agnes Rae	put ig
	William Marshell	ab[434]
	Agnes Lindsay	
	John Macklure	ab
	Jean Johnston	ab
	David Park	b
	Katharin Maule	ab
	Walter Murray	ab[435]
	Mary Ker	
	Thomas Murray	
	Richard Gibson	ab[436]
	Margaret Riddoch	
	Mary Gibson	
	James Monteath	ab[437]
	Isobell Gibson	
	Margaret Bruce	
	William Paul	ab[438]
	Christian Frazer	
	Jean Maitland	ab[439]
	Magdalen Litle	

433 'ab' refers to the entire household.
434 'ab' refers to the entire household.
435 'ab' refers to the entire household.
436 'ab' refers to the entire household.
437 'ab' refers to the entire household.
438 'ab' refers to the entire household.
439 'ab' refers to the entire household.

111	Robert Pedison	ab[440]
	Agnes Blair	
	Andrew Nicoll	ab[441]
	Margaret Bennet	
	Margaret Mercer	
	Thomas Hay	ab[442]
	Margaret Stewart	
	Adam Darlen	ab[443]
	Jean Ballard	
	Agnes Mitchell	test
	Mary Mitchell	b
	Giles Mitchell	b
	Marion Rodger	~~b~~ ig:
	Thomas Murray	ab
	Janet Pringle	~~ab~~ v
	James Lauson	v
	Marg[are]t Murray	~~ab~~ b
	Elspet Adam	b
	Mris Grier	ab
	George Scot	ab
	David Kid	ab[444]
	Isobell Burn	
	Isobell Fiffe	ab
	Bessie Broun	ab
	Elspet Pringle	b
112	Thomas Livingston	b
	Magdalen Collen	b
	Robert Livingston	ab

440 'ab' refers to the entire household.
441 'ab' refers to the entire household.
442 'ab' refers to the entire household.
443 'ab' refers to the entire household.
444 'ab' refers to the entire household.

	Hugh Ker	ab[445]
	Agnes Rutherfoord	
	Magnus Red	ab[446]
	William Forsyth	
	Janet Miller	
	Isobell Broun	v
	Margaret Richardson	ab
	Henry Broun	ab[447]
	Katharin Byers	
	John Colvill	ab[448]
	Barbara Henderson	
	John Mackrankin	ab[449]
	Janet Johnston	
	John Taylor	ab[450]
	Agnes Borthick	
	Archbald Bunton	ab
	Agnes Wingel	ab
	John Bunton	young
113	John Red	ab
	Margaret Cook	ab
	Thomas Murray	b
	Bessie Borleans	b
	Isobell Bain	ab
	John Anderson	ab
	Christian Broun	

445 'ab' refers to the entire household.
446 'ab' refers to the entire household.
447 'ab' refers to the entire household.
448 'ab' refers to the entire household.
449 'ab' refers to the entire household.
450 'ab' refers to the entire household.

	Elspet Kenlie	v
	Katharin Hardie	b
	James Bigger	ab[451]
	Agnes Spence	
	Marg[are]t Tail	
	Helen Duncan	ab[452]
	William Richardson	
	William Richardson	you[nge]r
	William Wood	ab[453]
	Agnes Lyll	
	Bessie Gowens	ab[454]
	Barbara Auchterlaunie	
	Katharin Rosse	ab
114	David Chisholme	ab[455]
	Martha Stevenson	
	James Borthick	ab[456]
	Margaret Paterson	
	Robert Borthick	
	Gilbert Patersone	ab[457]
	Janet Thomson	
	Archibald Wedderburn	ab[458]
	Agnes Bruce	
	James Hunter	ab[459]
	Margaret Hamilton	

451 'ab' refers to the entire household.
452 'ab' refers to the entire household.
453 'ab' refers to the entire household.
454 'ab' refers to the entire household.
455 'ab' refers to the entire household.
456 'ab' refers to the entire household.
457 'ab' refers to the entire household.
458 'ab' refers to the entire household.
459 'ab' refers to the entire household.

	Marg[are]t Mitchell	test
	Robert Hutton	ab[460]
	Marjory Dick	
	Gilbert Tam	test
	Andrew Hutton	ab[461]
	Christian Gourley	
	William Rosse	ab[462]
	Helen Weer	
	Thomas Rosse	
	Robert Greg	ab[463]
	Janet Gibb	
115	Patrick Hacket	
	Helen Ireland	
	John Chrystie	ab[464]
	Phyllis Wood	
	Marg[are]t Lightharness	ab[465]
	Marg[are]t Blair	
	Marg[are]t Wood	
	Jean Wood	
	Walter Broun	ab[466]
	Janet Bridge	
	Agnes Hunter	
	Richard Rae	ab[467]
	Marg[are]t Smeiton	

460 'ab' refers to the entire household.
461 'ab' refers to the entire household.
462 'ab' refers to the entire household.
463 'ab' refers to the entire household.
464 'ab' refers to the entire household.
465 'ab' refers to the entire household.
466 'ab' refers to the entire household.
467 'ab' refers to the entire household.

	James Heriot	ab[468]
	Elizabeth Scot	
	Janet Heriot	
	John Loughton	ab[469]
	Marg[are]t Greg	
	Janet Bridge	ab[470]
	John Mathers	
	Marg[are]t Wilson	
	Helen Blakewood	ab[471]
	Elizabeth Marshell	
116	William Mackomie	ab
	Marg[are]t Davidson	b
	John Harrower	ab[472]
	Marg[are]t Beveridge	
	James Hoyl	ab[473]
	Marg[are]t Chrystie	
	Anna Gillies	ab
	James Gray	ab
	Isobell Couper	b
	Janet Mackomie	ab
	Katharin Webster	ab[474]
	Mary Moorhead	
	John Broadie	ab
	Marion Glover	

468 'ab' refers to the entire household.
469 'ab' refers to the entire household.
470 'ab' refers to the entire household.
471 'ab' refers to the entire household.
472 'ab' refers to the entire household.
473 'ab' refers to the entire household.
474 'ab' refers to the entire household.

	Sylvester Lesly	p
	Marg[are]t Gentleman	
	Widow Cowie	ab[475]
	Agnes Hart	
	John Hutcheson	ab
	Marion Wilson	
117	Janet Scot	v
	Jean Cochren	ab
	Geo[rge] Mill	ab[476]
	Jean Guthrie	
	John Couper	
	Helen Hamilton	
	Robert Hamilton	ab[477]
	Mary Newlands	
	John Jackson	ab[478]
	Elizabeth Kellie	
	Sarah Hay	
	John Williamson	
	Christian Souter	
118	**4 Quarter**	
	Elizabeth Dewell	ab
	Isobell Hutcheson	b
	Richard Hutcheson	b
	David Bell	ab
	William Laing	ab
	Andrew Sheills	b
	Margaret Purves	ab
	Thomas Martin	young
	Agnes Martin	young

475 'ab' refers to the entire household.
476 'ab' refers to the entire household.
477 'ab' refers to the entire household.
478 'ab' refers to the entire household.

	William Broun	ab
	Jean Smyth	ab
	David Ivory	ab
	Richard Dick	ab
	Andrew Rae	v
	Agnes Broun	test b
	John Wallace	ab
	Janet Turren	b
	Laurence Scot	b young
	Barbara Turpie	v
	Quinten Adam	ab
	Grisel Montgomery	ab
	Christopher Butler	ab
	Helen Potter	ab
119	Isobell Gairnes	ab
	William Ker	test ab
	Barbara Ker	b
	Christian Ker	ab
	Elspet Paterson	b ~~test~~
	James Ker	ab[479]
	Margaret Marstoun	
	William Macknab	ab
	Marg[are]t Oats	ab
	Janet Scot	~~test~~ b
	Marion Hunter	ab
	Searjeant Mackintosh	ab
	Beatrix Mackintosh	pop
	Helen Davidson	ab
	John Landels	pop
	Anna Duncan	pop

479 'ab' refers to the entire household.

	John Allen	pop
	Elizabeth Hay	pop
120	Agnes Oliphant	put b
	Helen Borthick	put v
	John Esquire	b
	Isobell Jameson	ab
	Patrick Blaikie	ab
	Janet Halliway	b
	Anna Paterson	b
	James Sheill	ab
	Beatrix Sheill	ab
	Margaret Bain	ig
	Alex[ande]r Smyth	ab
	Isobell Jameson	b
	Marjory Smyth	ab
	William Dickson	ab
	Jean Cockburn	b
	Elspet Whitton	test ab
	Jean Wood	ab[480]
	Isobell Mitchell	put b
	Martha Mitchell	b put
	John Mitchell	
	William Shaw	test put b
	Mary Macklean	test ig
121	Robert Fulton	ab[481]
	Barbara Mathieson	
	Francis Provence	pop
	Dorothie Provence	pop
	Janet Rae	ab
	Mary Rae	ab

480 'ab' refers to the entire household.
481 'ab' refers to the entire household.

	John Tail	ab[482]
	Janet Wan	
	Jean Tail	
	Bessie Tail	
	Bessie Smyth	test
	William Holms	test
	Alex[ande]r West	ab[483]
	Alison Mitchell	
	Mary Somervill	ab
	James Walker	ab[484]
	Janet Allen	
	James Marnoch	ab[485]
	Jean Simm	
	John Grier	ab[486]
	Marg[are]t Dinn	
122	Janet Broadfoot	ab
	Abraham Turren	ab[487]
	Anthony de Bougie	
	Janet Weer	test
	Priscilla Johns	ab[488]
	William Jackson	
	William Laurie	ab[489]
	Elspet Sympson	
	Christian Walker	

482 'ab' refers to the entire household.
483 'ab' refers to the entire household.
484 'ab' refers to the entire household.
485 'ab' refers to the entire household.
486 'ab' refers to the entire household.
487 'ab' refers to the entire household.
488 'ab' refers to the entire household.
489 'ab' refers to the entire household.

	William Markoon	ab[490]
	Mary Arnot	
	Jean Buchannan	test
	Robert Hay	ab
	Margaret Armstrong	b
	Robert Gibson	ab
	Jean Windram	put ab[491]
	Margaret Dalyeal	
	Isobell Gyvelock	
	Walter Sheills	ab
	Margaret Clerk	b
	Alex[ande]r Gordon	b
123	James Cutbertson	ab
	Agnes Baxter	ab
	William Borleans	b
	Jean Depster	test b
	Mris Cowlie	ab[492]
	Janet Grieve	
	Margaret Jack	
	Janet Kennedy	test
	Isobell Dickson	
	Barbara Stevenson	test
	Alexander Thomson	
	Alison Turk	
	Margaret Thomson	young
	Christian Thomson	young
	Geo[rge] Borthick	ab
	Andrew Falconer	ab
	Marg[are]t Rae	ab
	John Lindesay	b
	Nicholas Rosse	b
	Isobel Couper	b

490 'ab' refers to the entire household.
491 'ab' refers to the entire household.
492 'ab' refers to the entire household.

	Archibald Falconer	b
	Robert Ramsey	ab[493]
	Marion Wilson	
	Anna Ramsey	
	Henry Mitchell	ab
	Janet Bell	
124	Andrew Sim	ab
	Janet Watson	ab
	James Sim	ab
	Geo[rge] Sim	young
	Alexander Sim	young
	John Watson	ab
	Janet Murray	b
	James Burn	
	Barbara Henderson	ab[494]
	Gilbert Gray	
	Margaret Gordon	
	Jean Gray	
	Margaret Rollo	ab[495]
	Katharin Barber	
	Robert Straiton	ab[496]
	~~Katharin~~ Christian Dennison	
	Patrick Mackarroch	ab
	Helen Watson	ab
	Mary Mackarrah	ab
	Christian Mitchell	b
	Mathew Wedderburn	ab
	Mary Mitchell	ab put ab
	Margaret Mitchell	b

493 'ab' refers to the entire household.
494 'ab' refers to the entire household.
495 'ab' refers to the entire household.
496 'ab' refers to the entire household.

	Giles Wedderburn	young b
125	Janet Ker	ab[497]
	Helen Borthick	
	John Turnbull	
	Janet Wood	ab
	John Yeats	ab[498]
	Isobell Moncreif	
	Jean Rae	
	Marg[are]t Borthick	
	Gilbert Bryson	
	Anna Fraser	
	Margaret Hardie	test
	Robert Smyth	ab[499]
	Sarah Liddel	
	James Couper	
	Alexander Prentine	test
	Mris Park	
	Jean Spence	~~ab~~ b
	Elizabeth Park	young
	Laird of Newtoons family	
	Barbara Clerk	ab
	Thomas Parkshire	put b[500]
	Widow Mitchell	ab
	John Rolland	v
	William Murray	b
	Anna Mitchell	young
	John Smyth	b
	Margaret Borleans	ab
126	Henry Colt	ab[501]

497 'ab' refers to the entire household.
498 'ab' refers to the entire household.
499 'ab' refers to the entire household.
500 Name and marginalia written in a different hand.
501 'ab' refers to the entire household.

Elizabeth Sympson
John Colt

Henry Ker ab[502]
Barbara Walker
Mr Campbell
Anna Chisholm

John Clerk ab
Agnes Miller ab
John Sutherland v
James Wilkinson v
William Watson ab

Robert Duncan ab[503]
Lillias Skinner
Marg[are]t Duncan

Joachim Johnston ab
Marg[are]t Ballantine ab
William Johnston b
Mary Drysedale forn: ab
Robert Bell ~~ab x~~ young

John Bishop ab[504]
Janet Duncan
James Bishop

George Tail ab[505]
Agnes Adamson
Margaret Tail
Janet Broun test

127 Thomas Todd ab[506]
Margaret Patersone
Janet Patersone

502 'ab' refers to the entire household.
503 'ab' refers to the entire household.
504 'ab' refers to the entire household.
505 'ab' refers to the entire household.
506 'ab' refers to the entire household.

	John Mason	ab[507]
	Mary Turner	put b
	Alexander Mathieson	ab[508]
	Christian Auld	put b
	Margaret Henderson	ab[509]
	Elspet Hay	
	James Sutherland	ab[510]
	Eupham Scot	
	Mary Burrell	ab[511]
	Janet Dinn	put b
	William Urchart	ab
	Christian Gordon	ab
	Marjory Knolls	~~ab~~ test b
	Adam Urchart	~~ab~~ young
	Lady Bogies family	
	Agnes	ab
	Lady Innervylies family	
	Janet Mackeinyie	test ab[512]
	John Craig	
128	Mr John Row	pop ab[513]
	Mary Ridge	
	Euphan Marshell	
	Margaret Grant	
	Margaret Wilson	
	Quarter Mr Dalmalnys family	
	Margaret Gardiner	put b

507 'ab' refers to the entire household.
508 'ab' refers to the entire household.
509 'ab' refers to the entire household.
510 'ab' refers to the entire household.
511 'ab' refers to the entire household.
512 'ab' refers to the entire household.
513 'pop ab' refers to the entire household.

James Farcherson

Captain Strauchans family ab[514]
Janet Wilson
John Kier test
Christian Gillespie test
Helen Mason test

Michael Ziglar ab
Amphylis Zyglar ab
Mary Ziglar ab
Geo[rge] Ziglar b
Amphylis Zyglar b
Katharin Zyglar b
Thomas Arthur b
Margaret Tam ~~ab~~ b
Mary pop

James Heriot ab[515]
Helen Aikman
Margaret Red test

Widow Carrin ab[516]
Margaret Sheills

129 E[arl] of Airlies family
William Urchart ab[517]
Mris Winchester pop
Janet Henry
David Rae
William Black
John Ogilvie
John Wishart
Francis Ogilvie
James Anderson b put
Alex[ande]r Taylor
John Gordon
William Gray put ig

514 'ab' refers to the entire household.
515 'ab' refers to the entire household.
516 'ab' refers to the entire household.
517 'ab' refers to the entire household.

	David Both	
	William Nobles	
	James Milln	
	Marg[are]t Balfour	
	Christian Herrieson	
	David Caskie	ab[518]
	Elizabeth Lundie	
	Beatrix Gordon	
	Bessie Primrose	
	Marg[are]t Young	
	Agnes Stewart	
	Mr Irvins family	ab[519]
	Beatrix Hodge	
	Violetta Campbell	
	John Sim	ig
	Marg[are]t Sympson	ig
	Margaret Simm	ab
130	William Carnegie	b
	Marg[are]t Hamilton	b
	William Carnegie	b
	Elizabeth Carnegie	ab
	James Atcheson	ab
	Agnes Ainsley	b
	William Herries	b
	Alex[ande]r Steven	ab[520]
	Sarah Phiddes	
	Daniel Bain	ab[521]
	Christian Sinclare	
	Isobell Sinclare	put b
	Katharin Bruce	

518 'ab' refers to the entire household.

519 'ab' refers to the entire household.

520 'ab' refers to the entire household.

521 'ab' refers to the entire household.

	Peter Grant	ab[522]
	Margaret Walker	
	John Airth	ab[523]
	Lillias Olyphant	
	John Dougall	v
	Margaret Thomson	b
	George Glover	young
	John Mackie	ab[524]
	Janet Glover	
131	John Hamilton	ab
	Janet Ainsley	b
	Marg[are]t Moor	test ab
	Collen Craig	ab[525]
	Janet Fiffe	
	William Morgan	ab[526]
	Marjory Fiffe	
	Charles Litlejohn	ab[527]
	Janet Melvill	
	Helen Litlejohn	
	James Taylor	ab[528]
	Marion Ogilvie	
	Charles Mackarnoch	pop[529]
	Elizabeth Martin	
	Anna Rosse	ab

522 'ab' refers to the entire household.
523 'ab' refers to the entire household.
524 'ab' refers to the entire household.
525 'ab' refers to the entire household.
526 'ab' refers to the entire household.
527 'ab' refers to the entire household.
528 'ab' refers to the entire household.
529 'pop' refers to the entire household.

	William Barron	ab[530]
	Janet Grieve	
	John Eiston	
	James Johnstoun	put b ab[531]
	David Adam	
	Giles Johnston	
	James Boyd	
	Helen Nidrie	put b
	Marion Craig	
132	David Mastertown	ab[532]
	Janet Henrie	
	Robert Couper	ab[533]
	Helen Mackgee	
	Marg[are]t Opter	ab[534]
	Francis Opter	
	Mary Opter	
	Geo[rge] Oliphant	ab[535]
	Margaret Yessin	
	Thomas Johnston	ab[536]
	Margaret Neiven	
	David Rollo	ab[537]
	Bethia Laurie	
	David Rollo	
	Isobell Sutherland	
	Agnes Grahm	ab
	John Harvie	

530 'ab' refers to the entire household.
531 'ab' refers to the entire household.
532 'ab' refers to the entire household.
533 'ab' refers to the entire household.
534 'ab' refers to the entire household.
535 'ab' refers to the entire household.
536 'ab' refers to the entire household.
537 'ab' refers to the entire household.

Isobell Douglasse ab
Isobell Red test b
John Broun ab
Katharin Harvie b young

~~John Dingwall~~
~~Isobell Taylor~~
~~Barbara Taylor~~

133 **Potterow Quarter**

Tho[mas] Greve ab[538]
Thomas Meek

William Carstairs ab[539]
Beatrix Sympson
William Lauriston put b
Beatrix Carstairs

George Ogilvie ab[540]
Christian Watson
Walter Mair

George Cuthketle ab

Alex[ande]r Black ab
Nicholas Lindesay ab
John Weer b

134 James Robertson ab
Helen Creighton ab
John Robertson b
And[rew] Robertson b
Daniel Moorhead b
Alexander Gill ab

Robert Stevenson
Helen Thomson
Michael Stevenson young b

538 'ab' refers to the entire household.
539 'ab' refers to the entire household.
540 'ab' refers to the entire household.

	Barbara Stevenson	young b
	John Robertson	b
	Bessie Scot	test ab
	David Key	ab[541]
	Margaret Alexander	
	Margaret Gilchrist	
	Robert Aiken	ab
	Margaret Robertson	b
	Elspet Welsh	v
	Andrew Cassle~~hill~~law	ab[542]
	Mary Douglasse	put b
	Janet Pringle	test
	Will[iam] Melvill	
	Isobell Thomson	b
	Isobell Melvill	ab
	John Stirlen	b
135	David Ireland	b
	Katharin Hastie	ab
	Thomas Ronald	b
	Helen Man	ig:
	William Rodger	ab[543]
	Janet Jameson	
	George Gargill	ab
	Katharin Jackson	v
	John Murray	ab[544]
	Agnes Cleves	
	Robert Lauson	ab[545]
	Janet Laurie	

541 'ab' refers to the entire household.
542 'ab' refers to the entire household.
543 'ab' refers to the entire household.
544 'ab' refers to the entire household.
545 'ab' refers to the entire household.

	Marg[are]t Carmichael	v
	Janet Locke	ab
	William Davidson	ab[546]
	Elspet Ramsey	
	Janet Malcolm	ab
	Bessie Pringle	
	Katharin Pringle	
136	Robert Sympson	ab[547]
	Christian Webster	
	Robert Red	
	James Scott	ab[548]
	Agnes Pringle	
	Andrew Melvill	
	Alex[ande]r Heriot	
	Helen Wood	
	Andrew Herring	v
	Anna Broun	ig
	James Wood	ab
	Katharin Red	ab
	John Rutherfoord	ab
	L. of Ithingtouns family	ab[549]
	Margaret Tail	
	Duncan Melvill	
	William Turpie	ab
	Jean Douglasse	ab
	William Mackell	b
	Elspet Donaldson	test

546 'ab' refers to the entire household.
547 'ab' refers to the entire household.
548 'ab' refers to the entire household.
549 'ab' refers to the entire household.

	William Broun	ab[550]
	Marion Bell	
	James Broun	
	William Wast	
137	David Martoun	ab[551]
	Katharin Thomson	
	William Macklearen	ab[552]
	Elspet Imbrie	
	Baillie Laudors family	
	William Lamb	ab[553]
	Margaret Air	
	Anna Johnston	
	Anna Ker	
	Mr John Wishart	ab[554]
	Barbara Murray	
	Christian Smyth	
	Marg[are]t Dunlapp	
	John Dunbarton	
	Alex[ande]r Calhoun	

550 'ab' refers to the entire household.
551 'ab' refers to the entire household.
552 'ab' refers to the entire household.
553 'ab' refers to the entire household.
554 'ab' refers to the entire household.

INDEX OF NAMES

Note: The index includes names that have been partially or completely scored out in the parish list. Names that have been partially scored out have been indexed by the full name given, e.g. John ~~Duncan~~ is indexed as 'Duncan, John' and Marie ~~Brooks~~ Macklachan is indexed as 'Macklachlan, Marie Brooks'.